Peter Norton's®
Complete Guide to Linux

Peter Norton and Arthur Griffith

SAMS

A Division of Macmillan Computer Publishing
201 West 103rd Street, Indianapolis, Indiana 46290

Peter Norton's® Complete Guide to Linux

Copyright © 2000 by Peter Norton

International Standard Book Number: 0-672-31573-4

Library of Congress Catalog Card Number: 99-60948

Printed in the United States of America

First Printing: October 1999

01 00 99   4   3   2

Trademarks

Warning and Disclaimer

Associate Publisher
Michael Stephens

Acquisitions Editor
Angela Kozlowski

Development Editor
Matt Larson

Managing Editor
Charlotte Clapp

Senior Editor
Karen A. Walsh

Copy Editor
Pat Kinyon

Indexer
Chris Barrick

Proofreader
Cynthia Fields

Technical Editor
Jason Wright

Interior Design
Gary Adair

Cover Design
Aren Howell

Copy Writer
Eric Borgert

Production
Stacey DeRome
Ayanna Lacey
Heather Miller

Contents at a Glance

iv

Contents

About the Authors

Computer software entrepreneur and writer **Peter Norton** established his technical expertise and accessible style from the earliest days of the PC. His Norton Utilities was the first product of its kind, giving early computer owners control over their hardware and protection against myriad problems. His flagship titles, *Peter Norton's DOS Guide* and *Peter Norton's Inside the PC* (Sams Publishing) have provided the same insight and education to computer users worldwide for nearly two decades. Peter's books, like his many software products, are among the best selling and most respected in the history of personal computing.

Peter Norton's former column in *PC Week* was among the highest regarded in that magazine's history. His expanding series of computer books continues to bring superior education to users, always in Peter's trademark style, which is never condescending nor pedantic. From their earliest days, changing the "black box" into a "glass box," Peter's books, like his software, remain among the most powerful tools available to beginners and experienced users alike.

In 1990, Peter sold his software development business to Symantec Corporation, allowing him to devote more time to his family, civic affairs, philanthropy, and art collecting. He lives with his wife, Eileen, and two children in Santa Monica, California.

Arthur Griffith received a Bachelor of Science in Computer Science and Mathematics from Northeast Louisiana State University in 1976. For several years he specialized as a compiler writer. His first encounter with operating system software was in the early 1980s when he maintained and enhanced embedded and dedicated systems. He has also worked with several flavors of UNIX as a system level programmer, and he is now working on two Linux projects.

Dedication

For Mary.

Acknowledgments

I need to thank the Linux community at large. Not only do they provide the software itself, but they also provide information—it seems that some knowledgeable person is always available to answer a question or clear up a point of confusion. There is an amazingly large body of knowledge out there on the Internet. In particular, the technical assistance of Jason Wright and Aron Hsiao were invaluable.

I owe special thanks to Angela Kozlowski at Macmillan Publishing and to Margot Maley at Waterside Productions. And I need to thank Rebecca Mounts and Karen Walsh for their unique combinations of patience and persistence. Matt Larson continuously created organization out of chaos. Pat Kinyon has a magic ability of looking at a sentence and figuring out what the writer really meant—and then fixing it so it actually says that.

—Arthur Griffith

Tell Us What You Think!

As the reader of this book, *you* are our most important critic and commentator. We value your opinion and want to know what we're doing right, what we could do better, what areas you'd like to see us publish in, and any other words of wisdom you're willing to pass our way.

As an Associate Publisher for Sams, I welcome your comments. You can fax, email, or write me directly to let me know what you did or didn't like about this book—as well as what we can do to make our books stronger.

Please note that I cannot help you with technical problems related to the topic of this book, and that due to the high volume of mail I receive, I might not be able to reply to every message.

When you write, please be sure to include this book's title and authors as well as your name and phone or fax number. I will carefully review your comments and share them with the author and editors who worked on the book.

Fax: 317-581-4770

Email: office_sams@mcp.com

Mail: Michael Stephens
          Sams Publishing
          201 West 103rd Street
          Indianapolis, IN 46290 USA

PART I

Introduction and Installation of Linux

Introduction to Linux

It seems like Linux is everywhere. It is certainly different things to different people. It is being applied to everything from hand-held devices to clusters of large-capacity computers handling millions of transactions. And, with the improvements that have been made to the GUI interface, Linux is making its move to the desktop.

There is a lot of speculation about what caused the Linux success. After all, there were other free (or very cheap) UNIX-like operating systems abroad in the land before Linux arrived. It's difficult (and probably useless) to attempt to determine any one overriding reason for its success, but there are a number of factors that contributed to it. One is that it works—it is fast, solid, and stable. Also, its complete source code is freely available to anyone who wants it. There's also a lot to be said for timing—the advent of Linux coincides with the explosive growth of the Internet. Another fortuitous circumstance is the fact that the GNU Project has written its huge collection of utility programs with free source. There is also an intangible factor—the fact that the kernel of the operating system was initially developed by one person. The feeling that Linus Torvalds is doing some things that no software company in the world is capable of doing adds to the Linux magic and mystique.

A while back, when I was starting to become acquainted with Linux, I came across something in the user interface that was an irritant to me. It worked okay as it was, but I would have preferred it to work in a different way. After all the years of working with closed operating systems, my first thought was, "I wish they would fix that." Then I realized, to paraphrase Pogo, "I have met the Linux programmers, and they are us!" This is my operating system, too. So I made the change to the source code that I use, and have been using it that way ever since. Linux is your operating system as well.

What Is Linux?

Linux. A word you hear more and more as the pundits ponder and the analysts analyze both its future and its past. Once considered an operating system for only the more "geek" amongst us, it is now making inroads into the heart of the computer industry as both a desktop workstation and server operating system. Current estimates put the growth rate of Linux higher than all other operating systems combined, with no signs of letting up in the near future.

At the lowest level, there is the Linux kernel. In the simplest of terms, the kernel's job is to load programs into memory and start them running. But this is a gross oversimplification. The kernel performs the juggling act that allows more than one program to be in execution at any one time, attaches software drivers to the appropriate hardware, processes inter-process communications, prevents one program from interfering with another, and protects itself from programs that have gone bad.

But the kernel—as its name implies—is just the seed from which a full-blown Linux can grow. Linux is expanding rapidly from its UNIX heritage. It offers many of the features found in commercial operating systems, as well as many that have never appeared anywhere else. Much of this variety can be attributed to the open source model of software development, but much also comes from software companies porting versions of their applications to the Linux platform.

You might say that Linux is a family of environments. It can be installed as a standalone server that sits in the corner and quietly receives, processes, and transmits data messages. You can get an ASCII console by using any number of command line shell programs. If you prefer a graphical interface, there are a number of them you can configure to control your screen and mouse, and you can do windows. The Linux user environment can be molded and shaped to just about anything a user would like. This extreme flexibility has resulted in Linux going into unanticipated locations and doing unexpected things.

Linux represents a new model of computing as well as distribution. With the advent and proliferation of the Internet, we are now seeing new ways to look at software development and the sharing of ideas on a global scale. The success of Linux is directly tied to this phenomenon because it is also largely responsible for its existence. Linux has now become the primary vehicle ushering in this "new way" of computing.

As you will find from the rest of this book, Linux's meteoric rise is well deserved. Linux offers many of the features found in commercial operating systems, as well as many not found until now. Many of these features are direct manifestations of the changing models and modes of software development brought on by Linux and the Internet. It can be shown that Linux is actually a new way of looking at old concepts and ideas. With its roots grounded firmly in the UNIX model of computing, Linux departs from these concepts with a flair that is certainly all its own.

More than just a kernel or operating system, Linux is an environment. It is an environment that is wholly owned by its operator—you, the user. This is a concept that is distinctly different from the more popular offerings by commercial software companies today. The Linux environment is one that can be molded and shaped to extremes never before known to the general computing public. This level of freedom and expendability has given rise to a movement with the power to take on multi-billion dollar corporations for the very hearts and minds of the computing public.

As a consumer, you truly do own Linux. You have the right to do with it what you will. This is possible because Linux returns to you one of your most fundamental rights, freedom of use.

In The Beginning

Where did Linux come from? What company could have spawned such a phenomenon? Who's responsible for this global movement changing the way we use computers?

Like many great ideas or inventions, Linux was born of humble beginnings. This brings us to University of Finland student Linus Torvalds, circa 1991. Originally inspired by the work of Andrew Tanenbaum's Minix (miniature UNIX) operating system, Torvalds began working on an operating system of his own. His first prototype, version 0.01, was born in August of 1991.

Torvalds' next move could well have been one of the most important events in the history of Linux. Torvalds posted his results, freely, on the Internet newsgroup comp.os.minix. This move gave other developers the ability to scrutinize his work as well as to contribute to it. As we now know, the latter is certainly true today. This was the germination of a software development system that had the ability to harness the intellectual minds of many people in a short amount of time. Changes to the system could be made and posted on the Internet, sometimes within minutes. This process enabled rapid development by many people. This was open source software development.

The first official version of Linux, version 0.0.2, was released on October 5, 1991. This version allowed a few GNU (a recursive acronym for "Gnu's Not UNIX") programs, like bash and gcc, to run. While these first versions were limited, they did attract the attention of many developers as the Linux phenomenon continued to grow.

After many very unstable versions, the first version claiming to be stable, version 1.0, was released. This release was also the start of a development cycle that is still in place today. Linux kernel releases follow a development phase that is denoted by their version numbers. The development phase—denoted by odd numbered versions such as 1.1, 2.1, 2.3, and so on—is the period in which kernel features are being added and developed. The stabilization phase—denoted by even numbered versions such as 1.2, 2.2, 2.4, and so on—is where smaller modifications are made to the kernel. These changes occurred mainly to fix bugs or optimize kernel performance. As of this writing, the current stable kernel is 2.2.10, and the current development kernel is 2.3.8.

Today, Linux has evolved into a full-blown operating system that, in many ways, rivals commercial systems. With the amount of interest it has garnered, Linux has now become an actively developing and improving system. While many people do contribute to the development of Linux, kernel features are still controlled by Linus Torvalds.

The Future

The future looks bright for Linux. To a user, the purpose of a computer is the running of an application, and Linux has lots of applications. There are new ones every day. Many of them are free and have source code available, but there are also many commercial applications appearing as companies port existing applications to Linux. If Linux runs the application suite required by the user, this will continue to feed the growing trend toward Linux and its model of computing for the foreseeable future.

Linux itself is perpetually in development. While many commercial operating systems offer updates a couple of times a year, the Linux kernel, the GUI interfaces, utility programs, compilers, and so on, are updated sometimes weekly. Every release is available for download, with source code, for free.

It seems that hardly a day can go by without hearing about a company announcing support for Linux. There almost seems to be rush to Linux, a state of rapid growth ushering in changes at a pace never seen before. These changes can only be good for the end user, offering advancements and opportunities that did not exist previously.

The Linux kernel is perpetually in development. While many commercial operating systems offer updates a couple of times a year, the Linux kernel is sometimes updated weekly. Every release is available for download with source code, for free.

Why Use Linux?

There are many reasons to use Linux. The following are some of the most compelling.

Power

Linux, more than any other operating system going, has the ability to transform your legacy hardware into a powerful, well-tuned machine. Take that old 486 or Pentium and turn it into a fully multitasking crash-free system. Linux does this because of several factors. Linux was designed from the ground up to provide very low level access to your hardware and its peripherals. The design philosophy of Linux is one of tight, very efficient code based on the UNIX model of computing. What this gives you, the end user, is an operating system capable of out-gunning even the best of the commercial breeds—all with the added benefits of rock-hard stability and reliability.

Price

Linux is free. Yes, free. Linux is developed by volunteers for free and maintained by volunteers for free. Nearly every Linux distribution comes with thousands of dollars worth of software, all for the price of a download. Of course, you can also buy Linux distributions for next to nothing compared to commercial operating systems. The price-to-performance advantage Linux gives you is immeasurable.

Development

Linux offers some of the most mature, well-respected development tools you can find today. Along with the famous GNU development suite, there are many other environments available free from the Internet. The toolkits, IDEs, and libraries available are too numerous to list here. This is one of the many reasons Linux is so popular today. Linux is virtually a developer's dream with which to work.

Networking

Our world is constantly becoming smaller. This is due, in great part, to the proliferation of the network. Linux offers some of the most powerful advantages today in the area of networking. As I write this sentence, my Linux system is running servers offering up mail, Web, print, file, database, news, FTP, and NFS services all at once. Linux was designed for the network, on the network, and by the network.

Portability

Perhaps more than any other operating system known to man, Linux runs on many different architectures. By looking at the Linux kernel tree in `/usr/src/linux/arch`, you can see that Linux supports

- i386—Intel x86 architecture, also including compatible processors by Cyrix, IDT, AMD, UMC, ST, IBM, NexGen, and others
- Alpha—Digital's DEC Alpha CPU, the fastest commodity CPU on the market today
- Arm—The Arm RISC CPU
- m68k—The Motorola 68000 series CPU, used in all older Macintosh computers through Quadra/Centris series
- mips—The MIPS processor, used in SGI computers
- ppc—The PowerPC CPU, used in Apple's Macintosh computers
- sparc—The Sparc CPU, used in Sun workstations and servers

What this means for the end user is a wide array of hardware possibilities for running Linux. No commercial operating system can even come close to claiming such portability. You can run Linux on most any type of computer available today.

The Source

Linux comes with all of the aforementioned advantages, plus one more very important one. Linux comes with source code. If you don't like a particular way the system works, change it yourself and recompile. Worried about Y2K? Open the source and check for yourself. No commercial operating system can offer this advantage. Linux is *open* in the true sense of the word. This gives you total freedom and releases you from the world of proprietary software and the many problems that go along with it.

One of the first things new Linux users notice is its awesome multitasking. Linux handles many applications at once without even blinking an eye. The variety of user interfaces is also without equal in Linux. There are many X-Windows window managers available for Linux, all with an incredible degree of "tweakability." Some with near cult followings, these window managers offer user interface features quite new and refreshing.

Of course, talk is only talk. You need to have tactile experience before you can make an informed conclusion. Linux offers one of the best computing experiences around. The "look and feel" aspect of Linux is certainly one of its strongest selling points. And, if you don't like the way it looks, change it. You have the source.

The GNU Difference

Linux distributions typically contain many other added applications and system tools. The most common set of tools contained within Linux distributions are the GNU utilities. A description of GNU and its purpose follows from the GNU Web site at `http://www.gnu.org`:

> The GNU Project started in 1984 to develop a complete free UNIX-like operating system. Variants of the GNU system, using Linux as the kernel, are now widely used; though often called "Linux", they are more accurately called GNU/Linux systems.

The founder of GNU, Richard Stallman, is seen by many to be one of the principal architects in this new way of thinking about software development.

The GNU project is funded by the Free Software Foundation whose description follows:

> The Free Software Foundation (FSF) is dedicated to eliminating restrictions on copying, redistribution, understanding, and modification of computer programs. We do this by promoting the development and use of free software in all areas of computing—but most particularly, by helping to develop the GNU operating system.

These are very radical concepts in today's world of multi-billion dollar software monopolies. The philosophies of GNU and the FSF can be further understood by reading Appendix B, "The Open Source Definition."

Principal among GNU's many contributions to computer science are

- *The GNU Emacs Editor*—One of the most powerful editors you can find today
- *The GNU C Compiler*—A compiler that now supports 7 languages and over 30 different architectures
- *Ghostscript*—An interpreter for the PostScript and PDF graphics languages.
- *The Gimp*—The GNU Image Manipulation Program, a Photoshop-like graphics application, only better

- *Gnome*—The GNU desktop, a graphical user interface for the desktop that includes many different useful applications

This is but a small portion of the entire GNU contribution. A full list with descriptions is far beyond the scope of this book, however, a visit to http://www.gnu.org is recommended.

The Best Things in Life Are Free

The Linux kernel, and major portions of all distributions, are licensed using the GPL (GNU Public License) or LGPL (Library General Public License). These licenses are covered in detail in Appendix A, "The GNU License."

Because of these licenses, you can get Linux, and all of its source code, free. Again, all for the price of a download. This is a freedom granted to you by the authors of software who choose to license through GNU and the GPL. This license essentially gives you the right to modify any source code, for any reason, as long as you contribute your changes back to the community.

Using this method of licensing removes the tired and worn-out methods we have in place at many major software companies today. In effect, the power to change the course of computing is taken out of the hands of a few select individuals and thrust squarely into the heart of the community. This enables anyone, even you, to contribute to the future of software technology, if you're so inclined.

Freedom is the secret to the power of the Linux revolution. In effect, you belong to a collective consciousness, a community of people who do what they do because they want to and not because they have to. This is the Open Source difference, and this is what is going change the world of computing forever.

Linux Distributions

Contrary to popular belief, Linux is really just the kernel portion of the operating system. The Linux kernel is packaged into distributions, with added applications and utilities. These distributions are maintained by both commercial companies and volunteers.

Most of these distributions are available both free and for retail purchase. On the surface, there are several advantages to purchasing distributions from a retailer, as opposed to downloading it for free. Among them are

- *Technical support*—Most distributions offer technical support for installation and beyond. This can be very beneficial to the beginning Linux user. Alternatively, you can find out nearly anything you want by just perusing public newsgroups pertaining to Linux. Often, the newsgroups are a wonderful source of knowledge, because usually you're able to find help on any subject you can think of.

- *Manuals*—Most distributions also offer very nice manuals. Installation and configuration can be much less painful with the addition of printed documentation. Of course, you could just go to one of the many Linux documentation Web sites and print whatever you'd like. There's always a choice.

- *Added Value*—Finally, many distributions offer additional software packages with your purchase of their distribution. Products such as WordPerfect, StarOffice, BRU Backup, and many more are often included. While some of these applications can be downloaded for free, it is nice to have them all in one place at one time and ready to install.

Remember though, this is Linux and it is free. You can still simply download and burn your own system CD-ROM for yourself, as many people do. Because the price of Linux distributions is so low in comparison to other operating systems, it's really just a matter of preference.

What follows is a short, but not complete, list of Linux distributions.

Red Hat Linux

Red Hat Linux is probably the most popular of all Linux distributions. Started in 1995, Red Hat has quickly become known for its quality and ease of installation. Red Hat is well respected in the Linux community, because it was one of the first and certainly most high-quality distributions for Linux. Today, Red Hat's distribution is available both free for download or commercially for a small price.

One of Red Hat's most important contributions to the Linux community was the RPM, Red Hat Package Manager. RPM is a tool to make installing and removing software in Linux easier and less error prone. The Red Hat installer is also an important contribution, as can be witnessed by the fact that other distributions sometimes use it with small modifications. Red Hat also offers Linux certification and training in the form of the "Red Hat Certified Engineer Program."

The current version of Red Hat Linux, as of this writing, is version 6.0. Red Hat distributions continually improve in quality, and Red Hat has become a major player in the exciting world of Linux.

To find out more about Red Hat Linux, visit http://www.redhat.com.

Caldera OpenLinux

Caldera Linux is known primarily as a distribution aimed at deployment for businesses. Offering one of the most polished installers around, Caldera's product has certainly come of age.

Caldera's installation program has many features not found in other distributions. First of all, it runs from Windows. Caldera assumed that many people buying OpenLinux would have Windows on their computers. Secondly, they include a special edition of Partition Magic, a tool to make room for Linux on an already existing Windows installation. These two factors are great pluses for the first-time Linux user. OpenLinux also includes COAS, the Caldera Open Administration System, for ease of administration.

Perhaps more than any other Linux distribution, Caldera has made great strides toward bringing Linux to the general public with its OpenLinux product.

To find out more about Caldera's OpenLinux, check out `http://www.calderasystems.com`.

SuSE Linux

Rapidly growing as one the largest selling Linux distributions, SuSE Linux is definitely worth a try. SuSE Linux is know for its "everything but the kitchen sink" approach. SuSE includes a great deal of free and commercial software in its distributions, which, as of the current 6.1 version, includes a total of five CD-ROMs—all totaling nearly 1,000 applications and utilities.

SuSE is also a very well-put-together distribution with a great deal of attention paid to the "out-of-the-box" experience. Among SuSE's unique features is the ability to save your installation preferences onto a floppy disk for later use.

In many regards, SuSE Linux seems to be catching up in many regards to the popularity of Red Hat Linux. Having won distribution contracts with major retailers for its commercial version, SuSE's sales are certainly growing at a very fast pace. SuSE Linux is also offered in German.

To find out more about SuSE Linux, visit `http://www.suse.com`.

TurboLinux

TurboLinux is a fairly new distribution in the world of Linux. Based in San Francisco, TurboLinux Inc. has managed to create a quality distribution. Founded in 1992 (formerly Pacific High Tech), TurboLinux Inc. claims to have shipped more than two million units of TurboLinux since 1998. The main focus of TurboLinux Inc. is beyond the Pacific Rim, into countries like China and Japan.

TurboLinux claims the distinct honor of being the only Linux distribution to ship in three languages—Chinese, Japanese, and English. The Japanese version of TurboLinux even includes an English-Japanese/Japanese-English dictionary on CD-ROM.

The TurboLinux installer is based on the Red Hat installer, with custom modifications suited to its various distributions. In a departure from most Linux distributions, TurboLinux comes in both workstation and server versions.

For more information on TurboLinux, visit http://www.turbolinux.com.

Debian Linux

Debian Linux has been around for quite a while. Debian is known as more of a developer's distribution, because a large majority of its user base is developers. The Debian distribution is well maintained and offers a large amount of add-on software.

The Debian Linux distribution is second only to Red Hat in staying on the cutting edge. Debian also has one of the most thorough testing periods of all distributions.

It's also worth noting that Debian is the only true free distribution mentioned here, as there is no commercial version of it.

The current stable version of Debian Linux is 2.1r2. For more information on Debian Linux, visit http://www.debian.org.

Slackware Linux

Slackware Linux is one of the first and oldest distributions around. Many longtime Linux users will tell you that their first introduction to Linux was through Slackware. Started and still maintained by Patrick Volkerding, Slackware remains very popular among many in the Linux community.

Slackware aims at being the most UNIX-like of any distribution. While not the most cutting edge of the Linux distributions, Slackware is certainly very stable and well maintained. The latest version, 4.0, includes many enhancements and is very well put together. Slackware also maintains a 2.0.x kernel distribution—Slackware version 3.9.

For more information on Slackware Linux, check out http://www.slackware.com.

Choices, Choices

While there are many Linux distributions available, finding out which is the best for you can be a little tricky. Like anything else, it involves a bit of research. One of the best ways to ascertain which distribution is best for you is to check the public newsgroups. They contain a wealth of information by users, such as yourself, who have already gone through the installations and setups of many of these distributions. Another very good source is the Linux.org site at http://www.linux.org.

The main difference among all of these distributions is really the installation process. Many of them offer different packages or add-on commercial packages, but the Linux experience is pretty much the same once you've booted into your new system. There will always be small differences here and there, but, in the end, it's always Linux.

Summary

The world of Linux is new and ever–changing. While many have viewed Linux as merely a fad or flavor of the month, people around the globe are discovering the power that lies within Open Source software and Linux. Whether they be students, developers, scientists, or just hobbyists, Linux is accessible to them. More than ever, Linux is becoming an operating system for the user. As great strides are continuously being made in the area of user interface, Linux will become more and more popular with the public at large.

As part of the collective consciousness that is Linux, you're willing to put up with unfinished software. You're willing to forgive incomplete documentation. It's not really an issue, because you know that the machine will produce—and produce it does, with an almost dizzying display of speed and effectiveness. This is something we've never seen before in the world of computers. It is a movement with a philosophy, almost with a mind of its own, taking on all of our preconceived notions about software development and distribution.

I hope that you discover Linux and the many wonderful tools and applications that it has inspired. Linux is a wonderful place to start your in-depth journey into the world of computer software. It's a fresh, needed change that has been a long time coming. It's finally here—Linux.

Installation Requirements

UNIX was developed to be portable from day one. While many versions of UNIX have come and gone, Linux has done more to bring this goal to fruition than any other operating systems—UNIX or otherwise. At last check, Linux runs on a variety of computing platforms unmatched by any other operating system. A short list of major platforms includes;

- Intel x86
- PowerPC
- MIPS
- Sparc
- Motorola 680x0
- StrongArm
- DEC Alpha

The versions of Linux that run on these platforms vary in stability and completeness, with the Intel x86 version as the most stable. The PowerPC and Alpha ports follow close behind in stability and compatibility. For instance, the PowerPC team will have support for the newest Macintosh models by the time you read this. That support includes advanced features such as USB, Firewire, and support for the G3 processors.

The MIPS 680×0 did not arrive until later in the development. Not all distributions currently include support for this platform.

Because the Intel version of Linux is the most popular, this chapter will focus on hardware requirements for that platform followed by PowerPC, Sparc, and Alpha.

Linux, in general, has very minimal requirements compared to the other mass market operating systems. Linux can be booted from a floppy and run in a stripped down fashion on a machine with as few as 4MB of RAM. Linux can also support machines with gigabytes of RAM and terabytes of hard drive storage. On Intel machines, the minimal requirement for CPU is a 386-series CPU, although a 486 is a better choice for performance reasons. Linux supports CPUs from many manufactures, including the genuine Intel as well as x86 clones from AMD and Cyrix. Support for the clone vendors has been problematic in the past but has gotten better with recent kernels. The main source of compatibility problems in the older processors has revolved around the math co-processor support, but even those have been dealt with in the recent kernels. Linux is a high-performance system and can bring out the deficiencies of a particular piece of hardware better than Windows or DOS. Try to pick the best hardware you can or, better still, buy a complete machine from one of the Linux hardware vendors. Buying from a respected Linux vendor can save hours of incompatibility headaches and hardware troubleshooting.

If you simply must experience the fun of building your own box, make sure you check the hardware compatibility lists of the distribution you will be using. Red Hat, Debian, and SuSE post lists of supported hardware on their respective Web sites. Additionally, there are Web sites springing up to provide information on hardware with which Linux works well and problems people have had. Linux portal sites like www.linux.org and www.linux.com can provide you with links to these valuable resources.

A minimal Linux machine can look like the following:

- 386 CPU
- 4MB of RAM
- Floppy drive
- VGA video

This system can boot Linux from the floppy and run quite happily, in a limited fashion. Some Linux users have added an ethernet card to this bare configuration and used it for a variety of functions, from a network gateway machine to a basic router.

A typical Linux workstation machine looks more like the following:

- Pentium class or equivalent CPU (such as an AMD K5 or Cyrix Cx586).
- 64MB of RAM
- Floppy drive
- CD-ROM drive
- 4GB hard drive
- IDE or SCSI disk controllers
- SVGA graphics card
- Ethernet card or modem
- 17-inch color monitor

A typical Linux server configuration looks something like the following:

- Pentium II class processor or equivalent CPU (such as an AMD K6-2 or Cyrix M2).
- 128MB of RAM
- Floppy drive

- CD-ROM drive
- 9GB SCSI hard drive or multi drive RAID array
- Ethernet card or modem
- VGA graphics card
- Tape backup drive

For server configurations, it is always best to stick with SCSI. Some Linux users opt for all SCSI drives, even the CD-ROM. SCSI typically provides better performance and stability than IDE drives, as well as supporting multiple drives on one disk controller. Most motherboards only support a maximum of 4 IDE devices. If cost is a major consideration, IDE is a still a good option. Current Linux kernels support the most advanced IDE features. If you are buying an older IDE CD-ROM, make sure that the kernel supports it. Many older non-ATAPI CD-ROMs need special support from Linux to work. Older IDE CD-ROM drives that are 1x or 2x should be looked at for compatibility; these units are usually the drives that may require special support.

There are a large number of SCSI controllers supported on Linux. Again, checking compatibility is a matter of checking your chosen distribution's Web site. The Linux kernel is frequently updated, but most distributions ship one or two versions behind. Skilled Linux users can also check the www.kernel.org Web site and check the current development kernels support for the hardware in question. Installing a new kernel is not for the novice, and should be done with care.

Choice of motherboard is usually not a real issue with Linux. However, some motherboard chipsets have been known to give Linux problems, due to the lack of specifications from the manufacturers. Intel, VIA Apollo, and Ali Aladdin chipsets are among the ones that work with Linux. However, it is always important to check any key components to your Linux system against the hardware compatibility lists to ensure that they are supported.

RAM is another component that has few problems with Linux. The only snag would involve marginal or substandard memory. Linux supports current state-of-the-art memory features like ECC and ECO. Linux will currently support up to 2GB of memory on the Intel platforms with support for more on the way.

Almost all hard drives work just fine with Linux, as long as they conform to the IDE or SCSI specifications. The only drives that require special Linux driver support are removable drives such as the Iomega Zip and Jaz drives and high end tape drives such as DLT. The Iomega Zip and Jaz are fully supported under Linux. There is also support for the newer removable technology, such as LS120. Support for devices such as these changes rapidly, so make sure to check on the compatibility Web sites for current compatibility information.

RAID is a special case of a disk controller that has seen recent stable support under Linux. Several RAID controllers are now supported under Linux. Cards from Mylex, IPC, AMI and others are well supported, with some manufacturers providing user-level tools that run under Linux.

Video support under Linux is a complex issue. PC video cards do not enjoy the standard-ization of other components like disks or memory. This makes the life of a Linux kernel programmer difficult but challenging. At the minimum, Linux needs a VGA card to which to display kernel boot output. In the 2.2 version of the Linux kernel, there is sup-port for directing output and input through the serial ports. This is a great feature that obviates the need for a video card or even a local presence on the machine. A typical Linux machine will have a VGA or SVGA video card for running X (also known as the X Window System). If you are only running in text mode, almost any VGA video card will do. Running X has its own special requirements, as there must be an X server that supports the video card of choice. The XFree86 project, which provides Linux with its X support, maintains a list of currently supported video cards at www.xfree86.org. Most of the major vendors' cards support Matrox, ATI, S3, Diamond, and others. Support varies from card to card, so if you plan on running X, you must check on support for the card you want to install. The other component to the video option is a monitor. Unfortunately, Linux still requires you to know a few technical things about your monitor, like refresh rates and resolutions. Any monitor that supports VGA output will work in some fashion with Linux. X configuration is where things get tricky with the monitor. Knowing the technical specifications previously listed can save problems at this point.

Sound support under Linux comes down to one thing—Sound Blaster compatibility. The best bet for using sound under Linux is to get a Sound Blaster-compatible card. Several other sound cards are supported, such as those from Gravis, Adlib, and others. Also, onboard sound chips are becoming popular with motherboard manufacturers these days, and Linux supports a number of the most popular brands. Intel seems to prefer the Crystal Audio embedded sound chips, which are generally well supported under Linux. Linux also has support for various synth modules that come as part of the sound chipset. There is support for the Yamaha OPL FM synth chips as well as others in Yamaha's line. There are drivers for MIDI devices, input/recording devices, and for playing audio CDs.

The final piece in the component puzzle is a networking option. Unless you are at work or have a high speed Internet connection, you will probably be using a modem for net-work access. Having at least some kind of access to the Internet is important for running Linux for the obvious reasons. If you must use a modem, there are a few guidelines you should follow. First, never get a Winmodem. This is a type of modem that has part of the hardware functionality emulated in software. This software requires some variety of Microsoft Windows, so you are out of luck trying to use this type of modem under Linux. The second guideline will save you hours of trouble—get an external modem. An external modem has status LEDs on the front. This makes it a lot easier to tell what your modem is doing than if it is inside the computer. Setting up a modem under Linux can be tricky, so you want an easy way to get all the information you can on what the modem is doing. On top of the easy troubleshooting features of external modems, they are also eas-ier to upgrade than internal modems. Linux supports any modem that supports the stan-dard Hayes AT command set, as well as the various speeds from 1200 to 56,000 baud. Just stay away from winmodems, and you will be fine.

Ethernet cards are the second network option. Linux supports a wide range of 10/100 ethernet cards, with everything from PCMCIA ethernet all the way up to multiport ethernet cards. Ethernet cards require a driver for the kernel, so check those compatibility lists. Linux also has support for Gigabit ethernet, Token Ring cards, infrared, and several other proprietary or otherwise out-of-date network technologies. Linux's forté has always been as a network operating system, so if there is a open specification for it, Linux probably supports it. There are drivers for most of the major card vendors, including 3Com, NE1000 clones, Bay Networks, DEC, IBM, and numerous other chipsets.

A necessary adjunct to hardware requirements are a few software requirements. First, pick a distribution. Linux has many packaged versions, which individuals and companies have put together, that bundle compiled programs and source with the Linux kernel and drives. These packages are called distributions. There are several major Linux distributions and some new up-and-coming ones. Popular distributions seen in the community are Red Hat, SuSE, TurboLinux, Debian, Caldera, and Slackware. This is by no means a complete list. There are many different distributions, and each may appeal to you for different reasons. There seem to be as many distributions as there are different personalities in the Linux community. Try a few out and see which one fits. Major differences in the distributions are in two areas—package management and installation. Red Hat has a very easy to use installation program, and its RPM package format is also used by SuSE and Caldera, among others. The Debian distribution has its own format call DEB. Slackware uses a format based on tar and GNUzip, which is common to most UNIX flavors. TurboLinux has packaged several Asian language distributions, and SuSE has a very popular German variety. All the distributions differ in small details, but not enough to throw you when moving from one to another.

One of the great things about Linux is the capability to download the entire system from the Internet for free. If you have the network requirements, this is a fun way to install Linux. Most people still like to have something physical to hang onto, so several of the distributions come on CD-ROMs. Red Hat, SuSE, and Caldera sell nice shrink-wrapped packages that you can find in your local electronics store or bookstore. These boxed distributions come with a manual, several CD-ROMs, and other items.

Lastly, get prepared to do some reading. A good manual, like this one, is essential to getting the maximum benefit from Linux. Linux also comes with extensive online documentation. While it is making real headway on ease of use and GUI tools, at its heart, Linux still relies on a command line interface for real control of the system. Linux and UNIX, in general, are probably the best documented operating systems around because of that command-line heritage. A facility for reading and a love of words go almost hand in hand with Linux mastery.

The following are URLs for hardware-related resources for Linux:

- The Linux Kernel Web site: `http://www.kernel.org`
- LinuxCare: `http://www.linuxcare.com`

- The Linux DocumentationProject: http://metalab.unc.edu/LDP/
- Red Hat Software: http://www.redhat.com
- SuSE: http://www.suse.com
- Caldera: http://www.caldera.com
- Debian: http://www.debian.org
- Slackware: http://www.slackware.org

Summary

There are many options available to you when building your Linux system. It is important to build your system to suit your needs; this includes installing hardware that will handle what you want to do. We have discussed many popular types and brands of hardware that you can build into your Linux system, but remember, these are just suggestions. It is always advisable to check out the hardware compatibility lists available to you when deciding on a specific hardware component. Do your research!

On Your Own

If you are building your system, or just installing Linux on a computer you already own, go to the sites listed in the chapter and check out the hardware you are intending to use with Linux against the hardware compatibility lists.

Installing Linux

Understanding the Various Installation Methods

There are many different ways to install Linux on a computer. The installation media can be CD-ROM, hard disk, or even another computer over the network (this is done via FTP or NFS). There are also a few choices for when you boot to the install screen, some of which include floppy disks and bootable CD-ROMs.

The easiest and most common way of installing Linux is from a CD-ROM. CD-ROMs are inexpensive and are sometimes distributed freely. The main advantage of using a CD-ROM is that oftentimes users can boot off the CD-ROM and therefore do not need a make a bootable floppy disk. This method is also one of the fastest.

Another way of installing Linux is from a partition on your hard drive. This is also a very easy-to-use method, but it requires that you have an existing operating system to copy all of the files there. Although this is the fastest way of installing, it might not be the best option for some users because you must use extra drive space to hold the Linux distribution.

The final option for installing Linux is from a network. This option is only viable for users who have a direct connection to the Internet or have a LAN (local area network) wherein there is a server from which to download all of the files. When doing a network install of Linux, there are usually two protocols you can use: NFS or FTP. Both methods are equally fast, but slower than any other install method (with the exception of installing from a set of floppy disks, which was done in older distributions). With most distributions, you must have a working network card (and double-check to make sure it is supported under your distribution of Linux). You also have the choice of using BOOTP, DHCP, or static IP addressing to configure the network. For more information on these, consult your network administrator.

Starting the Installation Process

Before you begin your installation, there are a few requirements you must fulfill:

- If you are installing via floppy or bootable CD-ROM, you must have a CD-ROM of the distribution you want to install.

- If you want to install via NFS or FTP, you must know of a site that contains the full distribution you want to install.

- If you are installing via NFS or FTP, you must have an Ethernet card that is supported, and also you must have a direct connection to the site from which you wish to download. This means that you cannot use a modem to do a network install.

- You must have enough hard drive space on which to install Linux. This means that for a standard install, you will need anywhere from 300–1000MB, depending on which packages you plan to install. The installation program will tell you exactly how much space you need.

- If you plan on using a bootable CD-ROM, your BIOS must support the El Torrito Bootable CD-ROM Standard. Generally, most Pentiums and faster processors have this.

- If you are installing with floppy disks, make sure that you have two blank floppy disks that you can use. You will also need access to another computer to write the boot disks.

Installing Red Hat Linux

When installing Red Hat Linux, you have two options for booting up the install screen: you can make a bootable floppy disk, or you can use a bootable CD-ROM (if you boot off the CD-ROM, the installation media must be either that CD-ROM or a hard drive partition; you do not have any network options). However, there is also a third option, you can use the "autoboot" feature to boot from DOS or Windows 9x.

Booting

You should now select which installation method is right for you. Keep in mind the type of media you will be installing from and your available resources.

Using Floppy Disks to Boot

If you plan on using floppy disks to boot Red Hat Linux, you will need only one of them and a computer where you can format the disk and make it bootable. If you plan on installing over a network, you must use a floppy disk to boot the installation program.

To do this under Windows, you will need to find the directory on your Red Hat Linux install medium that contains the disk images (CD-ROM, hard drive, network). If you are using a CD-ROM, the images are located in X:\images (where X is the drive letter of your CD-ROM drive). Here there should be four images to pick from if you are installing Red Hat 6.0. The four files are as follows:

- `boot.img`   Users who are installing from either CD-ROM or hard disk should use this image.

- `bootnet.img`   Users installing from over a network should use this image. This file differs from `boot.img` because it contains drivers for network cards.
- `pcmcia.img`   Users who are installing Linux onto a laptop should use this file. This image contains support for PCMCIA cards.
- `rescue.img`   Users who have already installed Linux and have been unable to boot because of some error should use this image. This image enables you to recover your installation.

After you have selected your boot image, you should copy it to a temporary directory on your hard drive. Next you need a utility called `rawrite`. `rawrite` copies a disk image and writes it to floppy. `rawrite` can be found on the Red Hat CD-ROM under `X:\dosutils\` (where `X` is the letter of your CD-ROM drive). Copy the `rawrite.exe` file from this directory into the same directory on your hard drive where you copied the image file.

Next you must run `rawrite`. It will now say "Enter Disk Image Source File Name." You must type the name of the image that you want to use (for instance, `boot.img`) and the path to this image if it is not in the same directory as `rawrite.exe`. Next, it will ask you the drive to which you want to write this image. You must now insert a blank floppy disk into your floppy drive and give `rawrite` the path to your floppy drive (for instance, `A:\`). It will now start to write the image to your floppy drive.

You can also make a boot disk using UNIX. To do this, copy the image file to a temporary directory on your system. Next, insert a blank floppy disk into your drive and type **dd if=*image.img* of=/dev/fd0 bs=1440k**, where *image.img* is the name of the image file you plan on using.

You now have a bootable floppy disk. You must now place the floppy in your drive and make sure that your BIOS is set up to boot off the floppy drive. Reboot your computer, and soon you should see a message saying "Welcome to Red Hat Linux." If you do not see this message after a few minutes, the computer might have failed to boot due to a bad disk. Try using another floppy disk (preferably new), make sure to format it, and then write the image to it again. If you have successfully started the install program, you can now skip to the section titled "The Installation Program."

Using a Bootable CD-ROM to Boot

If you have a commercial version of Red Hat Linux 6.0, it is definitely bootable. However, if the CD-ROM you are using is a copy, there is a chance that it is not bootable, and you must then use a floppy disk to boot. The best way to find out is to try it.

First you must make sure that your BIOS supports the El Torrito Bootable CD-ROM standard. Most newer computers (Pentium and faster) do. The next step is configuring your BIOS to boot off the CD-ROM. To do this, you must enter the CMOS setup utility. This is done on most computers by pressing either Delete or Esc when the computer is first booting up (when it is counting memory, there is usually a message that says which key to push to enter setup). Here you should set your first boot device to be your

CD-ROM drive (your second should be your floppy drive, and your third should be your hard drive). If you are using a SCSI CD-ROM drive, you will need to enter the SCSI BIOS to make sure that the CD-ROM drive is set to boot. Remember, not all SCSI controllers will be able to do this.

Finally, put your CD-ROM into the drive and reboot the computer. Now some text should scroll down the screen, and finally a message saying "Welcome to Red Hat Linux" should appear on your screen. Congratulations, you have successfully booted. Now proceed to the section titled "The Installation Program."

Using autoboot to Boot

There is one more way of booting to the install program: the autoboot feature. This only works if you have DOS or Windows (Windows NT will not work because you cannot use DOS) installed on the computer on which you plan to install Linux. This option is only applicable if you plan to use a CD-ROM or a hard disk as your installation media.

Included on the Red Hat CD-ROM is a file located in X:\dosutils\autoboot.bat (where X is the letter of your CD-ROM drive). This is a batch file that will start the install program when this script is run form DOS. This script can only be run from DOS, which means that if Windows 9x is being used, you must reboot to DOS. From DOS, go to the directory where autoboot.bat is located and execute it by typing **autoboot.bat** at the prompt.

If all goes well, you should see the installation screen appear in a few seconds. It should say "Welcome to Red Hat Linux." You should now proceed to the next section, "The Installation Program." If something goes wrong, it might be a good idea to use one of the other methods of booting mentioned previously.

The Installation Program

Once the installation program has started, you must first choose which language you want to use. You can use the arrows to scroll through the menu, and after you have chosen a language, simply press the Enter key. The next option to enter is the type of keyboard you are using. Anyone using an American "qwerty" keyboard should choose us.

The next selection is very important; here you enter the type of media from which you are installing Red Hat Linux. Anyone who used boot.img or pcmcia.img has a choice between Local CDROM and Hard Drive. If you have a CD-ROM that contains the entire distribution, you should go with the former. The latter should be chosen if you do not have a CD-ROM, but have the distribution copied to a partition of your hard drive instead.

Installing from a CD-ROM

If you are installing from a CD-ROM, the install program will now search for your CD-ROM drive. If the installer did not locate your CD-ROM drive, be sure that the disk was inserted correctly and try again. If it still does not locate it, it might ask for the type and location of your CD-ROM drive. Enter the location in the form seen in Table 3.1.

Installing from a Hard Drive Partition

If you are installing from a partition on your hard drive, you must first specify whether or not you have any SCSI controllers (this is crucial if you have a SCSI hard disk). If you do have a SCSI adapter, you must select your adapter from the list that it gives you. If your adapter is not listed, it may be unsupported or under a different name (be sure that you know the chipset that is on your adapter). Consult the Red Hat Hardware Compatibility List to see if your adapter is supported. This can be found either on its Web site (`http://www.Red Hat.com`) or on the CD-ROM.

Next, you must enter the drive, partition, and path where the files are. The drive is of the form `/dev/hdx#` if it is IDE. The *x* stands for the drive, as can be seen in Table 3.1.

Table 3.1   Format for Naming Drives Under Linux

Drive	Location
/dev/hda	Master drive on the primary IDE bus
/dev/hdb	Slave drive on the primary IDE bus
/dev/hdc	Master drive on the secondary IDE bus
/dev/hdd	Slave drive on the secondary IDE bus

The # stands for the partition number that the distribution is on (if there is only one partition on the drive, the number is 1). So to use the second partition on the master drive on the primary IDE bus, you would use `/dev/hda2`.

If you are using a SCSI hard drive, you must enter the device name in the form `/dev/sdx`, where *x* corresponds to the order in which the device is found at boot time. This means that the device with the lowest SCSI ID number would be the first device found by the SCSI BIOS. For instance, `/dev/sda` would be a SCSI hard drive with the lowest SCSI ID of all the devices found by the controller. The partition numbering scheme is identical to the one for IDE disks, wherein a number for the partition follows the device. For example, `/dev/sdb2` corresponds to the second partition of the SCSI hard drive, which is the second device on the SCSI chain.

The next part to be entered is the path. If you copied the distribution to your hard drive, the directory structure must be preserved for the installer to find it. The installer wants you to enter the path to the root of the distribution, which means that if you copied the contents of the entire CD-ROM to `C:\temp\` (this means that in this directory is a directory called Red Hat in which reside two more directories, RPMS and base), you would type `/temp/`. If the installer is unable to locate the directory, make sure that you double-check the path and the drive to which you copied.

Installing over a Network

If you choose to install via NFS, FTP, or HTTP, you must select your network card from the list provided after you have selected your installation method. If you do not see your card in this list, first find out what the chipset of your card is, and then see if there is a driver for that chipset (rather than for the actual model that you have). If this does not work, it would be wise to consult the Red Hat Linux Hardware Compatibility List to see if your card is even supported. If your card is not on the list, it is possible to just select NE2000 and Compatible, as many cards will work with this driver.

Once the drivers for your card are found, the installation program needs to detect your card to see if it can be found. In most cases, selecting Autoprode should work; however, you may need to enter special parameters if it does not detect it. The special parameters needed might include IRQ, IO Address, and so on. Please consult the documentation included on the Red Hat CD-ROM or on the Web site (http://www.Red Hat.com) for information on parameters specific to your card.

Now that your network card has been detected and drivers have been installed, you must tell the installation program how to set up IP addressing. For this, you have three options: Static IP addressing, BOOTP, and DHCP. For both DHCP and BOOTP, there must be a server on the subnet that will be detected. If you select either BOOTP or DHCP, the install program will search the local network for the server and then addressing will be configured automatically. However, if you are using a static IP address, you must enter certain information that was assigned by your network administrator (IP address, subnet mask, gateway, DNS server). After all of this is entered, you must enter your hostname and the domain name. After these are entered, you have the option of entering secondary and tertiary name server addresses. If you have none, leave these spaces blank.

Installing via NFS

Now that everything is configured for using the network, it is time to enter the information regarding the NFS server you are using. In the first space on this page, you must enter the name of the NFS server (for instance, server.host.net). You can also enter just the IP address of the server. Next you must enter the path on the NFS server to the directory named Red-Hat. For example, if the directory on the server is /nfs/Red Hat/i386/Red Hat, enter **/nfs/Red Hat/i386/**. At this point it should successfully find the server, so you can now skip to the "Partitioning and Installing" section in this chapter. If it does not find the server, recheck the name and directory and also try a mirror site.

Installing via FTP

If you are choosing to do an installation from an FTP site, you are required to enter two things: the name or IP address of the site, and the path to the Red Hat directory. If you are installing from the official Red Hat site, you would enter **ftp.Red Hat.com** for the site name and **/pub/Red Hat/current/i386/** if you are installing on an Intel-based computer. The installation program should connect to the FTP site and start to download a few files; this could take a few minutes. If it cannot find the right directory or site, re-enter everything or try another site. If you are using a private server to access the distrib-ution and require a password and username to log on (rather than using anonymous FTP), you must check the box at the bottom of the page where you entered the server name. You can also use this page to enter information regarding a proxy server if you are behind a firewall. If all is successful, go on to the "Partitioning and Installing" section later in this chapter.

Installing via HTTP

The procedure for installing over HTTP is almost identical to the one used for installing from an FTP site. However, you may need to enter information regarding a proxy server if you are behind a firewall. If this is the case, check the box at the bottom of the page where you enter information regarding the address of the HTTP site. When you enter everything on this page, it will open a new page where you can enter the name and port of the proxy server to use.

Partitioning and Installing

By now you have reached a screen that is asking you if you want to upgrade or install. If you choose Install, your installation program will let you reformat and repartition your hard drive, and then it will install all the needed system files and the packages that you select. If you choose Upgrade, it is assumed that you already have a working system. Therefore, you cannot repartition or reformat your hard drive, and certain system files will not be changed on your system. If you choose Upgrade, you can skip to the next section, "Selecting Packages."

There should be a list of options on your screen regarding the Installation Class. Your choices are Workstation, Server, and Custom. These options only change the way that your hard drive will be partitioned. If you choose Workstation, the installation program will delete all existing Linux partitions (this means that all data in these partitions will be deleted too!) and create a 64MB swap partition. (A swap partition is used like virtual memory is used in Windows.) It will also create a 16MB partition that it will mount as /boot; this directory will contain the kernel and related files. If you are installing on a DEC Alpha system, instead of /boot, a 2MB partition will be created that will be mount-ed as /dos. This directory will hold the kernel and MILO, the Linux loader for Alpha. All remaining unpartitioned space will be made into the main Linux partition. The Workstation install will also try to locate any other OS on your computer and will try to make the computer dual-boot to both Linux and the other OS. You will need at least 600MB to use the Workstation Class Install.

The Server install will completely erase any partitions on your hard drive. It will then create a 64MB swap partition and a 16MB partition mounted as /boot that contains ker-nel files (if you are using an Intel-based system). If you are using an Alpha system, there will be a 2MB partition mounted as /dos, just as in the Workstation Class installation. The difference is, now there will be a 256MB partition mounted as the root directory (/) and another 256MB partition mounted as /var. There will also be two partitions of at least 512MB each mounted as /home and /usr. This means that you will need a minimum of 1.6 gigabytes of disk space.

Both the Workstation and Server Class installations will automatically select the packages that will be installed on your system. If you are planning on installing either the Workstation or Server Class, you might want to skip ahead to the "Configuring Your System" section.

The Custom Class installation gives you the most control of what goes onto your system. Here you can specify how big you want your swap and main partitions to be. You also can specify what packages go on your system. If you choose the Custom Class installation, your next step is to partition your hard drive. You have the option of using Disk Druid or fdisk.

Partitioning with Disk Druid

Disk Druid lets you partition your disk with a character interface (a very primitive graphical user interface). On the main screen, you will see that a list of all of your partitions is displayed. If your disk has no partitions on it (it will have no data on it), it will just say free space. You must make at least two partitions for your installation to work. To do this, first make sure that you have enough free space (you can also delete existing partitions, but all data will be lost). It is recommended that you have between 64–128MB of space for a swap drive and around 1GB for the main Linux partition.

To add a partition, move the cursor to the Add button (the controls are the same as the installation program for moving the cursor) and press Enter or F1. A new dialog box appears. The first space to fill in here is the mount point for the new partition; if it is to be the root Linux partition, enter /. Select the next field and enter the size of the partition in megabytes. The next field is a check box where you choose whether or not you want the partition to be able to grow to the size of the drive. The next field allows you to enter the type of partition that you are creating; if this is your root partition, you must enter **Linux Native**.

To set up a swap partition, you must follow the same procedure, except that you don't need a mount point and must make sure to set the type to Linux Swap. Be sure to set the size somewhere between 64–128MB. It is often advised to make a swap partition that is the same size as your physical memory, but many distributions do not allow you to create a swap partition greater than 128MB. If you want more than 128MB of swap space, you can create multiple swap partitions. When you are finished, select OK to save all your changes.

> **Warning:** If you deleted or altered any existing partitions, all data will be deleted.

Partitioning with fdisk

fdisk is almost identical to its DOS counterpart; it is a command-line partitioning utility. When you select fdisk at the menu, the installation program will show you a list of all of the hard drives on the system. Select the drive that you want to partition, move the cursor to Edit, and press Enter. You will notice that you have entered text mode. You can press M at any time to see a list of all the commands you can use in fdisk. You can now press P to print out a list of all existing partitions. If none are listed, there is nothing on this drive. However, if there are other partitions on this drive that contain data you want to preserve, you must proceed carefully. Assuming that you have adequate disk space, press N to add a new partition. fdisk will ask you if you if this is a primary or extended partition. Choose primary by pressing P, and then type the number of the partition. If this is the first partition on the disk, it is best to use #1; however, if other partitions exist, just use the next available number.

Now you must enter the starting and ending point for this partition. Unlike Disk Druid, fdisk does not display the partitions' sizes in megabytes. By default, fdisk uses cylinders. To find the number of megabytes, notice that when the partition information was printed out, it said something like the following:

```
Disk /tmp/had: 255 heads, 63 sectors, 1229 cylinders
Units = cylinders of 16065 * 512 bytes
```

This tells you how big each unit is (your unit size will most likely be different from the example). In this case, one unit is about 8MB (16065 * 512 = 8225280 bytes). You can use this to enter the size of your new partition. It is generally a good idea to start each partition right at the end of the previous partition, or, if you are creating the first partition on the drive, start it at the first unit, as shown in the following:

```
Disk /tmp/had: 255 heads, 63 sectors, 1229 cylinders
Units = cylinders of 16065 * 512 bytes
```

Device Boot	Start	End	Blocks	Id	System
/tmp/hda1		*		1	1214	9751423+ 83
Linux native					
/tmp/hda2				1215	1229	120487+ 82
Linux swap					

After you have created your root partition (make sure that you saved space for your swap partition), you can print out the partitions to the screen by pressing P. Make sure that it says Linux native after it. If it does not, press T to change the type of the partition. fdisk will now ask you which partition number you would like to change; enter the number of the partition here. You are then asked for the Hex code for the partition type. The code for Linux native is 83; you can see for yourself by printing out all of the codes (press L). After it is changed, you can press P again to make sure the partitions were created correctly.

Now you are ready to set up your swap partition. Add a new partition as you did before (by pressing N), and make sure it is a primary partition. You should make sure to make the size somewhere between 64–128MB, depending on how much physical memory you have. You should try and make the swap space the same size as your physical memory. Some distributions will not allow swap partitions greater than 128MB. Therefore, if a larger-sized swap partition is desired, multiple swap partitions can be created. When you are done, you must make sure to change the type for this new swap partition. By default, all new partitions are Linux native. This is done as shown before (by pressing T and entering the partition number). However, make sure to make the partition type Linux swap (Hex code #82).

Now you must save the partition table on your hard drive by exiting fdisk by typing W (to write to disk). At this point there is no turning back. Once the new partitions are written, all old partitions that were edited or deleted will be permanently gone. If you do not want to write the table, you can press Q to quit without saving changes.

Now that you have set up Linux partitions, you can select Done from the menu. This will bring up all of the information on your partitions in Disk Druid. This must be done so that you can select a mount point for your new partition(s). Keep in mind that the swap partition does not use a mount point. From Disk Druid, you want to set the mount point for the root partition to be /. To do this, you must select the partition and click the Edit button. When finished, select OK to save and exit.

Congratulations, you have now set up your partitions!

Formatting

After you have set up your partitions, the installation program will look at your partition table to find all partitions that are going to be used for swap drives. You will see a list of these in the new window that appears; the size of each partition will appear to its right. Simply check the box by the partition name if you would like to use it. The installation program is now going to format your swap space; however, it might be a good idea to have it check for bad blocks on this partition if you are using an older drive. Click OK to continue, but the installation program will wait until you have selected which packages you would like to install before it starts to format.

Now a similar dialog box appears. This one should have a list of all of the Linux native partitions on your system. Just like the previous dialog box, you have an option to format and check for bad blocks. This is only necessary on older drives, and the time that it takes is directly proportional to the size of the drive.

Selecting Packages

Now that you have prepared your hard disks, it is time to actually choose what gets installed on your system. Before you should be a list of available packages. Table 3.2 lists these options and what they do.

Table 3.2 Packages for Red Hat Linux

Option	Description
Printer Support	Allows you to print to either a local printer or a LAN printer
X Window System	Required for a graphical interface
GNOME	This is an optional desktop environment that can be used with X
KDE	This is an optional desktop environment that can be used with X
Mail/WWW/News Tools	A group of programs for reading newsgroups, checking email, and browsing the Web
DOS/Windows Connectivity	Allows you to easily access DOS/Windows files and share them between OSs
File Managers	Utilities for managing files on your system
Graphics Manipulation	Utilities for doing image editing and layout
Console Games	Games that can be run in text mode
X Games System	Games that must be run from the X Window
Console Multimedia	Utilities that enable multimedia to be used from the text console
X multimedia support	Utilities for using multimedia in the X Window System
Networked Workstation	Network utilities for a workstation on a LAN or WAN
Dialup Workstation	Programs needed to create a dialup workstation
News Server	Programs needed to create a news server
NFS Server	Programs needed to create an NFS server
SMB (Samba) Connectivity	Programs that enable networked Linux workstations and servers to communicate with Windows machines (Network Neighborhood) over a network

continues

Table 3.2 Continued

Option	Description
IPX/Netware(tm) Connectivity	Utilities to enable your Linux machines to communicate with Netware machines using the IPX protocol
Anonymous FTP Server	Programs needed to create an anonymous FTP server
Web Server	Programs needed to create an HTTP server
DNS Name Server	Programs needed to create a DNS server
Postgres (SQL) Server	Programs needed to create an SQL server
Network Management Workstation	Programs needed for managing a network from this Linux workstation
TeX Document Formatting	Document layout utilities
Emacs	The Emacs text editor (text mode)
Emacs with X windows	The Emacs text editor (X Windows)
C Development	Compilers and associated files for the C programming language
Development Libraries	Programming libraries
C++ Development	Compilers and associated files for the C++ programming language
X Development	Files to aid in development of the X Windows System
GNOME Development	Files to aid in development of the GNOME Desktop Environment
Kernel Development	Linux kernel source code and associated files
Extra Documentation	README files, HOWTOs, and other documentation
Everything	All of the aforementioned packages

After you have selected which packages you want to install, you have the option of looking at the individual files rather than the groups listed in Table 3.2. You may decide that you do not want certain things on your system, so it might be a good idea to browse through here. When you are done, simply click OK. If there are any file dependencies that need to be fulfilled, the installation program will tell you now and should automatically install them with your permission. If everything else is okay, the installation program should begin to copy files to your hard drive. You will notice that it gives a description of each package as it installs it. You may also notice that there are estimated completion times in the bottom-right portion of the dialog box.

Configuring Your System

Now that all of the packages are installed on your system, it is time to configure it. The first thing that you must be do is install drivers for your mouse (if you have one). Generally, the installation program will auto-detect it. If this is the case, you still have to select it from the list that comes up in the next dialog box (even if it does not automatically detect your mouse, you can select it from the list). You also have the option of emulating a three-button mouse if your mouse only has two buttons. If this option is selected, when you click the first and second button simultaneously, it will act as if you clicked a third button.

The next part of the system that must be configured is your LAN (local area network). This is only applicable if you have a NIC (network interface card) in your system. If you only use a modem or have no network connections, you should skip this section. If you installed Red Hat Linux from a network, this should already be set up.

The first thing to enter here is the type of NIC you will be using. If you do not see your card on the list, check the chipset of your card and see if that is on the list. It is also a good idea to check the Red Hat Linux Hardware Compatibility List to make sure that your card is supported. If your card is not on the unsupported list, it might be a good idea to try the NE2000 and Compatible driver, because most generic cards should work with it. Now that the driver is installed, the installation program will try to communicate with your card; you should select Autoprobe for this. If there are any problems, you might need to enter extra parameters. Now you must specify how you obtain an IP address. Your options are Static IP, BOOTP, and DHCP. If you choose either BOOTP or DHCP, there must be a server on your local subnet for this to work. If you choose to enter a static IP, this must be assigned by your network administrator. You will need to enter your IP address, subnet mask, gateway, and the primary nameserver. After this is entered, you will then need to enter the domain name followed by the hostname, and then any additional nameservers (optional). All of this information can be obtained from your network administrator.

The next step in configuring your system is to set the time zone. You must select your proper time zone from the list provided. You also have the option to set your clock to GMT.

The final step is to set a password for the root account. This is extremely important because the root account has special privileges; the password should be hard to guess. You must then retype the password just to be sure you didn't mistype anything.

Rescue Disks

You now have an option to make a special bootable floppy for your system. This is a very good idea. To do this, simply insert a blank high-density (1.44MB) floppy disk into your disk drive at the prompt and click OK. The installation program will write the disk. This disk will come in handy whenever there is a system failure. Simply use this disk to boot your system and correct whatever malfunctioned.

X Configuration

The next step in setting up your new installation is to configure X Windows. X is the name of the graphical interface for Linux and other distributions of Linux. You have the option of using Linux from just the command prompt (text mode) or with X. If you have installed all of the required files for X, the installation program will now ask you questions about your video hardware. The first thing to be entered is the name of the video card you are using. If you do not see your card in the list, you should first check to see if it is supported (either check the hardware compatibility guide or go to http://www.xfree86.org/ to check the list). If your card is supported but you do not see it, find the chipset of your card and try installing drivers for a similar card with the same chipset.

The next step is to select your monitor's model and manufacturer from the list provided. This is important in determining refresh rates for X, so try to find the exact model in the list. If you do not see your monitor listed, select Custom. This will give you the opportunity to enter the specific specifications for your monitor, which are provided in your monitor's documentation.

Now you must enter the amount of video memory on your video card. If you do not know this information offhand, you can find it in the documentation that came with your card. Next you must enter a clockchip setting. Most users do not need a clockchip setting. You will find out if you need one in the next step.

The next step is to probe the video card for information such as clockchip settings, type of video card, or any other special options. This step can cause your computer to crash. If it does, simply reboot and skip this part next time. When you probe the card, your monitor should flicker and go blank for a little bit. If your screen does not come back after a few minutes, your computer may need to be rebooted.

When your screen comes back, there may be some numbers displayed regarding clockchip settings; just wait a few seconds for the screen to clear and a new dialog box should appear. Here you must enter the default resolutions for each video mode listed. Consult your video card's documentation to find out the limitations of your card. Remember: 8-bit color is 256 colors, 16-bit is 65,536 colors, and both 24-bit and 32-bit are 16,777,216 colors. After all of this information is entered, the installation program will test your configuration by starting X. If everything is working properly, you should see a dialog box telling you to click Yes. Do so. You will then be asked whether or not you would like to launch X automatically when the computer is rebooted. If you choose No, you will start up in the future in text mode and will have to start X by typing **startx** at the prompt.

Congratulations! Your installation is complete. Your computer will now reboot itself and should start Linux. You will know if it works if it says something like the following:

```
LILO boot:
Loading linux..........
Uncompressing Linux... Ok, booting the kernel.
```

After a minute or so, you should be at a login prompt (either in X or in text mode). Right now, the only account you may log in with is root. Be sure to enter the same password you set up during the installation.

Making Rescue Disks

If you run into any problems after your system is set up, you can use a rescue disk to try to recover your system. It is also good to keep these disks up-to-date. Inserting a blank disk into your drive and typing the command mkbootdisk -*kernel_version* will make a new or updated rescue disk. Simply replace *kernel_version* with the version number of your kernel. If you do not know the version, you can type uname -a to get a list of important system information, as shown in the following:

```
%uname -a
Linux myhost.local.net 2.2.5-15 #1 Sat Jul 24 22:21:09 EDT 1999
```

Or you could just use uname -r to find the release number by itself:

```
%uname -r
2.2.5-15
```

As can be seen, this is Linux 2.2.5-15. To make a boot disk, you would need to type mkbootdisk 2.2.5-15 and press Enter. You will now be asked to put a floppy disk in the drive and press Enter to start making the disk. The kernel will now copied from a specified location in /etc/lilo.conf to the floppy disk. It should take a few minutes for it to finish.

Now you should have a working boot disk. By default, this disk can be used two ways: you can boot this disk and type linux at the LILO prompt, or you can type rescue. If you type linux, LILO will load your previous settings, all of your existing startup files, and your previous kernel image that your system was using when you created the boot disk. This is helpful if there is a problem with the boot sector on your hard drive (such as if LILO wasn't written properly and you can't boot). If you use the rescue option, you will be prompted for a root floppy disk. This is because the rescue image is using only startup files from the floppy disks to boot. You would use this option if more than LILO wasn't working—if you were able to boot, but the system later crashed for another reason.

To be able to use the rescue option, you will need to make this second root disk. Writing an image called rescue.img to a new floppy does this. The image file can be found on your Red Hat Linux installation media, whether it be CD-ROM, hard drive partition, or network site. It can be found in the images directory on whichever media you used. It may be a good idea to copy this file to your system if it is not already on your hard drive. Simply enter the following to copy from a CD-ROM drive:

```
%mount /dev/cdrom /mnt
mount: block device /dev/cdrom is write-protected, mounting read-only
%cd /mnt/images
%cp rescue.img /tmp/
```

This rescue.img file is now located in /tmp/. The next step is to write this image to a floppy disk. This is done using the dd command, as shown in the following:

```
%cd /tmp
%dd if=rescue.img of=/dev/fd0 bs=1440k
1+0 records in
1+0 records out
%
```

You must remember not to remove the disk from the drive until both the command prompt has returned and the light on the floppy drive has gone out. Otherwise, you risk removing the disk before the files have been completely written to it. You now should have a working rescue disk set.

These disks can be used for two different reasons: either for attempting to fix Linux when it won't boot properly, or for saving important files when something goes wrong and you want to reformat and reinstall everything. One very common reason for using the rescue disks is because you've built a new kernel, LILO did not get reinstalled properly, and you are unable to boot; or maybe another operating system deleted LILO from the MBR (master boot record). This is common when you're using Windows 9x on another partition. If it is only a matter of reinstalling LILO, you might only need to use this rescue disk as a standard boot disk (this way it will only load the kernel from the floppy and all other system files will be loaded from the hard drive). To do this, simply insert the rescue disk into your floppy drive, reboot, and press Enter when prompted. It will then boot normally.

To boot to rescue mode, simply put your boot disk in the floppy drive and turn your computer on, making sure that the BIOS is set to boot off the floppy drive first (before the hard drive, anyway). Once you see the LILO prompt, simply type **rescue** and it will slowly load Linux from the floppy disk. After a minute or two, you will be asked to insert your root disk:

```
VFS: Insert root disk to be loaded into RAM disk and press ENTER
```

At this point you must insert your root disk and press Enter. It should now say that it found a compressed image at block 0. You will now see the system boot up, except that the hard drive will not be mounted because the root filesystem will be loaded from the floppy disks. You can now repair your system.

Troubleshooting

If anything does go wrong with your system, you should now be able to either recover your files and/or fix the problem. However, there are two more ways of booting up your system if anything goes wrong, in addition to using the rescue disk set. You can boot to single-user mode and emergency mode. This can be done by typing either mode at the LILO prompt after you type linux, as shown in the following:

```
LILO
boot: linux single
```

Single-user mode is for users who need to recover their systems because of problems with the network, problems with startup files, or any other problem where the computer will boot but will not allow any user to log in. In single-user mode, the system will boot as usual, except the network will not be activated and there is no login prompt. This mode should be used to attempt to repair the system.

Emergency mode is for users whose systems boot but do not function at all. This is for emergency situations only, because it is used for copying important files off the system onto floppy disks or other backup media. This mode is used as a last resort before reinstalling the system. The system will be booted, but very few services will be run, and the hard drive(s) will be read-only. You can enter emergency mode, as shown in the following:

```
LILO
boot: linux emergency
```

As in single-user mode, the system will boot and you should see a prompt. Here you must either enter the root password or press Ctrl+D to start the system normally. If the root password is entered, you will be able to bypass many system initialization routines. You should soon see a prompt and be able to copy any important files off the system.

Installing Caldera OpenLinux

Caldera OpenLinux is attractive to many users because it is the only distribution that features a fully graphical installation program and boot loader. On the downside, however, the only way to install Caldera OpenLinux is from CD-ROM or from hard disk. When you launch the installation program, you might notice that it is checking for SMB or NFS installations. However, these features are not yet fully implemented.

Booting

Caldera OpenLinux is a little more limited than Red Hat Linux in terms of the number of your installation choices. This is because it has a very complex directory system, so the easiest way to obtain it is on a commercial CD-ROM (as opposed to copying it yourself). The installation program itself is a bit easier to use than most other distributions because almost everyone will be installing from CD-ROM.

There are three choices for booting to the installation program: You can use a bootable CD-ROM if your computer supports it, you can make two floppy disks, or you can launch the installation program from Windows by opening the CD-ROM from My Computer.

If your computer supports the El Torrito Bootable CD-ROM Standard (usually on Pentiums and newer computers), you simply configure the BIOS to boot from the CD-ROM drive. Now just insert the CD-ROM into the drive and reboot your computer. You should now see the installation program start to load.

If you plan to use floppy disks from which to boot, you will need a working computer to create a boot disk set. If you are planning to use Windows to copy the files, it might be a good idea to first copy the disk images to your hard drive. Do this by inserting your Caldera OpenLinux CD-ROM into the drive and copying `install.144` and `modules.144` to a temporary location. These files should be located in `X:\col\launch\floppy\` (where `X` is the letter of your CD-ROM drive). To use these files to make two floppies, you must use a program called `rawrite`. `rawrite` should be located in the same directory where you found the disk images. You may want to copy this file to the same temporary directory as the images. Now, simply insert a blank floppy disk into your drive and execute `rawrite.exe`.

The program will display the following prompt:

```
Enter disk image source file name.
```

You must type the name of the image for the boot disk, **install.144**, and the path to this image if it is not in the same directory as `rawrite.exe`. Next, the program will ask for the drive to which you want to write this image. You must now enter the path to your floppy drive (for instance, `A:\`). It will now start to write the image to your floppy drive.

After the boot disk is done, it is necessary to create the second disk. Put a second floppy disk in the drive and run `rawrite` as you did for the first disk. This time, however, you need to enter **modules.144** for the image filename. When program is finished writing, remove the disk and insert the first disk you created into the computer on which you will be installing Caldera OpenLinux (it may be a good idea to label these disks at this point). Make sure that this computer is set to boot off of the floppy drive, and reboot it. The computer should boot to the OpenLinux installation program. It will take a few minutes to load files, and eventually it will display something like the following:

```
Loading kernel............................ Ok
Booting kernel............................ Ok
Mount modules floppy...................... Wait
```

As soon as it says `wait`, you must quickly insert the modules disk if you plan to use it. This disk adds extra drivers, such as SCSI adapters, Ethernet cards, and proprietary CD-ROMs.

At this point, make sure you have inserted your Caldera OpenLinux CD-ROM into your drive because it must be detected by the installation program.

The Installation Program

As soon as the installation program starts, it will ask you to choose a language for the program. You will notice immediately that, unlike any other distribution, Caldera OpenLinux has a completely graphical installation program in which you can use the mouse. Simply click the box for the language that you speak and click Next. On this next page, make sure to move the mouse around a little bit, very slowly. This way, the installation program can detect your mouse more easily. If you have a PS/2 mouse, you may need to scroll through the list of options to install your specific mouse. If you have a serial mouse, you should enter whether or not it's Microsoft- or Logitech-compatible. You will also have to enter the serial port it is on if it has not been detected. To do this, use Table 3.3 to determine its serial port under Linux.

Table 3.3 Serial Port Names Under Linux and DOS/Windows

Serial Port Under Linux	Serial Port Under DOS/Windows
/dev/ttyS0	COM1
/dev/ttyS1	COM2
/dev/ttyS2	COM3
/dev/ttyS3	COM4

After you have selected your mouse, you have the option of testing it. Simply move the pointer into the box that says Test Mouse Here and click each button to make sure it is detected correctly. If everything works, click Next to continue. If for some reason your mouse does not work, you probably either selected the wrong driver or serial port (if applicable).

Partitioning

The next step is setting up your hard drive partitions. To do this, you have three options. You can use your entire hard drive for Linux (selecting this option will completely reformat your entire hard drive and any existing information will be lost), you can install on existing Linux partitions (this will not harm any other partitions), or you can choose Custom to create your own partitions.

Using the Entire Hard Drive

If you choose to use your entire hard drive, the installation program will create at least three partitions, all of which will be used by Linux. There will be a root partition, where the main filesystem will be held (similar to c:\ in DOS/Windows). The size of this partition is dependent on the amount of space you have on this drive. You will also have a partition for /home, which contains all of the users' home directories (the size is dependent on the amount of space available on the drive). Finally, there will be a 120MB swap partition that Linux will use for virtual memory.

You now should see a list of hard drives and their sizes in the main window (Table 3.4 shows how to identify these drives). Click the one on which you want to install Linux, and then click the button labeled Prepare Selected Disk for Linux. The installation program will now partition your entire hard drive and reserve it for Linux. This process may take a few minutes. You will know it has finished when you are able to click the Next button to proceed to the next step.

Table 3.4 Drive Names Under Linux

Drives	Description
/dev/hda	Master drive on the primary IDE bus
/dev/hdb	Slave drive on the primary IDE bus
/dev/hdc	Master drive on the secondary IDE bus
/dev/hdd	Slave drive on the secondary IDE bus
/dev/sda	First detected SCSI device
/dev/sdb	Second detected SCSI device

Using Existing Linux Partitions

If you plan to install onto existing partitions, select that option and you will notice a window showing all of the Linux partitions on your drive. Remember, you must have existing Linux partitions on your hard drive to use this option. Now, you must select which one you want for the root filesystem, and then click Next. On the next page, you must select another partition for swap space (virtual memory). You should use between 64–128MB of space for this. You should make swap partitions equal to the amount of physical memory that you have. If you have more than 128MB of memory, you must make multiple swap partitions because a single partition cannot exceed 128MB. You also have the option of selecting any other partition you want. You then must specify a mount point if one isn't already specified. A mount point is a directory where this partition will show up on your filesystem. You must now format each partition by selecting the partition and then clicking the button at the bottom of the screen. When you are all done, click Next to proceed to the next step.

Making Custom Partitions

Customizing your own partitions is only recommended if you do not have existing Linux partitions on your hard drive and you have other non-Linux partitions you do not want to delete (so you cannot use the other partitioning options). To do this, you must have existing space on your drive or some partitions you want to delete. All of the drives on your system are shown in this main window in the format shown in Table 3.4.

To delete a partition, simply click it and then click the Delete button labeled on the right. To create a new partition, click one of the partitions listed below the drive that you want to use (click one of the ones that says Not Used by it). Click Edit to bring up a dialog box that will help you to customize this partition. You should make all of your partitions right next to each other, each one starting where the previous one ends. The dialog box will show you how much space there is and where it is possible to make a new partition, so start at the first possible point. You should leave 64–128MB of space so that you can make a swap partition (virtual memory). However, keep in mind that you need at least 1 gigabyte to install Linux with Caldera OpenLinux. Next, the system type should be set to Linux, and the mount point should be set to /. If there are no other operating systems installed on this computer, make sure that you check the box that says Bootable. If you have Windows 9x or DOS, you may also check this box and then read the "Installing and Configuring LILO" section later in this chapter. However, if you have NT on another partition, do not check this box because you may not be able to use NT again (there will be no way of booting it). If you have NT and hence did not make the partition bootable, you should not turn off your system after Linux starts up until you read the section on making your computer dual bootable between NT and Linux (found in the "Installing and Configuring LILO" section, later in this chapter).

Now you must make a swap partition. Edit another unused partition on this or another drive and make it between 64–128MB in size, depending on the amount of physical memory that you have (the swap space should be the same size). If you need more than 128MB of swap, make multiple partitions because the maximum size of a single swap partition is 128MB. Next, change the system type to Swap. That is all that must be done. Click OK to close the box. Now, click the Write button (bottom-right corner) to save all the partitions that you created/edited. When that is done, click Next to proceed. You will now have to select the root partition (this is the partition where you set the mount point to be /). Click the partition from the list, and then click Next to proceed.

You will now have to format all of the new Linux partitions that you created. To do this, highlight them from the list and click the button labeled Format Chosen Partition, located on the bottom. This may take a few minutes depending on the size and speed of your hard drive. When it is finished, you can click Next.

Selecting Installation

Now you are at the point where you must decide what software will be installed on your system. You have four options. The minimum installation puts only the necessary files and programs for getting Linux working and takes 160MB of disk space. Installing all the recommended packages will install everything needed, plus extra programs and utilities that will most likely be used regularly; this installation takes about 580MB of disk space. The third option is to install all of the recommended packages, plus Corel, WordPerfect 8, and StarOffice 5; this installation uses 780MB of disk space. The fourth option is to install everything possible. This includes everything from the third option, plus extra recreational programs and documentation. This installation takes up 1GB of space on your hard drive.

After you have selected your installation type, you must enter your keyboard type and layout. The type of keyboard is in the Type box. If you are unsure of your keyboard type, select Generic 101-key PC. Select the language that your keyboard is in from the box below. Proceed when ready.

Video Setup

Next, you must enter information regarding your video card. The type of card is auto-detected and should be shown in the top field. If this is incorrect, click the Probe button. Do not be alarmed when the monitor turns black when you probe, this is normal. The amount of onboard video memory usually should be entered manually (if you do not know this information, consult the documentation that came with your card). You do not need to worry about the Mode Clocks. These will be set when you probe the video card. After probing, you should go to the next page, where you can select the monitor that you are using. There are hundreds of models listed here, but if you do not see your monitor, you can select Typical Monitors and edit the specifications accordingly for your monitor (as found in the monitor's documentation).

On the next page, you must enter the modes for your video card. This is basically the resolution, depth, and refresh rate you want to use. You should make sure that you have Show All Usable Modes selected (bottom of screen). Now click a mode you want to use and test it to see if it works well and looks good. If the mode does not work, you will just have a black screen and will need to either wait 10 seconds or click the left mouse button to return to the menu. If you do see the screen, press any key to return to the installation program. If you are happy with your selection, click Next. If not, try another mode until you find one that you like.

Accounts

The next step is to configure system accounts. The first thing that must be done is to pick a password for the root account. The root account is the system administrator's account, so make sure you pick a very secure password. You confirm the password by retyping it in the next box.

The next step is setting up a regular user account. Because the root account is reserved for administrative purposes, making it unadvisable to use it on a daily basis, Caldera OpenLinux forces you to create a regular user account to proceed with the installation.

In the first dialog box, you enter your full name. The next box is where you enter the username you want to use. This is generally all lowercase and is often a first or last name or your handle. Next you must select a password and retype it in the next box (it is advised that you use a different password from the one you selected for the root account). Finally, you must select the default shell for this user. The shell is the command interpreter, the program that you type all of the commands into. Most users should select Bash. When everything is entered, click Add User to save this information.

Networking

Now you must decide whether or not you will be using a network of which your Linux machine will be a part. If you are not using a network, or are only using a modem for Internet access, select No Ethernet and continue. If you are on a network, you must find out how your computer is going to handle IP addressing. If IP addresses are configured dynamically, you should select to use DHCP to configure addresses (you must have a DHCP server on your subnet for this to work). However, if you have a static IP address, you must fill in the spaces provided (you might need to contact your network administrator to get some of the IP addresses needed to complete this section). Regardless of your ID addressing configuration, you must enter the hostname, followed by the domain name, in the box at the bottom of the page.

Time Zones

Next you must select your time zone from the map provided. Simply move the mouse across the map and you should see the names of cities appear. Click any city in your time zone. Next, you have the option of setting your system clock to the selected local time zone or to GMT.

Entertainment!

Congratulations, you are done configuring the system. You can now sit back and play some Tetris while the installation completes itself. You can use the arrow keys to move, the up arrow to rotate, and the spacebar to drop a block. When the installation is completed (you can tell by the status bar at the bottom), you can click Finish to complete the installation. Good luck!

First Startup

If all went well, your system should have booted up and started Caldera OpenLinux for the first time. It may take a few minutes for everything to load, but eventually you will get a login screen. Here it might be a good idea to log in with the root account so you can become more familiar with the system.

You should now be using KDE (the K Desktop Environment) with X. The first thing that should come up on your screen is the KDE Setup Wizard. You can use this to customize your desktop environment.

Congratulations, you have successfully installed and configured Caldera OpenLinux!

Troubleshooting

If you have any problems during the installation, it might be a good idea to start over and pay careful attention to the advice that the installation program gives you in the right bar. For any problems regarding your hardware, you should consult your hardware's documentation to get specifications.

Installing SuSE Linux

SuSE Linux is very similar to Red Hat Linux, except that the installation program is much more straightforward and probably easier for first-time users. When you first boot to the installation program, you can boot two ways (like every other distribution): via bootable CD-ROM or bootable floppy disks. You also have four options for the installation method: CD-ROM, hard disk partition, or over a network using either NFS or FTP. Unlike Red Hat Linux, if you boot off the CD-ROM drive, you can still do a network installation.

Booting

If your system is capable of booting from a CD-ROM (usually found on Pentiums and newer machines), simply put your CD-ROM into the drive and set your BIOS to boot from the CD-ROM drive before the hard drive. If you are using a floppy disk to boot, there are a few options in terms of which disk you will require. Located on the CD-ROM (`X:/disks/` where `X` is the letter of your CD-ROM drive) are 36 different disk images. To select which one you need, consult Table 3.5.

Table 3.5   Disk Images for SuSE Linux

Image	Description
eide01	Most users who are using an IDE hard disk to install on should use this image.
eide02	This is the same as `eide01`, except that it offers support for many more IDE chipsets (use this if `eide01` fails).
eide03	This is the same as the previous two images, except that it doesn't provide support for a PCI-BIOS. This should be used on really old computers where the previous images don't work.
scsi01	Adaptec AIC-7xxx series chipsets (found in the 274x, 284x, and 294x series of SCSI adapters).
scsi02	All BusLgic SCSI controllers.
scsi03	This works with the NCR 53C78xx series of adapters.
scsi04	This works with the NCR 53C8xx series of adapters.
scsi05	Adaptec 1542 SCSI adapter.
scsi06	Adaptec 1740 SCSI adapter.
scsi07	Adaptec 1505, 151x, 152x, and 2825 SCSI Adapters.
scsi08	EATA EISA PM2011/021/012.
scsi09	EATA EATA-DMA DPT, NEC, AT&T, SNI, and similar cards.
scsi10	AM53C974 adapters.
scsi11	Future Domain 16xx series of adapters.
scsi12	All Advansys SCSI cards.
scsi13	DTC 3180 and 3280 cards.
scsi14	EATA-PIO DPT PM2001 and PM2012A cards.
scsi15	Always IN 2000.
scsi16	All Pro Audio Spectrum SCSI adapters.
scsi17	For use with an Iomega Parallel Port ZIP dive.
scsi18	Qlogic FAS cards.

Image	Description
scsi19	Qlogic ISP cards.
scsi20	For use with the Seagate ST-02 and Future Domain TMC-8xx cards.
scsi21	Trantor T128, 128F, and T228 adapters.
scsi22	UltraStor 14F and 34F cards.
scsi23	Alternative UltraStor driver if scsi22 doesn't work on your hardware.
scsi24	For use with the Western Digital 7000 FASST.
scsi25	For use with a GDT SCSI Disk Array (ICP Vortex).
scsi26	For use with NCR53c406a chipsets.
scsi27	For use with NCR5380 and NCR53c400 chipsets.
scsi28	For use with the Tekram DC-390(T).
scsi29	For use with AMI Megaraid controllers.
scsi30	For use with SCSI cards with the Initio chipset.
rescue	Rescue Disk.
modules	This provides extra drivers in case your hardware does not fall under the other categories. Simply insert this disk when the installation program starts.
thinkpad	This disk provides support for the IBM Thinkpad series of notebooks. Not all Thinkpads need this disk. It is best to try the eide disks before resorting to this.

After you have selected one of the preceding disk images, you will need a blank floppy disk (two if you need to make a modules disk) and a working computer. You can write the disk image to disk with either a DOS/Windows computer or UNIX workstation.

To make the disk under DOS/Windows, you will need to use the rawrite program included on the CD-ROM (X:\dosutils\rawrite\rawrite.exe). At this point, it might be a good idea to save both the rawrite executable and your chosen disk image to a temporary directory. Now execute rawrite.exe and follow the instructions. You should first insert a blank disk into your floppy drive. Next, you must enter the location of the image file. If it is in the same directory on your hard drive as the rawrite program, enter the name of the image (for example, eide01). Otherwise, you must enter the full path to the image (for example, X:\disks\eide.img). Next, you have to enter the drive letter of your floppy drive (usually A:\). The program will now begin to write the image to the floppy. Do not remove the floppy until the program has finished and the drive's light is out. Now put the disk into the machine on which you plan to install Linux and turn it on (making sure that it is set to boot off the floppy drive first).

The Installation Program (YaST)

After the installation program has started, you must first select the language that you want the installation program to use. Next, you must specify whether or not you have a color monitor (only so that the installation program can be in color). Then you must select the type of keyboard that you are using.

After you have entered the previous information, the main menu appears. Proceed to the Kernel Modules section if you plan on loading any modules (there are some modules on each of the boot disks, so use these first before trying the modules.img disk). The System Information menu only shows you information about what hardware was detected on your system. There is nothing to configure there. At the Modules menu, it might be a good idea to have the system try to load any modules needed by the system if you do not know specifically what you need. It will read the modules from the disk and prompt you each time it finds a module compatible with your hardware. Otherwise, you can always specify exactly what modules you need, and the program will load them from the disk and tell you if it was successful. Remember, if you plan on doing a network install, be sure to add drivers for your Ethernet card.

When you have completed loading modules, start the installation from the main menu. From this menu you have four options: you can install SuSE from scratch, you can boot an already-installed system, you can try to rescue a corrupt system, or you can use a system already installed on the CD-ROM (this is just a base system, known as a "Live CD," and is included on a second CD-ROM with the official distribution of SuSE Linux). Most users who are installing for the first time should choose the first option.

Installation Media

After you have determined how you plan to boot the installation program, you must select the type of media from which you will be installing. You can install locally and use either an existing hard drive partition or a CD-ROM. Or, you can install over a network and use either an NFS or FTP server.

Installing from CD-ROM

If you plan to install from CD-ROM, insert your CD-ROM into the drive and select CD-ROM for your source media. The installation program will now mount your CD-ROM and load some files into memory. That is all that must be done to install from a CD-ROM. You can now skip to the "Partitioning" section later in this chapter.

Installing from an NFS Server

If you are using NFS to install SuSE Linux, you must first determine how IP addressing is set up on your system. For this, there are two options: IP address can be obtained from a BOOTP server on your local subnet, or IP addresses can be static and configured statically. If you do not know which option to choose, consult your network administrator. If you are using BOOTP, the installation program will try to locate a BOOTP server on your LAN. If it fails, you should contact your network administrator. If you are using static IP addressing, you must now enter the IP address of the machine on which you are installing Linux. Next, you must enter the subnet mask and gateway (if a gateway is not used, enter the IP address of the machine), and the DNS server must be entered (if you do not use a DNS server, press Esc). Next, enter the IP address of the NFS server you are using, and then enter the directory on the server where the distribution is located.

Installing from an FTP Server

As with NFS, you must have an Ethernet card installed and configured on your system to do an FTP install. After you select the FTP install option from the menu, you must configure your network. There are two different ways you can configure IP addressing with the installation program: you can obtain an IP dynamically from a BOOTP server on your local network, or you can manually enter a static IP and related information (DNS, gateway, and subnet mask). If you choose BOOTP, the installation program will try to find a server on your LAN. If you want to use static IP addressing, you must first enter the IP address you want to use for your new Linux machine. Next, you must enter a subnet mask and then an optional gateway can be entered; use the IP address you chose for your machine if no gateway is going to be used. If you plan to use a DNS server, enter the IP address when asked, or press Esc if you do not want to use a DNS server. Finally, you must enter the IP address and directory of the FTP server from which you are going to be installing. After you enter the IP address, you must specify if you are using anonymous FTP (if not, click Yes). If you are behind a firewall, you also may need to specify your settings for an FTP proxy (if you are unsure, contact your network administrator). Finally, you must enter the directory of the distribution on the FTP site. The directory should be the root directory of the distribution (for instance, /pub/suse/i386/current/ if you are using ftp.suse.com). This should be identical to the root directory of the official CD-ROM. It should now connect to the server and begin to download some files and put them into memory. If there are any problems, double-check the directory and IP addresses. If all is successful, proceed to the "Partitioning" section later in this chapter.

Installing from an Existing Hard Drive Partition

If you are not using one of the installation options, you can install SuSE Linux from an existing partition on your hard drive. This is by far the fastest way of installing, but you must have adequate drive space to hold both the new installation and the entire distribution. To do this, you must either copy the distribution from the FTP site or from the CD-ROM to your hard drive. This can take up to 650MB of disk space. First, select Hard Drive as the installation media from the menu. Next, enter the name of the partition on your hard drive. This must be in the format shown in Table 3.6.

Table 3.6 Format for Naming Drives Under Linux

Device Name	Device Location
/dev/hda	Master drive on the primary IDE bus
/dev/hdb	Slave drive on the primary IDE bus
/dev/hdc	Master drive on the secondary IDE bus
/dev/hdd	Slave drive on the secondary IDE bus
/dev/sda	First detected SCSI device
/dev/sdb	Second detected SCSI device

This format shows only the location of the drive. You must follow that with a number to specify the partition. For example, /dev/hda3 is the third partition of the master drive on the primary IDE bus. You must enter this now. Next, enter the directory where the distribution is on that drive. This directory should be the root of the entire distribution (for example, there should be directories named suse, disks, setup, and so on in the directory you specify). If there are any problems with the installation program locating the right directory, double-check both the partition number and the directory.

Partitioning

You're now ready to set up partitions on your hard drive on which to install Linux. You have three options: You can install from scratch (all new users should choose this), you can upgrade your existing Linux system, or you can use the Expert mode (not recommended for new users). If you choose to upgrade your existing system, you do not need to repartition your hard drive and can skip this section.

Because you will need a portion of your hard drive to be formatted for Linux, you will need to make some space if you have an existing operating system on your hard drive. To continue, you must either have unpartitioned space on your disk or be willing to delete partitions.

Either way, unless you already have Linux partitions set up, you should select to partition your drive when the installation program asks you. If you plan to use only Linux on the entire hard drive, you might as well tell it to use the entire disk. This will now automatically set up Linux partitions and swap space (virtual memory). If this is your choice, you can skip the rest of this section.

If you plan to make your own partitions, you must enter the partitioning program (this comes up automatically when you choose to partition your hard disk manually). You will need about 1GB of disk space for a decent-sized installation and plenty of working room. Also remember to leave room to make a swap partition (64–128MB is recommended). Your swap partition should be the same size as your amount of physical memory. If you require greater than 128MB of swap space, you must create multiple swap partitions because most distributions will not allow creation of swap partitions greater than 128MB.

If you want to delete an existing partition to make some space, select that partition, press F4, and confirm the deletion (all data on this partition will be lost). If you want to create a new partition, press F5 to bring the window up; you should select Primary Partition. Choose one of the available partitions from the menu. It does not matter which one, as long as you remember which partition is which. The partitioning program will now ask you to enter the size and location of this partition on the hard drive. It is recommended that you put it at cylinder #1 if available, or right at the end of any partitions before this one (for example, if /dev/hda1 starts at cylinder #1 and ends on ready cylinder #583, you should create /dev/hda2 starting at cylinder #584). After you have specified the starting cylinder, it might be easier just to specify the size you want this partition to be, rather than typing the ending cylinder. This can be done by typing +xM in the second box, where x is the size of the partition in megabytes. Remember to leave space for your swap partition!

You should now see your new partition in the main partition window. Finally, you must create a swap partition. To do this, press F5 again to make another partition. Select Primary, if available, and select a partition number for your swap partition. You now must specify the beginning and ending cylinders, as you did earlier. It is advisable to make this partition sit right after your main Linux partition(s), so set the starting cylinder to follow the other partition(s). For the ending cylinder, specify the size (+xM, where x is in megabytes). When you are done, select the newly created swap partition from the main window and press F3. You must change the swap partition to Linux Swap Partition. You can now click Continue to write the new partitions to your drive. The installation program should locate the swap partition, and then you must select to format it. This can take a few minutes to format, but when it is done it will bring up a window for editing the other Linux partitions.

You will now see your other partition(s) in the window. You need to designate at least one drive to be the Root Filesystem. To do this, select the drive and press F4 to edit the mount point. You need to set the mount point on the main drive to be /. Any other drives you are using under Linux should have mount points created here as well. The next thing to set up on your partition(s) is inode density. An inode is the same as a cluster in DOS or Windows—it is the smallest size a file can take up. In Linux, you can set the inode density to be 16,384, 8,192, 4,096, 2,048, 1,024, or 512 bytes (SuSE will not allow inode densities of 512 bytes during installation). The smaller the inode density, the more space you have available on your hard drive. For example, if you had 100 files that were each 300 bytes on a drive formatted with an inode density of 1,024 bytes, these files would take up exactly 100KB. However, on a partition formatted with an inode density of 16,384 bytes, those same files would take up about 1.6MB! However, the smaller the inode density, the slower the drive is when doing tasks such as formatting or checking for bad blocks. Also, the smaller the inode size, the larger the FAT (file allocation table). This can take up many megabytes. So when you're choosing an inode density, be sure to consider the pros and cons of very small densities.

After you ready select your inode density for the drive, you must format the drive by pressing F6. You're now given an opportunity to check the drive for bad blocks before it formats. Checking for bad blocks is only suggested on older drives, but it is a good precaution because it will prevent data corruption if there is something wrong with your drive. However, it might take a while, depending on the size and speed of your drive. Once the program is done formatting (the drive light goes out), be sure to repeat these steps for all other Linux partitions you want to use and then proceed.

Copying Files

At this point, the installation program is almost ready to start copying files to your hard drive. If you are installing over a network, there should now be an onscreen window confirming the location of the installation media. You can press F5 to check all of the settings on the screen. Everything should be okay unless you changed some settings, the site has gone down (or has changed IP addresses), or the location of the installation media has changed. If everything is okay, press F10 to proceed with the installation.

There is now an onscreen window for configuring what will be installed on your system. It is recommended that you go to Load Configuration to pick any of the five prearranged package configurations. Or, you can go to Change/Create Configuration to manually select everything that you want to be installed. If you are using any of the prearranged configurations, the SuSE Minimum system Is Required and the SuSE Default System choices are highly recommended. You may highlight any of these configurations and press F2 to get a list of every package included in it. When you are ready, click Add and then make sure to Check Dependencies to make sure you haven't forgotten to install something that is required.

After you have decided which packages you want to be installed, select Start Installation to begin copying files. It may take a few minutes to copy files, depending on how fast your system is and how much you have chosen to install.

When the installation program is done installing packages, you must go back to the main menu to finalize the installation. You now have to install a kernel to use with your new installation. The list contains the same ones that could have been used for the boot disks, so it's a good idea to use the same boot disk you used to start the installation (assuming that it works). Each kernel contains a description. Most users who are using an IDE hard disk should select the first choice. Next, you have the option to make a boot disk. This is highly advisable because it will help you boot your system if something ever goes wrong, with the kernel or LILO. If you choose to make a boot disk, insert a blank floppy and follow the instructions.

Installing LILO

Next, you must configure LILO if you haven't done so already in a previous installation. If you have not, you will not be able to boot from the hard drive. When the new window opens up for configuring LILO, you usually don't need to fill in the first text box. The next box, which must be filled in, is the location to which to install LILO. If Linux is the only OS on this computer, select Master Boot Record. Also select this if you are using Windows 9x or DOS on another partition. If you have NT installed on another partition, your only choice (if you want to boot without a floppy) is to install to the boot record of the `root` partition. The next text box contains the amount of time LILO should wait before automatically booting the default OS (which is Linux unless you have LILO configured to dual boot, and the other OS is the default).

You must press F4 now to add any operating systems on your computer to LILO (Linux and any other OS to which you want to dual boot). In the first field, enter the name of the OS (in this case, Linux). In the next field, select Boot Linux. In the field after this one, enter the location of the `root` partition. This is usually detected automatically and filled in, but you may have to specify it if it isn't. Then select Continue to proceed.

If you have Windows 9x, DOS, or OS/2 on another partition, you must configure LILO to dual boot them if you plan to use them in the future. To do this, press F4 again to create a new configuration. Create a name for this new configuration (maybe `windows`). Next, select either boot `DOS/win` or boot `OS/2`, depending on which OS you have installed. Next, you must select the partition where your other OS is installed, and then double-click Continue to close this window and complete the installation of LILO. If everything is successful, LILO will output something like the following:

```
Added Linux *
Added windows
```

The asterisk (`*`) by `Linux` means that it will be booted by default.

Finishing the Configuration

Next you must enter your time zone from the onscreen list. You now have the option of setting your computer clock to the local time zone or to GMT. Then you must enter the hostname and domain name for your computer, regardless of whether or not you will be connected to a network. When you enter the hostname, make sure that you only put the hostname and do not follow it by the domain name (in other words, `myhost`, not `myhost.domain.net`). Next, you must decide whether you will be using a real network (not a modem). If you have are permanently connected to a network, select Real Network; otherwise, select Loopback Only.

If you are on a network, you must specify how IP addressing is to occur. You can use either DHCP or static IP addressing. If you choose DHCP, you don't need to enter anything more. If you use static IP addressing, you must enter some addresses on the next page. The first option that must be entered is the type of interface you are using to use the network. If you plan to use an Ethernet card, select `eth0`. If you are using a parallel port, select `plip`. You also have the option of configuring an Arcnet network or a Token Ring network by selecting either `arc0` or `tr0`, respectively. If you selected anything but `plip`, you must enter the specified addresses. If you do not know them, contact your network administrator. If you selected `plip`, you must specify which parallel port you are using (`plip0=parallel port 1`, `plip1=parallel port 2`, and so on). You also must specify the IRQ and base IO address of this parallel port. If you do not know this information offhand, it can usually be obtained from the BIOS or from the system information box from the main setup menu. In older kernel versions, the parallel ports are given names according to their I/O base addresses. For example, 0×378 corresponds to `plip0`, and 0×3bc corresponds to `plip1`.

The next option is whether or not to start `inetd` at boot time. If you do not, you will not be able to use your machine as a server because Linux will be unable to handle any incoming network requests. Most users should choose Yes here. For similar reasons, you should also start the `portmapper` at boot time. You now must decide if you are going to use your computer as an NFS server (Network FileSystem), which provides for file sharing over a network.

You should choose Yes for the next question. You also must specify if you are going to use a DNS server. Most users who are going to be connecting to the Internet should choose Yes here. Now enter the IP address of your DNS server (if you do not know it, contact your network administrator). If you are using a network, you now have to select what type of network card you are using so that drivers can be loaded. Select your card from the list. If you do not see it there, try to find the chipset of your card and see if it is on the list. If you still cannot get your drivers to load, you should check the hardware compatibility lists to see if your card is even supported.

Next, you have three options for sending mail from your new Linux machine. Most users should select the first option. If you are not planning on sending mail at all from this machine, you might want to use the last option and not install `/etc/sendmail.cf`.

The installation program now launches a new window and finishes configuring your system. Your computer will now boot up the newly installed version of SuSE Linux. It will start to load, and then you must add a password for the root account. This is very important because this account is used for administrative tasks. You will then have to confirm your password. Next, you have the option of setting up a modem if you have one. If you have a modem, all that will happen is that a link will be created between the serial port that your modem is on and `/dev/modem`.

Next, you will set up your mouse. If you do not see your mouse in the list provided, you should try either Microsoft Compatible Serial Mouse or PS/2Mouse, depending on whether you have a serial or PS/2 mouse, respectively. You can now choose to launch GPM at boot so that you can use the mouse while in text mode. Next, you can test your mouse's configuration by launching GPM. If your mouse does not work, you may need to try a different driver.

Your system will do some final configuring. This is done automatically. YaST, the installation program, will now terminate itself. The system will do some more configuring and will then prompt you to press Enter to finish configuring scripts. Do so and then wait a few minutes while this takes place.

Congratulations! You should now see a login prompt and can now log in with the `root` account.

Troubleshooting

If anything goes wrong with the installation, you should be able to restart the installation program easily. If you are having a problem with hardware, it might be a good idea to consult the compatibility lists to make sure that your hardware will even function under Linux. If you are having problems configuring network settings, you should consult your network administrator to double-check everything.

If, after you've changed some settings, your system does not boot for some reason, there are three ways to fix it. At the LILO prompt when you boot, you can enter either single-user mode or emergency mode. Single-user mode allows you to load the system with minimal settings and no network connectivity. This mode is for fixing bad scripts, drivers, or network problems. You must know the `root` password to enter this mode. To start single-user mode, reboot your computer andtype `linux single` at the LILO prompt to start up the system.

Emergency mode allows you to recover any important files that you have on your system if the system is broken beyond repair. Emergency mode will start up and mount the main partition in read-only mode and load just the bare requirements. You can now back up anything important that you have on your system to floppy disk or another type of backup source (tape, zip disk, and so on). However, you cannot write to the main Linux partition. This mode should only be used before reinstalling the entire system. You can enter emergency mode by typing `linux emergency` at the LILO prompt. You will need the `root` password to enter emergency mode.

You have a third option if something goes wrong on your system—you can use a rescue disk. A rescue disk can be used if your kernel is corrupt, LILO is corrupt, or all of your startup files are corrupt so that you cannot boot at all. A rescue disk can be made from one of the images on the CD-ROM: `rescue.img`. Simply write this image to a floppy using either `rawrite` or the `dd` under UNIX (and Linux). Insert this disk into your drive and boot from it.

Installing and Configuring LILO

LILO stands for "Linux Loader" and is the program that allows you to boot from your hard drive to Linux. LILO reads a few configuration options from `/etc/lilo.conf`, and then, when you type `lilo` at the prompt, it configures your system to boot Linux. The following is an example of the `/etc/lilo.conf` file that will boot only Linux:

```
      %cat /etc/lilo.conf
1     boot=/dev/hda
2     read-only
3     prompt
```

```
4        timeout=100
5        vga=normal
6        #Beginning of Linux section
7        root=/dev/hda1
8        image=/boot/vmlinuz
9        label=linux
```

Line 1 simply specifies where to write LILO. In this case, it is being written to the beginning (first 512 bytes) of /dev/hda, also known as the Master Boot Record (MBR). The MBR is where the BIOS usually looks when it is trying to load the operating system from the hard drive.

Line 2 specifies that the hard drive should be mounted as read-only. This is so that it can run fsck (to check for bad blocks) at startup. The operating system will then remount it as read-write.

Line 3 makes it okay to display the boot prompt without any prior keypresses. If this is omitted, LILO will boot the first OS specified in /etc/lilo.conf by default.

In line 4, the number given after timeout is the time to wait at the boot prompt (in tenths of a second) before loading the default OS. There's only one OS is shown in the example, so it is the default. In this example, LILO will wait 10 seconds before booting Linux. To specify a default OS if there are more than one listed in the configuration file, add the default=imagename line.

In line 5, the vga= setting specifies the default resolution in which to display everything. There are three commonly used settings: Normal (80×25 text mode), Extended (80×50 text mode), and Ask (prompts user for a custom resolution that can be entered numerically).

Line 6 is a comment added to the file showing that the next three lines specify information regarding the OS and are not customization options for LILO. Any text in this file that's preceded by a # cannot be read by LILO and is only there to help the reader understand the file better.

Line 7 tells LILO which partition is going to be mounted as the root partition. It needs the location of the root directory because the /etc, /var, and /sbin directories are all located there (they cannot be mounted from separate partitions). These directories contain programs, scripts, and other setup files needed to start Linux.

Line 8 tells LILO the location of the kernel. In this case the kernel is /boot/vmlinuz.

Line 9 tells LILO what to call this operating system. If you have multiple operating systems installed under LILO, you simply type linux at the boot prompt to start it (label=linux in this example).

If you ever edit this file, it is important that you always type lilo when you are done so that the new changes are written to the drive. Otherwise, although the file has changed, LILO will use its old configuration.

It also might be a good idea to have an entry in LILO for a backup kernel (one that you know works) in case you decide to upgrade with a bad one. This can be done by simply adding another entry for Linux in LILO:

```
%cat /etc/lilo.conf
boot=/dev/hda
read-only
prompt
timeout=100
vga=normal
#Beginning of Linux section
root=/dev/hda1
image=/boot/vmlinuz #new kernel
label=linux
#Beginning of Backup section
image=/boot/backup #backup kernel
label=backup
```

Notice that it is not necessary to define where the root partition is twice. This is only if both kernels are on the same partition. To use this backup kernel in case something goes wrong, simply type backup at the boot prompt within ten seconds (otherwise the first kernel will boot by default).

Dual Booting Windows 9x/DOS

If you have another operating system, such as Windows 9x, DOS, or OS/2, LILO has the ability to boot to this OS or Linux when you turn on your computer. To do this, look at the example /etc/lilo.conf file that follows:

```
      %cat /etc/lilo.conf
1     boot=/dev/hda
2     read-only
3     prompt
4     timeout=100
5     vga=normal
6     #Beginning of Linux section
7     root=/dev/hda1
8     image=/boot/vmlinuz
9     label=linux
10    #Begin DOS section
11    other=/dev/hdb1
12    label=DOS
```

The last two lines are all that you need to boot another OS. Line 11 specifies the location of the alternate OS, /dev/hdb1 in this case. Line 12 does the same thing when used for Linux. It specifies what needs to be entered at the boot prompt to boot this alternate OS. In this case, to start DOS or Windows (whichever is on /dev/hdb1), type **DOS** at the boot prompt. You can set a flag, default=DOS, if you want this OS to start by default.

Dual Booting Windows NT

If you are using NT on another drive, you cannot use the previous method for installing LILO. This is because LILO is being written to the MBR, and NT must be booted from the MBR (LILO will write over NT, causing NT to be unreachable). If you have already written to the MBR, your only way of recovering NT is to use an NT rescue disk (it prompted you to make one during your installation of NT, or you can always borrow one from someone else). Then you must recover the MBR with this disk.

To dual boot NT and Linux, you have two options: you can either boot Linux from a floppy each time, or you can install LILO in a special way. To make a floppy disk, the easiest method is to type the following:

```
%cat /boot/vmlinuz > /dev/fd0
```

Assuming that your kernel is /boot/vmlinuz, this will directly write the kernel to a floppy disk.

You must now make sure that the kernel is configured to mount the root filesystem correctly. This is done with the rdev command. After you have written your kernel to a floppy disk, you should type something like the following:

```
%rdev /dev/fd0
Root device /dev/hda1
```

As you can see, the root device for this boot disk will be /dev/hda1. If you are shown the incorrect location of your root partition, you can type rdev /dev/fd0 [root partition], as shown in the following:

```
%rdev /dev/fd0 /dev/hda2
%rdev /dev/fd0
Root device /dev/hda2
```

You can now reboot the system and boot from this disk without having to configure or install LILO at all.

The second way of dual booting is a bit more complex and involves installing LILO, but not on the MBR. The trick is to install LILO at the beginning of the hard drive where Linux is installed (the first 512 bytes). Hypothetically, let's say that Linux is installed on /dev/hdb1. You would edit /etc/lilo.conf so that the first line reads boot=/dev/hdb. You would then make sure that the rest of the /etc/lilo.conf file has only Linux configured (there should only be an entry for Linux; there should be nothing set up here for NT). Then write LILO to the drive by typing **lilo** at the command prompt.

Next, you must copy the first 512 bytes of your drive (where you wrote LILO) to a file that you can then use to boot Linux from the NT boot loader. This is done by issuing a command similar to the following:

```
%dd if=/dev/hdb of=/tmp/lilo.img bs=512 count=1
```

This assumes that LILO wrote to /dev/hdb and then creates an image of LILO located in /tmp. This file is now known as lilo.img. You should now copy this file to a floppy disk and boot Windows NT. From NT, you must copy lilo.img from the floppy to the hard drive, preferably to C:\. Now you must manually edit the C:\boot.ini file and add an entry for Linux. To do this, you must first change boot.ini to read-write mode (it is in read-only mode by default). Do this done by right-clicking it and selecting Properties. You should now add a line so the file looks like the following:

```
[boot loader]
timeout=3
default=multi(0)disk(0)rdisk(0)partition(1)\WINNT
[operating systems]
multi(0)disk(0)rdisk(0)partition(1)\WINNT="Windows NT Workstation Version4.00"
C:\lilo.img="Linux"
```

Now, make sure to save this file and change it back to read-only mode. If you do not, NT might not boot correctly next time. You must also check that lilo.img has been copied to your hard drive in the location specified in boot.ini. You're now ready to reboot. When you reboot, you can either select Windows NT or Linux from the NT boot loader. If Linux is selected, LILO will be started and Linux should boot up.

Uninstalling LILO

If for some reason you want to delete Linux from your hard drive (or want to delete LILO for another reason), you can reformat the disk. However, LILO will remain there and will attempt to boot Linux every time you start from that drive (even though all of the files have been deleted). This will only occur if it has been written to the MBR. To delete LILO, there are two methods.

From DOS, you can run fdisk and have it clear the MBR for you by typing the following:

```
C:\fdisk /MBR
```

This will completely flush the MBR, taking LILO with it. There is also a way of doing it from Linux, by typing the following:

```
%lilo -U
```

This copies the original boot record, which is saved in /boot/boot.0300, back to the MBR, thus deleting LILO from the system. You can manually do this by typing the following:

```
%dd if=/boot/boot.0300 of=/dev/had bs=512 count=1
```

Summary

By now, you should be familiar with installing your chosen distribution. Do not worry if it takes more than one try to successfully install Linux; this is very common, even among experienced users. If you run into problems along the way, the best way of dealing with them is to first read the documentation that came with your distribution. If that does not help, you might want to check online for help. There is a vast amount of information and help for new and experienced users online. Another option might be to find a LUG (Linux Users Group) in your area. A LUG can answer your questions about Linux and also help you to become a more experienced Linux user. To find the nearest LUG, try going to http://www.linux.org/users/.

On Your Own

Since you have a working system now, it might be a good idea to familiarize yourself with Linux. You can experiment with some of the commands and read through some of the configuration files in /etc to get a feel for the system (but don't change anything if you don't know what you're doing). Remember, the man pages are one of your biggest resources. Use them.

PART II

Up and Running with Linux

Configuring Your Linux System

In this chapter, you will learn how to customize your Linux system to meet your computing requirements. In the previous chapter, you learned how to install Linux. Fortunately (or maybe unfortunately) there are many different ways to configure a Linux system once it is installed. You can configure Linux as a workgroup server, using it to share disk drives and printers between users on the network. Or you could configure it as a full power Web server, handling multiple customers connecting to it across the Internet to view your latest Web pages. You could also configure it as a simple single-user workstation with high-resolution graphics and sound capabilities. Each situation uses the Linux software, but the Linux system is configured differently in each instance. It takes time and patience to properly configure a Linux system, but it is well worth it. You would not want to waste valuable memory and processor time running Web server software when all you want to do is play Xchess.

Setting Up Your System

Most Linux distributions have special options available during the install phase to help customize the system. Depending on your goals, you can select options to load programs intended for workstation or server use. These options are pretty generic though, and to properly configure your Linux system, you must still decide exactly what programs you want to be running. The main difference between a server configuration and a workstation configuration is the programs that are running in background. These programs are called processes, and are started by a special process called init. You will learn more about init in Chapter 9, "Administrative Tasks." For now, it is enough to know that init is the program that starts the programs that you tell Linux to run in background. You will see these processes load on the console display when the Linux server boots. The processes are often loaded by using scripts that display messages on the console to let the user know if the process loaded properly. There are several processes that must run by default. For instance, once your Linux workstation boots, you probably want to be able to log in to it from the keyboard. That requires a special program running in background. The getty, mgetty, and mingetty programs run in the background to watch the terminal (keyboard and monitor on a PC) and wait for a user to log in. Once they see a login attempt, they pass the login information to the login program for validation. Removing any of these processes could be interesting if you only use your keyboard to access your system. Actually, this process is so important that Linux uses a technique called "respawning" that automatically restarts these processes if they are accidentally killed by an unsuspecting user.

Determining Running Processes

To view the processes that are currently running on your system, you use the ps command, a special command that any user on the system can use on a normally configured Linux system. It gets running process information by querying the /proc filesystem. The /proc filesystem is a special area where Linux keeps real time information about the system, such as hardware configuration, running programs, and memory resources used. The ps command lists pertinent information from the /proc filesystem in a more user-friendly format. The ps command has the following format:

```
ps  [-]  [lujsvmaxScewhrnu]  [txx]  [O[+¦-]k1[[+¦-]k2...]]  [pids]
```

The - is shown as optional, but in practice, don't use it. It is being deprecated for another purpose, and is currently there only for old system administrators who have problems remembering not to use it. The options used in ps are explained in Table 4.1.

Table 4.1   ps Command Options

Option	Description
l	Use the long format to display information
u	Use user format (shows user name and start time)
j	Use job format (shows process gid and sid)
s	Use signal format
v	Use vm format
m	Displays memory information
f	Use "forest" format (shows processes as a tree)
a	Show processes of other users on the system
x	Show processes without displaying controlling terminal
S	Show child CPU and time and page faults
c	Command name for task_struct
e	Shows environment after command line and a +
w	Use wide output format
h	Do not display the header
r	Show running processes only
n	Show numeric output for USER and WCHAN
txx	Show the processes that are controlled by terminal ttyxx
O	Order the process listing using sort keys k1, k2, and so on
Pids	Show only the specified pids

As you can see, there are lots of ways to display information about the processes running on the system. Listing 4.1 shows the output from a sample ps command.

Listing 4.1   Sample ps Command Output

```
1   [haley@shadrach haley]$ ps ax
2    PID TTY STAT TIME COMMAND
3      1  ?  S    0:02 init [3]
4      2  ?  SW   0:00 (kflushd)
5      3  ?  SW<  0:00 (kswapd)
6      4  ?  SW   0:00 (md_thread)
7      5  ?  SW   0:00 (md_thread)
8     38  ?  S    0:00 /sbin/kerneld
9    221  ?  S    0:00 syslogd
10   230  ?  S    0:00 klogd
11   252  ?  S    0:00 crond
12   263  ?  S    0:00 inetd
13   274  ?  S    0:00 lpd
14   286  ?  S    0:00 rpc.mountd
15   295  ?  S    0:00 rpc.nfsd
16   322  ?  S    0:00 sendmail: accepting connections on port 25
17   334  ?  S    0:00 httpd
18   350  ?  S    0:00 smbd -D
19   358  ?  S    0:00 nmbd -D
20   376  2  S    0:00 /sbin/mingetty tty2
21   377  3  S    0:00 /sbin/mingetty tty3
22   378  4  S    0:00 /sbin/mingetty tty4
23   379  5  S    0:00 /sbin/mingetty tty5
24   380  6  S    0:00 /sbin/mingetty tty6
25   381  ?  S    0:00 /sbin/mgetty -D -s 38400 -n 6 ttyS0
26   383  ?  S    0:00 update (bdflush)
27   439  1  S    0:00 /sbin/mingetty tty1
28   470  ?  S    0:00 in.telnetd
29   207  ?  S    0:00 portmap
30   241  ?  S    0:00 /usr/sbin/atd
31   342  ?  S    0:00 httpd
32   343  ?  S    0:00 httpd
33   344  ?  S    0:00 httpd
34   345  ?  S    0:00 httpd
35   346  ?  S    0:00 httpd
36   471  p0 S    0:00 -bash
37   487  p0 R    0:00 ps ax
38   413  ?  S    0:00 ora_pmon_abc
39   415  ?  S    0:00 ora_dbw0_abc
40   417  ?  S    0:00 ora_lgwr_abc
41   419  ?  S    0:00 ora_ckpt_abc
42   421  ?  S    0:00 ora_smon_abc
43   423  ?  S    0:00 ora_reco_abc
44   430  ?  S    0:00 /u01/app/oracle/product/8.0.5/bin/tnslsnr LISTENER -
➥inherit
45  [haley@shadrach haley]$
```

In Listing 4.1, all of the processes running on the test Linux system named shadrach are displayed (because you used the a option). Line 3 shows our friend init. It is running as process ID (PID) 1. It is always the first process to run on the system, and is responsible for starting all other processes. As each new process starts, it is given a new PID. Processes that are shown in parenthesis have been swapped out of memory to disk due to inactivity. Linux will do this automatically to conserve hardware memory and help speed up the performance of running processes. Of course the downside to that is that when a process has been swapped out, it must be copied back into memory to run—thus incurring a performance penalty.

You can tell a lot about a Linux system from looking at the running processes on it. Breaking down the example system in Listing 4.1, you see

- Lines 20–24 and 27 show the mingetty process waiting for users to log in to the system. This server has six virtual sessions available to log in on (all of which are on the console).

- Line 12 shows the inetd process running. This program watches for IP network connections and passes the connections to the appropriate network programs to handle them.

- Lines 18 and 19 show the smbd and nmbd processes running. These programs are used to provide Microsoft Networking files and print sharing capabilities on the Linux server.

- Lines 17 and 31–35 show the httpd process running. This program provides Web server functionality for the Linux server. Multiple copies of the same program can run concurrently to service more clients with improved performance.

- Lines 38–44 show the Oracle database server processes running. These programs run in conjunction with an online Oracle database installed on the system.

- Lines 36 and 37 show the processes used for our login session. Line 36 shows the bash shell that we are running, and Line 37 shows the ps command we executed (complete with options).

By examining the running processes, it could be deduced that this Linux system is configured to perform network server functions. It provides Web server functions via the httpd program, Microsoft Networking functions via the smbd and nmbd programs, and database functions via the Oracle programs. You would not expect to see all of these processes running on an ordinary Linux workstation. You can also note what processes are not running—no X Window servers, no soundcard processes, and no user processes (except our own). You would expect a Linux workstation to have a lot more user processes running.

Adding and Deleting Processes

The first step in properly configuring your Linux system is to decide which processes you want to have running at boot time. After you have decided what you want running (and what you don't want running), you must let the Linux system know. Normally, this involves a complex system of files and subdirectories. Linux follows the System V method of initializing processes. This provides for having several different run levels, each with a subdirectory of startup scripts. Each process that you want to start at a particular run level must have a startup script in the proper subdirectory (or a link there to the original script's location). Chapter 9, "Administrative Tasks," will explain this method more thoroughly. Fortunately, most Linux distributions come with a handy graphical utility that takes all the pain out of this process for you. All you need to do is select which processes you want started from a menu list. You must be running the X Windows system to use these distribution-specific programs. Figure 4.1 shows the Caldera Open Administration System (COAS) daemon configuration window used on Caldera OpenLinux systems. As you can see, it is extremely easy to pick and choose which process you want to have running in the background when your Linux server boots. Just place a check mark in the boxes of the processes you want running. The startup scripts are configured and located automatically by the system.

FIGURE 4.1

The Caldera Open Administration System (COAS) daemon configuration window.

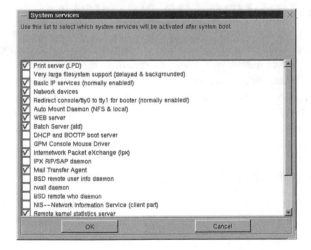

A similar function for Red Hat Linux users is in the linuxconf package. The "control service activity" option in linuxconf allows the user (assuming that he or she has root privileges) to select which processes start at boot time. Figure 4.2 shows the linuxconf "control service activity" screen. Be careful—the dimples mean "on," and the raised buttons mean "off"—don't get them confused or you might be unhappy. Again, selecting these options allows you to automatically start particular processes at boot time.

FIGURE 4.2
*The Gnome
linuxconf
control service
activity screen for
Red Hat Linux.*

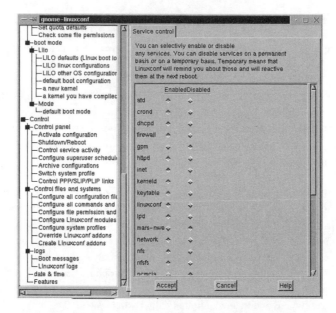

Configuring the Network

Normally, if Linux detects an Ethernet card in the system during the install process, it will automatically configure the kernel to use the card and load the appropriate network software. If you did not have a network card in your system at install time, and then decide later that you want your Linux system to talk with other devices on a Local Area Network (LAN), it is your responsibility to perform the additional configuration required. This is usually a two-step process. First, you must ensure that Linux recognizes the new network card installed, and then you must configure the system to operate properly with your network.

Configuring the Network Card

When Linux recognizes your new network card during the install, it automatically asks you network questions and configures the software accordingly. If you want to (or need to) configure the network card yourself, you can do the same things manually.

The basic program used to configure the network card is ifconfig. This sets the necessary parameters in the kernel table, so Linux knows how to communicate with your network card on your network. There are two formats of the ifconfig command. They are as follows:

```
ifconfig [interface]
ifconfig interface [aftype] options ¦ address ...
```

The first format for ifconfig displays the current network configuration information for the entire system (if no interface is included), or for a specific interface if it is. Listing 4.2 shows the output of an ifconfig command for a Linux system with an active Ethernet interface.

Listing 4.2   Sample ifconfig Command Output

```
1  [barbara@shadrach barbara]$ /sbin/ifconfig
2  lo        Link encap:Local Loopback
3            inet addr:127.0.0.1  Bcast:127.255.255.255  Mask:255.0.0.0
4            UP BROADCAST LOOPBACK RUNNING  MTU:3584  Metric:1
5            RX packets:45 errors:0 dropped:0 overruns:0 frame:0
6            TX packets:45 errors:0 dropped:0 overruns:0 carrier:0
7            collisions:0
8
9  eth0      Link encap:Ethernet   HWaddr 00:00:C0:54:62:B0
10           inet addr:192.168.1.1  Bcast:192.168.255.255  Mask:255.255.0.0
11           UP BROADCAST RUNNING MULTICAST  MTU:1500  Metric:1
12           RX packets:418658 errors:0 dropped:0 overruns:0 frame:7
13           TX packets:1047 errors:0 dropped:0 overruns:0 carrier:0
14           collisions:0
15           Interrupt:9 Base address:0x310 Memory:e0000-e4000
16
17 [barbara@ishadrach barbara]$
```

Line 1 shows the ifconfig command as typed at the command prompt (you may have to include the path). Line 2 shows the configuration of the first network interface—lo. This is a special device called the loopback device. It is automatically configured by Linux to provide network connectivity to itself (thus the term loopback). The IP address 127.0.0.1 is a special loopback address. You can test this on your system by TELNETing to IP address 127.0.0.1. If you have the inetd process running, you should get a login prompt from your own machine. Linux can use this feature to communicate between processes and to emulate network functionality without having to have the machine actually on a network. Line 3 shows the IP address information for the loopback interface. The status of the loopback interface is shown on Line 4. This indicates that the loopback interface is UP (operational).

The configuration parameters for the installed Ethernet network card start on Line 9. This shows the device name of the card (/dev/eth0), as well as the hardware MAC address. The MAC address is unique for every Ethernet card manufactured. Line 10 shows the IP address information for this device on your Ethernet network. You must make sure that the IP address and subnet values are appropriate for your network, or your Linux server will not be able to communicate with other devices. Line 11 shows the network status of the device. Lines 12–14 show network statistics for the interface. This is a handy troubleshooting tool in case of any network problems. If you cannot communicate with other devices, but see the TX (transmit) and RX (receive) packet counts increasing, it is usually an indication that you messed up the IP address on your system. If you see a large amount of errors and collisions, it is a good indication that you have a network media problem, such as a bad cable or defective network hub. Line 15 shows the hardware configuration of the network card. Different network cards communicate with Linux using different methods, so be careful on how your particular card works. Many newer PCI plug-and-play cards will be autoconfigured when Linux boots. If this happens, you need to pay close attention to the boot messages to see what values are assigned to the network card. Usually that is not a problem.

The second format of the ifconfig command allows you to manually set the configuration parameters of the network card. The available options are shown in Table 4.2.

Table 4.2 ifconfig Command Option

Option	Description
Interface	Specify the interface name
Up	Causes the interface to attempt to become active
Down	Causes the interface to attempt to become inactive
[-]arp	Enables (or disables) the ARP protocol
[-]promisc	Enables (or disables) promiscuous mode
[-]allmulti	Enables (or disables) multicast functionality
metric N	Sets the metric of the interface for routing purposes
mtu N	Sets the maximum transfer units of the interface (1500 for Ethernet)
dstaddr addr	Sets the remote IP address for a point-to-point link (PPP)
netmask addr	Sets the IP netmask
add addr/prefixlen	Adds an IPv6 address to the interface
del addr/prefixlen	Deletes an IPv6 address from the interface
tunnel aa.bb.cc.dd	Create a new SIT (IPv6-in-IPv4) device, tunnelling to the given destination
irq addr	Sets the interrupt line used by the device
io_addr addr	Sets the start address in I/O space for the device
mem_start addr	Sets the start address for shared memory for the device
media type	Sets the physical port or medium type to be used by the interface
[-]broadcast addr	If an address is given, set the broadcast for the interface to addr, otherwise clear the IFF_BROADCAST flag for the interface

Option	Description
[-]pointopoint *addr*	Enables (or disables) the point-to-point mode using addr as the protocol address of the remote side
hw class *addr*	Sets the hardware address of the device
multicast	Sets the multicast flag
address	Sets the IP address of the interface
txqueuelen length	Sets the transmit queue length of the device

As you can see, there are lots of specific parameters that can be used to configure the network card. The way that ifconfig recognizes parameters may seem a little strange at first. There are no dashes (-) involved in the parameters, just commands. The following is an example of an ifconfig configuration command:

```
ifconfig eth0 192.168.1.1 netmask 255.255.0.0 broadcast 192.168.255.255
```

This command sets the IP address on the /dev/eth0 interface to 192.168.1.1 using 255.255.0.0 as the subnet mask, and 192.168.255.255 as the local broadcast for the network.

If your network has a router to enable you to get to other networks, you can manually configure that also. The command that does that is the route command. The Linux system maintains an internal table of routes. The route command allows you to add and delete entries to that table. The following are the three formats of the command:

```
route [-CFvnee]

route  [-v]  [-A  family] add [-net¦-host] target [netmask
       Nm] [gw Gw] [metric N] [mss M] [window W] [irtt  I]
       [reject] [mod] [dyn] [reinstate] [[dev] If]

route  [-v]  [-A  family]  del [-net¦-host] target [gw Gw]
       [netmask Nm] [metric N] [[dev] If]

route  [-V] [--version] [-h] [--help]
```

This allows you to add and delete routes for entire subnets, as well as individual hosts into the system routing table. The first format of the route command will list the system routing table. Listing 4.3 shows the output from a sample route command.

Listing 4.3 Sample route Command Output

```
1  [katie@shadrach katie]$ /sbin/route
2  Kernel IP routing table
3  Destination     Gateway         Genmask         Flags Metric Ref    Use Iface
4  192.168.0.0     *               255.255.0.0     U     0      0       15 eth0
5  127.0.0.0       *               255.0.0.0       U     0      0        2 lo
6  default         192.168.10.1    0.0.0.0         UG    0      0        9 eth0
7  [katie@shadrach katie]$
```

Line 6 shows a destination called `default` that uses router `192.168.10.1` and can be found on the `eth0` interface. The default route is special IP address `0.0.0.0`. By pointing that address to the default router, all IP traffic not destined for your internal network will be sent to the default network router. The command would look like the following:

```
route add -net 0.0.0.0 192.168.10.1 255.255.0.0 1
```

This shows that we will use router `192.168.10.1` for all IP destinations not on the `192.168.0.0` network. The `1` at the end of the command is the metric. You can use this to specify multiple routes to the same network. The primary route would use a metric of 1, and all other backup routes would use higher values, depending on their hierarchy.

Now you should have a fully functional network card. There is only one problem—each time you reboot your Linux system, you will have to re-enter these values. That quickly becomes annoying. There must be a better way. There is! If you remember, the `init` process can run startup scripts for each run level that the Linux system enters. The `ifconfig` and `route` commands are perfect candidates for placing in a startup script and running at boot time.

Configuring the Network Card the Easy Way

Before you start writing your scripts, there is an easier way to get the `ifconfig` and `route` commands automatically started. If you are running an X Window system, most Linux distributions include graphical utilities that take the hassle out of network interface configuration.

Figure 4.3 shows another piece of the Caldera Open Administration System (COAS) that is used to configure network interfaces on Caldera OpenLinux systems. As you can see, all that needs to be done is to type in the IP address, subnet mask, and default router. Then, if you enable the `Init` at Boot Time function, presto—instant network interface scripts configured and installed.

FIGURE 4.3
Caldera Open Administration System network interface configuration.

Figure 4.4 shows what Red Hat Linux users can use to make network life simpler. The netcfg program is an X Windows program that, like COAS, allows you to easily configure the network interfaces. Each network interface is listed and can be selected and edited. Be sure to enable the Atboot option, so that the interface will be loaded at the next boot (and every boot thereafter).

FIGURE 4.4
Red Hat netcfg *network interface configuration program.*

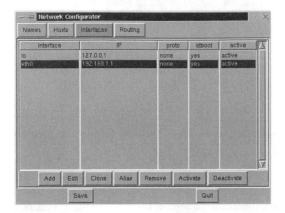

Configuring a Printer

One of the most complicated pieces of configuring the perfect Linux system is getting the printing right. Again, fortunately there are tools available to help, but before we discuss them, let's see what Linux printing is all about.

Most computer users are familiar with the DOS method of addressing printers connected to a PC. The first printer is usually LPT1, the second LPT2, and the third is LPT3. Linux has not adopted this naming convention. Table 4.3 shows how Linux sees the standard printers.

Table 4.3 Linux Parallel Printers

Linux Device	DOS printer
/dev/lp0	LPT1
/dev/lp1	LPT2
/dev/lp2	LPT3

Once Linux recognizes that a printer is present, it must be able to communicate with it. There is a special process that Linux uses to continuously watch for print jobs and send them to the printer. The lpd process runs in the background (assuming you elected to start it) and monitors print queues for jobs to send to the appropriate printers. How does it know what jobs to send to what printers? That is where it gets tricky. The lpd process reads a special configuration file called /etc/printcap that has specific definitions for each printer to which the Linux system can print. Creating the perfect /etc/printcap file is where the art of Linux printing comes in. Listing 4.4 is a sample /etc/printcap file.

Listing 4.4   Sample /etc/printcap File

```
1  [jessica@shadrach /etc]$ cat printcap
2  #
lp:mylp:\
4           :lp=/dev/lp0:\
5           :sd=/var/spool/lpd/lp:\
:mx#0:\
:sh:\
8           :if=/var/spool/lpd/lp/filter:
9  [jessica@shadrach /etc]$
```

Line 3 defines the name of the printer. The first one listed is the normal printer name. You should have one printer named lp. This is used as the default printer. Any other names listed are aliases for the printer. Lines 4–7 define the characteristics of the printer for lpd. Each line starts with a capability code. There are lots and lots of options that can be configured into a printcap file to define a printer. The man page for printcap defines all of the options available. Table 4.4 lists some important options that you will most likely encounter.

Table 4.4   printcap Capabilities

Name	Description
af	If using accounting, the name of the accounting file used
br	If serial printer, the baud rate
if	Name of the text filter file
ff	Defines the string to send for a formfeed
fo	Sends a formfeed when the printer is first opened
lf	Name of the error logging file
lo	Name of lock file
lp	Device name to use if printer is a local printer
mx	Maximum print file size (0 = unlimited)
of	Name of output filter file
pl	Printer page length in lines
pw	Printer page width in characters

Name	Description
rm	Machine name if printer is a remote network printer
rs	Restrict printer users to those with local system accounts
sb	Print a short banner (one line) before the print job
sc	Suppress multiple copy requests to the printer
sd	Name of spool directory
sh	Suppress printing of the burst page header

If there are multiple printers on the system, each printer will have its own section in the /etc/printcap file. The example shown in Listing 4.4 indicates that the printer is connected to LPT1 (/dev/lp0). It also uses /var/spool/lpd/lp as its spool directory, can accept any size print file, and uses the file /var/spool/lpd/lp/filter as an input filter. Input filters are extremely difficult to create. They control the way the print data is presented to the printer. Each type of printer uses a different type of input filter to format the print data for the printer. A laser printer needs the data in a different format than an inkjet printer. Fortunately, ghostscript is a program that can pass postscript files to printers without complicated formatting by the user. Most printer input filters make use of this program to help in formatting printer output.

Configuring Printers the Easy Way

Most Linux distributions help by providing graphical utilities to install and configure printers. Figure 4.5 shows how COAS configures printers for Caldera OpenLinux systems.

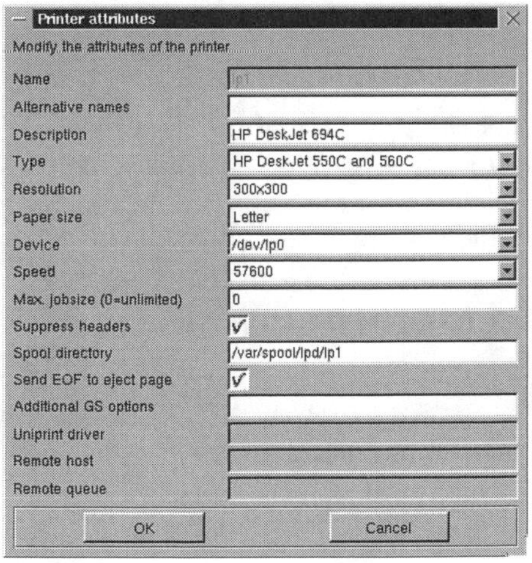

FIGURE 4.5
Caldera Open Administration System printer configuration helper.

Again, Red Hat users also have a graphical tool to help them configure printers. The printtool utility allows you to install and configure printers on your system. This utility will also try to autodetect your printer for you. Figure 4.6 shows a sample screen used in this process.

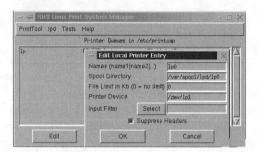

One very nice feature of these utilities is that they also produce the proper input filter file for many different types of printers. You do not need to labor over how to get your data to the printer and in what format. It has already been configured for you.

Sending Print to a Printer

After the printer is configured for the system, you can start sending print jobs to it. The lpr command is used by programs to send print to the lpd process using the definitions in the /etc/printcap file for the specified printer. You can also manually print using the lpr command. The following is the format to do so:

```
lpr [-Pprinter] [-#num] [-C class] [-J job] [-T title] [-U user] [-i
        [numcols]] [-1234 font] [-wnum] [-cdfghlnmprstv] [name ...]
```

The –P option tells lpd which printer to which you want to print. If it is not present, the print jobs will go to the default printer named lp. The -# option tells lpd how many copies you want to print (unless of course the printer uses sc in its definition to suppress multiple copies). Other options are used to further define the print job to the system. See the lpr man pages for further details of each option.

Commands to Monitor Printing

Linux also has commands that can be used to monitor the printer when you think that things might have gone wrong. The lpq command can be used to display the current jobs in the print queue for a given printer. Listing 4.5 shows sample output of the lpq command.

Listing 4.5 Sample lpq Output

```
1  [rich@shadrach rich]$lpq
2    Printer: lp1@shadrach
3    Queue: 3 printable jobs
4    Server: pid 827 active
5    Unspooler: pid 828 active
6    Status: printed all 21 bytes at 13:27:06
7    Rank    Owner/ID             Class Job  Files           Size Time
8  active  rich@shadrach+826       A   826 test.txt         21 13:27:06
9  2       rich@shadrach+838       A   838 test.txt         21 13:27:19
10 3       rich@shadrach+843       A   843 test.txt         84 13:27:54
11 [rich@shadrach rich]$
```

The first job shows that it is active, which means that it should be currently printing. The other jobs just pile up in the print queue quietly waiting their turn. But what about if you accidentally send a 100 page report to the printer and then change your mind? Don't worry, Linux uses the lprm command, which can be used to delete jobs waiting their turn in the queue. Notice from Listing 4.5 that each print job is assigned an internal job number (column 5 on Lines 8–10). Once you know the job number, you can delete the job by using the lprm command using the syntax shown in Listing 4.6.

Listing 4.6 Sample lprm Output

```
1  [rich@shadrach rich]$lprm 843
2  Printer lp1@shadrach:
3  checking 'rich@shadrach+843'
4  checking perms 'rich@shadrach+843'
5  dequeued 'rich@shadrach+843'
6  killing subserver '862'
7  [rich@shadrach rich]$
```

This example deletes job number 843 from the default printer queue. Unless you are the root user, you can only delete jobs that belong to you. Be careful when trying to delete an active job (one that is currently printing). Unpredictable things can occur. Many modern printers have internal memory that accepts data faster than they can print. Even if you manage to kill the job in the print queue, you may still have pages printing from the printer memory. Some printers allow you to power them off to clear the memory area. Unfortunately, some fancier printers try to "help out" and retain the memory area and pick up printing where they left off when they are turned back on. Sometimes progress turns into inconvenience.

Configuring Standard User Features

A standard feature of Linux is the ability to add multiple users and to configure each user differently. Each user can have his or her own specific X Window desktop, environment variables, PATH statement, and lots of other individual characteristics. The key to individuality on Linux is "hidden" files in the user's home directory. The files aren't really hidden, they just take a little extra effort to see. Some beginning Linux users think that by using the standard ls command to view a directory, you see a list of all the files in that directory. That's not true. Hidden files are files that begin with a period (.). These files do not appear on a plain ls listing of the directory. There is a way to display them, and it's not too complicated—just use the -a option on ls.

When you create a new userid, you must specify a default directory for the user. You can specify the same home directory for all of your users, but that would not lend itself to being very customizable (nor user friendly). The most common system is to use the /home filesystem. Each user has his or her own directory under a common /home directory. For example, Chris's home directory would be /home/chris, Matthew's would be /home/matthew, and Riley's would be /home/riley. Each user would be able to read and write to his or her own directory, but only be able to read others, so no user could mess with another's files.

User-Specific Shell Configuration

Once a user's home directory is created, user-specific hidden files are kept there to customize the Linux environment. These files apply only to that user, and each user has his or her own set. If the user is using the bash shell, three hidden files are created by default for him or her—.bashrc, .bash_history, and .profile from the /etc/skel template. The .profile file is used to initialize environment variables when logging in to the system. If you want to initialize your own environment variables or execute your own scripts during log in, you can create a .profile-private file in your home directory. The last thing that the .profile script does is call the user's .profile-private script (if it exists). The .bashrc file is executed when a non-login shell is created (for example, when you start a new terminal session in X Windows). The .bash_history file is very interesting. Did you notice that you can recall previous commands from the command prompt using the up arrow key? Each command executed in the shell is cached in memory during your shell session so it can be recalled. When you exit the shell, the history cache is appended to .bash_history. The next time you bring up a new shell, you can then recall commands used in previous shells. Sometimes progress is pretty cool.

User-Specific Program Configuration

The use of hidden files to save user-specific configuration information is not limited to the bash shell. Many programs utilize this method of saving configuration information. Listing 4.7 shows the hidden files found in a user's directory after several programs within an X Windows session were run.

Listing 4.7 Sample Home Directory Listing

```
1  total 2395
2  drwxr-xr-x  14 alex    users    1024 Jul 22 19:33 .
3  drwxr-xr-x   8 root    root     1024 Jul 10 13:43 ..
4  -rw-------   1 alex    users      70 Jul 22 19:06 .Xauthority
5  -rw-r--r--   1 alex    users     946 Jul 22 19:07 .bash_history
6  -rw-r--r--   1 alex    users      49 Nov 25  1997 .bash_logout
7  -rw-r--r--   1 alex    users     577 Feb 12 10:29 .bashrc
8  -rw-r--r--   1 alex    users     580 Nov 25  1998 .config
9  -rw-r--r--   1 alex    users     647 Nov 25  1998 .cshrc
10 drwx------   3 alex    users    1024 Jul 13 21:06 .ddd
11 -rw-r--r--   1 alex    users    7790 Apr  3 18:16 .gcalrc
12 drwxr-xr-x  11 alex    users    1024 Jul 22 13:16 .gimp
13 -rw-r--r--   1 alex    users     111 Nov  3  1997 .inputrc
14 -rw-r--r--   1 alex    users       2 Jul 22 19:06 .kaudioserver
15 drwxr-xr-x   3 alex    users    1024 Jul 10 19:11 .kde
16 -rw-r--r--   1 alex    users    2218 Jul 22 19:06 .kderc
17 -rw-r--r--   1 alex    users     417 Nov 24  1998 .login
18 -rw-r--r--   1 alex    users      51 Nov 25  1997 .logout
19 drwx------   5 alex    users    1024 Jul 19 21:27 .netscape
20 -rw-r--r--   1 alex    users     793 Feb 12 10:36 .profile
21 drwxr-xr-x   2 alex    users    1024 Jul 10 13:33 .seyon
22 -rw-r--r--   1 alex    users     809 Nov 25  1998 .tcshrc
23 -rw-r--r--   1 alex    root       4 Jul 22 19:06 .wmrc
24 drwxr-xr-x   2 alex    users    1024 Jul 14 18:24 .wprc
25 drwxr-xr-x   2 alex    users    1024 Jul 15 21:18 .xcdroast
26 -rw-------   1 alex    users    9196 Jul 22 19:06 .xsession-errors
```

As you can see from Listing 4.7, it did not take Alex long to acquire a lengthy list of hidden configuration files. Also, notice how some applications create entire hidden subdirectories for their own configuration files. What can be frustrating is spending hours getting a configuration for a particular application "just right" and then losing the configuration file. If you have applications that you have fine-tuned to perfection, it would not be a bad idea to copy the hidden configuration files onto a floppy disk (if they fit) for safekeeping. Then, the next time you accidentally crash your hard drive and have to rebuild (that's what Linux is for, isn't it?), you can retrieve your applications' configuration files in no time and be back in production mode.

Summary

The standard Linux install procedure produces a running Linux system, but to maximize your applications' performance, you should take the time to fine-tune the system. Background processes are the core of the Linux system. They define the functionality of the system, whether it is a server or a workstation. Most Linux distributions include graphical utilities to select individual processes to run in background. Unnecessary processes should be turned off to conserve memory and processor time. Also included are graphical utilities to configure network interfaces and printers. Normally these can be configured during the install phase, but if they were not present during the install, they can be added later using the utilities. Lastly, many applications save specific user preferences as hidden files located in the user's home directory. These files can be saved on removable media in case they need to be restored, either to bring back a broken configuration or when replacing a hard drive.

On Your Own

After a successful Linux install, run your Linux distribution's graphical process control utility (COAS for Caldera, or linuxconf for Red Hat). Watch what processes are enabled by default, and decide what processes you want to have running on your system. Be careful not to disable anything that you need the next time you boot. Next, use the other graphical utilities to view your network interface settings (if applicable) and your printer settings (if applicable). Open a terminal window and type ls -al. Do you have any hidden files yet? Start a few X Window applications and check again. Before long, you will have as long of a list as Alex does in his home directory.

Adding Hardware to Your Linux System

Introduction

Adding hardware to Linux can be surprisingly easy or difficult. While there are several methods, picking the best one is dependent on your current configuration as well as the type of hardware you're adding.

Linux has the great distinction, among UNIX and UNIX-type operating systems, of supporting the widest range of hardware devices. Many cards, printers, scanners, joysticks, hard drives, modems, and sound cards will work right out of the box. Linux enjoys this distinction because of its wide-spread support throughout the industry. As Linux becomes more popular with both users and developers, you can expect hardware support on a level with any of the commercially available operating systems today.

Many Linux hardware drivers receive support from hardware vendors, and many do not. In the case where they do not, hardware drivers are often reverse-engineered to make devices work properly in Linux. This process has yielded surprisingly good results for many of the drivers contained within Linux. While very time-consuming, sometimes reverse engineering is the only way.

Note: Reverse engineering is a process by which a developer deciphers the inner workings of a hardware device, through various development methods, usually without the help of the hardware manufacturer.

This chapter will help you get the most out of your Linux system and the hardware you attach to it. The goal is to have you up and running with any sort of hardware you may want to attach to your Linux system.

Basic Process for Adding New Hardware

Adding hardware in Linux is a combination of both hardware and software procedures. This process begins with, of course, adding the actual device to your hardware. In Linux, as with most operating systems, this must always be done with the system shutdown and powered off. Depending on what kind of device you're adding, you must also be cognizant of proper safety procedures for handling and installing your hardware. All steps should be taken to ensure your own safety, as well as the safety of the hardware you'll be installing.

> **Caution:** Electrostatic discharge, or ESD, kills computers dead. The most effective way to guard against ESD is to use an anti-static wrist band. These can usually be purchased at any neighborhood electronics store. Anti-static wrist bands should always be used when installing memory or hard drives. In the absence of an anti-static wrist band, you can also periodically touch your still plugged in computer case to eliminate static.

Many factors go into adding hardware to your Linux system. For a complete understanding, a primer on Linux and the way that it handles your hardware device drivers is in order.

Everything is a File

In Linux, as with most UNIX-based operating systems, everything is a file. This includes your devices. If you look at the /dev directory on your system, you'll see many files representing devices that may or may not be in your computer. These files can be written to and read from just like any other file. The difference is that they actually represent things like a printer, serial port, hard disk, CD-ROM drive, ethernet card, and so on. The following are commonly used devices and their prefixes in the /dev directory:

- cdrom   A CD-ROM drive (actually a symbolic link)
- dsp   Sound card audio device
- eth   An ethernet port

- `fd` The floppy disk
- `hd` IDE controller hard disks or CD-ROM drives
- `sd` SCSI hard disks
- `scd` SCSI CD-ROM drives
- `ttyS` A serial port (as of kernel ver. 2.2.x)

By reading and writing to the device files, you are actually reading and writing to hardware devices. Linux sees no distinction between these and your real hardware.

> **Note:** The `/dev/null` file is a special device. This device, sometimes called the "bit bucket," is actually just as it's name implies[el]nothing. By writing to `/dev/null`, you are essentially throwing away anything you've written. Many script writers use `/dev/null` as a means by which to discard output or errors when not needed.

Before the Linux kernel can use these devices, it must know how to connect them, via device drivers, to your physical hardware. This process is accomplished by connecting your Linux device drivers to hardware resources on your computer. These resources and a short description of each follow.

DMA

DMA, or Direct Memory Access, is only found in older ISA-type devices. DMA is a process by which a device takes over the main memory from the CPU and transfers bytes into it. When a device makes a DMA request, the system knows which device is making the request by a number that is assigned to it called the *DMA channel*. This method of using main memory is very inefficient, because only one device can do so at a time. Not all ISA devices can do DMA. DMA is often found in older ISA sound cards.

> **Note:** The PCI (peripheral component interconnect) bus does not use DMA. It does, however, use a much improved method of access called bus mastering. While still sometimes referred to as DMA (UltraDMA Hard Drives), bus mastering is a far more efficient process whereby devices do not have to request a channel for taking over the bus. The PCI bus automatically delegates bus mastering ability to devices connected to it, as it knows which devices are currently bus mastering and which devices request bus mastering.

IRQ

IRQ, or interrupt request, is the number assigned to devices that lets a device driver know where it is located on the bus. Once the device driver knows this number, it is able to successfully communicate with the device. Interrupts are really just one of sixteen numbered wires connecting to the bus. Once this number is stored on the device, the device's driver knows how to communicate with it. This way, the driver listens for an interrupt from the device on the particular numbered wire, facilitating direct communication between the two whenever needed.

Older ISA-based devices must have separate IRQ assignments. With the more modern PCI bus, devices are allowed to share IRQ numbers. Be aware that while this is allowed, not all PCI devices and motherboards support this feature.

I/O Addresses

I/O Addresses, or input/output ports, are one of the three memory spaces contained within in a modern PC. Computers contain memory spaces designated by I/O memory, main memory, and configuration. Configuration is a PCI address space. Most devices will use the I/O memory space. Once the device driver obtains an I/O address, it tells the hardware device what to use, enabling the two to further communicate with each other. The address of this information is stored on the hardware device in one of its own registers. This I/O base address is usually configured via a jumper on the device.

Memory Regions

Finally, there are memory regions that can be assigned to a device. These regions are in main memory, as opposed the address space that is reserved for I/O. When you use a device that uses main memory for transfers, the device creates a shared area for direct transfer of data between it and the CPU. This method requires that the card and the device driver each know where this region of memory resides.

The proc Filesystem

The proc filesystem is usually mounted in the /proc directory in Linux. This is not a true filesystem, it is really an interface into the currently running kernel's data structures. Nearly everything about your current kernel can be ascertained by looking at entries in the /proc directory. Using /proc, you will be able to find out which resources are being used and which are available to you for adding new hardware.

To get a good idea of where you stand with regard to IRQ assignments, try the following.

From your running Linux system, you can issue the following command:

```
cat /proc/interrupts
```

This will give you a list of devices and interrupts that looks something like the following:

```
          CPU0
   0:     714270          XT PIC   timer
   1:      16496          XT PIC   keyboard
   2:          0          XT PIC   cascade
   5:          1          XT PIC   soundblaster
   8:          2          XT PIC   rtc
  10:       5058          XT PIC   eth0
  11:      12748          XT PIC   aic7xxx
  12:     246851          XT PIC   PS/2 Mouse
  13:          1          XT PIC   fpu
 NMI:          0
```

The important pieces of information in this printout are the first and last columns. The first column shows you the interrupt with its corresponding device in the last column. This is the best way to see, from a hardware standpoint, what IRQ resources your peripherals are currently using.

To see serial port information, issue the following command:

```
cat /proc/tty/driver/serial
```

This should give you a printout that looks something like the following:

```
0: uart:16550A port:3F8 irq:4 tx:0 rx:0
1: uart:16550A port:2F8 irq:3 tx:0 rx:0
```

Certain IRQs are generally the same in most computers. Serial ports one and two will use IRQs 4 and 3, respectively. The keyboard is also usually assigned IRQ 2. While these can be changed, it is recommended that they not be.

Next, take a look at which I/O addresses are in use by issuing the following command:

```
cat /proc/ioports
```

This returns a printout similar to the following:

```
0000 001f : dma1
0020 003f : pic1
0040 005f : timer
0060 006f : keyboard
0070 007f : rtc
0080 008f : dma page reg
00a0 00bf : pic2
00c0 00df : dma2
00f0 00ff : fpu
0170 0177 : ide1
01f0 01f7 : ide0
020b 020b : PnP read port
0220 022f : soundblaster
02f8 02ff : serial(auto)
0330 0333 : MPU 401 UART
```

```
0376 0376 : ide1
0388 038b : OPL3/OPL2
03c0 03df : vga+
03f6 03f6 : ide0
03f8 03ff : serial(auto)
0620 0623 : sound driver (AWE32)
0a20 0a23 : sound driver (AWE32)
0e20 0e23 : sound driver (AWE32)
e800 e8be : aic7xxx
ec00 ec7f : eth0
ffa0 ffa7 : ide0
ffa8 ffaf : ide1
```

This shows you what I/O addresses are being used by which devices and their drivers. Remember, once the driver obtains this address, it gives it to the hardware device that stores it in its own registers via jumpers on the device.

Finally, use the following command,

```
cat /proc/dma
```

which produces something similar to the following:

```
1: SoundBlaster8
4: cascade
5: SoundBlaster16
```

This shows that a sound device is using two DMA channels on the system. The system this command was run on was, in fact, using an older ISA-type sound card. This is why there are used DMA channels being shown.

While the previous steps are not necessary, they do give a good starting point from which to troubleshoot any future hardware problems. The information gained here can be invaluable when and if the time comes that you need it. With that in mind, a good practice would be to print these various command line outputs. If you already have a working printer, the easiest way to print this information is to pipe any of the previous outputs to the lpr command:

```
cat /proc/interrupts ¦ lpr
```

Armed with all of this information, you're ready to proceed to the next step.

Dealing with the Kernel

The Linux kernel is where all of the magic happens. This is where the drivers are loaded into the operating system, making themselves available to you and any software you plan to run.

There are two ways in which the Linux kernel loads drivers into the system. The first is to have the drivers directly compiled into the running kernel. Second, and most preferable, is to have the driver compiled as a module for loading and unloading to and from the kernel. As you can imagine, having the code dynamically load and unload itself is a great savings on resources for your system. Not only does this make the size of your running kernel very small, it enables you add support for hardware in a very clean and efficient manner. This is why the module method is preferred.

Most Linux distributions come with a default kernel that has support for many different types of hardware. Your system may recognize your hardware without you even having to interact with the kernel. The kernel does this by probing common base addresses for each device at startup and listening for interrupts to respond. This will give the kernel a good idea of what is installed in your system. Once identified, Linux will try to load a module for the specific piece of hardware.

As of kernel 2.2x, the method Linux uses for loading kernel modules has changed from a standalone daemon, called kerneld, to a kernel thread called kmod. When the kernel requests a module, using the system call request_module(), the kmod thread is awakened to load the module into the running kernel. kmod uses the program depmod to figure out on which modules the requested module depends. Finally, depmod uses the program insmod to insert the modules. While this procedure sounds a bit complicated, it is actually very simple and efficient.

If your kernel does not have module support compiled in, you will have to re-compile it to use modules. An in-depth discussion on how to accomplish this is included in Chapter 24, "Kernel Hacking."

At boot time, Linux prints a number of lines giving you information about the hardware that was recognized on your system. You may miss all of the information as it scrolls by during startup, but there is way to see it once your system is fully booted. From the console, or a terminal in X Windows, you can issue the following command:

dmesg

This will show you the messages from the latest boot of your kernel. Using this printout, you can see quite a few interesting things about your system. The following is an example dmesg output:

```
Linux version 2.2.10 (root@cw326456 a) (gcc version egcs 2.91.66 19990314/Linux
(egcs 1.1.2 release)) #2 Wed Jul 7 09:32:22 PDT 1999
Detected 334095623 Hz processor.
Console: color VGA+ 80x25
Calibrating delay loop... 333.41 BogoMIPS
Memory: 128316k/131072k available (796k kernel code, 412k reserved, 1500k data,
48k init)
CPU: Intel Pentium II (Deschutes) stepping 00
Checking 386/387 coupling... OK, FPU using exception 16 error reporting.
Checking 'hlt' instruction... OK.
```

```
POSIX conformance testing by UNIFIX
mtrr: v1.35 (19990512) Richard Gooch (rgooch@atnf.csiro.au)
PCI: PCI BIOS revision 2.10 entry at 0xfdb81
PCI: Using configuration type 1
PCI: Probing PCI hardware
PCI: Enabling I/O for device 00:3a
Linux NET4.0 for Linux 2.2
Based upon Swansea University Computer Society NET3.039
NET4: Unix domain sockets 1.0 for Linux NET4.0.
NET4: Linux TCP/IP 1.0 for NET4.0
IP Protocols: ICMP, UDP, TCP
Starting kswapd v 1.5
Detected PS/2 Mouse Port.
Serial driver version 4.27 with no serial options enabled
ttyS00 at 0x03f8 (irq = 4) is a 16550A
ttyS01 at 0x02f8 (irq = 3) is a 16550A
pty: 256 Unix98 ptys configured
Real Time Clock Driver v1.09
(scsi0) <Adaptec AHA 294X Ultra SCSI host adapter> found at PCI 17/0
(scsi0) Wide Channel, SCSI ID=7, 16/255 SCBs
(scsi0) Downloading sequencer code... 413 instructions downloaded
scsi0 : Adaptec AHA274x/284x/294x (EISA/VLB/PCI Fast SCSI) 5.1.17/3.2.4
       <Adaptec AHA 294X Ultra SCSI host adapter>
scsi : 1 host.
(scsi0:0:0:0) Synchronous at 20.0 Mbyte/sec, offset 8.
  Vendor: SEAGATE    Model: ST15150W        Rev: 0023
  Type:   Direct Access             ANSI SCSI revision: 02
Detected scsi disk sda at scsi0, channel 0, id 0, lun 0
  Vendor: MATSHITA Model: CD R  CW 7502    Rev: 3.10
  Type:   CD ROM                    ANSI SCSI revision: 02
(scsi0:0:1:0) Using asynchronous transfers.
(scsi0:0:2:0) Synchronous at 5.0 Mbyte/sec, offset 8.
  Vendor: SONY      Model: SDT 5000       Rev: 3.26
  Type:   Sequential Access         ANSI SCSI revision: 02
scsi : detected 1 SCSI disk total.
SCSI device sda: hdwr sector= 512 bytes. Sectors= 8388315 [4095 MB] [4.1 GB]
tulip.c:v0.89H 5/23/98 becker@cesdis.gsfc.nasa.gov
eth0: Digital DS21140 Tulip at 0xec00, 00 00 c0 a8 68 f9, IRQ 10.
eth0:  EEPROM default media type Autosense.
eth0:  Index #0   Media MII (#11) described by a 21140 MII PHY (1) block.
eth0:  MII transceiver found at MDIO address 3, config 3100 status 782f.
eth0:  Advertising 01e1 on PHY 3, previously advertising 01e1.
Partition check:
 sda: sda1 sda2
VFS: Mounted root (ext2 filesystem) readonly.
Freeing unused kernel memory: 48k freed
Adding Swap: 128516k swap space (priority 1)
st: bufsize 32768, wrt 30720, max buffers 4, s/g segs 16.
Detected scsi tape st0 at scsi0, channel 0, id 2, lun 0
eth0:  Advertising 01e1 on PHY 0 (3).
eth0: Setting full duplex based on MII Xcvr #3 parter capability of 01e1.
```

This output shows a wealth of information about the currently running system. From this output, you can see that there are several SCSI and IDE devices on this system. Note how the kernel assigns device names like sda, hda, tty, and eth to the devices after it recognizes them. Because drivers for these devices have been loaded at boot time, they are available to the system from the /dev directory.

Dealing with Plug-and-Play

Some devices can pose quite a challenge when adding them to your Linux system. Plug-and-play ISA devices are particularly troublesome, while PCI devices usually are not. While Linux does have support for plug-and-play, it is quite new and not completely reliable. In addition, not many hardware drivers in Linux support plug-and-play. This is surely an issue that will be resolved in time because there are a great many devices using the plug-and-play standard today.

The Concept

Plug-and-play is a very simple concept. The basic premise is that plug-and-play drivers find plug-and-play hardware connected to the system and establish the channels of communication between them. Plug-and-play drivers automatically allocate the resources needed to make the hardware devices functional within the system. This allows the CPU to talk to the devices while they remain under control of their respective device drivers.

This process requires not only that the system be plug-and-play aware, but also that the drivers and devices be aware. Most of the problems stemming from plug-and-play have their root in the old ISA bus. Unfortunately, the plug-and-play standard has, in effect, kept the ISA bus around for longer than it should have been. Because the ISA bus was not designed for plug-and-play, as the PCI bus was, its implementation is very complicated. The lack of resources available on the ISA bus make it very hard to implement plug-and-play drivers for it. The supposed replacement for ISA, PCI, is much superior in almost every way. With PCI, the BIOS can configure plug-and-play, as well as make it easy for device drivers to find their respective hardware devices on the bus. PCI was designed from the ground up to support plug-and-play.

With all of this history coming into play, you now have two separate implementations to deal with when configuring plug-and-play devices. Because Linux does not currently fully support plug-and-play, you may have to sometimes "jump through hoops" to make your devices work with the kernel.

BIOS: To Plug-and-Play or Not to Plug-and-Play

On most modern PCs today, there is usually an option in the BIOS asking whether or not you are using a plug-and-play operating system. Where Linux is concerned, you most certainly are not.

Telling your BIOS that you do have a plug-and-play operating system will have a couple of side effects that will most likely cause you a great deal of trouble in Linux. In this instance, the BIOS configures only the disk, video, and keyboard, so you're actually able to boot your system. From there, the BIOS expects that your operating system will take over the rest of the configuration. Additionally, the BIOS may "isolate" devices on your ISA bus to be further configured by your plug-and-play operating system. Once your Linux kernel boots, your ISA devices may then be disabled, as well as some of your PCI devices. This is certainly an unwanted situation for a healthy Linux system.

The solution is to tell your BIOS that you do not have a plug-and-play operating system. This gives the BIOS the chance to configure all of the devices it can, allocating resources to them before the operating system takes control. The BIOS stores this configuration information in a database called ECSD (Extended System Configuration Data). This database is usually stored in a non-volatile chip on your motherboard. This way, the BIOS can use the ECSD at each boot to successfully allocate resources.

Plug-and-Play Linux Tools

While all of this sounds good on paper, it is not necessarily as smooth in the real world. There are often still problems with plug-and-play devices, especially ISA ones, that must be addressed by the host operating system. In Linux, this is done by a suite of applications, isapnptools, developed for just such a reason.

The isapnptools are a suite of programs that allow you to specifically set the resource allocation of ISA plug-and-play devices when your system boots. By using the pnpdump program, you can find out all the resources configurations that the devices on your system support. Pnpdump builds a configuration file template for you that can be used by another program in the isapnptools called isapnp. The following is an example of the command used to create the dump file and place it in its proper destination:

```
/sbin/pnpdump > /etc/isapnp.conf
```

This will create a configuration file readable by isapnp. From there, you will need to edit the file by uncommenting the right configuration based on the resources available in your system. To get a better understanding of what resources are available, refer to the "The Proc filesystem," section, earlier in this chapter. A thorough explanation of the isapnp.conf file is beyond the scope of this book, however, you can gain a better understanding of it by viewing the isapnp.conf man page.

After you have finished your /etc/isapnp.conf file configuration, you need to make sure that isapnp runs at boot time for it to affect your ISA devices. The easiest way to do this is to, as root, issue the following command:

```
echo "/sbin/isapnp" >> /etc/rc.d/rc.local (for SysV type systems)
```

This will allow isapnp to run when your system is booted, giving your ISA devices the new resource allocations as defined in /etc/isapnp.conf. From there, you can load your devices into the kernel as modules and have access to them like any other device.

The Windows Solution

Finally, there is another way to manage plug-and-play devices in Linux. This method requires that you have a dual-boot setup on your system consisting of Windows and Linux. Because Windows is a fully plug-and-play operating system, you can leverage this ability by having Windows configure your devices and then boot into Linux via the loadlin program.

loadlin is a DOS-based application that effectively kicks Windows out of your system and loads Linux. The great advantage to you here is that Windows can plug-and-play configure your devices, while Linux takes advantage of this by booting via loadlin. Among the disadvantages to this approach are

- Booting in this way can be very slow compared to a normal Linux boot time.
- This method requires a licensed copy of Windows.
- It will not work on all devices.

To use loadlin, you need the following:

- A fully installed and bootable Windows system is required.
- A fully installed and bootable Linux system is required.
- You need the loadlin.exe program.
- An image of your kernel is needed to load into memory.

Once you've met these requirements, you can execute loadlin as shown in the following:

```
loadlin.exe drive:\your_kernel root=/dev/linux_boot_partition ro
```

While not the most elegant of solutions, this will boot you into Linux with your Windows-configured plug-and-play devices.

Adding a New Hard Drive

One of the most common additions to a running system is a new hard drive. The process for adding a new hard drive is as follows:

1. Connect the disk to your SCSI or IDE bus.

2. Set up your BIOS to recognize the drive.

3. Compile support for SCSI or IDE into the kernel (if needed).

4. Create a filesystem on the new drive.

5. Assign a mount point to the new filesystem.

The steps for adding a new hard drive are not that difficult. They can, however, cause unexpected results. Care must be taken at all times.

Dealing with Hardware

The first step in adding a new hard drive is to prepare the drive itself for addition to your existing installed drives. For IDE-based hard drives, this involves either setting the drive to be a master or slave. The IDE bus usually has two different segments defined as bus 0 and bus 1. Each bus can have only two total devices connected to it. One of these drives must be defined as a master. If another drive is added, it would be defined as a slave. You must make the appropriate jumper connections for your particular hard drive based on this configuration constraint. For most hard drives, the instructions for making them master or slave can be found within documents that came with the drive. Instructions can also often be found in the form of a diagram on the top of the actual drive. This step is very important, because your system will malfunction if these types are not correctly defined.

For adding a SCSI-based hard drive, there are also design constraints involved. The SCSI bus is usually made up of one "chain" of devices. This chain has a total of seven possible devices, each with its own ID ranging from 0–6. Most SCSI controllers also define ID 7, which is used by the actual controller itself. Any drive that you add to your SCSI chain must have its own ID. How you define this ID depends on whether the drive is internal or external. Most external SCSI devices will have a switch, usually at the rear of the device, that allows you to select the drive ID. For internal drives, this task can be accomplished by jumper settings. Again, consult the documentation for your particular device for instructions on how to set hardware jumpers. Some SCSI devices also have diagrams on the top of the drive, showing the various jumper settings. Additionally, you must terminate the SCSI chain at both physical ends. This is accomplished either via a hardware jumper on an internal drive, or a hardware terminator for an external drive.

After attaching an IDE hard drive to your computer, you must make sure that your system's BIOS can recognize it. On most newer computers, this will be done automatically. You should see your BIOS auto-detecting the drive at startup, if auto-detect is enabled. If you do not, you need to enter the BIOS, and set it up so that it auto-detects on the particular bus to which you've installed your disk. You can enter the BIOS configuration usually by hitting the Delete key at startup. This procedure varies for different BIOSs, so be sure to check the documentation. For an older PC BIOS, you must manually enter the drive parameters. These parameters can usually be found on the outside of the drive or in the documentation that came with it.

If you're attaching a SCSI hard drive to your system, you should be able to see the drive when your SCSI BIOS loads at boot time. If not, verify that your SCSI chain is terminated and that your new drive has a unique SCSI ID. SCSI can cause many problems without these two parameters being taken care of properly.

Drive Detection

Next, boot into Linux. After the system comes up, check to see if the drivers for the new drive have been loaded and assigned an entry in the /dev directory. For example, use the dmesg command covered earlier to grep through the kernel messages looking for device entries specific to the kind of installed hard drive.

For an IDE-type hard drive, use the following:

```
dmesg ¦grep hd
```

This command returns the following output:

```
hda: Maxtor 92048D8, ATA DISK drive
hdb: Maxtor 91152D8, ATA DISK drive
hdc: FX320S, ATAPI CDROM drive
hdd: QUANTUM FIREBALL_TM3840A, ATA DISK drive
```

Reading this output, you can see that the system has found four IDE devices and has assigned the device names hda, hdb, hdc, and hdd to them. If you're installing a second IDE hard drive, you would see hda, for the original boot disk, and a new hd entry for your new drive. IDE bus hard drives are enumerated as shown in the following:

```
IDE bus 0 dev 1     /dev/hda
IDE bus 0 dev 2     /dev/hdb
IDE bus 1 dev 1     /dev/hdc
IDE bus 1 dev 2     /dev/hdd
```

You could possibly have even more drives, provided you were using an add-in IDE card for extra drive capacity. Kernel versions 2.2.x support up to four add-in IDE busses. The current development kernel, versions 2.3.x, support up to eight.

For SCSI hard drives, you can use the same method by grepping through the dmesg command for sd entries, as shown in the following example:

```
dmesg|grep sd
```

From the previous dmesg output, this would produce the following result:

```
Detected scsi disk sda at scsi0, channel 0, id 0, lun 0
SCSI device sda: hdwr sector= 512 bytes. Sectors= 8388315 [4095 MB] [4.1 GB]
 sda: sda1 sda2
```

You can see here that there is a SCSI device, detected as sda. The kernel also prints out the two partitions on sda as sda1 and sda2. You now know that the SCSI drive has been successfully detected by the kernel. You can now proceed to the next step.

> **Note:** If your kernel messages do not show your new drive, you may have to compile support for IDE or SCSI into your kernel. Please refer to the "Dealing with the Kernel" section, earlier in this chapter.

Partitioning with `fdisk`

Now it's time to partition the hard drive and prepare it for a filesystem. The easiest way to do this is with the Linux fdisk program. The fdisk's interface is somewhat arcane, but very useful.

> **Caution:** Using fdisk in the wrong way can seriously damage your system or any other systems you may have on your currently installed hard drives. Please use great caution to make sure that you are using fdisk on only your new hard drive. As always, the best policy is to have a complete backup of all the data on your system.

An fdisk takes the drive that you want to affect as its argument. If your new hard drive is /dev/hdd, drive no. 2 on your first IDE bus, you would enter the following:

```
/sbin/fdisk /dev/hdd
```

This will bring you to the fdisk prompt.

There are several ways to perform this next step. Before you can use your new drive, you must create a filesystem that Linux can recognize. Generally, you would want to create an extended2 filesystem because this is native to Linux. While you could create, for example an MS-DOS filesystem, you would not receive all of the benefits gained by using extended2. It is recommended that you use extended2 unless you have a need to use the filesystem from another operating system on a dual boot system.

Once you're in the fdisk program, you can type p to see the currently defined partitions on your drive. If your drive is new, you may have no partitions defined. If your drive does have partitions defined, you need to either remove them or add your new Linux partition after them, if there is room.

At this time, it's a good idea to make sure fdisk is seeing your drive with the proper amount of heads, cylinders, and sectors. This is commonly referred to as the *disk geometry*.

After typing p, for print, you'll get something like the following:

```
Disk /dev/hdd: 16 heads, 63 sectors, 7480 cylinders
Units = cylinders of 1008 * 512 bytes

    Device Boot    Start      End    Blocks   Id  System

Command (m for help):
```

This will print your currently defined partitions. Because this is a new drive, there are no currently defined partitions.

At the top of this printout, you'll notice the various drive parameters that fdisk sees for your particular hard drive. By consulting the documentation for your drive, you can verify that they are correct. If you need to change them, you must enter the advanced mode of fdisk by typing x, for extra functionality. Form there, typing m will give you a printout of the options needed to change your disk's geometry settings.

```
    COMMAND            ACTION
    c                  Change the number of cylinders

    h                  Change the number of heads
    s                  Change the number of sectors
```

By entering these commands individually, you will be prompted for the values your drive uses.

Note: You can actually calculate the exact size of your the drive by its geometry settings with the following formula.

Cylinders×Heads×Sectors×512 bytes

While this still holds true for drives below 8.4GB, the industry convention is to now define Cylinders/Heads/Sectors=16383/16/63 on disks above 8.4GB.

After setting the correct drive geometry, it's now time to create the new partition. For this example, you will be adding an extended2 partition. From the fdisk prompt, type the following:

```
new
```

This will give you a prompt that looks like the following:

```
Command action
   e   extended
   p   primary partition (1 4)
```

Select p, for primary, to make a primary partition.

Note: Linux has a limit of four primary partitions on any installed hard drive. When using an extended partition, it will be counted as a primary partition. The only limit for logical partitions within an extended partition is 15 on a SCSI drive and 63 on an IDE drive. Linux can be installed and booted from either primary or logical partitions on any installed hard drive.

Next, you will be asked which partition number you want to use:

```
Partition number (1 4):
```

There is a hard limit of four primary partitions from which to choose for any given hard drive within Linux. Because you are making one large partition and there are no existing partitions, select number 1. After selecting partition 1, you will be prompted for the beginning cylinder:

```
First cylinder (1 7480, default 1):
```

By entering 1, you are specifying that you want the partition to start at the beginning of the drive. Next, you are prompted for the end cylinder:

```
Last cylinder or +size or +sizeM or +sizeK (1 7480, default 7480):
```

By pressing Enter at this point, the default end cylinder, 7480, will be defined; fdisk makes this the default because it is the end of the drive.

Now that you have defined a partition, you need to define the type of filesystem with which the partition will be formatted. From the fdisk prompt, typing t will allow you to set the type of filesystem. First, fdisk asks which partition you want to affect. You have only defined one partition, so simply select 1. You are then prompted for the type:

```
Hex code (type L to list codes):
```

By typing L, you are given a list of file types from which to choose:

```
0   Empty           16  Hidden FAT16    61  SpeedStor       a6  OpenBSD
1   FAT12           17  Hidden HPFS/NTF 63  GNU HURD or Sys a7  NeXTSTEP
2   XENIX root      18  AST Windows swa 64  Novell Netware  b7  BSDI fs
3   XENIX usr       24  NEC DOS         65  Novell Netware  b8  BSDI swap
4   FAT16 <32M      3c  PartitionMagic  70  DiskSecure Mult c1  DRDOS/sec (FAT-
5   Extended        40  Venix 80286     75  PC/IX           c4  DRDOS/sec (FAT-
6   FAT16           41  PPC PReP Boot   80  Old Minix       c6  DRDOS/sec (FAT-
7   HPFS/NTFS       42  SFS             81  Minix / old Lin c7  Syrinx
```

8	AIX	4d	QNX4.x	82	Linux swap	db	CP/M / CTOS / .
9	AIX bootable	4e	QNX4.x 2nd part	83	Linux	e1	DOS access
a	OS/2 Boot Manag	4f	QNX4.x 3rd part	84	OS/2 hidden C:	e3	DOS R/O
b	Win95 FAT32	50	OnTrack DM	85	Linux extended	e4	SpeedStor
c	Win95 FAT32 (LB	51	OnTrack DM6 Aux	86	NTFS volume set	eb	BeOS fs
e	Win95 FAT16 (LB	52	CP/M	87	NTFS volume set	f1	SpeedStor
f	Win95 Ext'd (LB	53	OnTrack DM6 Aux	93	Amoeba	f4	SpeedStor
10	OPUS	54	OnTrackDM6	94	Amoeba BBT	f2	DOS secondary
11	Hidden FAT12	55	EZ-Drive	a0	IBM Thinkpad hi	fe	LANstep
12	Compaq diagnost	56	Golden Bow	a5	BSD/386	ff	BBT
14	Hidden FAT16 <3	5c	Priam Edisk				

As you can see, fdisk supports quite a few filesystem types. For your purposes, select type 83 for a Linux extended2 filesystem. This step is not necessary if you are adding an extended2 filesystem because ext2(83) is the default type.

Finally, typing w will write the partition table to the hard drive and quit fdisk. The disk now has a partition located at /dev/hdd1. You are now ready to proceed to the next step—formatting the disk.

Making a Filesystem

After the hard drive has been partitioned, you are ready to format the filesystem on the drive. Using the mkfs program will allow you to create an extended2 filesystem on the hard drive. The partition you created was the first and only partition of the /dev/hdd drive, so issue the following command:

```
/sbin/mkfs -t ext2 /dev/hdd1
```

Alternatively, you could use

```
/sbin/mkfs -t ext2 -c /dev/hdd1
```

to check for physical defects on the drive. This step is really not necessary, but it can be useful for a drive with bad blocks that need to be mapped out of the usable filesystem. If you are installing a previously used drive, this step is recommended.

Now that you've formatted the drive, you're ready to test it by manually mounting it. As root, create a mount point on your system, as shown in the following example:

```
mkdir /disk2
```

This gives you a directory from which to mount your newly created drive. By issuing the following command,

```
/sbin/mount -t ext2 /dev/hdd1 /disk2
```

the drive will be mounted and ready to use. You can verify the mounted drive by issuing the mount command:

```
/dev/sda1 on / type ext2 (rw)
none on /proc type proc (rw)
```

```
none on /dev/pts type devpts (rw,gid=5,mode=620)
/dev/hdd1 on /disk2 type ext2 (rw)
```

As you can see from this output, the last entry is your new drive, mounted on /disk2.

You can further verify the mount, as well as the available space on your new drive, by entering the following:

```
df -m
```

This will show how much of the drive is used, and how much is available. The -m switch tells df (disk free) to return the totals in megabyte values.

/dev/sda1	3836	3528	109	97%	/
/dev/hdd1	3558	0	3374	0%	/disk2

Automatic Drive Mounting

In Linux, filesystems can be automatically mounted at boot time. This is accomplished by the kernel reading the /etc/fstab file and mounting the partitions defined in it. Great care must be taken when editing this file—improperly formatting it may cause your system to malfunction. The following is an example fstab:

```
/dev/sda1        /              ext2    defaults      1 1
/dev/sda2        swap           swap    defaults      0 0
/dev/fd0         /mnt/floppy    ext2    noauto        0 0
/dev/cdrom       /mnt/cdrom     iso9660 noauto,ro     0 0
none             /proc          proc    defaults      0 0
none             /dev/pts       devpts  gid=5,mode=620    0 0
```

Each column in this fstab example, from left to right, has a specific purpose outlined in the following list.

- (fs spec)   This is the actual block device and partition to be mounted. In your example, /dev/hdd1.

- (fs file)   The mount point for the device. Using your example, this would be /disk2.

- (fs vfstype)   This is the type of filesystem contained on the device. Your example used the ext2(extended2) filesystem.

- (fs mntops)   This is the filesystem's mount options for the type of filesystem defined in fs vfstype. For your example, you can use the keyword defaults because it is sufficient for the ext2 filesystem. This will allow the partition to be automatically mounted at boot time.

- (fs freq)   The frequency field defines whether the filesystem needs to be dumped by the dump program. dump is a program that does backups of devices to disks, files, or tapes. A value of 1 will inform dump that the filesystem is to be dumped or backed up. You should use the value 1, to specify this in the fstab.

- (fs passno)   This parameter tells the system in what order the disk is to be checked by the fsck (filesystem check) program at boot time. The root device, /dev/sda1 in the previous example, should always be set to 1. All other devices should be set to 2 if they are persistently mounted devices such as hard drives. As this is the case with your device, use 2 to signify that this device will be the second device to be checked.

With all of these parameters for your device, you can build an fstab entry similar to the following:

```
/dev/hdd1                    /disk2                       ext2      defaults 1 2
```

The next step is to add this to your existing /etc/fstab. A good rule of thumb is to put this line after the root and swap partitions, because mount and other programs scan this file sequentially. This entry will mount your disk at /disk2 at boot time, as well as check it for any errors with fsck.

> **Caution:** Many people make the mistake of editing sensitive system files, like /etc/fstab, with an editor such as pico. This causes problems, because pico will add a return character at the point where the text wraps around your screen or term. Most of the time, this is around twenty-four columns long. This causes problems because most programs, such as mount, expect to have all of the options on the same line. It is recommended that Emacs, vi—or a vi derivative, such as vim—be used explicitly because none will have this nasty side-effect.

Adding a Modem

Adding a modem in Linux is perhaps one of the easiest hardware additions you can make. The only real difference comes when you have to load an internal modem as opposed to an external modem. Both options, however, are very similar and do not require a great deal of effort.

Preliminary Steps

Prior to setting up your modem, it's always a good idea to make sure that you have the latest BIOS version available. Most modern modems are equipped with a flashable BIOS. This enables the modem manufacturer to supply the end user with newer versions of the modem's core functionality. You can usually find Web site URLs in your modem documentation that will lead to manufacturer software for checking and upgrading your modem's flash BIOS.

First, you must physically connect the modem to your computer. When connecting an external modem, be aware of to which Com port you're connecting. This is important because Linux defines Com ports 1 and 2 (as of kernel versions 2.2.x) as ttyS0 and ttyS1, respectively. If you're connecting an internal modem, and you already have two external serial ports, you will most likely be using ttyS2 as your Linux serial device.

Note: Which modem is the best for Linux? Most external modems will work fine with Linux, as will internal ISA-type modems. Among the types that will not work in Linux are modems with the distinction or label "winmodem." Also known as DSPModem, HSPModem, Host Signal Processor, Windows Processor, P-Modem, or Mwaave modem, these devices do not work at all in Linux. While there is development under way in kernel 2.4.x for winmodem support, these modems will not work in the current kernel versions: 2.2.x. This is because winmodems implement a great deal of their functionality in software. This software implementation is, as the name implies, only Windows-based. PCI-based internal modems will usually not work in Linux either. While some people have been able to get them to work, they are very troublesome. Finally, avoid any USB-type devices because there is no current USB support in the Linux kernel.

Conflicts

With external modems, there is no need to worry about IRQ or port conflicts because the already-installed external serial port on your computer has probably already been defined. Internal modems, however, may cause a bit of a problem if they are plug-and-play type modems. Special attention has to be taken to check which IRQs are available, as well as I/O ports. A method on how to accomplish this is included in this chapter in the "Basic Process for Adding New Hardware" section. If you are installing an internal modem, you will most certainly have to deal with the assignment of resources for this device.

Many internal modems are also plug-and-play type modems. You may have to make adjustments, using third-party software, to your modem's BIOS to make it work. The methods outlined in the previous section ("Dealing with Plug-and-Play") will be of great use to that end.

Testing Your Modem

At this point, you need to boot into Linux to find out if your modem is functioning properly. Make sure the modem is turned on and a phone line is plugged into it. There are several ways to find out if Linux sees your modem on your particular serial port.

The easiest way is simply to try it out with some type of communications software. Most Linux distributions come with the `minicom` or `xminicom` program. `minicom` is simply a character-based interface to your modem. Before you use `minicom`, you need to define your connection parameters so `minicom` can find your modem. As `root`, launch `minicom` using the following command:

```
minicom -s
```

Or if you're in X, use the following command:

```
xminicom -s
```

This will launch minicom and allow you set up the communication parameters for your particular system. Once you're in minicom, you will be presented with a configuration dialog box (see Figure 5.1).

FIGURE 5.1

The xminicom configuration menu.

Next, you can select Serial Port Setup from the menu by using your arrow keys and pressing Enter. At this point, you are presented with a new dialog box containing several options that you can configure. By selecting the letter next to each category, you can modify its parameters (see Figure 5.2).

FIGURE 5.2

The xminicom communication configuration menu.

The only options you're concerned with here are

- A—Serial Device:
- E—Bps/Par/Bits:
- F—Hardware Flow Control:

Serial Device is the /dev file that corresponds to the serial port to which your modem is hooked. If you hooked your external modem to serial port 1, you would enter /dev/ttyS0 as this parameter. The default minicom value of /dev/modem can be used only if you have a symbolic link from /dev/modem to /dev/ttyS0. You could, for instance, create the following link as root:

```
ln -s /dev/ttyS0 /dev/modem
```

This gives you a pointer to your actual serial port so you don't have to remember where it is. You can just enter /dev/modem in any application without having to remember which serial port you used.

If your modem is internal, you would enter /dev/ttys2 as your serial port, because internal modems define their own new serial ports apart from your already installed ones.

Bps/Par/Bits is the final set of parameters that define modem-specific settings for bits-per-second, parity, and data bits. Table 5.1 is a guide you can use to set the appropriate speed for your particular modem

Table 5.1 ITU Standards and Their Equivalent Serial Speeds

ITU Standard	Serial Speed
56Kbps (V.90)	115200bps
28.8Kbps (V.34)	115200bps
14400bps (V.32bis)	57600bps
9600bps (V.32)	38400bps
less than 9600bps (V.32)	Use the highest speed your modem supports

The most common settings for parity and data bits is 8-N-1. For your current purposes, this is sufficient.

The Hardware Flow Control setting will nearly always be set to Yes with most modems. For the purpose of testing your modem, select Yes (see Figure 5.3).

FIGURE 5.3
Setting Hardware Flow Control in xminicom.

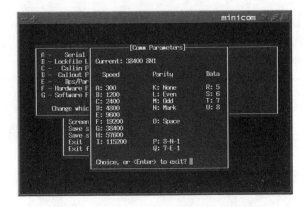

Finally, you can return to the configuration menu and select the option Save Setup as dfl. This will save your configuration so you don't have to modify it each time you use minicom. You can now select Exit Minicom to quit the minicom configuration session.

Now that your modem's communication parameters are set up, you can use minicom to test whether or not your modem is working correctly in Linux. From your terminal, launch minicom once again. You will now be in the minicom terminal session. To test your modem, simply enter the following modem command:

AT

After pressing Enter, you should see your modem respond with the following:

OK

This indicates that your modem is working with Linux and minicom. To test your line, you can enter the following modem command:

ATA

At this point, you should hear the dial tone for your line. You can hang up the line by typing shift +++ or ATH0. If you did not hear a dial tone, check to make sure that your phone line is connected to your modem in the correct port, usually labeled on the back of your modem.

Alternatively, if you have a number to dial into, you can use the following command:

ATDT 555-5555

Where 555-5555 is the number you want to dial.

If your modem failed any of these tests, you can troubleshoot it by using the methods outlined in the "Basic Process for Adding New Hardware" section, earlier in this chapter. The most common mistake people make with regard to modems is setting the communication parameters incorrectly.

Adding a Sound Card

Adding a sound card in Linux is sometimes more of a task than adding most hardware devices. Because of the incredibly wide variety of sound cards on the market, there really is no defined standard for how they work or how drivers for them should function. The Linux kernel does its best by supporting a wide range of sound hardware on the market today. As stated previously, Linux does support more devices than any other UNIX-type operating system today, especially if you're talking about multimedia devices such as sound cards.

> **Note:** While the Linux sound drivers are extensive, they are not necessarily the best option for adding sound to your system. One popular alternative is the set of commercially available sound drivers from 4Front Technologies. 4Front Technologies produces a set of drivers with a much larger selection of sound cards than the Linux kernel. These drivers, called the Open Sound System, are an attempt by 4Front to unify the sound architecture for most UNIX-based operating systems with a uniform sound API. The Linux kernel contains a subset of OSS called OSS Lite. You can find out more about 4Front Technologies and OSS by visiting http://www.4front-tech.com.

Unlike most devices, sound cards use several device entries for different parts of the actual sound chipset.

- /dev/audio   Actual audio inputs and outputs
- /dev/dsp   Sound card's digital sampling device
- /dev/mixer   Sound card's sound mixing device
- /dev/music   A high-level sequencer device
- /dev/midi   The raw MIDI port
- /dev/sndstat   Contains the status of the sound drivers

All these device entries will usually reside on your one specific sound card.

Installing the Card

The first step is to actually install the card on your system. Follow the card manufacturer's directions on installing the card onto your motherboard. Most cards also include a connector for your internal CD-ROM drive. If you are using an internal CD-ROM drive, be sure to follow the directions to properly connect it to your sound card. This step is required if you want to play audio CD-ROMs and have the sound output through your sound card. Finally, connect a pair of speakers to your sound card's speaker output so you'll be able to verify that it is functioning. Alternatively, you could use headphones in place of speakers.

Conflicts

Many older sound cards' resources are configurable by setting jumpers on the card. You may need to determine what resources you have available and set them appropriately to your particular card. To determine what resources you have available, refer to the previous section, "Basic Process for Adding New Hardware." You can use these methods as a guide when configuring your sound card's resources.

Today, however, most newer sound cards are plug-and-play. This means that you may need adjust the sound card's parameters via the methods outlined in "Dealing with Plug-and-Play," earlier in this chapter.

Kernel Sound Options

More likely than not, you will need to configure your kernel for sound. To accomplish this, you will have to recompile your kernel after selecting the appropriate sound card in the sound section of the kernel configuration. On some sound cards, you will also need to enter parameters for the card's resources. You can get more information on each card's specific parameters by selecting help for the device you are enabling from within the kernel configuration. For a guide on how to recompile your kernel, a thorough reading of Chapter 24 is recommended.

If you are using an ISA-based plug-and-play sound card, the card must be compiled as a kernel module. This is because the card's resources can only be configured after the kernel has already been booted. Once the card's resources are allocated, the device drivers will attach to it via the kernel module mechanism.

After compiling module support for your particular sound card, you are ready to test whether it was initialized and, finally, test the card for functionality.

Detecting a Sound Card

If you were able to compile your sound card into the kernel, as opposed to a loadable kernel module, you can use a couple of methods to verify that it was detected by the kernel. First, you will be able to see the sound initialization happen when the system boots. If your card is working, you will see a section like the following:

```
Sound Initialization Started
SoundBlaster AWE64 Gold at 0x220 irq 5 drq 1,5
OPL-2/OPL-3 FM at 0x388
SB MPU-401 at 0x330 irq 5
Emu 8000 Synthesizer Engine at 0x620
Sound Initialization Complete
```

If this information scrolls by too fast at boot time, you can find it by issuing the dmesg command and grepping for the word Sound (see the previous section, "Dealing with the Kernel").

If you see this section with nothing between the started and complete printouts, your sound card has not been initialized. This could indicate that you have compiled the wrong card into your kernel.

If you do not see the Sound Initialization Started and Sound Initialization Complete section, you probably have not properly configured your kernel for sound. If this is the case, go back, verify your kernel configuration, and recompile.

If your sound card was compiled as a loadable kernel module, you can verify its functionality by simply using cat to send the device a sound file, as shown in the following:

```
cat audiofile.au > /dev/audio
```

If you have speakers connected to the output of your sound card, you should hear the audio file being played. If you do not, you can further diagnose the status of your card by issuing the following command:

```
cat /dev/sndstat
```

This command should give you information about your sound card, similar to the following:

```
Card config:
Generic PnP support
SoundBlaster AWE64 Gold at 0x220 irq 5 drq 1,5
OPL-2/OPL-3 FM at 0x388
SB MPU-401 at 0x330 irq 5
Emu 8000 Synthesizer Engine at 0x620

Audio devices:
0: Creative SB AWE64 Gold (4.16) (DUPLEX)
1: SB secondary device (DUPLEX)

Synth devices:
0: Yamaha OPL-3
1: AWE32-0.4.2 (RAM4096k)

Midi devices:
0: Sound Blaster 16

Timers:
0: System clock

Mixers:
0: Sound Blaster
1: AWE32 Equalizer
```

While not all drivers support /dev/sndstat, most do and will give you information on your installed sound card.

This command will give you information about the various devices on your card, if it has been detected and initialized. If you do not get any information from /dev/sndstat, your sound card has not been initialized. At this point, you need to again verify your kernel compile, as well as any resources that are supposed to be allocated to your device. Any conflicting resources can cause your sound card to not work. The methods outlined in the previous sections can be a guideline for troubleshooting your installation.

Summary

Adding hardware to your system can often be a confusing and frustrating venture. While Linux does support a wide range of hardware, it is still comparatively very young as far as operating systems are concerned. This situation is further aggravated by the fact that many of Linux's device drivers have to be reverse-engineered because of the lack of hardware vendor support. This situation will surely not last long, as Linux continues to gain more and more popularity within the end user and developer communities.

The most full-proof way of overcoming problems adding hardware is to arm yourself with as much knowledge about the subject as you can. With an increased level of knowledge, you can certainly overcome any of the pitfalls or problems presented to you when adding hardware to your system.

As always, the Internet is a great source of information on subjects such as adding hardware to your Linux system. You can always find many people in the public newsgroups who have probably been through the same problems as you have. Using their experience, you will usually be able to find a solution to any problem you may come up against.

On Your Own

After successfully installing your new hard drive, try moving it to a different mount point. Make sure to edit the /etc/fstab file correctly to have it automatically mount at boot time. You can also try adding two partitions to your drive and mounting them at different mount points.

After installing your internal modem, try moving it to a different serial port. Then, configure and test it by dialing a remote computer using minicom or xminicom. When your modem is working, investigate any of the many communications applications that are included with most Linux distributions.

When your new sound card is installed, try playing various audio and MIDI files using the sox sound utilities. Then, try using your CD-ROM drive to play an audio compact disc. Once you've verified that your sound card works, try recording some audio using an external microphone. Check out the wealth of audio applications that you can find using any of the many Internet based Linux software distribution sites. For a great start, visit http://www.freshmeat.net.

Finally, using the methods described earlier in this chapter, make a note of what resources you have used with your new hardware. Also, make note of any resources that you may have remaining. This knowledge will give you a great starting point from which to tackle any future hardware installations with ease.

Installing the X Window System

The X Window System is the GUI interface for Linux. It was originally designed to provide mouse and windowing capabilities to UNIX. Every attempt was made to make the system as portable as possible in the hopes that the world would wind up with a single standard interface. With the exception of a proprietary system here and there (Apple and Microsoft, among others), X has largely succeeded. I believe that all UNIX systems now use it, and, of course, X is now considered an integral part of Linux.

Two projects at the Massachusetts Institute of Technology jointly developed the original version of X. Its purpose was to enable programmers to build applications without having to start from scratch to control the keyboard, graphics, and the mouse. Two sponsoring companies, IBM and Digital Equipment, supported the development. The year 1987 is considered to be the turning point—the X system became widely known and was adopted by several workstation manufacturers. It's in very good shape now because it has had a number of years to mature and stabilize.

> **Note:** It seems that there are some really big things in store for X in the future. Linux is constantly getting rave reviews everywhere. The only consistent criticism of Linux is the difficult interface (that is, the command line). The Linux community is responding to the criticism by adding more and more windowing options for system configuration and management, and all this windowing activity is being based on X.

The Names of X

X has many names. The name of the software system is simply X, but the problem is that the name is so short and non-descript that most people like to add a couple of syllables. The X Consortium requests that only the following names be used:

- X
- X Window System

- X Version 11
- X Window System, Version 11
- X11 (pronounced x-eleven)

You will see X referred to as both X10 and X11. The 10 and 11 are version numbers. X10 is probably not being used anywhere now because there were so many improvements made in X11. Beyond the version number, there are also revision levels, and these can also be included in the name. For example, for 6.3 of X11 you may see the name X11R6 or even X11R6.3.

Just What is X?

X is a client/server, network-transparent, vendor-independent operating environment supporting a mouse and keyboard interface to a set of overlapped windows.

It is client/server in the sense that an application program is the client and uses the display server to communicate with the user. The same server (display with mouse and keyboard) can communicate with several clients simultaneously. Normally, a client only talks to one server at a time—if another user wants to run the application, a new instance of it is started.

It is network-transparent in that an application can run on any computer in a network and use the display of any other computer in the network. The complete address of a display includes the name of the host computer and a number—the number is present in case there is more than one display attached to the host.

A computer that has a display, keyboard, and mouse that is used as the interface to X programs is called a *workstation*. There are also special terminals, called X-terminals, that are not computers, but are terminals that operate under control of the X protocols. There was a time when X-terminals were very common but, for various reasons having to do with cost and flexibility, they are not so common any more.

The display, mouse, and keyboard being referred to as the server, and each application being referred to as a client, may seem backward to you. And with all that has happened in client/server systems in the last decade, it probably is backward. It was named this way because of the designer viewpoint. Designers are people who think in terms of writing applications that need an interface to their users—the applications are thought of as clients, and the display is thought of as the server.

The diagram in Figure 6.1 is an overview of the flow of data through the X windowing system. The application is written using calls to the functions found in Xlib—the library of X windowing functions. All communications to and from the terminal are made through these function calls. There are functions that can be used to open windows, close windows, read the mouse, read the keyboard, display text or graphics, and much more. It is a very complete, but low level, set of windowing functions. There are other libraries (among them are the Xtoolkit, GTK+, and Qt) that are linked to the applications to supply a higher level interface to the low-level Xlib functions.

FIGURE 6.1

The basic architecture of the X system.

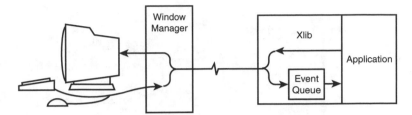

Here's how things work. The application starts running and, by making the appropriate library calls, establishes a connection with the window manager of the display server. As soon as the connection is established, the application calls a function with a detailed description of a window to display. The window manager reads the message, obeys the commands, and displays a window for the application. Then everything stops and waits. It is now up to the user.

The user, on seeing the window, presses a button on the keyboard, moves the mouse, clicks a mouse button, or some other action. The user action is formatted as an event and sent to the window manager. The window manager passes the event over the communications link to the application. The events come across the link asynchronously (that is, the program does not have to stop and wait for them) and are queued up by the software in Xlib. Whenever the application needs an event from the user, it calls an Xlib function to read the next event on the queue. The application then processes the event, redesigns its display, and the whole sequence starts over again.

As you might imagine, there are some other things than can happen. For one thing, if the mouse is clicked on something on the screen that does not belong to an application, the resulting action is determined by the window manager (it could be anything from a system menu to resizing a window). For another thing, the window manager can check the exact time of mouse clicks and convert ones that are close together into double-click events. To reduce the amount of traffic over the link from the application (graphics can get large, you know), once the initial window is displayed, Xlib will often send just the changes that need to be made.

The X system is in no way limited to a mouse, a keyboard, and a CRT monitor. There are facilities included to handle touch pads, joy sticks, track balls, or just about anything else. There is even the capability to use multiple screens with a single mouse and keyboard—more on this later.

A Few Words About X

There are some terms that are used to describe windowing in general, and X specifically. A typical display layout is shown in Figure 6.2. There are three X programs running: a calculator, a terminal emulator, and a clock.

FIGURE 6.2
Typical Display Layout

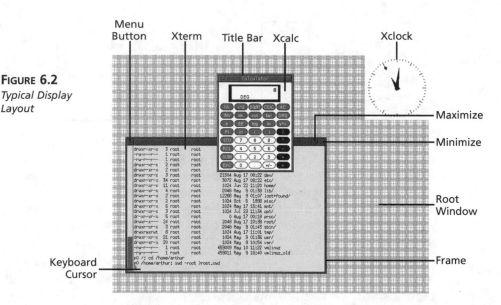

A *window* is a rectangular region of the display. A single application can have one or more of these windows on display. Windows can overlap and obscure one another. Smaller windows can be nested inside larger ones, and the contained windows appear in front of the containing windows.

There is one *root* window. It is the parent window—the containing window—of all the other windows on the display. It is the background window covering the entire screen. It cannot be resized or moved like other windows can. All other windows are displayed on top of it.

There is a program called the *window manager* (more on this in the next section) that controls the size and location of the windows and adds controls enabling the user to adjust the display.

Normally, the window manager places a *frame* around the windows to facilitate control by the user's mouse. In Figure 6.2, the window manager has placed a frame around xterm that has a menu button on the left—the menu contains the list of things the user can request the window manager do to this particular window. In the opposite corner of the xterm frame, there are buttons to Maximize (expand the window to its maximum allowable size) and Minimize (reduce the window to an icon on the root window) the window. Not all window frames are equal. Notice that the frame around xcalc does not have a Minimize button, and xclock has no frame whatsoever.

There are two cursors—the *keyboard cursor* and the *mouse cursor*. In common usage, the keyboard cursor is simply called the cursor, and the mouse cursor is called the mouse pointer or just the mouse. There is never more than one mouse cursor, but there can be a keyboard cursor in each of several windows.

A window is said to have *focus* if input from the keyboard is sent to it (well, sent to the application displaying the window). Only one window can have the focus at any one time. A window can be partially obscured by another window and still retain focus, as is the case for xterm in Figure 6.2. It is up to the window manager, but a window with the focus typically has a different colored frame or contains a different pattern than the other windows. There are different ways to change the focus from one window to another—it is under the control of the window manager.

A *widget* is a small window dedicated to a specific purpose—it is a single item performing a task inside another window. It can be a button, a pull-down list, a menu selection, a text string, or anything else that operates as a single unit. In Figure 6.2, for example, each of the calculator buttons is a widget, as are the maximize/minimize buttons and the scrollbar on the left of the xterm window. A widget is programmed with special functions that are called from Xlib so both the window manager, as well as the application, can communicate directly with the widget.

A *dialog box* is a window that has data input and output fields of some sort. It can be anything from a simple information window with a single OK button to a scrolling screen full of buttons, pull-downs, pop-ups, and text editing widgets. In Figure 6.2, the calculator window is a dialog box.

What Is a Window Manager?

The window manager is a program that controls everything that appears on the display. It fills the entire screen with a root window and displays all other windows on top of it. The window manager controls the position and size of every window, whether or not a window shows as an icon, the background color or pattern, the shape of the mouse pointer, and so on.

Because this one program is completely in charge of the display, it is possible for a very different window manager to be working with an application. The application doesn't decorate the window—the window manager does. The application's window can have a set of buttons in the corner to halt the application, reduce it to an icon, or whatever. The decoration—the bar across the top and the frame around the edges—is completely at the discretion of the window manager.

The window manager has so much control that many of the messages coming from an application are taken has hints and suggestions. For example, an application can issue a request for its window to be a certain size, but the window manager is under no obligation to obey—the application can only suggest.

Everything is a window—every button, pull-down list, dialog box, pop-up tab, and text area. Each of these items is managed separately by the window manager, so each one of them can take on an entirely different appearance in different window managers.

As shown in Table 6.1, there are a number of window managers. There are many more than just those listed. Some window managers are designed for a special purpose to do things like tile the windows instead of overlapping them or convert colors to shades of gray for a monochrome display. No single Linux distribution will have all of the window managers listed in Table 6.1, and there may be some others that are not listed. There are dozens of window managers, and new ones are appearing all the time.

Table 6.1   Some Window Managers Available for Linux

Name	Full Name	Description
afterstep	AfterStep window manager	This window managers is designed to simulate the look and feel of the NeXTStep interface.
enlightenment		Window manager for GNOME The GNOME system a complete operating environment, and the enlightenment window manager is part of it.
fvwm	Virtual Window Manager for X11	This is an update of the twm window manager with changes made to use memory more efficiently and to provide a beveled-edge look to the graphical objects. This is the default window manager for most Linux distributions.
fvwm2	Virtual Window Manager for X11 Version 2	In addition to the features of fvwm, this updated version provides multiple virtual desktops. You can scroll around as if you screen were much larger than it really is.
mwm	Motif Window Manager veteran UNIX users.	This could be the most well-known of the window managers among It was the first one to use beveled edges on the buttons and the frame around an applications window. Mwm is not commonly found on Linux systems.
olwm	Open Look Window Manager	This is the default Window manager of older Sun workstations.
rtl	Tiled Window Manager	The windows are tiled and sized next to one another without overlapping.
twm	Tom's Window Manager	As window managers go, this is a fairly simple one. It handles the basic overlapped window management with a minimum of clutter. Buttons and borders are flat and non-textured. This is the window manager that is part of the X11 source distribution.

Name	Full Name	Description
uwm	Universal Window Manager	This was the first of the window managers, but it is seldom used now because it employs an older form of the communications protocol and it requires a special setup for installation.
windowmaker	GNU WindowMaker	This window manager is from the GNU project and is designed to emulate the NeXTStep user interface.

There are a number of advantages to this architecture with everything being under the control of the window manager:

- Each individual login can have its own configuration. Files in the home directory of a user determine the colors used for frames, decoration of the root window, what causes focus to change from one application to another, and even which window manager is used. Two people can be running the same program but have the screen look and act very differently. There are ways to individualize the settings for individual applications. Everybody gets what they want—the screen can be configured to work like a Macintosh or a Windows computer if desired.

- The X System was designed to run both locally and over a network. The client and the server (the display and the application) can be on the same computer or on two separate computers connected in a LAN, or even a remote computer connected over the Internet. It is not uncommon for a workstation display to simultaneously contain windows from three or four different computers.

- Distributed execution simplifies administration. Non-drastic administration tasks (like adding a new user or installing files) can be done remotely. This allows the system administrator to remain in one place and perform very specific administrative and system monitoring tasks.

- Distributed execution enables CPU load sharing. In cases where there are a number of CPU-intensive processes to be run, these processes can be spread across a number of computers on the network, effectively speeding up the entire process.

- The standard X communications protocol allows for a no-impact upgrade of the system. There can be new versions of applications, and even of the window manager, without disrupting anything. There is no requirement for everyone to suddenly switch to the new version.

Installing X Under Linux

It is really a very simple process to install X under Linux. You just need to load the files, set the path, define the termcap, and set a couple of environment variables. In fact, most of the installation is normally completed during the initial Linux installation. There are some things you are going to want to adjust because the default installation is usually less than elegant. There are a lot of options you can set, but all of them are in separate configuration files, and you can set them any time.

The X Files

The files are all kept in subdirectories of /usr/X11R6. Table 6.2 describes the content of these directories. If you have not already installed X11, you can do so now. The installation procedure will add files to the directories listed in Table 6.2. The exact installation procedure varies quite a bit from one distribution of Linux to another, so you will need to refer to the documentation that comes with your version.

Table 6.2   Installed X

Directory	Contains
/usr/X11R6/bin	Executable programs. This is everything from window managers to games.
/usr/X11R6/include	Sets of C language include files for use by programmers writing X applications.
/usr/X11R6/lib	Libraries containing the executable code of X. The libraries are used by X applications while they run.
/usr/X11R6/man	The manual pages.
/usr/X11R6/share	Programs and data from outside sources. These items are not strictly a part of X.

Set the Path Variable

If this was not already done as part of the Linux installation, the PATH environment variable needs to include the name of the directory holding the X executables. The name of the directory containing the binaries is /usr/X11R6/bin, and there is a link to it named /user/bin/X11. A path that points to either of these directories will do.

For the bash shell, the path can be defined in /etc/profile as the following:

```
PATH=$PATH;/usr/bin/X11
```

Or, if you prefer not going through the link, it can be done as the following:

```
PATH=$PATH;/usr/X11R6/bin
```

The C shell will need to have the path defined in /etc/csh.cshrc:

```
setenv PATH "${PATH}:/usr/X11R6/bin
```

Do Some Exploring

There is good news and bad news. The bad news is that there are several steps involved to configure X. The good news is that all the configuration information goes into a single text file. More good news is that there are some utilities that will help you set up the configuration. Even more good news is that Linux knows a lot of hardware by name, and may know yours.

Grab manuals on your computer. You will need to know the following:

- The name and model of the video card.
- The amount of RAM installed on the video card.
- Whether or not the video card is VGA compatible.
- The horizontal sync rate and the vertical refresh rate of the monitor.
- The protocol used by your mouse. This may be unnecessary because a plug-n-play mouse will be detected automatically.

A utility exists that can help you with some of the information. The program named SuperProbe will try to determine what kind of video adapter you have installed. It has the ability to recognized almost all of the adapters that are compatible with Linux and X. If successful, SuperProbe will tell you the type of video card, the chipset it uses, and the amount of memory it contains.

> **Warning:** Because SuperProbe deals directly with the hardware (trying to read information from the video card), it could trigger something that causes the system to lock up. If this happens, take a look at the man page for SuperProbe—there is some information there about how to proceed. Basically, if you use the -verbose option, you will see a trace of what is being probed, and this should tell you where it stopped. You then may be able to use the -excl option to have SuperProbe skip that particular port. There are also other options that can be used to limit the search.

There is a utility that is present in some Linux distributions. You may be able to use a command line program called mouseconfig to configure the mouse for your Linux system. This has the beneficial side effect of showing you the information about the mouse—information that will be needed for X configuration.

There is a wealth of information available to you in the directory /usr/X11R6/lib/X11/doc. There are documents that describe installation options, hardware compatibility, and other situations you can encounter during installation. You would be doing yourself a favor if you explored the files in this directory to get a better idea of what is required for the installation. In particular, there are a number of documents that pertain to specific video cards. There is even information about compatible versions of Linux.

XF86Config

The file named /etc/X11/XF86Config is a text file containing all the configuration information for X. The default version of the file that comes with the system contains configuration for a standard VGA card and monitor with 640×480 resolution. There is a file named /etc/X11/XF86Config.eg that is a duplicate of the original version of XF86Config and contains all the default settings—to start from scratch, copy XF86Config.eg to XF86Config.

There is software that can be used to help you edit this file. A program named xf86config can be used to make certain changes to the file. A utility named Xconfigurator comes with Red Hat Linux. Another utility named XF86Setup—an X application—can also be used to edit the file. If you find that you have one of these utilities on your system, you should use it to configure X.

> **Tip:** If you are new to all this, your best approach will be to read through this section and familiarize yourself with the format and contents of the XF86Config file. Then use one of the configuration software utilities to create an updated file. You can do this a number of times, experimenting with different settings—just make backup copies of XF86Config as you go, and you can restore any previously defined configuration.

The file XF86Config is divided into sections, and each section is named for what it holds. The sections of the file are listed in Table 6.3. Each section is described in the following sections.

Table 6.3   The Sections of XF86Config

Section Name	Contains
Device	Information on the graphics adapter. There can be more than one of these sections.
Files	The locations of various fonts and color name definitions.
Keyboard	Specification of the keyboard type and protocol.
Module	The names of libraries containing dynamically-loaded executable modules.
Monitor	The information on the monitor's horizontal and vertical frequencies. There are also tables of data for each mode of operation.
Pointer	Definition of access and protocol for the pointing devices (usually a mouse).
Screen	Name of the X server that will control the display, the size of the screen, and the color depth. There may be more than one of these sections.

Section Name	Contains
ServerFlags	Settings to enable or disable responses to signals and to certain keyboard sequences.
Xinput	Definition information for any special input devices, such as a stylus or a graphics pad.

In the file, each section begins with the word Section and ends with the word EndSection. For example, the Monitor section looks like the following:

```
Section "Monitor"
   . . .
EndSection
```

Any line that has an octothorpe (#) as its first non-blank character is a comment line. Fortunately, the distributed file is generously commented, making it much easier to read that it would be otherwise.

Section "Files"

```
# **********************************************************************# Files
section.  This allows default font and rgb paths to be set#
**********************************************************************

Section "Files"

# The location of the RGB database.  Note, this is the name of the
# file minus the extension (like ".txt" or ".db").  There is normally
# no need to change the default.

    RgbPath       "/usr/X11R6/lib/X11/rgb"

# Multiple FontPath entries are allowed (which are concatenated together),
# as well as specifying multiple comma-separated entries in one FontPath
# command (or a combination of both methods)

    FontPath      "/usr/X11R6/lib/X11/fonts/misc/"
FontPath      "/usr/X11R6/lib/X11/fonts/75dpi/:unscaled"
FontPath      "/usr/X11R6/lib/X11/fonts/100dpi/:unscaled"
FontPath      "/usr/X11R6/lib/X11/fonts/Type1/"
FontPath      "/usr/X11R6/lib/X11/fonts/Speedo/"
FontPath      "/usr/X11R6/lib/X11/fonts/75dpi/"
FontPath      "/usr/X11R6/lib/X11/fonts/100dpi/"

# For OSs that support Dynamically loaded modules, ModulePath can be
# used to set a search path for the modules.  This is currently supported
# for Linux ELF, FreeBSD 2.x and NetBSD 1.x.  The default path is shown
# here.

#    ModulePath    "/usr/X11R6/lib/modules"

EndSection
```

There is a file that defines the names of the colors. A color is defined as three numbers—one each for red, green, and blue. This allows you to use color names to configure the appearance of your system. The actual file name is /usr/X11R6/lib/X11/rgb.txt.

Fonts are referred to by name. There are a number of directories that contain fonts, and you can add more. This section contains a FontPath entry for each directory containing one or more fonts. The font directories are normally installed in the directory /usr/X11R6/lib/X11/fonts, and there may be some already there that are not included in the configuration list. In particular, the ISO8859 fonts are included along with example entries for the configuration file.

Section "Module"

```
# *********************************************************************# Module
section — this is an optional section which is used to specify# which
dynamically loadable modules to load.  Dynamically loadable
# modules are currently supported only for Linux ELF, FreeBSD 2.x
# and NetBSD 1.x.  Currently, dynamically loadable modules are used
# only for some extended input (XInput) device drivers.
# *********************************************************************
#
# Section "Module"
#
# This loads the module for the Joystick driver
#
# Load "xf86Jstk.so"
#
# EndSection
```

This section is normally not needed, but if you ever install a program that needs a dynamically loaded library as part of X, it can be listed here. This type of library normally has the extension .so (which is short for shared object library).

Section "ServerFlags"

```
# *********************************************************************# Server
flags section.
# *********************************************************************

Section "ServerFlags"

# Uncomment this to cause a core dump at the spot where a signal is
# received.  This may leave the console in an unusable state, but may
# provide a better stack trace in the core dump to aid in debugging

#     NoTrapSignals

# Uncomment this to disable the <Crtl><Alt><BS> server abort sequence
# This allows clients to receive this key event.

#     DontZap
```

```
# Uncomment this to disable the <Crtl><Alt><KP_+>/<KP_-> mode switching
# sequences.  This allows clients to receive these key events.

#    DontZoom

# Uncomment this to disable tuning with the xvidtune client. With
# it the client can still run and fetch card and monitor attributes,
# but it will not be allowed to change them. If it tries it will
# receive a protocol error.

#    DisableVidModeExtension

# Uncomment this to enable the use of a non-local xvidtune client.

#    AllowNonLocalXvidtune

# Uncomment this to disable dynamically modifying the input device
# (mouse and keyboard) settings.

#    DisableModInDev

# Uncomment this to enable the use of a non-local client to
# change the keyboard or mouse settings (currently only xset).

#    AllowNonLocalModInDev

EndSection
```

These are configuration flags that tell the X server how to react to certain stimuli. If the members of this section are all commented out, the default actions will be taken.

Section "Keyboard"

```
# **********************************************************************
# Keyboard section
# **********************************************************************

Section "Keyboard"

    Protocol    "Standard"

# when using XQUEUE, comment out the above line, and uncomment the
# following line

#    Protocol    "Xqueue"

    AutoRepeat    500 5

# Let the server do the NumLock processing.  This should only be required
# when using pre-R6 clients
#    ServerNumLock

# Specifiy which keyboard LEDs can be user-controlled (eg, with xset(1))
```

```
#     Xleds       1 2 3

# To set the LeftAlt to Meta, RightAlt key to ModeShift,
# RightCtl key to Compose, and ScrollLock key to ModeLock:

#     LeftAlt      Meta
#     RightAlt     ModeShift
#     RightCtl     Compose
#     ScrollLock   ModeLock

# To disable the XKEYBOARD extension, uncomment XkbDisable.

# XkbDisable

# To customise the XKB settings to suit your keyboard, modify the
# lines below (which are the defaults).  For example, for a non-U.S.
# keyboard, you will probably want to use:
#     XkbModel     "pc102"
# If you have a Microsoft Natural keyboard, you can use:
#     XkbModel     "microsoft"
#
# Then to change the language, change the Layout setting.
# For example, a German layout can be obtained with:
#     XkbLayout    "de"
# or:
#     XkbLayout    "de"
#     XkbVariant   "nodeadkeys"
#
# If you'd like to switch the positions of your capslock and
# control keys, use:
#     XkbOptions   "ctrl:swapcaps"


# These are the default XKB settings for XFree86
#     XkbRules     "xfree86"
#     XkbModel     "pc101"
#     XkbLayout    "us"
#     XkbVariant   ""
#     XkbOptions   ""

EndSection
```

If you don't know which protocol to use, just go with the standard. The rate that characters will repeat when a key is held down is defined as a pair of Autorepeat numbers—the
first on is the number of milliseconds to wait before starting to repeat, and the second is
the number of milliseconds between each repeat.

If you have a standard PC keyboard layout, you may want to uncomment the lines that
remap some of the keys. There are keys known to Linux, to other UNIX systems, and to
X that are not on the PC keyboard. Uncommenting the four lines (LeftAlt, RightAlt,

RightCtl, and ScrollLock) will give you the ability to type in the missing keys—it isn't common, but there are some applications that expect them.

If you have anything other than a standard English PC keyboard with 101 keys, you may need to do some customization. The directory /usr/X11R6/lib/X11/xkb contains the files controlling the configuration of the keyboard. Which files are chosen to configure the keyboard is determined by the settings of the Xkb definitions. In this directory you will find options for German, Japanese, Dvorak, and several other keyboard layouts.

Section "Xinput"

```
# ***********************************************************************# Xinput
section — this is optional and is required only if you# are using extended input
devices.  This is for example only.  Refer# to the XF86Config man page for a
description of the options.
# ***********************************************************************
#
# Section "Xinput"
#     SubSection "WacomStylus"
#         Port "/dev/ttyS1"
#         DeviceName "Wacom"
#     EndSubSection
#     SubSection "WacomCursor"
#         Port "/dev/ttyS1"
#     EndSubSection
#     SubSection "WacomEraser"
#         Port "/dev/ttyS1"
#     EndSubSection
#
#     SubSection "Elographics"
#         Port "/dev/ttyS1"
#         DeviceName "Elo"
#         MinimumXPosition 300
#         MaximumXPosition 3500
#         MinimumYPosition 300
#         MaximumYPosition 3500
#         Screen 0
#         UntouchDelay 10
#         ReportDelay 10
#     EndSubSection
#
#     SubSection "Joystick"
#         Port "/dev/joy0"
#         DeviceName "Joystick"
#         TimeOut 10
#         MinimumXPosition 100
#         MaximumXPosition 1300
#         MinimumYPosition 100
#         MaximumYPosition 1100
#         # CenterX 700
#         # CenterY 600
```

```
#          Delta 20
#      EndSubSection
#
# The Mouse Subsection contains the same type of entries as the
# standard Pointer Section (see above), with the addition of the
# DeviceName entry.
#
#      SubSection "Mouse"
#          Port "/dev/mouse2"
#          DeviceName "Second Mouse"
#          Protocol "Logitech"
#      EndSubSection
# EndSection
```

Unless you have some sort of special input device, there is no need to do anything with this section. There are provisions for a stylus and a joystick—there is even a way to install a second mouse. Even if you do have such a device, it would probably be best to install X without it just to make sure that everything works without the special device. You can come back and edit this file any time.

Section "Monitor"

```
# ***************************************************************************
# Monitor section
# ***************************************************************************

# Any number of monitor sections may be present

Section "Monitor"

    Identifier     "Generic Monitor"
    VendorName     "Unknown"
    ModelName      "Unknown"

# HorizSync is in kHz unless units are specified.
# HorizSync may be a comma separated list of discrete values, or a
# comma separated list of ranges of values.
# NOTE: THE VALUES HERE ARE EXAMPLES ONLY.  REFER TO YOUR MONITOR'S
# USER MANUAL FOR THE CORRECT NUMBERS.

    HorizSync    31.5  # typical for a single frequency fixed-sync monitor

#    HorizSync    30-64        # multisync
#    HorizSync    31.5, 35.2   # multiple fixed sync frequencies
#    HorizSync    15-25, 30-50 # multiple ranges of sync frequencies

# VertRefresh is in Hz unless units are specified.
# VertRefresh may be a comma separated list of discrete values, or a
# comma separated list of ranges of values.
# NOTE: THE VALUES HERE ARE EXAMPLES ONLY.  REFER TO YOUR MONITOR'S
# USER MANUAL FOR THE CORRECT NUMBERS.
```

```
        VertRefresh 60  # typical for a single frequency fixed-sync monitor

#       VertRefresh    50-100          # multisync
#       VertRefresh    60, 65          # multiple fixed sync frequencies
#       VertRefresh    40-50, 80-100 # multiple ranges of sync frequencies

# Modes can be specified in two formats.  A compact one-line format, or
# a multi-line format.

# A generic VGA 640x480 mode (hsync = 31.5kHz, refresh = 60Hz)
# These two are equivalent

#     ModeLine "640x480" 25.175 640 664 760 800 480 491 493 525

    Mode "640x480"
        DotClock    25.175
        HTimings    640 664 760 800
        VTimings    480 491 493 525
    EndMode

# These two are equivalent

#     ModeLine "1024x768i" 45 1024 1048 1208 1264 768 776 784 817 Interlace

#     Mode "1024x768i"
#         DotClock    45
#         HTimings    1024 1048 1208 1264
#         VTimings    768 776 784 817
#         Flags       "Interlace"
#     EndMode

# This is a set of standard mode timings. Modes that are out of monitor spec
# are automatically deleted by the server (provided the HorizSync and
# VertRefresh lines are correct), so there's no immediate need to
# delete mode timings (unless particular mode timings don't work on your
# monitor). With these modes, the best standard mode that your monitor
# and video card can support for a given resolution is automatically
# used.

# 640x400 @ 70 Hz, 31.5 kHz hsync
Modeline "640x400"     25.175 640  664  760  800   400  409  411  450
# 640x480 @ 60 Hz, 31.5 kHz hsync
Modeline "640x480"     25.175 640  664  760  800   480  491  493  525
# 800x600 @ 56 Hz, 35.15 kHz hsync
ModeLine "800x600"     36     800  824  896 1024   600  601  603  625
# 1024x768 @ 87 Hz interlaced, 35.5 kHz hsync
#Modeline "1024x768"    44.9  1024 1048 1208 1264   768  776  784  817 Interlace

# 640x480 @ 72 Hz, 36.5 kHz hsync
Modeline "640x480"     31.5   640  680  720  864   480  488  491  521
# 800x600 @ 60 Hz, 37.8 kHz hsync
Modeline "800x600"     40     800  840  968 1056   600  601  605  628 +hsync
```

```
+vsync

# 800x600 @ 72 Hz, 48.0 kHz hsync
Modeline "800x600"      50      800 856  976 1040    600 637  643  666 +hsync
+vsync
# 1024x768 @ 60 Hz, 48.4 kHz hsync
Modeline "1024x768"     65      1024 1032 1176 1344   768 771  777  806 -hsync -
vsync

# 1024x768 @ 70 Hz, 56.5 kHz hsync
Modeline "1024x768"     75      1024 1048 1184 1328   768 771  777  806 -hsync -
vsync
# 1280x1024 @ 87 Hz interlaced, 51 kHz hsync
#Modeline "1280x1024"   80      1280 1296 1512 1568   1024 1025 1037 1165 Interlace

# 1024x768 @ 76 Hz, 62.5 kHz hsync
Modeline "1024x768"     85      1024 1032 1152 1360   768 784  787  823
# 1280x1024 @ 61 Hz, 64.2 kHz hsync
Modeline "1280x1024"    110     1280 1328 1512 1712   1024 1025 1028 1054

# 1280x1024 @ 74 Hz, 78.85 kHz hsync
Modeline "1280x1024"    135     1280 1312 1456 1712   1024 1027 1030 1064

# 1280x1024 @ 76 Hz, 81.13 kHz hsync
Modeline "1280x1024"    135     1280 1312 1416 1664   1024 1027 1030 1064

# Low-res Doublescan modes
# If your chipset does not support doublescan, you get a 'squashed'
# resolution like 320x400.

# 320x200 @ 70 Hz, 31.5 kHz hsync, 8:5 aspect ratio
Modeline "320x200"      12.588 320  336  384  400    200 204  205  225 Doublescan
# 320x240 @ 60 Hz, 31.5 kHz hsync, 4:3 aspect ratio
Modeline "320x240"      12.588 320  336  384  400    240 245  246  262 Doublescan
# 320x240 @ 72 Hz, 36.5 kHz hsync
Modeline "320x240"      15.750 320  336  384  400    240 244  246  262 Doublescan
# 400x300 @ 56 Hz, 35.2 kHz hsync, 4:3 aspect ratio
ModeLine "400x300"      18     400  416  448  512    300 301  602  312 Doublescan
# 400x300 @ 60 Hz, 37.8 kHz hsync
Modeline "400x300"      20     400  416  480  528    300 301  303  314 Doublescan
# 400x300 @ 72 Hz, 48.0 kHz hsync
Modeline "400x300"      25     400  424  488  520    300 319  322  333 Doublescan
# 480x300 @ 56 Hz, 35.2 kHz hsync, 8:5 aspect ratio
ModeLine "480x300"      21.656 480  496  536  616    300 301  302  312 Doublescan
# 480x300 @ 60 Hz, 37.8 kHz hsync
Modeline "480x300"      23.890 480  496  576  632    300 301  303  314 Doublescan
# 480x300 @ 63 Hz, 39.6 kHz hsync
Modeline "480x300"      25     480  496  576  632    300 301  303  314 Doublescan
# 480x300 @ 72 Hz, 48.0 kHz hsync
Modeline "480x300"      29.952 480  504  584  624    300 319  322  333 Doublescan

EndSection
```

The values for the horizontal sync and vertical refresh rate are very important. The default values are for a generic VGA monitor, and, while that is typical, you should not simply allow the values to default. Make certain that you leave only mode lines with values that will work with your monitor. Incompatible settings can physically damage your monitor. A mode line can be eliminated by preceding it with a comment character. You will need a separate Monitor section for each monitor connected to your computer.

A monitor can be set up in different display modes—that is, different resolutions and numbers of colors. So X will be able switch from one mode to another, all of the possible modes should be listed. Normally, there is no need to make this kind of setting manually, but, if you must, the details of the Modeline settings are described in /usr/X11R6/lib/X11/doc/VideoModes.doc.

Section "Device"

```
# *********************************************************************
# Graphics device section
# *********************************************************************
# Any number of graphics device sections may be present

Section "Device"
    Identifier      "Generic VGA"
    VendorName      "Unknown"
    BoardName       "Unknown"
    Chipset     "generic"
#   VideoRam    256
#   Clocks      25.2 28.3
EndSection

Section "Device"
    # SVGA server auto-detected chipset
    Identifier      "Generic SVGA"
    VendorName      "Unknown"
    BoardName       "Unknown"
EndSection

# Section "Device"
#   Identifier      "Any Trident TVGA 9000"
#   VendorName      "Trident"
#   BoardName       "TVGA 9000"
#   Chipset     "tvga9000"
#   VideoRam    512
#   Clocks      25 28 45 36 57 65 50 40 25 28 0 45 72 77 80 75
# EndSection

# Section "Device"
#   Identifier      "Actix GE32+ 2MB"
#   VendorName      "Actix"
#   BoardName       "GE32+"
#   Ramdac      "ATT20C490"
```

```
#     Dacspeed    110
#     Option      "dac_8_bit"
#     Clocks      25.0  28.0  40.0   0.0  50.0  77.0  36.0  45.0
#     Clocks     130.0 120.0  80.0  31.0 110.0  65.0  75.0  94.0
# EndSection

# Section "Device"
#     Identifier     "Hercules mono"
# EndSection
```

This section will configure a graphics adapter card. If you have more than one, you will need more than one of these sections. Even if you have used one of the programs mentioned earlier to configure the adapter card, you should inspect this section and compare the values against those returned from SuperProbe. In particular, the actual amount of RAM could have been commented out.

Section "Screen"

```
# **********************************************************************
# Screen sections
# **********************************************************************

# The Colour SVGA server

Section "Screen"
    Driver      "svga"
    # Use Device "Generic VGA" for Standard VGA 320x200x256
    #Device      "Generic VGA"
    Device      "S3 Virge/DX"
    Monitor     "Cybervision"
    Subsection "Display"
        Depth      8
        # Omit the Modes line for the "Generic VGA" device
        Modes      "640x480" "800x600" "1024x768" "1280x1024"
        ViewPort   0 0
        # Use Virtual 320 200 for Generic VGA
    EndSubsection
    Subsection "Display"
        Depth      16
        Modes      "640x480" "800x600" "1024x768" "1280x1024"
        ViewPort   0 0
    EndSubsection
    Subsection "Display"
        Depth      24
        Modes      "640x480" "800x600" "1024x768" "1280x1024"
        ViewPort   0 0
    EndSubsection
    Subsection "Display"
        Depth      32
        Modes      "640x480" "800x600" "1024x768"
```

```
                ViewPort    0 0
        EndSubsection
EndSection

# The 16-color VGA server

Section "Screen"
    Driver      "vga16"
    Device      "Generic VGA"
    Monitor     "Cybervision"
    Subsection "Display"
        Modes       "640x480" "800x600"
        ViewPort    0 0
        Virtual     800 600
    EndSubsection
EndSection

# The Mono server

Section "Screen"
    Driver      "vga2"
    Device      "Generic VGA"
    Monitor     "Cybervision"
    Subsection "Display"
        Modes       "640x480" "800x600"
        ViewPort    0 0
        Virtual     800 600
    EndSubsection
EndSection

# The accelerated servers (S3, Mach32, Mach8, 8514, P9000, AGX, W32, Mach64)

Section "Screen"
    Driver      "accel"
    Device      "S3 Virge/DX"
    Monitor     "Cybervision"
    Subsection "Display"
        Depth       8
        Modes       "640x480" "800x600" "1024x768" "1280x1024"
        ViewPort    0 0
    EndSubsection
    Subsection "Display"
        Depth       16
        Modes       "640x480" "800x600" "1024x768" "1280x1024"
        ViewPort    0 0
    EndSubsection
    Subsection "Display"
        Depth       24
        Modes       "640x480" "800x600" "1024x768" "1280x1024"
        ViewPort    0 0
```

```
        EndSubsection
        Subsection "Display"
            Depth        32
            Modes        "640x480" "800x600" "1024x768"
            ViewPort     0 0
        EndSubsection
EndSection
```

This section is used to specify which X server is to be used to control the physical display. This includes settings for things such as the number of pixels and the number of bits per pixel. The number of pixels is normally expressed in terms of width and height, as in 640×480, 800×600, and 1024×768. The number of bits-per-pixel—the color depth—is usually 8, 16, 24, or 32.

Warning: Experience has shown this to be the most difficult section to configure by hand. Your best bet would be to try one or more of the configuration utilities described earlier. It doesn't happen very often, but it is possible to choose settings that drive your monitor beyond its capabilities and cause physical damage.

A screen section names the driver that will be used to talk to the display. There are also the names of the graphics card and the monitor.

There can be a number of "Display" subsections—each subsection has a different number of bits-per-pixel to represent colors. There can be more than one mode of operation (resolution), but there is only one pixel depth value. The subsection to be used is selected by the pixel depth. One of the modes will also be selected, but you can easily switch from one to the other while running X. Once you are up and running, you can switch from one mode to the other by holding down Ctrl+Alt and pressing either the plus or minus key on the keypad.

More Than One Way to Start X

It is possible to have X start when the system boots up. A program named xdm can handle logins by prompting for the user name and password. Another option is to have X start running automatically whenever you log in. It is also possible to start X yourself from the command line.

Starting X from the Command Line

There is a script named /usr/X11R6/bin/startx that can be used to start the X Window System. It sets up a few things and executes /usr/X11R6/bin/xinit that does the actual job of starting X. The startx script that is delivered with the system does little more than pass the arguments through to xinit and set up defaults if no arguments are supplied. If you need to customize the way to start X, simply edit startx.

When you start X this way, it reads and executes the commands found in the .xinitrc file found in your home directory. This file is a shell script, and it contains configuration settings and programs to be set into execution. The following is an example .xinitrc file:

```
#!/bin/sh
cpu=`hostname`
if [ -z $DISPLAY ]
then
    DISPLAY=$cpu:0
fi
export DISPLAY

xrdb -Dhostname=$cpu $HOME/.Xresources

xset c off s 600

fvwm &

sleep 5

xsetroot -bitmap /usr/X11R6/includde/X11/bitmaps/plaid -fg gray

xclock -update 1 -geometry -0+0

xterm -C -display $DISPLAY
```

The DISPLAY environment variable must be set so X will know the identity of the screen it is to use for display. X is quite aware of the network and any program can be run on any display. In this example script, the DISPLAY variable is set to the local host only if has not already been set. Notice that there is a colon and a zero added to the end of the name. That is the monitor number. If there is a second monitor connected to a computer, it will be number 1.

The program xrdb is used to set the values of the resource manager property. Many applications will retrieve data stored in the resource manager so they will know things such as the size of the screen and what colors they should use. There are more details about this in Chapter 7, "Running the X Window System."

The program xset is used to set the user preferences. The example shown uses the c option to turn the key click off and the s option to configure the screen blanker to activate after 600 seconds. A list of these options is presented in Chapter 7.

The window manager fvwm is started as a background process. The window manager has the job of displaying the windows and giving the user control over their size and positions. Depending on how you prefer to use your system, you can wait and start the window manager last, as described a little later.

There is a `sleep` command following the start of the window manager. You may or may not find this sort of thing necessary, but, if you have applications starting before the window manager is ready for them, you may wind up with inconsistencies in their operation. Sometimes they will get all their configuration information, and sometimes not. It is a race condition that you want the window manager to win.

The `xsetroot` program can be used to set all sorts of background colors and decorations. This example loads a bitmap file, which is a black and white patter, and sets the foreground display color to gray.

The `xclock` program is started in the background and told to update itself once each second. It is also instructed to display itself in the upper-right corner. This geometry option is available for the start of most X programs—there is more information on how it works in Chapter 7.

The last line of the file is the startup of an `xterm`. This program is a command line window that can be used just like a regular non-X terminal. It uses a shell program to prompt the user for input.

Notice that the `xterm` program has not been started in the background. This means that as long as `xterm` is running, the `.xinitrc` script will not proceed to the next statement. The next statement in `.xinitrc` is the end of the file, so when the `xterm` window is closed, the entire X session ceases. Many people use `xterm` as the program to shut down or close the X session, but you can use any program you would like. Some window managers will allow themselves to be used at the end of the file this way with the advantage that there is no other program that will cause the X session to close. Of course, to do this, the window manager itself will need to supply some way of allowing the user to shut it down.

Starting X by the Run Level

There is a program named `xdm` that, when launched, will take control of access to your system, start X running, and prompt for a login. Logging in through `xdm` will put you right into X, and logging out will cause `xdm` to display the prompt again.

Linux can be set to boot in one of several modes. These modes are called *run levels*. The configuration file `/etc/inittab` defines all the programs and settings for each of these run levels. The discussion here is limited to the modifications needed to start X at boot time. There is a more detailed discussion `/etc/inittab` in Chapter 14, "Getting Online with Modems."

A run level is defined by a single digit number. The `inittab` file can be used to set up any configuration for any run level, and different systems will use different default settings. There is a line toward the top of the `inittab` file that looks like the following:

```
id:5:initdefault;
```

Whenever you boot the system, the default run level is 5. The rest of the file consists of commands that are to be executed for each of the run levels (some commands execute for more than one level). If you want to have X start at the default run level of 5, include a line in the file that looks like the following:

```
x:5:respawn:/use/bin/X11/xdm -nodaemon
```

This command should be at or toward the bottom of the file so the other commands that set things up for level 5 (or whatever level you choose) will have already finished when xdm is started.

By default, xdm executes as a daemon process and, because it is security minded and in charge of system access, it takes certain actions as it starts. It will close all files and disassociate itself from any terminal putting itself in the background. This is not a desirable thing in this situation, so the -nodaemon option is chosen to suppress it.

With X configured this way, it is still possible to start and stop X from the command line. You can use init to change the runlevel to the one for X, as shown in the following:

```
init 5
```

In the same way, you can bring the X session down and revert to your previous level (in this case, level 3), as in the following:

```
init 3
```

If you forget the previous level, enter the command runlevel, and both the previous and current run levels will be displayed.

Another Way of Starting X at System Boot

There is a way to configure your system so that it ignores the run level and always starts in X. The xdm program will take control of the display and, using X, will prompt for the username and password.

The rc file is fundamental to the operation of Linux, so be careful how you edit it. To put X in charge of all logins, add the following command as the last line in the /etc/rc.d/rc file:

```
/usr/bin/X11/xdm
```

Whenever the system boots, the rc file is executed, which executes the xdm program. It is important that xdm be the last thing in the file because the xdm program will not cease execution until the system is shut down. The entire path is required because no path variables will have been set as yet.

> **Warning:** The program xdm has some security features and runs as a daemon. You can test it by starting it from the command line if you want, but, once it has started, it is hard to get rid of. After all, its purpose is to guard the system by validating usernames and passwords. Go ahead and test xdm, but be prepared to reboot after the test.

Whenever you log in using xdm, the script /etc/X11/xdm/Xsession is executed. This script will, in turn, execute a file in your home directory named .sessions. If .sessions does not exist, it will execute .Xclients. If .Xclients does not exist, it will execute your .xinitrc.

Starting X Automatically at Log In

If you are logging in from the command line, you can still have X start for you automatically. There are two things you must do. First, add the command startx as the last command in either your .cshrc or .bashrc file.

This has the same effect as if you had typed startx from the command line, so it will probably be necessary to create a .xinitrc file for it to read.

Summary

The X Window System is very mature and, once it is installed, a very solid and flexible windowing utility. There are some difficulties with the installation, only because there is no clear-cut way to detect the characteristics of your hardware—the key to a successful installation is have all the hardware information at your finger tips. There is no real standard one-size-fits-all procedure for installing X, so expect to spend a little time with it. Be patient, take your time, and read all the README files that are included with your software, because you never know when some little gem of information will be the very key to your installation.

On Your Own

If you have a network connection with another computer that is also running X, start a process running on it with the window being displayed on your local screen. To do this, start the program on the other system with the display option set. For example, start an xterm in the following way:

```
xterm -display <name>:0.0 &
```

Try the reverse action. Start a local process with a remote window. That is, start a process running on your local computer with the window appearing on another computer in the network.

Edit /etc/inittab to initialize X according to the run level and switch in and out of X by switching run levels.

Running the X Window System

Getting X up and running, as described in Chapter 6, "Installing the X Window System," is only half of the battle. The other half is setting things up to look and act the way you want them. There are lots of options for doing this. There are a number of projects developing desktop systems that can be used as interfaces with Linux.

While there are a number of desktop systems—in various stages of completion—there are two that seem to be in a dead heat for the number one position. This chapter is a brief introduction to these two: Gnome and KDE. They both appear to work quite well, even though KDE appears to be more mature and complete than Gnome.

Gnome

Gnome (GNU Network Object Model Environment) is a graphical user interface designed to enable users to easily configure and use the X Window System. There is a panel for starting applications and for showing the status of applications in progress. There are some standard utility programs that are a part of Gnome. Internally, there is a set of conventions to make it easy for applications to cooperate with one another.

The Look and Feel of Gnome

Figure 7.1 is the screen presented by Gnome. There are icons on the left side of the root window (sometimes called the desktop window), and there is a bar across the bottom. The two applications being displayed are the integrated help and the file managers.

The bar across the bottom of Figure 7.1 is the Gnome Panel and is used to control the system. The Panel can be moved to any edge of the screen—in fact, you can display more than one Panel at a time if you need the space.

The little arrows at each end of the Panel can be used to slide the panel out the of way, and slide it back in again (all of it can be hidden except for one little arrow). The contents of the Panel are configurable, but the one shown here shows a fairly standard setup. At the right end is a clock that can be set to display the time or the time and date. The four icons to the left of the clock start a terminal emulator, the Netscape Web browser, the Gnome configuration tool, and the Gnome help system.

The Gnome footprint button on the far left brings up the system menu shown in Figure 7.2.

FIGURE 7.1

The layout of the Gnome desktop.

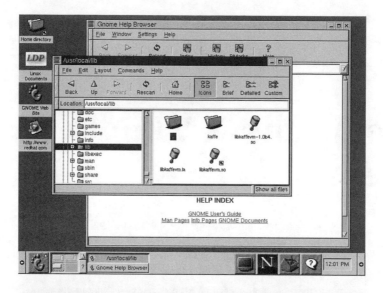

FIGURE 7.2

The Gnome system menu.

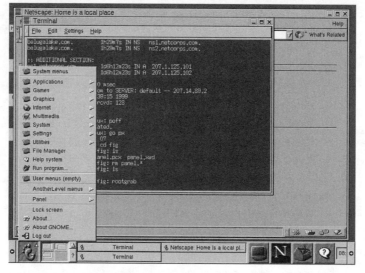

To the right of the Gnome footprint button in Figure 7.1 is the Pager. The Gnome Pager enables you to switch among four screens, and each screen can have several windows open.The Pager indicates (by the hash-mark shading) that the currently active window is the one on the lower left, and that there are applications displaying windows in both of the top screens. Switching the display from one screen to another is simply a matter of selecting one of the four screen indicators on the Panel.

The screens are not really independent of one another. It's more like one big screen that is four times the size of your display, and you can only look at one corner at a time. It is possible to move a window from one screen to another. If you grab and drag the bar at the top of a window, you can drag down or to the side so that part of it sticks into a neighboring screen and, when you switch to that screen, you will find the window there. Also, you can pull down the menu with the button at the left end of the title bar (or use the right mouse button on the title bar), select Desktop, and then select one of the four screens—the window will immediately jump to that screen.

To the right of the Pager's screen selector is a question mark and an upward-pointing arrow. Clicking the question mark brings up the window that can be used to configure the Pager. There are several settings available to set sizes and positions. The upward-pointing arrow brings up a list containing all the tasks in all the screens; selecting one will switch screens (if necessary) and bring the selected task's window to the top.

To the right of the upward-pointing arrow and question mark is a button for each task running on the current screen. These buttons can be used to bring an application to the front of the stack (de-iconizing it if necessary).

> **Tip:** It is possible that the default configuration of your system does not include the Pager. If not, when you iconize an application, the window simply disappears. To install the Pager, click the right mouse button on a clear space on the Panel and, on the menu that appears, select Add Applet, Utility, Gnome Pager.

Applications do not necessarily have to be written to be Gnome-specific—any X Window program can be run in a Gnome environment. For example, Gnome supports different drag-and-drop protocols, so it will be compatible with as many applications as possible. An application running in Gnome has control over its windows the same as it would have otherwise—it is the surrounding environment that is controlled by Gnome. Of course, there are some special Gnome facilities that can be used by programmers to integrate their applications more closely to Gnome.

> **Note:** There is a bit of standardization in the way the mouse is used. The left mouse button is used to select things such as windows and filenames. The right mouse button brings up a menu that is used to select the configuration settings for the selected item. The middle mouse button, when clicked on the root window, brings up a menu for starting applications. For example, to add and remove an item from the Panel, use the right mouse button to select it and a menu will appear. To configure the clock, select it with the right mouse button and a configuration dialog box will appear. The middle button seems to have been mostly ignored, except that it will bring up the main menu when used on the root window.

Getting Your Copy of Gnome

If you have the Red Hat distribution CD-ROM, you have a copy of Gnome. If you have something other than Red Hat Linux, you may or may not have Gnome. If you don't have it, you can download it from the Internet. Even if you do have it, you may still want to download a new copy, because there are new versions every week or so.

There is a lot of software included in Gnome, and it is divided into two packages. The base package contains the software that needs to be installed for you to use Gnome. The development package includes the software necessary to write Gnome applications.

Note: You may need the development package as well as the base package. You will certainly need it if you are going to be writing Gnome software. Even if you're not, there could be a cross-dependency inadvertently included in the base package. The software developer always has both packages installed, and if something is included in the base package that depends on something in the development package, the developer will never know it.

You can download the Gnome executable code for a specific version of Linux (at this writing, there were versions available for Red Hat, Debian, SuSE, PowerPC, and Sparc), or you can download the source code and compile it yourself.

Compiling Gnome from the source requires some work, so you only want to do this if there is not a binary form for your particular flavor of Linux, or if you want to dig around inside Gnome to change the way it works.

Gnome has a Web site that has information for both users and software developers at `http://www.gnome.org`.

The Gnome software is the same for every flavor of Linux, but the installation varies a bit. Also, the method of getting your copy of Gnome will vary from one flavor to the other. You can find updated information at `http://www.gnome.org/start/getting.shtml`.

Documentation

There is a lot of documentation but, to begin with, it is probably simplest to just get the user documents. The documentation comes in several forms such as postscript, pdf, and HTML. Each of these forms is packaged in more than one way—zip files and tar files. There are documents for everyone from users to programmers. Some of the documents are available in more than one language. You can download the documentation, in the form and language you want from `http://www.gnome.org/users-guide/project.shtml`.

Note: Everything in Linux has a version number. You can always look at any two copies of a software package and tell whether they are the same version or, if not, which one is newer than the other. Also, Linux is under constant development and there can be a new version of anything at any time, and the documentation often doesn't reflect the new version. Generally speaking, if your version number is larger than the one in the documentation, you are okay, because backward compatibility is always a consideration. However, to be sure that your software will play together, it is best to upgrade all the subcomponents when upgrading software.

Installing Gnome

It is really quite simple to install Gnome, but there are a couple of things you should know.

The installation of Gnome places files in several directories inside /usr. These directories are bin, doc, etc, include, info, lib, libexec, man, and share. The base installation will take up about 50MB. Adding the software development part will add another 10–20MB. At any time, you can see which parts, if any, of Gnome are installed with the following command:

```
rpm -qa ¦ grep gnome
```

Red Hat Installation

The software downloaded from the Internet, or found on your CD-ROM, is a collection of files with rpm extensions. If you downloaded the files, they should all be loaded into a single directory that you intend to use as a staging area for the installation. If the files you have are on a CD-ROM, you can leave them and perform the installation from there.

If you are using an earlier version of Red Hat (5.0 or 5.1), you will need to upgrade some updated libraries before you can successfully install Gnome. You will need the rpm files for gsl-0.3b-4.rpm, umb-scheme-3.2-7.rpm, guile-1.2-6.rpm, and xscreensaver-2.34-1.rpm. You can get the files at either ftp://ftp.redhat.com/redhat/updates or ftp://sun-site.unc.edu/pub/Linux/distributions/redhat/current/i386/RedHat/RPMS.

To install the updated libraries, put them in a directory by themselves, change to that directory, and enter the following:

```
rpm -Uhv *.rpm
```

The rpm command can be used to install all of Gnome. Change to the directory containing the rpm files and enter the command given earlier.

There are two problems with installing Gnome from the CD-ROM instead of a download. Depending on the age of your CD-ROM, you may not have the latest version of Gnome. If you download the files, you will always be getting the latest version. The second problem is that the rpm files for Gnome are stored in the same directory with all of the other rpm files. The wildcard command will cause the installation of everything possible, and you may not even have enough drive space to hold it all. You can prevent this from happening by installing each of the files independently (instead of using a wildcard name), but to do this, you will need to get a list of the names.

If you decide to install from the CD-ROM, insert the CD-ROM into the drive and enter the following command:

```
mount /mnt/cdrom
```

For this command to work, there must be an appropriate CD-ROM entry in the `/etc/fstab` file. If there is not, you can still mount the CD-ROM in the following way:

```
mount -t iso9660 /dev/cdrom /mnt/cdrom
```

The name of the installation directory on the CD-ROM is `/mnt/cdrom/RedHat/RPMS`. By the way, before you will be able to remove the CD, you will need to enter this command:

```
umount /mnt/cdrom
```

Change to the installation directory—the one containing all the `rpm` files—and enter the following command:

```
rpm -Uvh gnome*.rpm
```

This command will install everything having to do with Gnome. If you want to install only parts of it, copy the `rpm` files you want and use it as your install directory on a command line, as shown in the following:

```
rpm -Uvh *.rpm
```

Either of these commands will run `rpm` in the update mode (`-U`), tell you everything it is doing (`-v`), and even display sequences of `#` characters when it is busy but has nothing to tell you (`-h`). For the most part, you will get messages explaining things like the inability to delete non-existent directories. You may get a notification that some package or other cannot be installed because a newer (or the current) version number has already been installed. You may get a message that something is missing, and you will have to go find its `rpm` file and try again.

Non-Red Hat Installation

Red Hat is involved directly in the development of Gnome, so it installs very easily because the installation doesn't have to bother with some of the details (like which libraries are loaded). If you use a version of Linux other than Red Hat, the installation will still work, but it will probably be a little more time-consuming, because you may find a library or two that wasn't installed as part of your default Linux. It could also be more difficult to match the correct versions of the system libraries. The latest version of the Gnome files for different version of Linux can be found at `http://www.gnome.org`.

In particular, you will find special versions for SuSE at that Web site and also at

- `http://ceu.fi.udc.es:8000/suse/gnome.html`
- `http://www.tu-harburg.de/skf/Pub`

Make certain that you have installed the following packages from the CD-ROM:

```
libz [a]
texinfo [a]
libtiff [gra]
```

```
libjepg [gra]
libgif [gra]
imagemag [gra]
freetype [gra]
python [d]
```

The downloaded Gnome comes as a collection of .rpm files. One of the reasons for a special SuSE version of Gnome is that there is some version sensitivity with the rpm utility—you need to make certain that the files you get will work with your distribution of Linux. Place all the .rpm files in a single working directory and enter the following command:

```
rpm -Uvh *.rpm
```

This command will run rpm in the update mode (-U), tell you everything it is doing (-v), and even display sequences of # characters when it is busy but has nothing to tell you (-h). For the most part, you will get messages explaining things like the inability to delete non-existent directories. You may get a notification that some package or other cannot be installed because a newer (or the current) version number has already been installed. Unless you specify—force on the command line (and you shouldn't unless you know the previous installation is bad)—the installation will occur only if you are installing for the first time, or if you are updating to a newer version. You may get a message that something is missing, and you will have to go find its rpm file, install it, and then try again.

The Gnome files are always stored in rpm files. The rpm utility originated with RedHat Linux, but it is open source and is now available on almost every flavor of Linux. There are also versions of rpm on OS/2, Solaris, SCO, HP-UX, Beos, and others. To get a version of rpm for your system, see http://www.rpm.org/platforms.html.

Configuring Gnome

After the software is installed, there is only one thing left to do: You need to tell Linux how to start Gnome. If you want to use startx, you need to edit the .xinitrc file in your home directory, as shown in the following:

```
#!/bin/sh
cpu=`hostname`
if [ -z $DISPLAY ]
then
    DISPLAY $cpu:0
fi
export DISPLAY
xrdb -Dhostname=$cpu $HOME/.Xresources
xset c off s 800
exec gnome-session
```

Except for the last line, the contents of the .xinitrc file were described in Chapter 6. The last line uses exec to execute the program that is in charge of everything during your Gnome session.

If you want to log in using xdm, you will need to create or modify the .xsession file in your home directory. After xdm validates the login, it executes this script. It can contain the same sort of things you would put into .xinitrc, and it must end with

```
exec gnome-session
```

KDE

KDE (K Desktop Environment) is a graphical user interface to provide users with easy access to applications and the operating system. The letter K in the name doesn't stand for anything other than itself—like the X Window System, K is just has a one-letter name. KDE has its own window manager and implements such things as drag-and-drop and cut-and-paste. Mainly, it is a user interface providing system access with menus and toolbars.

The Look and Feel of KDE

Figure 7.3 shows the screen as it is presented by KDE. The icons on the left are on the root window (or desktop window, if you prefer), there is a button-bar along the top with one button per running application, and a toolbar along the bottom to provide access to the system and the KDE programs. In the figure, the window on top the KDE File Manager. The window behind the file manager is the starting page of the KDE help documentation.

FIGURE 7.3
A KDE screen in its default configuration.

The bar across the bottom is called the KPanel and consists of a row of icons and a special set of screen swapping buttons in the center. Each of these buttons, labeled One, Two, Three, and Four, represents one complete screen. Selecting one of these buttons will cause the display to immediately switch to another screen. The only difference in the screens is the application used to display windows. On each of the four screens, the icons on the desktop and the bars at the top and the bottom are identical, but an application can only call one screen its home.

The bar across the top has one button for each process running under KDE. Selecting the button of an application that doesn't currently have the focus will bring it to the top and give it mouse and keyboard focus. If necessary, KDE will switch to another screen to bring the window to the front. If the screen is on top and has focus, selecting its button will remove the window from the display. The window will stay hidden until the button is selected again.

Across the bottom is the KPanel. At its far left is a left-pointing arrow that, when clicked, causes the entire panel to slide to the left, leaving only a right-pointing arrow that can be used to make it visible again. The leftmost icon—the one with the letter K and the cogwheel, opens the system menu shown in Figure 7.4.

FIGURE 7.4
The KDE system menu.

To the right of the system menu button is a button that brings up a menu containing the same selections available from the button bar on top, because, as you can see in Figure 7.3, it is possible to obscure the button bar at the top. The next icon, the one with the little house, is the file manager. The next button brings up the KDE Control Center that is used to configure the KDE system (colors, shortcut keys, mouse properties, and so on). The next icon is a file finder. The icon that looks like an open box is a menu that contains a set of utilities shown in Figure 7.5.

FIGURE 7.5
*The Utilities
menu.*

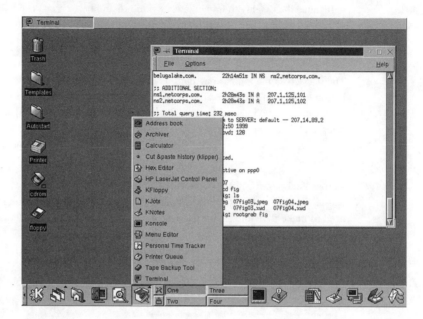

To the right of the utility icon are two small buttons, one above the other. The one on top that looks like the letter X can be used to log out. The padlock button can be used to lock the screen—the display goes blank and stays that way until the mouse is moved or a key is struck. To get the screen back, it is necessary to enter the password of the current user.

To the right of the screen-swapper is an icon that will bring up a terminal emulator that can be used to enter command-line commands. The next icon is for the help system shown in the background of Figure 7.3. The last five icons shown are the calculator, a sticky-note pad, another terminal emulator (a little different from the other one), a simple text editor, and an integrated email client program.

Getting Your Copy of KDE

If you have a distribution CD-ROM, you may already have a copy of KDE, even if your version of Linux normally installs with Gnome. However, open source software being what it is, you will need to go to the Internet to get the latest version.

The Web site for KDE is http://www.kde.org.

To get a copy of the KDE software, you need to find a download site. You can get the list of mirror sites at http://www.kde.org/mirrors.html.

There are a quite a few mirror sites, and they are listed by geography, so you should be able to find one near you. The following are a few of the mirror sites:

```
ftp://ftp.kde.org/pub/kde

ftp://ftp.us.kde.org/pub/kde

ftp://ftp.varesearch.com/pub/mirrors/kde
```

You will find several subdirectories inside the kde directory. There is a subdirectory, named unstable, that contains the next version of KDE but, as the name implies, it is not stable enough to be used on a regular basis—this is the version for KDE developers. If you want the latest stable release version, change to the .../kde/stable/latest/distribution directory.

From this point, you will need to choose which version to download, according to your version of Linux, and the software packaging method. For the Debian version, there are .deb files for the PowerPC and Intel. There are .rpm files for Caldera, RedHat, SuSE, and others. There are tar and tar.gz files for HPUX and openBSD. There are .pkg.gz files for Solaris on Intel and Sparc. Each of these can be loaded in a binary form, ready for installation, and as source code.

There is a readme file in each directory with specific installation and configuration instructions. KDE is mature enough that installation is very simple.

There is other software available that can be used with KDE. You may find some things you want in one of the following directories on the FTP site:

```
.../kde/stable/latest/apps

.../kde/stable/latest/contrib
```

There is user documentation for KDE online at
http://www.kde.org/documentation/index.html.

This URL contains extensive user-level documentation in the form of a FAQ, the Quick Start guide, and the User's Guide to KDE.

CDE (Common Desktop Environment)

The idea of having a common environment for all computers is an appealing idea. The X Window System, with its highly-configurable window manager, is a good starting point for basing a standard. An organization named COSE (Common Open Software Environment) was founded to come to consensus on what the environment should be like. Its efforts are supported by more than 70 companies involved with various flavors of UNIX, and with Linux. The companies that started COSE are HP, Sun, Novell (USL), IBM, and SCO.

One of the components of COSE is CDE (Common Desktop Environment). It is "...a specification for components and services to give the UNIX desktop common and consistent capabilities like those found in other widely used environments (Mac, Windows)."

CDE is based on X11 and uses the Motif window manager to control the display. But there's much more.

In the area of desktop management, there is a login manager to accept user names and passwords, a session manager to view and control active processes and open windows, a workspace manager for switching from one context to another, a front panel that can be used for quick access to often-use programs, a style manager to control things such as fonts and colors, and a file manager based on icons with drag-and-drop.

In the area of tools, there is a text editor, an icon editor, a help viewer to be used with application help files, a calendar, a mailer, a terminal emulator (an improvement to xterm), a windowing Korn shell, and the ability to create a custom icon associated with some user-defined action.

Most of the graphics area is covered by X11 and Motif. Motif defines dozens of widgets, but there are some new ones defined in the CDE. The drag-and-drop capabilities of Motif have been expanded. There are extensions to the X print server for printing graphics.

There are some other definitions in the CDE that describe things that already exist, but are included as part of the standardization process. Among these is the IPC (Interprocess Communications) facility, the standard messages to a window to close or iconify or whatever, define and detect file types, a list of standard fonts, and internationalization.

CDE is not GNU. Linux versions are available for purchase from more than one vendor. There is a commercial version for Linux by XiGraphics. You can see it at http://www.xig.com.

A site full of information about CDE (as well as X11 and much more) can be found at http://www.opengroup.org/.

Defining Resources

An X application has a certain number of default settings—things like fonts and colors—that can be modified to suit your taste. An application written specifically to run with Gnome or KDE will allow for settings to be made from the command line and often by selecting menu items with the mouse.

To configure a KDE application, use the application's menu or a text editor to modify either its global rc file, located in /opt/kde/etc/skel/.kde/share/config, or its local rc file, located in the ~/.kde/share/config directory. Each configuration file has the same name as the application, but with the letters rc appended to it—for example, the configuration file for kfind is named kfindrc. Each line of these files contains a keyword, an equals sign, and a value. For example, to place the menu bar on top and the status bar on bottom, enter the following:

```
Menubar=top
Statusbar=bottom
```

A Gnome program normally has configuration settings that can be made from a menu, and it always has some that can be made on the command line (because there are some that are built in to the Gnome programming library). The available command line options can be listed by executing the program with either —help or -? as its one argument. If you want to use the mouse to start an application with command line options, write a single-line startup script and add it to the menu or the desktop.

Applications not written specifically for a desktop environment, like Gnome or KDE, have a standard method for retrieving configuration information. Inside the X system is a resource manager that holds configuration information and passes it on to each application. The information is stored in a file (usually named .Xdefaults or, sometimes, .Xresources). The configuration information can be written to resource manager by the following command:

```
xrdb .Xdefaults
```

Each user can have personalized resources by having an .Xdefaults file in the home directory and having this line added to the startx script:

```
xrdb ~/.Xdefaults
```

Each entry in the .Xdefaults file contains the name of an application, the name of the attribute to be specified, and the new value for it. Whenever an X program starts running, the resource manager passes the appropriate entries from the .Xdefaults file to the application. It looks through the .Xdefaults file in your home directory to see if its name is there and, if so, overrides its internal settings with whatever values you have specified.

Command line options normally take precedence of any settings in the .Xdefaults file. This allows you to define a set of defaults and still have the ability to vary the settings for each copy of a program that you run. You may want to start several xterm programs running, but have them all use different background colors so you can tell which is which.

For example, the program xterm (a terminal emulator) can be instructed to include a scrollbar by being started with the following command:

```
xterm -sb
```

It can be told to not have a scrollbar by being started in the following way:

```
xterm +sb
```

If you start the program without specifying whether there should be a scrollbar, xterm will respond to the settings in the .Xdefaults file to determine whether or not to display the scrollbar. The following entry in the file tells xterm not to display a scrollbar:

```
xterm*scrollBar: false
```

The following tells xterm to display a scrollbar:

```
xterm*scrollBar: true
```

If the option is not specified either on the command line or in the file, the program will use its internal default (in this case, there will be no scrollbar).

In X Window terminology, these settings are called *resources*. For you to know what resources can be set for a particular application, it is necessary for the programmer to have listed it in the documentation. If you look at the man page for xterm, you will see a lot of command line options followed by an extensive list of resource settings. You have very detailed control—things like the column number that will ring a margin bell, size and position of the window, and even whether it will be iconized or a full window when it starts running.

The entries in the .Xdefaults file have a syntax that allows you some flexibility in the way the resources are applied. To define a resource value, you simply need to use the name of the application, an asterisk, the name of the resource, a colon, and the value you want to assign to the resource.

If you do not specify the application—that is, if you begin the line with an asterisk so it looks like the following:

```
*background: red
```

the leading asterisk shows that it is a wildcard definition and applies to all applications.

It is normal to have a number of settings in the .Xdefaults file to configure an application. For example, the following is a configuration for xterm that was taken from a copy of the .Xdefaults file shipped with X:

```
xterm*background: cornsilk2xterm*foreground: blackxterm*cursorColor:
orchidxterm*reverseVideo: falsexterm*scrollBar: true
xterm*reverseWrap: true
xterm*font: fixed
xterm*fullCursor: true
xterm*scrollTtyOutput: off
xterm*scrollKey: on
xterm*scrollBar: off
xterm*VT100.Translations: #override\n\
        <KeyPress>Prior : scroll-back(1,page)\n\
        <KeyPress>Next : scroll-forw(1,page)
xterm*titleBar: false
```

Font Resources

It is normal for a Linux system to have two thousand or more fonts from which applications can choose. And just because a font was available to the programmer, there is no guarantee that same font will be available on every system running the program. There is a way of specifying the name of a font in such a way that the "closest one" available will be chosen.

The names of the fonts have a standard form, making it easy to determine rather detailed information about the font itself. There is a program you can use to list the names of the fonts installed on your system. Enter the following statement from the command line:

```
xlsfonts ¦ more
```

You will get several screens full of font names that looks something like the following:

```
-adobe-avantgarde-book-o-normal—0-0-0-0-p-0-iso8859-1
-adobe-avantgarde-book-r-normal—0-0-0-0-p-0-iso8859-1
-adobe-avantgarde-demibold-o-normal—0-0-0-0-p-0-iso8859-1
-adobe-avantgarde-demibold-r-normal—0-0-0-0-p-0-iso8859-1
-adobe-bookman-demibold-i-normal—0-0-0-0-p-0-iso8859-1
-adobe-bookman-demibold-r-normal—0-0-0-0-p-0-iso8859-1
-adobe-bookman-light-i-normal—0-0-0-0-p-0-iso8859-1
-adobe-bookman-light-r-normal—0-0-0-0-p-0-iso8859-1
-adobe-courier-bold-o-normal—0-0-0-0-p-0-iso8859-1
-adobe-courier-bold-o-normal—0-0-100-100-m-0-iso8859-1
-adobe-courier-bold-o-normal—0-0-75-75-m-0-iso8859-1
-adobe-courier-bold-o-normal—10-100-75-75-m-60-iso8859-1
-adobe-courier-bold-o-normal—10-100-75-75-m-60-iso8859-1
-adobe-courier-bold-o-normal—10-100-75-75-m-60-iso8859-1
-adobe-courier-bold-o-normal—12-120-75-75-m-70-iso8859-1
-adobe-courier-bold-o-normal—12-120-75-75-m-70-iso8859-1
-adobe-courier-bold-o-normal—12-120-75-75-m-70-iso8859-1
-b&h-lucida-bold-i-normal-sans-0-0-100-100-p-0-iso8859-1
-b&h-lucida-bold-i-normal-sans-0-0-75-75-p-0-iso8859-1
-b&h-lucida-bold-i-normal-sans-10-100-75-75-p-67-iso8859-1
-b&h-lucida-bold-i-normal-sans-10-100-75-75-p-67-iso8859-1
-b&h-lucida-bold-i-normal-sans-10-100-75-75-p-67-iso8859-1
-b&h-lucida-bold-i-normal-sans-11-80-100-100-p-69-iso8859-1
-b&h-lucida-bold-i-normal-sans-11-80-100-100-p-69-iso8859-1
-b&h-lucida-bold-i-normal-sans-11-80-100-100-p-69-iso8859-1
-dec-terminal-bold-r-normal—14-140-75-75-c-80-dec-dectech
-dec-terminal-bold-r-normal—14-140-75-75-c-80-iso8859-1
-dec-terminal-medium-r-normal—0-0-75-75-c-0-dec-dectech
-sun-open look glyph— —-10-100-75-75-p-101-sunolglyph-1
-sun-open look glyph— —-12-120-75-75-p-113-sunolglyph-1
-sun-open look glyph— —-14-140-75-75-p-128-sunolglyph-1
-sun-open look glyph— —-19-190-75-75-p-154-sunolglyph-1
10x20
12x24
12x24kana
```

```
12x24romankana
variable
vga
```

Each line is a fully-qualified, descriptive name of a font. The list also includes some shorter names that do not follow the naming convention—these names are convenience aliases for some of the longer font names. Your system will have many more fonts than those shown in this list.

The name of a font is made up of fields separated by dashes. The meaning of a field is determined by its position in the name. Table 7.1 lists the fields as they appear from left to right in the font name. Any of the fields can be omitted in a font name (indicated by two back-to-back dashes).

Table 7.1   Fields of a Font Name from Left to Right

Field Name	Contents
Foundry	This is the name of the font manufacturer. This name is used to differentiate among otherwise identical fonts from different sources.
Family	This is the design of the typeface. Examples are times, courier, and helvetica.
Stroke Weight	This has to do with the thickness of the lines drawing the font. Examples are bold, medium, and light.
Slant	This defines the angle and manner with which each character has its top skewed to the right. The common settings are i for italic, o for oblique, and r for roman (no slant).
Set Width	This is a relative font-width measurement. A foundry may produce several versions of the same font, except that some are wider than others. Examples are normal, condensed, semicondensed, and narrow.
Additional Style	This is another style specifier and is probably the least used of all the fields. Some of the possibilities are sans, serif, r (for roman), and medium.
Pixels	The size of the font in terms of pixels.
Points	The size of the font in terms of tenths of a point.
Horizontal Resolution	The number of horizontal dots per inch.
Vertical Resolution	The number of vertical dots per inch.

Field Name	Contents
Spacing	A letter indicating the type of spacing used between characters. For example, the letter m is used for mono-space for fixed or variable width font, and the letter c is used for typewriter-like spacing with every character being the same width.
Average Width	An average of the width of every character in the font set. The value is in tenths of a pixel.
Registry	The name of the organization or standard registering the character set. This is usually iso8859, but it can also be adobe, dec, or some other registry.
Character Set	This extends the previous field by designating one set of characters within the registered ones. For example, iso8859-1 is the alphabet we know as Latin-1.

This naming convention has a purpose. When specifying a font, it is only necessary to specify the parts that are important and use wildcards for the rest. This allows the software to find the closest match, so programs don't have to know exactly which fonts are available. For example, the -fn option can be used with the xterm terminal emulator to specify a font, as shown in the following:

```
xterm -fn -adobe-courier-bold-r-normal—12-120-75-75-m-60-iso8859-1
```

For this to work, there must be an installed font with an exact match, and if no match is found, the program resorts to one of the standard fonts (usually a font named fixed). However, to broaden the search, you can use an asterisk as a wildcard to widen the search, as shown in the following:

```
xterm -fn -*-courier-bold-r-*—12-120-*-*-m-60-iso8859-1
```

This widens the search by not specifying a specific foundry, allowing for any width setting, and allowing for any horizontal and vertical resolution values. You can get quite simple with your request—for example, the following specifies a 120 point times font:

```
xterm -fn -*-times-*-*-*-*-*-120-*-*-*-*-*-*
```

> **Note:** In some font definitions, a missing field is indicated by having its surrounding dashes back-to-back with no space or value between them. If you want to match only fonts that have a missing field in your wildcard name, use the same form—that is, two hyphens back-to-back. An asterisk will match any field value, whether it is specified or not.

This wildcarding has the advantage of increasing the odds that you will locate a font. But you don't know exactly what font your expression will find, or what that font will look like. The utility program `xfd` will accept the name of a font on the command line and display information about it, as shown in the following:

```
xfd -fn -*-times-*-*-*-*-*-120-*-*-*-*-*-*
```

This command displays the window shown in Figure 7.6. The full name of the font is displayed across the top. Each character of the font is displayed, and you can select any character with the mouse and have information about it displayed at the top.

FIGURE 7.6

The xfd display of the characters of a font.

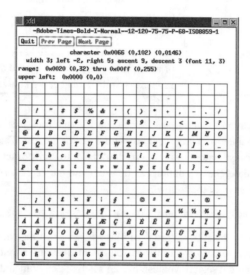

One of the most useful font utilities is `xfontsel` that can be used to help you create a font expression. Figure 7.7 shows the window. The top line—the list of the field names as they appear in a font description—is actually a list of pull-down menus that you can use to select the characteristics of your font. The line right below displays the values of the currently selected fields. You can see by the count in the upper-right corner that this specification matches three fonts, and the characters displayed are from the first of these three.

FIGURE 7.7

The xfontsel window for creating font expressions.

xfontsel is quite easy to use. When it starts running, it loads all of the available font descriptions and uses the information to construct the options available on the menus. The program grays menu selections that are not available in combination with choices you have already made. To speed up the process, start with your most important selections (usually size and the font family), because it is better to have your selection limited for the ones that are less important to you.

Color Resources

Compared to fonts, colors are easy. All of the color definitions are kept in a text file named /usr/X11R6/lib/X11/rgb.txt. To get a quick look at the contents of the file enter the following statement from the command line:

```
showrgb ¦ more
```

Each color is defined by three numbers and a name. The numbers, each ranging from 0–255, are the red, green, and blue components of the color—the larger the number, the more of that particular color is mixed in with the other two.

> **Note:** The standard color ranges are 0–255, with each color being represented by 8 bits. This means that a color can be represented in 24 bits (which is 16 million colors). This is quite sufficient for most purposes, but, depending on the hardware, it is possible to use a larger ranger of numbers for each color and have many millions more colors available.

The following are some example color entries from the file:

```
  0   0   0      black
 47  79  79      DarkSlateGray
 47  79  79      DarkSlateGrey
 47  79  79      dark slate gray
 47  79  79      dark slate grey
  0   0 139      DarkBlue
  0   0 139      dark blue
  0 139 139      DarkCyan
  0 139 139      dark cyan
139   0   0      DarkRed
139   0   0      dark red
139   0 139      DarkMagenta
139   0 139      dark magenta
144 238 144      LightGreen
144 238 144      light green
169 169 169      DarkGray
169 169 169      DarkGrey
169 169 169      dark gray
169 169 169      dark grey
245 245 245      WhiteSmoke
245 245 245      white smoke
```

```
248 248 255     GhostWhite
248 248 255     ghost white
255 228 225     MistyRose
255 228 225     misty rose
255 255 255     white
```

This is only a partial list—there are lots of colors and color names. There are 753 color names in the standard distribution. Some of the names are alternate spellings for the same color. For examples, in the previous list, the four names DarkGray, DarkGrey, dark gray, and dark grey all signify the same color.

Most applications allow you to specify the color on the command line. For example, an xterm window normally shows up as white with black letter but, you can reverse that with the following command:

```
xterm -fg white -bg black
```

The background will be black and the foreground (the text) will be white. There are names in the color list that contain spaces. To use one of these on a command line, it is necessary to surround it with quotes, as shown in the following:

```
xterm -fg white -bg "dark grey"
```

> **Note:** It is an easy thing to invent your own colors. All you have to do is add your color name and its values to the file. The only disadvantage is that if you have a script or an application that uses the name, it will not be portable to other systems. However, every application normally has a default color setting, so the program should still run—it will just use a different color.

Geometry Resources

You can use geometry settings on the command line starting an X process to control the size and position of its initial window. This is done by specifying the height and width of the window and the number of pixels the edges of the window are from the edges of the screen. The four numbers are formatted without spaces, as shown in the following:

```
widthxheight±xoffset±yoffset
```

For example, to start an xterm window that is 120 characters wide, 40 characters tall, 10 pixels from the right side of screen, and 350 pixels from the top of the screen, enter the following:

```
xterm -geometry 120x40-10+350
```

When used with the x offset, a minus sign indicates that the offset is to be measured from the right, and a positive sign indicates it is to be measured from the left. Similarly, when used with the y offset, a minus sign indicates the distance is measured from the bottom of the screen, and a plus sign indicates a distance from the top.

Note: Applications written specifically for a desktop environment, such as Gnome or KDE, usually have their own geometry setting syntax and may not respond to this request.

X Utilities

There are a number of utility programs that come with the standard distribution of X. These tend to be rather basic utilities, but can be very handy indeed if you need to diddle with fonts, dump the image of a window to disk, or complete some other fundamental task.

Setting the Background

The root window (sometimes called the background window or desktop window) can have its appearance set by the utility xsetroot. There are a lot of options. To set the background to a solid red, enter the following:

```
xsetroot -solid red
```

This command can be used with any available color (that is, the ones defined in the rgb file as described earlier in this chapter). You can use a bitmap to tile the background with a repeating pattern by using a command such as the following:

```
xsetroot -bitmap citadel.xbm
```

The usual file extension for a bitmap file is .xbm. You can find a lot of them in the /usr/X11R6/lib/X11/xfm/bitmaps directory, and you can create your own by using the utility program named bitmap. A bitmap is an image that has depth of one pixel—that is, a bitmap can only contain a black and white picture. However, using some xsetroot options, it is possible to set the background and foreground colors to display the bitmap instead of using the default black and white, as shown in the following:

```
xsetroot -bg blue -fg lightgrey -bitmap citadel.xbm
```

This command uses a bitmap that creates a pattern using a light gray drawing on blue background. You can create a grid pattern on the root window in the following way:

```
xsetroot -mod 5 10
```

The first number defines the width, and the second number defines the height. The numbers can vary from 1–16. To set the display back to the original default (the black and white mesh) enter the command with no arguments, as shown in the following:

```
xsetroot
```

X Window Graphic Images

Anything displayed onscreen can be saved to disk or written directly to a printer. The xwd utility captures displayed images and writes them to disk. The graphic image (sometimes called a *pixmap*, and sometimes called an xwd file) is saved to disk in a format known to several X utilities. For example, the xwud utility displays images written to a file by xwd. Also, there is a convert utility that will convert xwd files to and from other formats.

> **Note:** The convert utility, and its companion utilities display and identify, are probably already included with your distibution of Linux, but, if not, they are freely available from ImageMagick. If you are going to be working with graphic files, you will probably find these programs to be very useful. You can get information and a copy of the programs at http://www.wizards.dupont.com/cristy/ImageMagick.htm.

Dumping a Window to Disk

The xwd utility can dump a single window, or it can dump the entire display and all its windows. The simplest thing that can be done is probably to select the window with the mouse by entering the following command:

```
xwd -out dumpfile.xwd
```

The cursor changes to a sort of gunsight-looking shape. Use this to select the window you want to dump and, when you press the left mouse button, the selected window will be written to the file. You can view the file by using the xwud utility, as shown in the following:

```
xwud -in dumpfile.xwd
```

There are a number of options that can be used with xwd to dump images. For example, the following command will dump a single image that contains everything on the display—the root window and all its child windows:

```
xwd -root -out dumpfile.xwd
```

There are a couple of other options that control exactly what gets dumped. Every X window has a border around it (although it can be set to zero width), and around the border is the frame that is generated by the window manager. The default is to include the border, but omit the frame. The following will also omit the border:

```
xwd -nobdrs -out dumpfile.xwd
```

The following statement will include both the border and the frame:

```
xwd -frame -out dumpfile.xwd
```

There are some other options—listed in the man pages—that allow you to specify which display is to be the source of the dump, and to select the window by its name or its ID number. Also, there are a couple of beeps that occur during the dump. There is a single beep when the dump starts and a double beep when it ends.

Here's a little trick that will give you a time-delay for a screen dump. Say, for example, that you have an application running and you want a screen shot of one of its menus. Normally xwd takes control of the mouse, so there is no way to both pull down a menu and select a window for dumping. The following is a simple two-line script that will solve this problem:

```
sleep 5
xwd -out dumpfile.xwd
```

When the script starts running, it immediately goes into a five second sleep. This should give you time to pull down, or pop up, whatever it is you want to grab. After the five seconds is up, the cursor will change to the gunsight and you can choose the menu, or the window containing the menu, to be dumped.

Converting Image Files

There is a simple all-purpose utility that will convert a graphic file from one format to another. It is easy to use. For example, to convert an .xwd file to a .jpeg file, just enter the following at the command line:

```
convert dumpedfile.xwd showfile.jpeg
```

The file named dumpedfile.xwd is read from the disk, and a new file named showfile.jpeg is created. The new file contains the JPEG version of the image. The convert utility determines the type of output file by the file extension. If you don't supply an extension on the output file, or if the extension is not known to convert, the output type is the same as the input type.

The input type is not determined by the file extension—you can name the input file anything you want, because the convert utility examines the contents of the file to determine what kind it is. The convert utility can read and write a large number of image file formats. Because it examines the input file to determine its type, if you have some unknown image file, you will likely be able to convert it, even if you don't know what kind of file it is. On the other hand, if you want to convert an image to some specific file type, you may need to check the man page for convert to determine the file extension that identifies your target format. Also, there are several options that can be used to control assumptions and algorithms used during the conversion.

Identifying Image Files

You can discover inside information about an image file with a utility named identify. To output descriptions of the two files used on the previous convert command, enter the following:

```
identify dumpedfile.xwd showfile.jpeg
```

Depending on the characteristics of `dumpedfile.xwd`, the output will look something like the following:

```
dumpedfile.xwd 800x600 PseudoClass 256c 471kb XWD 2s
showfile.jpeg 800x600 DirectClass 91kb JPEG 1s
```

You can get even more information by using the verbose option, as shown in the following:

```
identify -verbose dumpedfile.xwd
```

This will display volumes of information about the image. The actual data displayed depends on the type of image file.

The Clipboard

A number of X programs and utilities use the built-in cut-and-paste system. Whenever you cut or copy data from an application, it goes to the clipboard. When you paste data into an application, the source of the data is the clipboard. The clipboard is always there, but you can open a window to display its contents with the following command:

```
xclipboard
```

A window will appear that displays the current contents of the clipboard.

Locking Your Terminal

You can lock your screen with the following command:

```
xlock
```

Your screen will immediately go blank (some screen blanker program will start running), and it wait for your return. When you touch the mouse or the keyboard, there is a prompt for your password, and your terminal will only be released to you when the proper password is entered.

Summary

This chapter is an introduction to the user interface of the X Window System. There are large families of programs that are integrated as desktop environments, as with Gnome and KDE. There are also standalone utilities that are a standard part of X. Also, if you need something special that was not included as a part of Linux, you are likely to find it somewhere on the Internet. There are more X programs appearing every day.

On Your Own

Install and run either KDE or Gnome. Either one of these packages supplies quick and easy access to your computer, not to mention the fact that a lot of software comes with each of them.

Using either KDE or Gnome, try starting applications in separate screens, not just separate windows. For example, you can have the Netscape browser fill all of one screen and then have a couple of terminal emulators in another.

Experiment dumping windows to a file and converting the image file to another format. Try converting image files into various formats and back again to see if there is any loss of picture quality.

PART III

Linux System Administration Guide

8

User Administration

If you have been setting up your Linux system while reading this book, you have no doubt been using only the root account to log in. While this is the only way to set up a system, it is unadvisable to continue using the system on an everyday basis with only the root account. The root account has Superuser access (something that other users do not have), and, therefore, gives you complete control over the system. This is not necessarily a good thing though, because it means that one little mistake can render the system completely unusable. It is for this reason that it is necessary to add other user accounts to your machine, regardless of whether or not you are the only user.

Because Linux aims at complete POSIX compliance, like any other flavor of UNIX, it is a very robust multiuser environment. However, users are not automatically added to the system. One of the first tasks in system administration in any UNIX environment is to add and remove users from the system. Although some accounts are created during the installation of Linux, these are for system use only and cannot be used by a regular user.

In this chapter, we will go over the basics of user administration. This not only includes adding and removing users, but also keeping up-to-date on system security and learning what goes into setting up a secure system.

Creating New Accounts from the Console

Under Linux, one needs only two programs to set up any user's account from the console: useradd and passwd. First, useradd is run to set up the basic account. This program comes with every Linux distribution and is located in /usr/sbin/.

```
useradd [-u uid [-o]] [-g group] [-G group,...]
[-d home] [-s shell] [-c comment] [-m [-k template]]
[-f inactive] [-e expire mm/dd/yy] [-p passwd] name
```

The useradd command requires that certain flags be passed to it, as can be seen from the previous syntax. The only mandatory command that is passed is the name of the user; for this example, we'll call him user1. The following is the simplest way of adding this user:

```
% useradd user1
```

By default, user1 now has a home directory in /home/user1, is using the bash shell, is in the users group, and gets the next available user ID number.

The home directory is where the user starts out when he or she logs in. The home directory serves as the place where the user stores his or her files; so, by default, the user only has permission to write, modify or delete files that are in his or her home directory. This does not prohibit the user from reading files in other directories. By default, almost every file is readable by any user on the system unless the permissions of the file are changed (this will be discussed later in this chapter). When adding an account, the user's home directory can be specified if the default location is not to your liking. This is done by passing useradd the -d flag, followed by the desired location for the user's directory. Remember, all flags must be passed before the username is entered; for example,

```
% useradd -d /home/users/joe user1
```

The shell is the program that provides communication between you and the kernel. When you type in the console, you are typing commands to the shell, which are then translated into something the kernel—the heart of your Linux system—understands. By default, /bin/bash is used, but this can be changed by using the -s flag in a similar fashion to the -d flag. Although most shells are very similar when it comes to simple commands, there are still some subtle differences. These differences include things like the ways you declare variables and what the prompt looks like. These differences will be discussed in more detail in Chapter 11, "Using the Command Line Shell."

Groups are a major part of user administration. Every user on the computer is a member of one or more groups. Groups allow for permissions to be set on files so that different levels of access can modify the files in different ways. On a newly installed system, every file has default permissions. The administrator (the person who can use the root account) can modify these files to change the level of access needed to read, write, execute, or delete such files. The amount of access to the file and who has the ability to change this access is written right in the file, as shown in the following:

```
% ls -al README
-rw-r--r--  1 user1     users      20819 Feb 12 20:08 README
%
```

From this, you can see that the file README is owned by user1 who is a member of the group users (this is the default group when new users are added). The file is 20,819 bytes long and was last modified February 12, at 8:08 p.m. This tells a great deal about the file, but the most important part is right at the beginning—the first ten characters tell how you can modify this file. The first character is the most important and tells you what kind of file this is. A - means that it is just a file (a d would mean a directory, a b would mean it was a block device commonly found in the /dev/ directory, a c would correspond to a character device usually found in the /dev/ directory, and an l would mean it was a link). The next three characters tell what you can do to this file: an r means you can read it, a w means you can write to it, and, because there is a - in place of the fourth character, that is all you can do. Had there been an x for the fourth character, it would mean the file was executable and was either a program or a script of some sort.

The next three characters indicate the permissions for the rest of the group for this particular file. These can be read just like the previous three characters. Because it has an r and two dashes, any user in group users can read the file, but cannot write to it like user1 can. Finally, the last three characters indicate what the permissions are for every other user on the system (besides those in group users). You can see that every other user has the same access as those in user1's group—read-only.

Notice that user1 is the owner of this file. This means that he or she has the ability to change the permissions so that others can read, write, or execute this file. This is done through the chmod command. The following is the syntax for chmod:

```
chmod {a,u,g,o} {+,-} {r,w,x} filename
```

As can be seen in this syntax, chmod requires four arguments: who the new permissions will affect, whether you are adding or removing access to the file, whether you are changing read, write, or execute permissions, and the name of the file. The first argument has five options: a, u, g, o, or nothing at all. The a stands for all users; this will change the permissions for all the users on the system (this modifies the last six characters). The u changes the permissions for the current user, g changes the permissions for the user's group (in this case users), and o changes the permissions for those not in the user's group (the last three characters). If you do not specify what users you are changing access for, Linux will modify access for all users by default.

The next argument is how you want to change the permissions, + adds access and - takes access away. After this, you must specify what kind of access is to be changed: read, write, or execute. Finally, you must type the filename of the file you are modifying. The following is an example of how to add write access for all users:

```
% chmod a+w README
% ls -al README
-rw-rw-rw-  1 serge    users      20819 Feb 12 20:08 README
```

It is also possible to use a numeric system to change the permissions on the file. This is done by using the chmod command followed by a four digit numeric code. The first number is always zero when modifying file permissions and can therefore be omitted, leaving only three numbers to worry about. These digits each correspond to permissions for the user, group, and everyone else, respectively. Each digit can have a value of 0–7, inclusive. Each digit is derived from adding the numbers 0, 1, 2, and 4 together. A value of 0 adds no permissions to the file, 1 makes the file executable, 2 makes it writable, and 4 makes the file readable. These digits can be added together to set the permissions for any file. For example, a value of 5 would correspond to being readable and executable, but not writable. This is because 4+1=5.

The following syntax makes the file README, readable, writable, and executable by the current user (the owner of the file). The file is now also readable and executable by all users in this user's group, and also by any other user on the system.

```
% chmod 755 README
```

Group information is all stored in the /etc/group file. If you print this file to the screen, you will notice that each line in the file consists of three parts and should look like the following:

```
root::0:root
bin::1:root,bin,daemon
daemon::2:root,bin,daemon
sys::3:root,bin,adm
adm::4:root,adm,daemon
users::100:user1
```

The first part of each line is the name of the group. The root group should have only one member—the root account. The users group is where all of the regular users of the system should go. However, you can also add your own groups for users (such as students, people, and so on). The remaining groups that are listed here should not be touched at all. The bin, daemon, sys, and adm are all groups that are used for system processes. Adding a user or modifying one of these can really mess up your system, by making them unreadable by system processes and cause your system to fail, so it is unadvisable to modify these groups.

The second part of each line has a place for a password. This makes it possible to require a password to join a group. It is not recommended to add a password to a group such as users, but it might be a good idea to put a password on route so that a user cannot change to that group with something such as the newsgroup command. An alternative to using a password is to put an asterisk in the password field itself. This will completely disable any other user from becoming a member of the root group. To do this, modify that line in /etc/group to read as follows:

```
root:*:0:root
```

The third portion of each line contains the group ID (GID). This is very similar to the user ID (covered next), but encompasses a whole group rather than one individual. This is how the system keeps track of groups internally, rather than remembering groups by name.

The last part of the line contains the members of each group. As you may or may not have noticed, a user can be a member of more than one group.

Now that you understand what groups and permissions are, the next step in creating a user is the user ID number. Every user on the system is provided a unique ID number. This number can either be specified by the system or by the administrator when an account is set up. The system keeps track of all users based on their user IDs most of the time, not their usernames. This is not very important at this point, but if you plan on setting up more than one Linux system, you may want to make sure that each user's ID is the same on all machines so some networking aspects will be easier to configure.

The next option when adding a new user to the system is the -m switch. When multiple users are created, the administrator may want to have certain files placed in each user's home directory. This can be done using the -m flag. The files to be copied are located in the /etc/skel/ directory, but the -m flag can be followed by a -k flag if another location is desirable.

In the interest of security, it may be desirable to set up an account password that will expire after a certain period of time. This forces users to frequently change their passwords. If the user does not add a new password after the old one has expired, the -f flag causes the account to be permanently disabled after a defined period of time. Following this flag with 0 makes this occur immediately, -1 will disable this feature. This feature is disabled by default.

Another security feature that can be enabled with the useradd command is an expiration date on the account. This is useful if you want to create a user account that will only be active for a defined period of time. This requires the -e flag. This flag is followed by the date that the account will expire, in MM/DD/YY format.

The last optional argument that will be passed is the password that will be put on the account. It is strongly recommended to put a password on every active account on your system. This can be accomplished from useradd by passing the -p flag followed by the desired password.

Congratulations! At this point you should now know how to add a new user to your system. However, unless you have used some of the optional arguments described so far, this user has no password on the account and therefore cannot log in yet. The Superuser has the ability to add or change the password on any account. This is accomplished via the passwd command. By itself, the passwd command will change the password for the current account you are using. However, the root user can type passwd followed by a username to change the password for any user on the system.

The passwd command changes the password defined in the password file located in /etc/passwd. This is a very important file that stores most of the information regarding a specific user. A line from this file may look like the following:

```
user1:kYoQE6k:1000:100:Joe User:/home/user1:/bin/bash
```

Much like the /etc/group file, this file has each line separated into distinct pieces. Each tells something different about the user. The first part is the username, which was specified when the account was created.

The next part contains the encrypted password for that user. Every password for a login is always encrypted. While the password file is readable by every account on the system, it is nearly impossible to decode the passwords by hand.

The third part of the password file consists of the user ID number, which was allocated by Linux when the account was created, or it could have been specified by the administrator when the account was added. The fourth part consists of the group ID number, which will match the ID number that is written in /etc/group. If it doesn't, something is very wrong.

The fifth part of this file is the name of the user. This was either added when the account was created using one of the methods that are going to be described on the next few pages, or it could have been added manually to the password file by the system administrator (only the system administrator has permission to write to the password file). If the user's name is not here, you may want to add it now. This helps for user identification in the future.

The sixth part of each line in the password file contains the user's home directory, which was created when the user's account was added. The last part contains the shell that will be started after the user logs in. The user can run any shell he or she wants after logging in, but the one he or she will use first is specified here. It is usually `/bin/bash`, but `/bin/tcsh` and `/bin/csh` are also very common choices. This option is set up by the system administrator.

Creating New Accounts with Red Hat 6.0

Now that you know how to add user accounts at the console under any distribution of Linux, let's focus on setting up accounts under X. Regardless of whether you chose to install KDE or Gnome with your copy of Red Hat 6.0, there is a very powerful tool called `control-panel`. This can only be run by the root user and also must be run in X.

1. You must first log in with `root`.

2. Now you must start X, if it is not already started. This can be done by typing **startx** at the command prompt.

3. Once X is up and running, it is necessary to open up `xterm` (or any other command terminal that is run under X) and type **control-panel &**. The ampersand (&) is necessary if you want to continue using that `xterm` window while `control-panel` is running.

4. A toolbar should appear that is similar to the one shown in Figure 8.1. Click the icon at the bottom (this icon will say System Configuration if you hold the mouse over it).

5. This icon will bring up a program called `linuxconf`. The `linuxconf` is an administration utility that allows you to fill in check boxes and forms and then modifies system files for you. As such, `linuxconf` is a very powerful tool that can also be used to remotely administer your computer.

6. Now locate the tree in the left panel labeled User Accounts. You may need to collapse some of the other branches to find it because it is located right in the middle. When you locate it, expand the branch labeled Normal. From here, click once on the branch right below it labeled User Accounts (it is a different branch from the first one).

7. You should now see that the panel on the right is filled with information about all the other accounts on the system (see Figure 8.2). All this information is obtained from the password file. Next click the Add button on the right panel.

FIGURE 8.1

The Red Hat Linux control-panel.

FIGURE 8.2

linuxconf displaying all the existing accounts on the system.

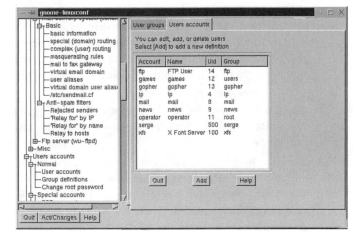

8. The panel should change to look something like Figure 8.3. It is only a matter of filling in all of the information for the new account now. In the space for Group, you have an option of creating a new group by filling in the space, or you can make the user a member of an existing group by clicking the arrow to the right of the box and selecting the appropriate group from the pull-down menu.

9. Because a user can be a member of more than one group, you can fill in the box labeled Supplementary Groups with any other groups that you want this user to become a member of. Next, you probably want to leave the box for the Home Directory blank and let Linux use the default new home directory for this user (/home/username). However, you also have the option to fill this in if you want another location.

FIGURE 8.3
Creating a new account with `linuxconf`.

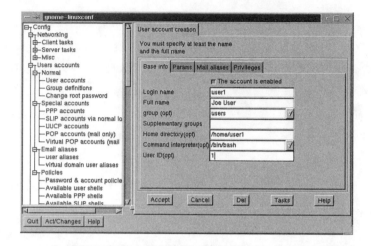

10. The next step is choosing a Command Interpreter (commonly called a shell). The default and most-used shell under Linux is `/bin/bash`. However, there is another pull-down menu that shows a list of all the available command interpreters from which you can choose. You access this menu by clicking the arrow to the right of the Command Interpreter text field.

11. You now have the option of selecting a user ID. This is completely optional, as stated before. If you do not select one, it will be provided by Linux based on the next available ID.

12. Then, you have the option of adding certain parameters to this account. To do this, click the Params tab. The right frame should look like the one seen in Figure 8.4. Here you have the option of adding an expiration date on the account and an expiration for the user's password. Currently, this is all completely optional, and not changing the current values that are shown in Figure 8.4 will disable these features.

FIGURE 8.4
Account expiration parameters that can be edited when creating a new account using `linuxconf`.

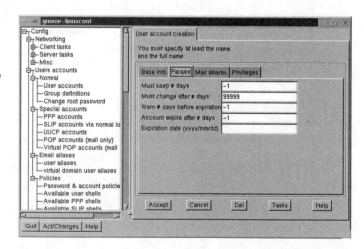

13. At this point, the account is ready to be created. Click the Accept button at the bottom on the Params tab. The account will be created, but it is not yet active. To activate the account, a password must be added. This procedure is exactly like the one described in the section titled "Creating Accounts from the Console," at the beginning of this chapter.

14. Now you must log in using root, if you have not already, and add a password for the user. Type **passwd *username***, where *username* is the username for the account that is going to be created.

15. Congratulations! You have successfully created an account using Red Hat Linux 6.0 and linuxconf.

Creating New Accounts with SuSE 6.0

SuSE is very similar to Red Hat in more ways than one. They not only both use the RPM package format, but also can use linuxconf to set up new user accounts. However, for the sake of being different, SuSE also has its own administrative utility. This is known as YaST, and can be run from both the command prompt and from X; both modes of execution lead to the same program.

By default, SuSE comes with KDE. The YaST icon can be found in the bottom-right corner of the KDE menu bar, as seen in Figure 8.5.

FIGURE 8.5

The YaST button found in the bottom menu bar in KDE.

Clicking this icon once will launch the program. However, if X is not set up yet, you can launch YaST by typing **yast** at the prompt. Setting up an account is very similar in each distribution of Linux, and is as follows for SuSE:

1. Upon launching YaST, scroll through the list of options until System Administration is selected. When you press Enter, a new list of options will come up.

2. From the second list of options, scroll down until User Administration is selected. This and the previous step can both be seen in Figure 8.6. Press Enter and a new screen will appear. If you have been following along closely, you will notice that the next screen has spaces for you to enter all of the standard information that is required to add a new user to the system.

FIGURE 8.6

Select System Administration and then User Administration from YaST to edit/create accounts with SuSE Linux.

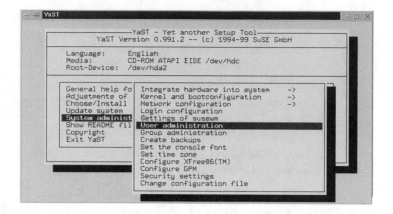

3. After entering the desired username for the user to be added, pressing Enter or Tab will take you to the next box, the user ID (see Figure 8.7). As always, if one is not specified, Linux will dynamically assign an ID to the new user. This can be seen immediately when the cursor flashes in that box. You can see in Figure 8.7 that the next available ID is 501.

FIGURE 8.7

Main window for creating/editing with YaST under SuSE Linux.

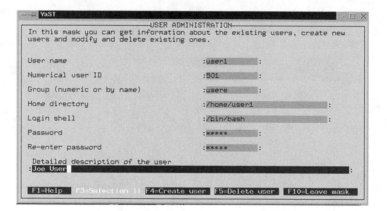

4. The next box lets you specify the group for the new user. By default, the group users is here. You may also notice that YaST gives you the option of entering the group by either the name or the number of the group.

5. As always, the next parts to be configured are the new users' home directory and the default login shell. The users home directory is /home/username by default, and the login shell is usually /bin/bash by default. It is only advisable to change these if there is good reason to.

6. Unlike some other methods of creating accounts, YaST lets you add a password for the new user as part of the whole process. This means that instead of manually

adding a password by using the passwd command, there is a space to fill it in when you use YaST. As always, you must confirm the password by retyping it.

7. The final field that should be entered is an area for comments. This is a good place to put the user's real name. When you complete this field, press F4 to add the new user. Then press F10 to leave the setup utility and return to the YaST main menu. Here you can safely exit the program from the menu.

You have now successfully added a new user to the system using YaST and SuSE. Although YaST is a very powerful tool, you still have the option of adding future users by using the console commands discussed at the beginning of this chapter.

Creating New Accounts with Caldera Open Linux 2.2

Although the installation program for Caldera Open Linux 2.2 requires that you add another user in addition to root before it finishes copying files, it is important that you know how to add other users once you are using Open Linux.

You may have already noticed that Open Linux automatically installs KDE on your computer. Within KDE there should be an icon on the bottom menu bar for Caldera Open Administration System (COAS). This utility will help you to do most of your configuration from within X. Click this icon and a menu will appear. Now click System and then Accounts (see Figure 8.8).

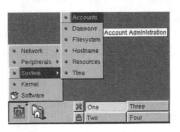

FIGURE 8.8

To create new accounts or edit existing ones, select System and then Accounts from the bottom menu bar where you see the COAS button in KDE with Caldera Open Linux.

Now you should see a box appear onscreen just like the one in Figure 8.9. This contains all the information about all the accounts on the system. This information is taken from your /etc/passwd file. As you can see, the program defaults to displaying all the accounts on the system, not just the user accounts. This can be changed so that only user accounts are displayed (excluding root) by clicking the View menu and selecting Regular Users. Now you should only see the account that you created when you first installed Open Linux and an account named Nobody.

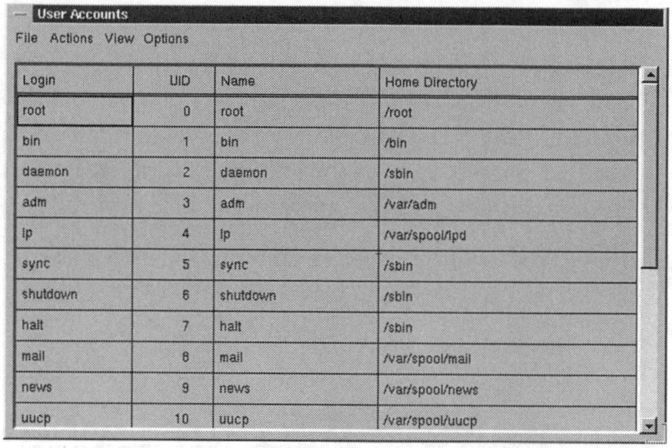

FIGURE **8.9**

*Sample list of all
existing accounts
on your Caldera
Open Linux
system.*

Login	UID	Name	Home Directory
root	0	root	/root
bin	1	bin	/bin
daemon	2	daemon	/sbin
adm	3	adm	/var/adm
lp	4	lp	/var/spool/lpd
sync	5	sync	/sbin
shutdown	6	shutdown	/sbin
halt	7	halt	/sbin
mail	8	mail	/var/spool/mail
news	9	news	/var/spool/news
uucp	10	uucp	/var/spool/uucp

To add a new account, select Actions from the top of the screen, click Create User, and a
new box appears asking for the username. After the username is entered, another box
will appear containing all the information for the account. All this information is pretty
standard; the first box is for entering the user's real name. Next comes the User ID
(UID)—by default the UIDs for new users start at 500, but you can enter another value
as long it is not already taken.

The next thing that needs to be entered is the group in which to put the new user. By
default, the group users is selected, but scrolling through the list of options in this box
can change this, or a new group can be added by typing it in. However, it might be a
good idea to make private groups for new users in the interest of security.

After you enter the group for the user, you must decide which shell you want this user to
use by default. The default option is the Gnu Bourne Again Shell, this is the same as
/bin/bash. It is recommended that you use /bin/bash for most users. However, you can
change this option if you scroll through the shell options. You will notice that all the
available shells on your system are listed by their full names rather than just the name of
the executable (for instance Cornell C Shell is the same as /bin/tcsh, and Z Shell is the
same as /bin/zsh). You can also use a shell that isn't listed by typing in the name and
location of the executable in the box (for example, **/usr/local/bin/customshell** if that
is a shell that you want to use).

The next thing to be configured is the password for this user. This is extremely straightforward—simply click the button to the right of the word Password. Now a new box
appears onscreen. Here you must enter the password for this user and then retype it in
the box below to make sure that you haven't mistyped it.

In the next box, you must enter the home directory for the new user. The default is
/home/*username* (where *username* is the username of the user to be added). However, this
can be changed if necessary. The box below this is an option inherent to Open Linux; you
have the option to disable this account when it is created so that it can be enabled at a later

time. By default, the account should be enabled (simply look at the button to the right of where it says Disabled—the button should say Enabled). The account can be disabled by simple clicking the Disabled button. All this information can be seen in Figure 8.10

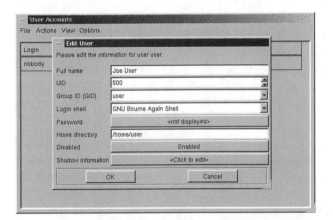

FIGURE 8.10
Window for creating new users or editing existing ones with COAS.

The final option when configuring an account for Open Linux is the information regarding password expiration. This is done by clicking the Click to Edit button to the right of Shadow Information. A new box appears that looks like the one in Figure 8.11. The first option in this box is to set the minimum number of days that must pass before the password can be changed. The next field has the maximum number of days before the password must be changed. The field after this indicates the number of days before the password expires to warn the user. The next field shows the number of days after the password has expired before the account will be disabled (if the account is never to be disabled automatically, simply enter a value of -1 here). This is a handy feature; if the user never changes his or her password when warned, the account is disabled and he or she is then forced to come to you (the system administrator) to get the account activated again. You should take this opportunity to explain the need for security on the system.

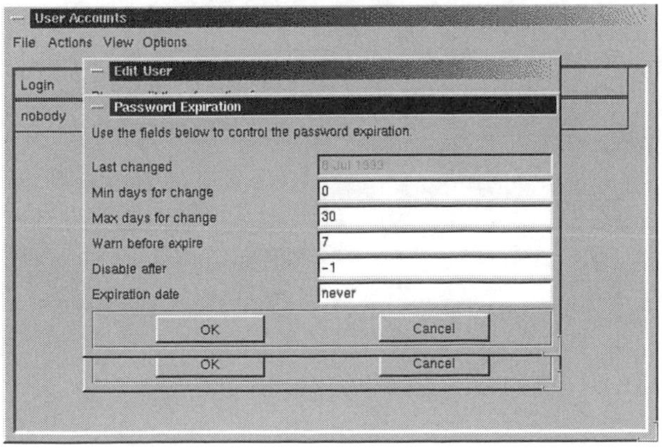

FIGURE 8.11
Setting password expiration parameters with Caldera Open Linux.

The final piece of information that must be entered here is the expiration date for the account. If the account is never to expire, simply type **never** here. After you check all of this information, click OK to go back to the previous box. Click OK again at this box to create the account. You should now see the new user listed in the list of all the regular users, as shown in Figure 8.12.

FIGURE 8.12
Sample list of all user accounts after the new user is added to the system.

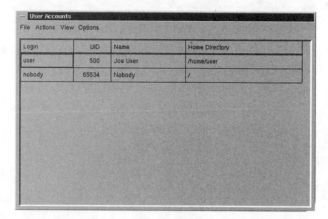

Now that you are familiar with creating new accounts under Caldera OpenLinux, it is important to know how to set up some of the defaults for creating other accounts in the future. Open the box showing all the user accounts again, if you closed it. Choose Options from the top of this screen, and click Preferences. A new box appears like the one shown in Figure 8.13.

FIGURE 8.13
Editing defaults for account creation.

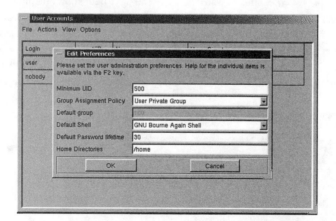

The first box contains the minimum User ID required when creating a new account. By default, this is set to 500 (which means that the first user added will have a UID of 500, the next will be 501, and so on). The next box is for configuring the default group for the user. There are two options here, Default Group and User Private Group. If User Private Group is selected, the new user will be in his or her own group (user joe will be in group joe). Default Group means that all new users will be in group users by default. The next box is only used when the user is to be placed in Default Group. This box is where you specify what the Default Group is. This can be done by entering the group name or the Group ID number (the default is 100, which is group users).

The next box to fill in is the default shell for the user. This box is identical to the one that is there when a new user is added. You can either pick one of the shells from the list or add your own custom shell. The next area to fill in is the Default Password Lifetime. This is where you enter the default number of days before the user must change his or her password. This option will only work if shadow passwords are enabled (the shadow feature will be discussed in the next section; it can be turned on and off from the Options menu in this box). The default here is 30 days. The final area that should be looked at is the default home directory for each new user. The default here is /home; this means that all new accounts get their home directories in /home/username (where username is the name of the new user). When you are finished, click OK to save this information and close the box.

Congratulations, you have successfully added a new user under Caldera Open Linux!

Security Concerns

Now that you know how to add users to your new system, you should be aware of a couple of concerns that have arisen. With many users on a system, there is a growing concern for system security. This becomes an issue with both malicious existing users and non-users who want to gain access to your system.

The most common way for getting a breach in security on your system is when an outside person learns the login and password for an existing account. When someone has access to the system, he or she can do anything that an existing user can do.

Believe it or not, the most often used way of getting a user's password is to randomly guess it. Surprisingly enough, it works a lot of the time. The best way to prevent an unauthorized user from gaining access to your system is to be sure that every existing user has a hard-to-guess password, and that he or she changes this password every few months.

Here are a few guidelines that you might want to follow to make your passwords hard to crack:

- Never make the password the same as the login. This is often the first thing that is tried when someone wants to access someone else's account. This also means that you should avoid using the user's real name for the password.

- Avoid using simple words for passwords. It's better to use random letters, a combination of punctuation/numbers and letters, or even just numbers and punctuation.

- Never tell anyone your password—not even people you trust. Everybody who knows your password is a potential security risk.

- Avoid logging in on machines using your account and letting others use the account unattended.

By following these guidelines, you should be able to keep your system fairly secure from an outside attack. However, there is still a threat of an existing user doing malicious things to your system. The main way to do something like this is by gaining access to the root account. This is one of the reasons why you should make sure to use the root account only when necessary—not on an everyday basis.

You may have already noticed that the /etc/passwd file is readable by all users on the system. This is a potential threat because any existing user can read every other user's encrypted password. With this information, a user can use a utility known as a "brute force cracker" to decode the password. This is a major security concern. However, the file permissions must remain readable because certain system components require access to this file. The way around this is to use the shadow utilities.

The shadow utilities should come standard with most distributions of Linux, but if you do not have them on your system, they can be downloaded from http://www1.itnet.pl/amelektr/linux/shadow/. This group of programs copies the encrypted passwords from /etc/passwd to /etc/shadow. The /etc/passwd file remains the same, except the area where each password was now has an x. The /etc/shadow file is readable only by the root user, so no one else can look at encrypted passwords. The shadow utility is invoked by typing **pwconv** at the prompt while logged in as root (pwunconv reverses the process and puts the passwords back into your /etc/passwd file, deleting /etc/shadow in the process). The following is an output of the shadow utility and shows how the /etc/passwd file is changed:

```
%cat /etc/passwd
root:1FkTK93k/$k:0:0:root:/root:/bin/bash
user1:kYoQE6k:1000:100:Joe User:/home/user1:/bin/bash
...
%pwconv
            %cat /etc/passwd
```

```
root:x:0:0:root:/root:/bin/bash
user1:x:1000:100:Joe User:/home/user1:/bin/bash
...
%cat /etc/shadow
root:1FkTK93k/$k:10780:0:99999:7:-1:-1:134537332
user1:kYoQE6k:10780:0:99999:7:-1:-1:134537332
...
```

You may have already noticed that the /etc/shadow file is similar to the /etc/passwd file as far as the data, in addition to the username and password. The first field after the encrypted password tells how many days it has been since January 1st, 1970 that the password has been changed. The next field contains the minimum number of days before the password on that account may be changed. The next field indicates how many days before the password must be changed, and the next field indicates how many days beforehand to warn the user of the password expiration. The next field shows how many days can pass after the password has expired and before the account is completely disabled. The final field is unimportant and carries no significance to anyone because it is reserved for the system.

Summary

By now, you might be familiar with adding users from both the command prompt and under X in your specific distribution of Linux. There are a few key things that you should remember:

- Only use the root account when it is needed (system administration). This means that the first thing you should do on every new system you will use is to make an account for yourself.

- Be sure to update key components of your system to ensure its stability. Bug fixes are released all the time, and these help to secure your system from crashes and unwanted intruders.

- Never give out any password to anybody. Also, remember to force users to update passwords regularly. This includes the passwords on the root account.

- Frequently remind your users to change their passwords often. Also, be sure to instruct them on how to create secure passwords (don't use words, use numbers and punctuation with letters). Some good examples of passwords that don't use real words but are still easy to remember are 'nix4evr!, Iluv-bash2, and I8sushi?.

Following these reminders will help you to set up and maintain a secure and powerful Linux machine.

On Your Own

It might be a good idea to now try and create an experimental account, so that you can try some of the steps discussed in this chapter. This will help you become more familiar with administering accounts under Linux and will help to familiarize you with the operating system as a whole.

From the console you can type something like the following:

```
%useradd -d /home/tempuser -s /bin/bash -c "Temporary User" tempuser
%passwd tempuser
Changing password for tempuser
Enter the new password (minimum of 5, maximum of 8 characters)
Please use a combination of upper and lower case letters and numbers.
New password:
Re-enter new password:
Password changed.
%
```

You should now have successfully created an account. The output (if created from the console) should look something like the previous sample.

Now it is highly recommended that you set up shadow passwords if they are not enabled already on your system:

```
%pwconv
```

Check to make sure that all of the passwords are now shadowed by displaying the shadow file (/etc/shadow) and the password file (/etc/passwd):

```
%cat /etc/shadow
```

```
%cat /etc/passwd
```

You should try to modify some file permissions to get accustomed to using chmod. Try making a file and then setting it as not readable by anyone, and then try viewing it. If everything is successful, you should not be allowed access to the file.

```
%echo "hello world" > test
%ls
test
%cat test
hello world
%chmod 000 test
%ls -al test
----------    1 tempuser     users          12 Sep  1 22:12 test
%cat test
cat: test: Permission denied
```

Next, you should try making the file readable by the current user only, and then try opening it up again:

```
%chmod u+r test
%ls -al test
-r--------      1 tempuser      users        12 Sep  1 22:12 test
%cat test
hello world
```

Finally, make the file readable and executable by all users on the system and then delete it when you are finished:

```
%chmod 755 test
%ls -al test
-rwxr-xr-x      1 tempuser      users        12 Sep  1 22:12 test
%rm test
%
```

At this point, hopefully you have mastered user administration and understand the basics of editing user accounts and file permissions. By following some simple security practices, you can have a very secure system. Good luck!

Administrative Tasks

The Startup and Shutdown Process

The Linux startup process begins with the kernel loading itself into the memory. This puts in place all the memory handling, file and device drivers, and everything else needed for basic system operation—but no user-accessible interfaces. These are all started by the init process.

The init Process

After the Linux kernel is done loading itself into the memory, it calls the init process. As the name suggests, the init process initializes the system by starting the various daemons, processes, and programs you need to use the system. For example, init will usually perform such tasks as initializing the network, starting network services, mounting remote file systems, and starting the getty processes that enables you to log on to the system from its console. init does this by looking at its configuration file (/etc/inittab) and running the init scripts found in its configuration files, normally located in the /etc/rc.d/ directory.

The init process is also called when shutting down or rebooting the system. At this time, it will attempt to terminate all running processes, unmount all file systems, and generally try and make sure you're shutting off the system cleanly, so that no data will be damaged.

Please note that this will not prevent data from being lost—shutting down the system while you have several files open in a word processor may not cause the word processor to automatically save them. It will just make sure it closes the files, usually in the fastest way possible, and exits.

The init Script

The init process uses many individual scripts to start the system's individual processes. You can expect to find several dozens of these scripts. They are normally shell scripts that will test whether all the necessary files exist and will then start the process. When called during shutdown, these scripts will, of course, terminate the process. On the more recent distributions, they will also create status files for the process, and can be queried as to whether or not the process is running.

Runlevels

Linux (like most other UNIX variants) has several different levels of operation, referred to as *runlevels*. You can select the default runlevel by editing your /etc/inittab file. On Red Hat systems, the following runlevels exist:

- 0　This runlevel is used to shutdown the system.
- 1　Single User mode—At this runlevel, only one person may log on, and that person will be operating as the Superuser. This mode is used mainly for maintenance and repair.
- 2　Multiuser mode—At this runlevel users are allowed to log on, but the network has not yet been initialized. Services that are usually started at this runlevel include Web servers, system loggers, the cron daemon, and the inetd daemon. Note that while the inetd daemon does provide network services, external connections cannot be made until the network has been initialized.
- 3　Full Multiuser Mode—At this runlevel, all the vital services and network connections have been initialized.
- 5　This runlevel will cause the machine to boot directly into the graphical X Windows System. If you have set up X Windows and the XDM services correctly, you may log in to the machine directly in that mode, bypassing the console.
- 6　This runlevel is used to reboot the machine.

Choosing the Default Runlevel

Selecting the default runlevel is done by modifying the initdefault parameter in the /etc/inittab file. This parameter is usually on the first non-comment line in the file and will look something like the following:

```
id:3:initdefault:
```

Simply replace the number (3) with the value corresponding with the runlevel you want the system to boot into.

Most distributions automatically set this to the Full Multiuser, text mode level, although recent distributions let you select runlevels during installation.

You will probably want to boot either into Full Multiuser Mode or into X. The other runlevels do not provide full functionality. In some cases, they may provide absolutely no functionality or even damage the equipment. For example, setting Reboot as the default runlevel will cause the machine to reboot endlessly.

Booting into Single User Mode

It may be necessary to boot into Single User Mode to repair damage to the system or to modify some parameters for programs before they start. You can achieve this by passing the single keyword to LILO at boot time. For example, if you want to boot into the kernel image linux, you would type the following:

```
LILO: linux single
```

This will halt the `init` process at runlevel 1. Depending on your system, you may be required to enter the Superuser password before accessing the system.

You may choose to continue into the default runlevel by logging out of your Single User session.

Changing Runlevels On–the-Fly

You may change runlevels at any time by issuing the `init` command followed by whatever runlevel you want. For example, if you want to reboot the system, you can type the following:

```
init 6
```

The `/etc/rc.d/` Directory Structure (Red Hat)

If you look in the `init-scripts` directory, the listing should look something like the following:

```
# ls -Fa /etc/rc.d/
./            rc*           rc.sysinit*   rc2.d/        rc5.d/
../           rc.firewall*  rc0.d/        rc3.d/        rc6.d/
init.d/       rc.local*     rc1.d/        rc4.d/
```

As you can see, each runlevel has a corresponding script directory named rc<number>.d. Take a look inside one of these.

```
# ls -Fa /etc/rc.d/rc3.d/
./            K65portmap@   S30syslog@    S65dhcpd@     S91smb@
../           K95nfsfs@     S40atd@       S75keytable@  S95httpd@
K20rusersd@   K96pcmcia@    S40crond@     S80qmail@     S99local@
K30mcserv@    S01kerneld@   S50inet@      S85gpm@
K40snmpd@     S10network@   S55named@     S90squid@
K55routed@    S20random@    S60lpd@       S90vmware@
```

During the startup process, as `init` progresses through runlevels, it will access each corresponding directory and run through all the scripts starting with S. Because it reads the filenames in alphabetical order, lower numbered scripts have a higher priority. For example, `S01kerneld` will be run first, whereas `S95httpd` will be run almost last. The process will call each of these files with the `start` keyword.

When the system is being shut down, `init` goes through the process in reverse and calls the files beginning with K, giving them the `stop` command.

You may have noticed that all these scripts are actually symbolic links—the rc<number>.d directories usually contain no actual files. The real files are all located in `/etc/rc.d/init.d`:

```
# ls -Fa /etc/rc.d/init.d/
./              gpm*            mcserv*         random*         syslog*
../             halt*           named*          routed*         vmware*
atd*            httpd*          network*        rusersd*
crond*          inet*           nfsfs*          single*
debug           keytable*       pcmcia*         smb*
dhcpd*          killall*        portmap*        snmpd*
functions*      lpd*            qmail*          squid*
```

The init process is controlled by having symbolic links to any of these files from one or more of the rc<number>.d directories, with an appropriate S<priority>process or K<number>process. Because these are shell scripts, they can be given a command line parameter by init, so the same script can be used to start, stop, or restart a process.

Manually Controlling a Process

You may want to manually start, stop, or restart any of these processes. All you have to do is run the appropriate init script with the appropriate command line parameter. For example, to stop your httpd process, type the following:

```
# /etc/rc.d/init.d/httpd stop
```

To start your httpd process again, type the following:

```
# /etc/rc.d/init.d/httpd start
```

Other valid command line options may include restart, status or reload, depending on your distribution and on what specific process you're trying to control.

Modifying the init Process

The most straightforward (and most complicated) way to modify the init process would be to manually set or delete the symlinks within /etc/rc.d/.

A common practice is to rename scripts you do not want to run into names beginning with a period (.)—not only will this prevent init from finding them, it will also cause them to be hidden from a regular ls command. Another common practice is to rename S files to a lowercase s. These methods are not very maintenance-friendly, however.

Using the chkconfig Utility (Red Hat)

The chkconfig utility can be used to display, activate, or de-activate init processes. It will actually manipulate the symlinks in the /etc/rc.d/ directory tree for you.

You can get a listing of all init processes known to the system (actually, scripts that are located in /etc/rc.d/init.d and contain information about what runlevels they think they should be run at) by issuing the following command:

```
# chkconfig —list
```

This will produce a long list of services, along with information about the runtimes on which they are active. To check on a particular script, use its name on the command line:

```
# chkconfig —list httpd
httpd 0:off 1:off 2:off 3:on 4:on 5:on 6:off
```

As you can see, httpd is active in runlevels 3, 4, and 5.

If you would like to disable a script, type the following:

```
# chkconfig httpd off
# chkconfig —list httpd
httpd 0:off 1:off 2:off 3:off 4:off 5:off 6:off
```

The script is now inactive in every runlevel.

To turn the script back on, type the following:

```
# chkconfig httpd on
```

Shutting Down the System

As stated before, you can simply call on init to shut down the machine for you. Simply type **init 0** to halt the machine, or **init 6** to reboot. You can also issue the halt command to the reboot commands to halt or reboot. If you are logged on to the machine's console, pressing Ctrl+Alt+Del can be configured as a shortcut to the reboot command. These methods are fine if you are the only user on the system.

However, if you are running a multiuser server and have users logged on who may have open files or applications, it might be polite to give them a short warning before shutting down. For this, you can use the shutdown command.

The shutdown command will wait until near the time you told it to shutdown. It will then send everyone on the system a warning (that you can also specify). You can tell it to wait a given amount of time after this, to provide people with time to log out of the system. Then it will call init to do the dirty work.

The syntax for the shutdown command is as follows:

```
# shutdown [-t delay] [-r¦-h¦-k¦-c] time message
```

The argument for the -t option is the delay, in seconds, between the warning and the actual shutdown.

You can use -r to reboot or -h to halt the system. The -k option will cause shutdown to send out messages, but not actually shut down. This is useful if you are writing a Linux guide and want to make sure you're using the correct syntax. The -c option cancels a running shutdown process. This is useful for the times you forget to use the -k option.

The time option can be given in two formats. You can either use an exact time (for example, 10:45), or you can specify a delay in minutes. For example, to shut down in 15 minutes you would use +15m. You can also type in now for an immediate shutdown.

The warning message is usually an explanation of why you are shutting down. You can be as descriptive as you like. If you are doing this on a large, multiuser system, you'll still get phone calls.

Formatting and Disk Partitioning

One of the things that seems to scare a lot of people away from Linux is drive partitioning. With more and more machines being delivered with another popular operating system pre-installed, less and less users are even aware of such a thing as a *partition*. This isn't very surprising—when icons and pointers have made even the concept of files blurry, why would you want to deal with something as complicated as a partition?

The truth is that with very little practice, you can repartition and format a drive for Linux in under two minutes—including the physical formatting time.

Device Names

To partition and format your hard drive, you will need to know the device name assigned to it by Linux. Under Linux (and, in fact, UNIX in general), all peripherals and devices are referred to as files, and all devices are kept in the /dev directory. IDE hard drives are referenced as hd devices, with letters referencing their location on the IDE chain, as shown in Table 9.1.

Table 9.1 IDE Drive Device Names

IDE Name	Device Name
Primary Master	/dev/hda
Primary Slave	/dev/hdb
Secondary Master	/dev/hdc
Secondary Slave	/dev/hdd

SCSI hard drives are referenced as sd devices and numbered according to their location on the SCSI chain, as shown in Table 9.2.

Table 9.2 SCSI Drive Device Names

SCSI Position	Device Name
First SCSI hard drive	/dev/sda
Second SCSI hard drive	/dev/sdb
...	...
Tenth SCSI hard drive	/dev/sdj

These device names refer to the entire hard drive. Once the drive has partitions, you can access a partition by appending the partition number to the device name, as shown in Table 9.3.

Table 9.3   IDE Drive Partition Device Names

Partition Number	Device Name
1	/dev/hda1
2	/dev/hda2
...	...
n	/dev/hda$n$

Some Notes About Fdisk

Although simple to use, you can still damage your data through incorrect usage of the fdisk program. Make sure you are entering the correct parameters.

If you are using a large hard drive and are not using it in LBA mode, fdisk will give you an error message. What this message says is that while Linux itself has no problems accessing such a configuration, other operating systems or programs might. If you are going to use your drive for nothing but Linux data, you can safely ignore this message. If, however, you plan on booting Linux from this drive, you should consider using it in LBA mode, just to be on the safe side, as the boot-loader software (LILO) might have problems accessing data which resides after the 1024th cylinder.

MSDOS's FORMAT program may have trouble accessing MSDOS partitions created with Linux's fdisk program. When you exit fdisk, it will issue a warning about this. Refer to the fdisk manual page (type 'man fdisk') for more information.

Using fdisk

You must determine the device name you want to work on and use it as the command-line parameter for fdisk. fdisk will, by default, work on /dev/hda.

Assume that you have decided to convert your Secondary Slave drive from another popular operating system to Linux. As root, type the following:

```
# fdisk /dev/hdd
```

You should now be presented with fdisk's Interactive Mode prompt. In this mode, you usually type single letter commands to create, delete, and list partitions. The first command you should try is the **p** command, shown next, which will print out the current partition table:

```
Command (m for help): p

Disk /dev/hdd: 15 heads, 63 sectors, 8912 cylinders
Units = cylinders of 945 * 512 bytes

   Device Boot    Start      End    Blocks   Id  System
/dev/hdd1    *        1      8912  4210888+   b  FAT32

Command (m for help):
```

As you can see, this drive only has one partition (/dev/hdd1). It is bootable, it ranges the entire drive, its size is approximately 4.3GB, and it is formatted as a FAT32 partition.

Because you want to use this drive for Linux, go ahead and delete this partition, using the d command, as shown in the following:

```
Command (m for help): d
Partition number (1-4): 1

Command (m for help): p

Disk /dev/hdd: 15 heads, 63 sectors, 8912 cylinders
Units = cylinders of 945 * 512 bytes

   Device Boot    Start      End   Blocks   Id  System

Command (m for help):
```

Now that the partition table is empty, you can go ahead and add Linux partitions.

Primary and Extended Partitions

Before adding partitions, you must decide what types of partitions you want.

Linux supports up to four primary (*real*) partitions. If you don't need a larger number than that, you can go ahead and make all of your partitions of that type.

If you need more than that, you can create one of your partitions as an extended partition. This partition type can hold many logical volumes. These act as regular partitions, but cannot be used to boot from.

Note that real partitions will be numbered 1 to 4. Logical Volume partition numbers start at 5.

Adding Partitions

You will now add three partitions to the drive. You're going to add a Linux Swap partition of 128MB and a Linux Data (or Linux Native) partition of 3GB. The remaining 911MB will be allocated as an Extended partition, in which you will create two logical volumes. They will both be FAT32 partitions of approximately 455MB in size.

You use two fdisk commands for this entire process. First, the n command creates new partitions. It will prompt you for partition type and number. It will also prompt you for the start cylinder and end cylinder. Don't worry about missing the correct cylinder and calculating bytes per cylinder; default start values will be provided, and the end parameter may be given in kilobytes.

The second command used is the t command, used to modify partition types. It will also prompt you for partition number, and ask you what type to which to change it. It can also display a list of known partition types.

Another useful command is the l command, which will show you the list of known partition types. You can consult it in advance to save time. For example, you are going to be using partition types 82 (Linux Swap), and b (FAT32). Using the l command is shown here before the rest of the process:

```
Command (m for help): l

 0   Empty            a   OS/2 Boot Manag  65  Novell Netware   a6  OpenBSD
 1   DOS 12-bit FAT   b   FAT32            75  PC/IX            a7  NEXTSTEP
 2   XENIX root       c   FAT32 (LB        80  Old MINIX        b7  BSDI fs
 3   XENIX usr        e   FAT16 (LB        81  Linux/MINIX      b8  BSDI swap
 4   DOS 16-bit <32M  f   Win95 Extended   82  Linux swap       c7  Syrinx
 5   Extended         40  Venix 80286      83  Linux native     db  CP/M
 6   DOS 16-bit >=32  51  Novell?          85  Linux extended   e1  DOS access
 7   OS/2 HPFS        52  Microport        93  Amoeba           e3  DOS R/O
 8   AIX              63  GNU HURD         94  Amoeba BBT       f2  DOS secondary
 9   AIX bootable     64  Novell Netware   a5  BSD/386          ff  BBT
Command (m for help): n
Command action
   e   extended
   p   primary partition (1-4)
p
Partition number (1-4): 1
First cylinder (1-8912): 1
Last cylinder or +size or +sizeM or +sizeK ([1]-8912): +128M

Command (m for help): n
Command action
   e   extended
   p   primary partition (1-4)
p
Partition number (1-4): 2
First cylinder (279-8912): 279
Last cylinder or +size or +sizeM or +sizeK ([279]-8912): +3072M
```

```
Command (m for help): n
Command action
   e   extended
   p   primary partition (1-4)
e
Partition number (1-4): 3
First cylinder (6937-8912): 6937
Last cylinder or +size or +sizeM or +sizeK ([6937]-8912): 8912

Command (m for help): n
Command action
   l   logical (5 or over)
   p   primary partition (1-4)
l
First cylinder (6937-8912): 6937
Last cylinder or +size or +sizeM or +sizeK ([6937]-8912): 7924


Command (m for help): n
Command action
   l   logical (5 or over)
   p   primary partition (1-4)
l
First cylinder (7925-8912): 7925
Last cylinder or +size or +sizeM or +sizeK ([7925]-8912): 8912

Command (m for help): t
Partition number (1-6): 1
Hex code (type L to list codes): 82
Changed system type of partition 1 to 82 (Linux swap)

Command (m for help): t
Partition number (1-6): 5
Hex code (type L to list codes): b
Changed system type of partition 5 to b (Win95 FAT32)

Command (m for help): t
Partition number (1-6): 6
Hex code (type L to list codes): b
Changed system type of partition 6 to b (Win95 FAT32)
Command (m for help): p

Disk /dev/hdd: 15 heads, 63 sectors, 8912 cylinders
Units = cylinders of 945 * 512 bytes

    Device Boot    Start      End    Blocks   Id  System
/dev/hdd1              1      278   131323+   82  Linux swap
/dev/hdd2            279     6936  3145905    83  Linux native
/dev/hdd3           6937     8912   933660     5  Extended
/dev/hdd5           6937     7924   466798+    b  Win95 FAT32
/dev/hdd6           7925     8912   466798+    b  Win95 FAT32

Command (m for help):
```

That's just about it for creating partitions. The only thing left to do now is write the partition table to the disk. You do this by using the w command. The fdisk program will write the new partition table to the drive and will then make a few system calls to make sure Linux sees the new partition table. It will also issue the aforementioned warning regarding creating or modifying old FAT partitions.

With older versions of fdisk and the Linux kernel, it is recommended that you reboot your machine to make sure the changes have taken effect. Those versions of fdisk will usually print out a message if that is the case. If you want to verify that the changes have been saved, you can run fdisk with the -l command line switch; this is equivalent to running the p command within fdisk.

Formatting Your Partitions

Although there are Linux utilities for formatting many partitions and filesystem types, you will only concentrate on the Linux native types: Swap Space and the Second Extended File System (ext2).

Formatting Swap Filesystems

To format a partition for use as swap space, you run the mkswap program and supply what partition on which to work. For example, to format the swap partition you created earlier, type the following:

```
# mkswap /dev/hdd1
```

If you would like mkswap to check for bad blocks while formatting, use the -c command line switch, as shown in the following:

```
# mkswap -c /dev/hdd1
```

Naturally, this will take longer.

Formatting ext2 Filesystems

The ext2 filesystem is Linux's native filesystem. Your data will normally reside on this type of filesystem. You use the mke2fs command to format this type of partition.

Much like mkswap, the only parameter required is the name of the partition you want to format. The -c command line switch can also be used if you want to check for bad blocks. This is highly recommended if you are not completely sure the drive is in perfect condition.

```
# mke2fs -c /dev/hdd2
```

Unlike mkswap, the mke2fs command will, by default, print out a lot of information while formatting. For example, it will give you a list of blocks on which it will store backups of the superblock. This is a block containing the filesystem information. There are many backup blocks for this information, in case the filesystem gets damaged. Although very rarely necessary, you may want to write a few of these down, or even print out the entire list and keep it in a safe place.

If you run the command with the `-c` option, `mke2fs` will provide a progress report as it works.

Checking Your Filesystem—e2fsck

During the startup process, Linux will check its native filesystems before mounting them, and, if errors are found, attempt to repair them. You might occasionally need or want to perform this task manually. For example, you might want to check an unmounted filesystem, or, on rare occasion, the startup process may fail to repair damage caused by a violent reboot.

When a filesystem is unmounted, the partition is marked as `clean`. By default, `e2fsck` will not check a filesystem marked `clean`. Instead, it will just print usage statistics, as shown in the following:

```
/dev/hdd2: clean, 11/789504 files, 104462/3145729 blocks
```

You can force `e2fsck` to check a filesystem by giving it the `-f` command line option, as shown in the following:

```
# e2fsck -f /dev/hdd2
e2fsck 1.10, 24-Apr-97 for EXT2 FS 0.5b, 95/08/09
Pass 1: Checking inodes, blocks, and sizes
Pass 2: Checking directory structure
Pass 3: Checking directory connectivity
Pass 4: Checking reference counts
Pass 5: Checking group summary information
/dev/hdd2: 11/789504 files (0.0% non-contiguous), 104462/3145729 blocks
```

As you can see, `e2fsck` goes through five separate phases while repairing a partition.

If `e2fsck` finds an error, it will print it out and ask you whether or not to repair it. You will usually want to say yes, unless you have some reason for leaving the drive unrepaired (you might want to run an external utility on the drive, for example).

Filesystems that were not cleanly unmounted will usually produce a large amount of errors, requiring a large amount of intervention. You can instruct `e2fsck` to attempt to automatically repair all errors by giving it the `-y` command line option, as shown in the following:

```
# e2fsck -y /dev/hdd2
```

Damaged Superblocks

As briefly explained before, the superblock contains various filesystem information. It is roughly equivalent to the FAT on old MSDOS filesystems.

Because this information is extremely vital, the `ext2` filesystem saves backups of the superblock. You can see a list of these blocks when you format the partition, and the bigger your partition is, the more backup superblocks you'll have.

If `e2fsck` says it can't find the superblock, you can tell it which backup superblock to use via the `-b` command line option, as shown in the following:

```
# e2fsck -b 8193 /dev/hdd2
```

If you saved the backup superblock list from the time when you formatted the drive, you can use any of those values at this time.

Once `e2fsck` is done, you may want to run it again—just to be sure.

Backups

Not too long ago, "UNIX Backups" were synonymous with "SCSI Tape Drives." This is no longer the case, especially not with Linux. Practically any PC hardware solution can work with Linux—SCSI tapes, IDE tapes, CD-Writers, Rewritable CD-ROMs, ZIP/JAZ drives, and far too many more to mention.

Linux support for most of the aforementioned devices can be achieved simply by compiling support for them into the kernel. CD-Writers will require additional software to create and write data to the CD-ROMs. Such software is freely available and comes with most distributions (quick pointers: look for `mkisofs`, `cdrecord`, `xcdroast`, and many more. Also, read the `CD-Writing-HOWTO`).

Naturally, you will need to know the UNIX device name for the device you intend to use for backups. The documentation that comes with the Linux kernel should provide this. Most of the obscure and outlandish devices you can use with Linux will probably have a `HOWTO` file—you might want to read the appropriate `HOWTO` file for your device.

The following sections concentrate on some of the built-in UNIX utilities that come with Linux—`cpio`, `dump/restore`, and `tar`.

cpio

The word `cpio` stands for *Copy In/Out*. That's simplistic, but that is precisely its function—it will copy files into or out of archives. It has three modes of operation:

- Create and archive
- Extract from an archive
- Passthrough mode

Create an Archive

In this mode, `cpio` will take a list of files and create an archive file containing them. The list of files is provided on `stdin`, so you have great flexibility.

For example, to create an archive of all the HTML files in the current directory, you would type the following:

```
# ls *.html | cpio -ov > archive.cpio
```

You use the `ls` command to generate the list of files you want to archive. The `o` option tells `cpio` that you are creating an archive, and the `v` causes verbose operation.

This command will create a file named `archive.cpio` in the current directory, which now contains all the HTML files that you passed to `cpio` using the `ls` command.

As useful as creating archives of your files is, you might want to back up your data to removable media. All you have to do is substitute your back up device's name for the filename. For example, to back up to the first floppy drive (drive A), type the following:

```
# ls *.html ¦ cpio -ov > /dev/fd0
```

Don't worry if your data takes up more space than a floppy disk, `cpio` will prompt you to change media, and then type in the device name again.

Extract from an Archive

To extract all files from the archive created above, type the following:

```
# cpio -iv < /dev/fd0
```

The `i` command tells `cpio` you are extracting files from the archive. Once again, the `v` option causes verbose operation.

You might want to check what files are in the archive. To do this, type the following:

```
# cpio -i --list < /dev/fd0
```

This will give you a listing similar to the `ls` command. If you supply the `v` option, the listing will contain more information, similar to the `ls -l` command.

Passthrough Mode

Although not a backup in the traditional sense, this mode is usually used to copy all files from one directory tree to another while maintaining file modes and permissions. This is useful, for example, if you are moving a filesystem to a larger hard drive and would like to copy all the files over to the new drive.

For example, assume the 400MB partition you have been using to house home directories (`/home`) is now no longer sufficient due to system growth. You have installed, partitioned, and formatted a 4GB filesystem to house it and mounted it on `/mnt`. Assuming you are currently in the `/home` directory, issuing the following command will copy all the information over to the new drive:

```
# find . -print ¦ cpio -pd /mnt
```

You can supply the `v` option in this mode, too, for verbose operation. This will cause `cpio` to print out the name of each file as it copies. If you want a progress report but don't want your screen cluttered with filenames, you can substitute the `v` command with an uppercase `V`. This will cause `cpio` to print out a dot (`.`) instead of a filename.

dump/restore

Of the three utilities covered in this chapter, dump is the one most suitable for large, multilevel backups. On many small systems, searching the crontab will reveal a dump command running at least once a week.

The dump command is very elaborate, and only its outline is presented here. You should read the manual page for more flexible backups (man dump).

dump supports incremental backups. This means that, over time, it will only back up files that are newer or have been modified recently. Because this functionality is somewhat complex, I will only mention that dump supports up to ten backup levels, starting at level zero which does a full back up. This level is used in the examples. The dump level must be provided on the dump command line.

For incremental backups to work, you must provide dump with the u option on the command line. This will tell dump to update its dump database, which usually resides in /etc/dumpdates.

The next command line option you will pass to dump is the f option—it is followed by the device name to which you are backing up. In the example, the first SCSI tape, /dev/nst0, will be used.

The last value you use is the filesystem you want to back up. dump will only work on filesystems. You need to use multiple dump processes for multiple filesystems. This is why you use the system's non-rewind tape device (/dev/nst0 rather than /dev/st0). This will allow you to put more than one filesystem on one tape—providing you have enough space on the media, of course. The /home filesystem will be used for the example.

So, putting it all together, to run a level 0 dump of the /home filesystem to the first SCSI tape, enter the following:

```
# dump 0uf /dev/nst0 /home
```

If dump runs out of space on the backup media, it will prompt you to change the media and continue.

The counterpart to dump is the restore utility. Again, you should refer to the manual page (man restore) for the more elaborate options.

The restore utility can be run with no other options other than giving it the device name to restore from using the f option, much like dump. However, you might want to also give it the v option, to prompt verbose operation, and the i option, to get into interactive mode, as shown in the following:

```
# restore ivf /dev/nst0
```

Interactive mode lets you interactively select which files to restore. While in interactive mode, you can move within the backed up filesystem as if you were in a real one—using commands such as ls, cd, and pwd. When you see a file or directory you would like restored, type

add <filename>

You may later change your mind by typing

delete <filename>

You can terminate the restore process by typing

quit

One you've selected all the files and directories you want, type

extract

This will initiate the restore process.

If your backup spans more than one media, restore will prompt you to enter other media as needed.

tar

The version of tar that comes with Linux, GNU tar, is superior to the plain UNIX version of tar in many ways, not the least of which is the ability to compress files it is archiving on-the-fly.

While widely used to create distribution files for software packages (now known as *tarballs*), tar is still used to back up to high-capacity media, such as tape drives.

As usual with UNIX utilities, especially the GNU version, tar has a incredibly huge amount of optional switches. Only a very short few of them are covered here, please refer to the manual page for more (man tar). The syntax you'll use for tar is

tar t¦x¦c [z][v]f tarfile list-of-files

You must supply one of the c, x, or t commands. They are used to create, extract or test, respectively.

The z option tells tar you're either creating or extracting from a compressed archive. Trying to extract from a compressed archive without providing the z option will cause tar to fail.

The v option will cause tar to operate in verbose mode. In this mode, it will print out a list of files while it is creating or extracting from an archive.

The f option is followed by the filename you are creating or the device name to which you are backing up.

For example, to create a tar file called /tmp/files.tar.gz containing all the files in the /usr/local/bin directory, type

```
# tar czvf /tmp/files.tar.gz /usr/local/bin
```

To check what files are contained in an uncompressed tar archive contained on a tape in the first SCSI tape drive, type

```
# tar tvf /dev/st0
```

To extract the files from the same archive, type

```
# tar xvf /dev/st0
```

Installing Software

As Linux has developed, software installation has become considerably easier. With most, if not all, modern distributions offering some sort of package management utilities, installing precompiled binary executable files has become practically painless. And with the ever growing popularity of tools such as GNU Autoconf, compiling software packages from source code is easy even for novice users.

There's also a lot more documentation available.

Using the rpm Program

The rpm program can be used to install, upgrade, or check the status of software. It can also provide information about uninstalled rpm files.

Querying an rpm Package

The first thing to know about rpm is how to check what packages are installed. You do this by using rpm's Query mode by using the -q option.

Typing

```
rpm -qa
```

will list all packages installed on your system. If you want to browse this list, you can pipe the output to the more command, as shown in the following:

```
# rpm -qa ¦ more
```

Or, you can use grep to look for specific packages, as shown in the following:

```
# rpm -qa ¦ grep apache
```

If you know the name of the package you're looking for, you can supply that to rpm:

```
# rpm -q basesystem
basesystem-4.9-2
```

This tells you that the basesystem package is installed (it should be on all Red Hat systems), and that the version you have is 4.9, build 2.

The Query mode has two more useful modes. The i subcommand, shown next, will print out information about the installed package:

```
# rpm -qi fileutils
```

The other mode, which you access by specifying the l subcommand shown next, will list all files owned by the package.

```
# rpm -ql fileutils
```

These last two modes can be run on an rpm file by adding the p subcommand, shown in the following:

```
# rpm -qip zsh-3.0.5-10.i386.rpm
```

Installing or Upgrading an rpm Package

The advantage of a package management system is that it won't let you install packages that depend on other packages you don't actually have installed. It will also not let you remove packages on which packages you are not removing depend.

The rpm Install mode is activated by supplying the -i switch. That is actually all it takes, along with the filename you are trying to install, as in the following:

```
# rpm -i zsh-3.0.5-10.i386.rpm
```

You might want some feedback on the installation process. In this case, type

```
# rpm -ivh zsh-3.0.5-10.i386.rpm
```

rpm will check its database before installing a package and will not install a package that is already there, even if you are trying to install a newer version. You have to specifically tell rpm you are upgrading a package. You do this by using the U switch, shown in the following:

```
# rpm -Uvh zsh-3.0.5-10.i386.rpm
```

Uninstalling an rpm Package

Removing an rpm package is straightforward:

```
# rpm -e zsh-3.0.5-10
```

Please refer to the "Querying an rpm package" section for instructions on how to locate an rpm package.

Overriding rpm

Sometimes rpm will refuse to let you install or remove a package. It will usually have good reasons—you might be trying to remove a package that will break other packages, or you may be trying to install a package that requires newer versions of packages you have. When this happens, rpm will tell you what you might be breaking or what other packages you need to upgrade or install.

You might want to override rpm's internal overprotectiveness. While installing, you can tell rpm to ignore inter-package dependencies by supplying the -nodeps switch, shown in the following:

```
# rpm -ivh —nodeps zgv-3.0-8.i386.rpm
```

You can do the same thing when removing software:

```
# rpm -e —nodeps zgv-3.0-8.i386.rpm
```

Installing Software Packages Manually

This section will give a brief overview of the process required to install a package downloaded as source code. Please note that the actual process of software development and compilation is extremely complicated, and while the process of installation from source-code packages is getting more and more standardized, this process might not work with all packages. This section also assumes you have installed the compilers and development options that came with your distribution.

Overview

Most software packages released to the Linux community rely on the GNU autoconf utilities to create a uniform installation process. These packages are usually distributed as a compressed tar file (a .tar.gz or .tgz file), referred to as a *tarball*. This file will contain the source code, and usually include some documentation—namely two files called README and INSTALL. These files will usually contain a more verbose version of this section, but some packages may have additional instructions. You should definitely read these files before moving to the next installation steps.

The tarball will also contain an executable shell script called configure. This file will attempt to configure the package for compilation on your machine. It will search the system for the libraries and header files it needs. The INSTALL and README files should tell you which you need to have installed and may tell you where to get them, too.

Once the configuration process is over, you can start the actual compilation process.

Here are some detailed, step-by-step instructions. These instructions assume you have already downloaded a tarball, which you'll call tarfile-1.0.tar.gz. You should have a directory designated specifically for source-code packages. Most people put this in /usr/local/src.

Why /usr/local?

By default, system-installed files go in the /usr directory. If you are using Red Hat's rpm package, it will also install into that directory. It is a common convention that packages you install manually go in the /usr/local directory tree so that you won't accidentally overwrite system-installed software. It is always a good idea to have a clear distinction between your software and the system's software.

Please note that most tarball packages will automatically install in /usr/local. You might want to make sure that the /usr/local/bin directory is in your search path.

Step 1: Untarring the Archive

Issue the following command to uncompress the tarball:

```
# tar xzvf tarfile-1.0.tar.gz
```

You will see a list of the files contained in the archive. Uncompressing tarballs usually creates a new directory containing those files, usually having a very similar name to the actual tarball file. In this case this would be tarfile-1.0. You now want to enter this directory by typing

```
# cd tarfile-1.0
# ls
```

You should examine the output from the ls command to make sure all the required files are there. Check for files named configure, README, and INSTALL. If the README and INSTALL files are present, read them now, as they may contain specific instructions.

Step 2: Running configure

On many UNIX systems, the current directory is not in the search path (this is done for security reasons). To run the configure script, type

```
# ./configure
```

The INSTALL file might give you a list of optional configuration switches. Common available options include exclusion or inclusion of specific packages and pointing to installation directories.

If the configure script exits without errors, you are ready to move on to the next step. If you did get an error, configure will usually tell you what the problem is. You may be required to upgrade certain packages.

If you run into any specific problems, you should always refer to the documentation that came with the package.

Step 3: Compiling the Source Code

Unless the documentation provided says otherwise, you can start the compilation process by simply typing

```
# make
```

Compiling software can take a long time and can output a large variety of messages. Error messages are usually easy to spot because they are accompanied by many asterisks and will terminate the compilation process. It would be impossible to anticipate all the errors you might get during compiling; again, please refer to the documentation.

You might see a lot of "Warning" messages while compiling. As a rule of thumb, these can be ignored.

Step 4: Installing

If the compilation went well, you can type

```
# make install
```

This will install the package on your system, usually to the /usr/local/ directory tree.

You might want to run the installation script in test mode, just to see if everything is going to go where you thought it would. To do this, type the following:

```
# make -n install
```

Step 5: Updating the System

In many cases, step 4 is the end of the installation process. However, you might need to perform some additional actions to make the system aware of the new installation. Don't worry, you will not need to reboot.

Binary Files

If you have installed binary program files and are now trying to run them, the system may be unable to find them. This may be because the installation directory is not in your search-path, or because some shells cache the filesystem information for faster access.

The solution for the first problem is to add the directory to your search-path. If you are using the bash shell, type the following:

```
# export PATH=$PATH:/usr/local/bin
```

If you are using a C-shell variant (such as csh or tcsh), you can type

```
# rehash
```

to reread the filesystem cache. If all else fails, you can always type in the full path.

Libraries

You will definitely have to notify the system about new libraries.

You might need to update the system's main library search paths. These are contained in the file /etc/ld.conf.so. Be very careful with this file—damaging it could cause your entire system to become unusable.

Some systems may not have the /usr/local/lib path in this file. This is a common cause to library failure. You can use the cat command to check the content of the file, as shown in the following:

```
# cat /etc/ld.so.conf
```

If the required path is not in the file, add it using your favorite text editor.

If the directory is in the file (or if you've just added it), update the library information using the following command:

```
# ldconfig -v
```

This will rebuild the library cache in the system's memory. The -v option will cause it to visibly show you a list of all the libraries it finds on your system, so you can check to see the newly installed ones are actually loaded.

Summary

It is impossible to cover every aspect of installing software from source code. As mentioned before, the documentation that came with the software should be your primary resource. It may contain pointers to Web sites, mailing lists, or other information that could be extremely useful in installing that particular piece of software.

Over the past few years, the process of source-code installation has become a lot easier, mainly thanks to the GNU autoconf utilities. Unless you are trying to install a non-standard type of package, you should have a (relatively) easy time.

System Accounting and Logging

Introduction

This chapter contains information on how to check your system's usage. This includes

- Per-user usage information
- The system logs
- Quotas
- Monitoring utilities

This chapter will concentrate mainly on checking what's going on, rather than modifying system configuration.

System Accounting Functions

Because Linux is a multiuser, multitasking system, you will probably need to be able to check who is logged on and what processes are running.

Monitoring Currently Logged In Users

Unless specifically configured not to, the system will keep a log of user activity. This lets you check when a user logged in or out, how long he or she was logged in for, where he or she logged in from, his or her total login time, and so on. The system will save this information in a file called utmp that resides in the system log directory, which is usually either /var/log or /var/adm.

There are several utilities for monitoring currently logged in users.

who

The simplest way of checking who is currently online is the who command. It will tell you who is logged on, what tty they are using, and when they logged in:

```
$ who
paul      tty2     Jun 24 21:11
george    tty3     Jun 24 21:12
dusty     tty4     Jun 24 21:12
john      ttyp5    Jun 24 21:46
```

w

The w command provides more detailed information than who. It will provide system information in addition to user information, and it will tell you what programs the users are running.

The first line of the output contains information about the system: current time, uptime information, number of users, and system load.

The user information section will tell you who is logged on, what tty they are using, where they logged in from, when they logged in, how long they have been idle, how much CPU time they are using, and what process they currently have controlling their tty:

```
 9:54pm  up 3 days,  8:58, 4 users,  load average: 0.05, 0.06, 0.07
USER      TTY      FROM          LOGIN@   IDLE    JCPU    PCPU   WHAT
paul      tty2                   9:11pm 42:03    0.10s   0.10s  -bash
george    tty3                   9:12pm 37.00s   0.13s   0.02s  pine
dusty     tty4                   9:12pm 41:01    0.12s   0.12s  -bash
john      ttyp5    localhost     9:46pm  0.00s   0.16s   0.06s  w
```

finger

The finger command can provide a lot of useful information about users on your system and can also check information on remote servers. Typing finger with no command-line arguments will provide a list of people currently logged on. It will show their login names, their real names, what tty they are using, how long they've been idle, and the date and time they logged in. If the users were created with extended information, such as office number, finger will show this, too:

```
$ finger
Login     Name                 Tty  Idle  Login Time    Office     Office Phone
dusty     Dustin Stein         4          Jun 24 21:12
george    George C. Sheppard   3          Jun 24 21:12
john      John                 p5         Jun 24 21:10
paul      Paul Smith           2    1     Jun 24 21:11  D-211      288
```

You can also use finger to get information about a specific user. It will tell you the user's full name, home directory, and default shell.

It will give you information about the user's current login session, or, if the user isn't logged in, it will tell you when the last login session was.

It will also tell you if the user has mail or not (it will only check for mail on the local server).

If the user has created a `.plan` file in his or her home directory, its content will be displayed.

```
$ finger george
Login: george                          Name: George C. Sheppard
Directory: /home/george                Shell: /bin/bash
On since Thu Jun 24 21:12 (CDT) on tty3   18 minutes 34 seconds idle
No mail.
No Plan.
```

From a remote machine, you must supply a hostname. For example, to get the same output from a remote machine, type the following:

```
$ finger george@mymachine.mydomain.com
```

Note that the remote `finger` service is usually turned off for security reasons.

By default, `finger` will search for the name you provide in the `login` field and in the `real name` field. If `finger` finds more than one match, it will display the information for all the users it has found. If you know the exact username, you can restrict `finger` to the `login` field only by supplying the `-m` command-line option. On systems with many users, this will be considerably faster.

```
$ finger -m john
```

Monitoring Past System Logins

Linux will also maintain a log of all logins to the system, including login time, date, and duration. This information is saved in the `wtmp` file, which also resides in the system's logging directory, normally `/var/log` or `/var/adm`.

Please note that some systems, notably Red Hat systems, will rotate this log every few days, and will delete old logs. If you want to save a long history of system usage, you should check your system's log rotation utilities (on Red Hat systems, check in `/etc/logrotate.conf` and `/etc/logrotate.d/`).

last

The `last` command will give you a listing of every login to the system since the last time the log file was rotated. It will show the time, date, and duration of the login, as well as the `tty` used and where the user logged in from:

```
$ last john
john      ttyp3      localhost        Tue Jun 29 19:31    still logged in
john      tty3                        Tue Jun 29 19:23 - 19:23   (00:00)
john      ttyp3      localhost        Tue Jun 29 19:22 - 19:22   (00:00)
john      ttyp3      localhost        Tue Jun 29 19:22 - 19:22   (00:00)
john      ttyp5      localhost        Thu Jun 24 21:46 - 01:57   (04:11)
john      ttyp5      localhost        Thu Jun 24 21:10 - 21:33   (00:22)

wtmp begins Sat Jun 12 12:08:19 1999
```

Running last without a username will show logins by all users. If your system is heavily used or your log file is not getting rotated, the resulting list can be huge.

ac

The ac command can produce a wide variety of user accounting information. Basically, it provides total login times, but it can provide those on a per-user, per-day, or system total basis. Running ac with no parameters will give you the total amount of time used on the system, in hours, by all users:

```
$ ac
        total    2520.45
```

You may provide ac with a username to get information for that user:

```
$ ac john
        total       2.95
```

Or, you can request a day-by-day listing for that user:

```
ac -d john
Jun 24  total       2.61
Today   total       0.35
```

Or you can tell ac to give you a day-by-day listing for each user individually:

```
$ ac -p -d
```

Because the results from this command can be long, they are not included here.

Configuring System Quotas

On large, multiuser systems, you might want to restrict the amount of disk space each user can take up. Remember, no matter how much disk space you have, there's more than enough data out there to fill it up.

This is where quotas come in. You can limit the amount of space available on each filesystem on a per-user or per-group basis. You can implement soft and hard limits, and you can set a grace period.

Setting Up Quotas

A lot of distributions will automatically install all components required to use quotas. You can use this section as a checklist.

Making Sure Your System Is Ready

You will need to have Quota Support compiled into the kernel for quotas to work. The standard kernel in nearly every distribution will already contain quota support, but if you are compiling your own kernel, answer Yes to Quota support (CONFIG_QUOTA) when configuring.

You will also need to have several utilities installed to implement quotas. These utilities are usually available with your distribution. If your distribution uses rpm, you can check for their existence by typing the following:

```
# rpm -qa ¦ grep quota
```

Preparing the Filesystem

If you want to enforce quotas on a particular filesystem, you must first change its entry in the /etc/fstab file to include quota options. You must specify whether you are going to be using user quotas, group quotas, or both. For example, if the current entry is

```
/dev/hdd2    /home    ext2    defaults    1 1
```

you would have to modify the defaults parameter to

```
/dev/hdd2    /home    ext2    usrquota,grpquota    1 1
```

This will implement both user and group quotas. You can, of course, omit either one.

You must then create the quota database files. These files reside in the top-level of the filesystem. They are not readable by humans, but you only need to create empty files. These files should be owned by the Superuser and are not accessible by any other user.

There are two separate files for group and user quotas; you only need to create the ones you will be using:

```
# touch /home/quota.group
# touch /home/quota.user
# chmod 600 /home/quota.group /home/quota.user
```

Adding Quota Support to the System Initialization Process

You will want the system to turn quotas on and check for users who are over their quotas while booting. To do this, you need to add several commands to the system's initialization process.

Depending on your distribution, you may already have these commands. For example, the Red Hat initialization process will automatically check whether or not quotas are installed, and will perform the required instructions if they are.

The commands you will want in your initialization process are

```
quotacheck -avug
```

and

```
quotaon -avug
```

Please see the following sections for an explanation of these commands, and Chapter 9, "Administrative Tasks," for instructions on modifying the init process, should you need to do that.

If you have just compiled a new kernel, you should reboot your system for the changes to take effect. Otherwise, you can just run these commands manually.

Managing Quotas—the Quota Utilities

There are several utilities that allow you to manage quotas. They will let you enable or disable quotas, check how much disk space users are occupying, and edit individual quota settings. There is also a utility that users can use to check their own quota.

quotaon/quotaoff

These programs will, respectively, enable or disable quotas for a given filesystem. You must run quotaon during the init process for quotas to take effect. If you choose to disable them later on, you can use quotaoff.

By default, these programs will only affect user quotas. You must tell them to affect group quotas by supplying the -g option.

You can enable or disable quotas for all filesystems by supplying the -a option, rather than supplying each filesystem individually.

To turn on all group and user quotas for all filesystems that have quotas enabled, type the following:

```
# quotaon -aug
```

You can also supply the -v option, which will cause a more verbose operation.

quotacheck

This program should also be run during the init process. It goes through the filesystems and actually checks how much space users are occupying. If this program is not run, quotas will not be updated.

This program can be told to check user or group quotas by selecting the -u and -g options. The -v option will cause verbose operation, and the -a option will cause the program to check all quota-enabled filesystems. If you do not specify the -a option, you must supply the filesystem name.

quota

This program allows users to check how much of their quota they are using. It will tell the user how many blocks are in use, and what their soft and hard limits are:

```
$ quota
Disk quotas for user john (uid 507):
    Filesystem blocks  quota  limit  grace  files  quota  limit grace
     /dev/hdd2   242*    100    300   none      2      0      0
```

This user is using 242 blocks (1 block = 1 KB) out of a maximum of 300. His or her soft limit, however, is 100 blocks, so he or she is being warned.

The Superuser can use the quota command to check on other users' quotas:

```
# quota -u john
```

edquota

This command is used to set users' quotas. It is only available to the Superuser.

As mentioned previously, the quota database files are not readable by humans. This utility will extract the quota definitions for the user from this file and allow you to edit them using the default editor. Running

```
# edquota -u john
```

will bring up the following text:

```
Quotas for user john:
/dev/hdd2: blocks in use: 242, limits (soft = 100, hard = 300)
        inodes in use: 2, limits (soft = 0, hard = 0)
```

You should only edit the soft and hard limit values; anything else will either be ignored or cause an error (in effect, that will be ignored, too). Note that a value of 0 means no limits will be imposed.

Logging Features

On those rare occasions where something happens while you're away from your machine, you can check the system logs to see what happened.

syslogd

The system logger, syslog, is a daemon via which other programs can save their own logging information. Rather than having every program try and save its own log in its own format in various locations, syslog can accept this information from them and save it in a pre-designated area. This is also a way of providing non-privileged processes to write logging information to a location that is only accessible by the Superuser.

The syslog daemon can also send or accept logging information to or from remote hosts. This means you can have one central syslog file for hundreds of servers and workstations.

Please note that while syslog is available to all programs, some programs will prefer to use their own native log format. On most systems, you can expect syslog to contain information from the kernel, FTP servers, DNS, syslog itself, and more.

Configuring syslogd

When a program wants to save its logging information, it must supply syslog with its name and with a logging level. Logging levels include debug, info, notice, warning, err, crit, alert, and emerg. Programs should use the log level most appropriate for the entry they are sending.

The syslog daemon can sort log messages into separate files and locations based on these two parameters. For example, you can cause all info level messages to be saved to a file named info.

The /etc/syslog.conf file contains these instructions. It is usually well commented. As an example, a line in this file might look like the following:

```
*.info                          /var/log/info.log
```

This will cause all info messages to go into /var/log/info.log.

Another line commonly found in syslog configuration files is

```
kern.*;*.emerg                  /dev/console
```

This will cause all kernel messages and all emergency messages to be displayed on the system console.

Note: With older versions of syslogs, it was necessary to use tabs, not spaces, to separate entries in this file.

Reading syslog Files

The location and names of the default system log files is fairly standard. On Red Hat systems, the files will be in the /var/log/ directory, and the main file will be called messages. On other systems, /var/adm/ may be the directory name, and the system log file will be named syslog. You should check both of these directories to see in which files your system keeps the log files. If you can't find what you're looking for, check your system's /etc/syslog.conf file.

The system logs are saved in plain text format, so they are readable by humans. This means that writing programs that will search through or manipulate your log files is easier.

It also means that you can use any text editor or paging utility to view log files. For example, if all you need is to dump the content of a log file to the screen, type the following:

```
# cat /var/adm/syslog
```

However, because system logs can become very large in a very short time, you may want to load them into your favorite text editor and use its Search function.

You could also use a paging utility such as more or less; paging utilities are usually smaller and take up less resources than a full-fledged text editor.

```
# less -MM /var/log/messages
```

A simple way to filter specific information out of a log file is to use the grep command. For example, if you want to see only the entries pertaining to your FTP server, you can type the following:

```
# grep ftpd /var/log/messages ¦ less
```

Monitoring Log Files in Progress

It is sometimes useful to see the data entering the log file as it happens. For example, you might be running a program that sends its debugging information to syslog or are trying to track down illegal attempts to enter your system.

To get continuous output from a text file, type the following:

```
# tail -f /var/log/messages
```

This will continue to print out new lines that get added to the file until you send the break signal (usually by pressing Ctrl+C).

System Load and Current Processes

High system load can cause slower operation. This section explains how to check what the current system load is, as well as finding out the cause to high system loads.

Load Average

I will be referring to the "load average" as the means to determining system load. This is actually the average number or processes that had to wait for the CPU in a given amount of time. Normal system loads mean the load average is lower than one (1).

Although it is possible for a relatively low load average to bring a system down to its knees, please note that it is possible for the load average to soar to great heights without causing a noticeable performance degradation.

The uptime Command

The output of uptime is the same as the first line of the w command. It will tell you the current time, the amount of time the system has been up, how many users are logged on, and the load average for the past 1, 5, and 15 minutes.

```
# uptime
 9:03pm  up  1:59,  21 users,  load average: 0.00, 0.04, 0.07
```

The top Command

top will provide a live view of the most CPU intensive processes currently running on the system. It will also tell you how many processes are running and will provide memory and CPU statistics and the load average.

```
 9:09pm  up  2:04,  21 users,  load average: 0.61, 0.18, 0.10
```

```
66 processes: 59 sleeping, 7 running, 0 zombie, 0 stopped
CPU states: 90.5% user,  9.3% system,  0.0% nice,  0.3% idle
Mem:  127848K av, 121232K used,   6616K free, 41332K shrd,   7256K buff
Swap: 130748K av,    768K used, 129980K free              65176K cached

  PID USER     PRI  NI  SIZE  RSS SHARE STAT  LIB %CPU %MEM   TIME COMMAND
```

The ps Command

Another way of getting a list of running processes is the ps command.

Because this is another extremely complex command, I will only concentrate on some common uses. You should refer to the ps manual page (man ps) for more information.

Typing ps by itself will give you a list of processes you are running:

```
$ ps
PID TTY STAT TIME COMMAND
 5723  p3 S    0:00 -bash
 5734  p3 R    0:00 ps
```

For a more detailed listing, use the u option:

```
$ ps u
USER      PID %CPU %MEM  SIZE   RSS TTY STAT START   TIME COMMAND
john     5723  0.0  0.6  1196   784 p3 S    21:22  0:00 -bash
john     6345  0.0  0.3   868   508 p3 R    21:41  0:00 ps u
```

This option causes ps to also display the username associated with each process. This is useful if you ask ps to display a list of all running processes:

```
$ ps au
```

By default, ps will only display processes associated with a tty. You can override this by using the x option:

```
$ ps aux
```

ps will also truncate each entry so it will fit on one line. You can override this by providing the w option. Each w on the command line enables the output to be one line longer. The following is a good command to view all processes currently running:

```
$ ps auxwww ¦ less
```

Summary

Without the ability to monitor and log, multitasking and multiuser systems would become almost unusable. From solving obscure email errors that only occur at midnight to detecting attempts to crack your system, the system logs and accounting features are always there to help—make sure you keep them well-maintained.

On Your Own

You might want to run some of the programs and utilities mentioned in this chapter to get more familiar with their options and output. For example, look at all the different amounts of output generated by the following:

```
# ps
# ps a
# ps ax
# ps awux
# ps awwwwux
```

Try using the w, who, and finger commands, and look at the different information each program provides.

Try running top and then running CPU-intensive programs and look at the output.

Using the Command Line Shell

In Linux, a shell program is one that displays prompts on the screen and waits for input from the keyboard. Once it gets the input, it obeys the entered command. When the command has been completed, the shell prompts and waits for another.

Linux has, as its default shell, the `bash` shell. The `bash` shell is compatible with the original UNIX shell, the Bourne shell, but has some very useful extensions. In fact, `bash` is an acronym for Bourne-again shell. This chapter describes the syntax and commands that are a part of the `bash` shell. Chapter 12, "Introduction to Shell Programming," describes how to use these and other commands to write shell scripts.

It probably won't surprise you that there is more than one Linux shell from which to choose. They basically all do the same things, but the syntax and some of the commands differ from one to the other. Linux includes `ash` which is a version of the standard UNIX System V Bourne shell called `sh`. There is also `tcsh` which is an implementation of the Berkeley UNIX C shell `csh`—it has C-like syntax, filename completion, and command-line editing.

There is also a special purpose shell used for remote computing. When started, `rsh` is given the name of remote host. By redirecting the input and output, commands can be executed on the remote host just as they would be on the local machine.

Command Line Basics

The shell program displays a prompt. This prompt can be almost anything from a single character to several lines of information. The contents of the prompt are determined by the environment variables PS1 and PS2. The user enters the command in response to the prompt, and the shell obeys the command.

The first item on every command line is one of three things: the name of an executable program, the name of a script file holding further commands, or the name of a command built into the shell. More often than not, you will not know which is which—you just type in a command and the job gets done. For example, to get a list of the users currently logged in, type `who`.

This will execute the program `/bin/who`. The output of the program will look something like the following:

```
root        tty1      Apr  9 11:18
arthur      tty2      Apr  9 15:10
```

The `who` utility simply displays some lines of text and quits. Each line is the name of a currently active login. There are hundreds of these small utilities in Linux that perform this sort of simple task, and they can be hooked together in ways that perform complex tasks.

It is possible to put several commands on one line by separating them with semicolons. The following is an example of using two:

```
date; who
```

The `date` command runs and, when it has finished, the `who` command runs. The output looks like the following:

```
Fri Apr  9 16:22:07 AKDT 1999
root        tty1      Apr  9 11:18
arthur      tty2      Apr  9 15:10
```

Not everything is as simple as `date` and `who`—most commands have arguments that go with them. For example, to copy a file named `fromound` to a file and `tomound`, the command would be

```
cp fromound tomound
```

Not all commands are quick and simple. It is possible to enter commands that run long enough that you would rather not wait for them to finish. You don't have to. For example, if the file named `rawlist` has thousands of lines of text, and you want to sort them into a file named `sortedlist`, you could do it with the following command:

```
sort -o sortedlist rawlist &
```

The `-o` on the command line means that the name following it is to be the name of the output file. The next name—the one with no option letter preceding it—is the input file. At the end of the command line, there is an ampersand. This tells the shell that the sort routine should be spun off as a background process and not interfere with what you are doing. Every process in Linux is assigned a number, and your background process is no exception. The number is displayed looking something like the following:

```
[1] 856
```

This is job number 1 with a program ID of 856. The job is your local number (the count always starts at one) and the program ID is the system-wide number of the process.

When the background command completes its execution, you will be notified with a line that looks like the following:

```
[1]+  Done        sort -o sortedlist rawlist
```

Redirection and Pipes

Every Linux program has three data streams open when it starts running. They are standard input, standard output, and standard error. By default, standard input is the keyboard and the two outputs are the display, but the shell knows how to redirect both incoming and outgoing data. It turns out that this relatively simple mechanism is one of the most flexible and capable tools at your fingertips. The set of redirection commands are listed in Table 11.1.

Table 11.1   The Shell Redirection Syntax

Syntax	Means
>file	Standard out is written to the named file.
>>file	Standard out is appended to the named file.
<file	Standard in is read from the named file.
p1 ¦ p2	The standard out of p1 is redirected to the standard input of p2.
n>file	The output from data stream number n is written to the named file.
n>>file	The output from data stream number n is appended to the named file.
n>&m	The output from data stream number n is redirected to the same place as data stream number m.

A right bracket is used to redirect standard output to a file. For example,

```
ls >namelist
```

will list the names of the files and directories found in the current directory and, instead of displaying them on the display, will write them to a file named namelist. A new file is created—if there is already a file by that name, it will be overwritten. This output redirection can be used with any command that displays text onscreen.

A variation on this is

```
ls >>namelist
```

This command does everything the same as the previous example except that if the file already exists, the new information is appended to the end of it.

The input can also be redirected. It is a matter of using the left bracket shown in the following:

```
mail harvey <lettertext
```

The contents of the file `lettertext` will be emailed to the user named `harvey`. The result is the same as if you had typed it in from the keyboard.

Using a command with standard output redirected has a disadvantage. An error message sent to the display via standard output would go to the redirected target instead of going to the display, so another output stream is available to be used for error messages. But even it can be redirected, as shown in the following:

```
ls -j 2>errorfile
```

There is no `-j` option for `ls`, so an error message is produced and written to the file `errorfile`. The number 2 in front of the right bracket tells the shell that the redirection is to be done from standard error instead of standard out. You can redirect them both at once, as in the following:

```
make >mlist 2>merror
```

This command will run the `make` utility, have the listing for the actions it takes written to a file named `mlist`, and have any error messages written to a file named `merror`.

> **Note:** Every Linux program opens at least three files, and every file opened is assigned a number. The first one opened is the standard input, so it is always number 0. The second one opened is standard output, so it is always number 1. The third one is standard error, which is always number 2. Programs can open other files. Each one is assigned the next available number, and they can all be redirected by using their numbers. Of course, you will need to know the program well enough to know what file numbers are used.

There is a special construct that will redirect the output from both standard out and standard error into the same file. This can be useful when there is a lot of data because, with the error messages included with the data, you can get a better idea of the cause of the error. This command will mix the two outputs:

```
make >makelist 2>&1
```

Standard out from `make` is redirected to a file named `makelist`, and standard error is redirected to wherever standard out goes.

The ability to pass the standard output from one command into the standard input of another can be used to build a single-line command that does some very nice things.

This technique is known as a *pipe* because it serves as a connection from one application to another. The following is an example:

```
ls -l /bin ¦ grep sh
```

The ls command with the -l option lists the names—and other information—of the files in the /bin directory. The vertical bar redirects the standard output from ls into the standard input of grep. The grep command omits any line of text that does not contain the letters sh. The resulting output looks like the following:

```
-rwxr-xr-x    1 root       root           62660 Aug 28  1998 ash*
-rwxr-xr-x    1 root       root          153752 Aug 28  1998 ash.static*
-rwxr-xr-x    1 root       root          353944 Oct 12 15:23 bash*
lrwxrwxrwx    1 root       root               3 Feb  4 05:10 bsh -> ash*
lrwxrwxrwx    1 root       root               4 Feb  4 05:14 csh -> tcsh*
lrwxrwxrwx    1 root       root               4 Feb  4 05:10 sh -> bash*
-rwxr-xr-x    1 root       root          262756 Oct  2  1998 tcsh*
```

As it turns out, only the shell programs in the /bin directory have sh in them, so only information about the shell programs is listed.

Note: There is some information that can be garnered from this output. There is a right-pointing arrow that indicates which shell names are simply aliases of other shells. This kind of entry is part of the Linux file system and is called a *symbolic link*. This kind of link can be used to assign an alias to any file in any directory.

There is no need to stop with a single pipe on the command line. What follows is an example that uses ls and grep to select files that have "to" in their names, and displays the list one page at a time:

```
ls -l /usr/bin ¦ grep "to" ¦ more
```

Depending on which Linux options you have installed, there can be a lot of files in /usr/bin with "to" in their names because of a number of graphics conversion utilities (like giftopnm and pnmtotiff). There may be so many files that they cannot all be displayed on one screen. Adding another pipe and sending the output of grep into more allows you to view the list one screen at a time.

Any program can be written to use standard I/O and allow redirection and piping, but not all programs do. For example, the file command used to examine the contents of a file determines its type. The command will accept a list of filenames from the command line, as shown in the following:

```
file mmo*
```

However, the file command will not accept the filenames through a pipe, as in the following:

```
ls ¦ file          *** Wrong ***
```

Environment Variables

The shell has the ability to store data. The stored data takes the form of two strings: one is the key, and the other is the value associated with it. These are called the *environment variables* because they are used by the shell, and by other programs, to do things like locating files and determining modes of operation.

Because the environment controls the way programs operate, you need to have some control over the setting and clearing of environment variables. For example, you can use this to set a variable named DATAFILE to the location of a file:

```
DATAFILE=/home/pxlim/belulist
```

The value of the environment variable can be viewed with the following:

```
echo $DATAFILE
```

This will set the environment variable only for the current shell—any shells that are started by this one will not have this variable set, unless it is exported with the following:

```
export DATAFILE
```

Once a variable name is exported, it will be inherited by all child processes and their child processes.

There is another situation that is almost the opposite of exporting a variable. You can *source* a file and have it execute its commands just as if it were inline in the current shell. Say, for example, you have a file named baludefs that contains a set of environment variable definitions, and you want them to be defined in the current shell. Enter the following command:

```
source baludefs
```

There is a very odd little synonym for source. The same thing can be done with a period, like the following:

```
. baludefs
```

Sourcing a file will affect more than just the environment variables—it actually executes the file as a shell script, it just does so without spawning a new shell. To see instances of this being used, take a look in the setup files in your home directory. In particular, the .bashrc file commonly sources /etc/bashrc if it exists.

The env and the set commands can be used to display all of the environment variables currently set in your shell. The env command displays the environment variables that were defined in the startup files when the shell was first started, along with any that have been set on the command line. The set command shows all the environment variables, including the ones set internally by the shell itself. Table 11.2 contains a description of the environment variables that are always set by the shell.

Table 11.2   The Environment Variables Set by the Shell

Variable Name	Description
BASH	The full pathname used to invoke this shell.
BASH_VERSION	The version number of the shell.
EUID	The effective user ID of the current user.
HISTCMD	The number, or index, of the current command in the history list.
HOSTTYPE	A unique identifier of the kind of machine on which the shell is running.
LINENO	A counter of the number of command lines entered. The first is number 1.
OLDPWD	The complete path of the previous working directory.
OPTARG	The built-in command optarg stores the index of the last argument that was processed.
OPTIND	The built-in command optarg stores the index of the next argument to be processed.
OSTYPE	The name of the operating system.
PPID	The process ID of this shell's parent process.
PWD	The complete path of the current working directory.
RANDOM	A random number. It changes each time you read it.
REPLY	By default, the read command stores input here.
SECONDS	The number of seconds since the shell was invoked.
SHLVL	The level number of the current shell. The login shell is always 1. A child shell will be 2, its child will be 3, and so on.
UID	The user ID of the current user.

Table 11.3 contains a list of environment variables the shell uses to direct its own actions. It is not required to set all of these, because the shell itself sets default values for the ones that are necessary. You can use these environment variables to customize the shell.

Table 11.3   Environment Variables Used by the Shell

Variable Name	Description
CDPATH	If a relative filename is used on the cd command, it will look in each directory in the colon-separated list to find the requested directory.
ENV	The full pathname of a file to be sourced by the shell whenever the shell is to execute a script. -
FCEDIT	The name of the editor for the fc command.
FIGNORE	A colon-separated list of filename extensions to be ignored when doing filename completion.
HISTFILE	The name of the file containing the history. (See the "HISTORY" section that follows.) The default is .bash_history in the user's home directory.
HISTFILESIZE	The maximum number of lines allowed in the history file. The default is 500.
HISTSIZE	The number of commands to remember. The default is 1000. (See the "HISTORY" section that follows.)
HOME	The home directory of the current user.
IFS	The internal file separator. The character or characters used to separate items on the command line. The default is <space><tab><newline>.
IGNOREEOF	The number of EOF (Ctl+D) characters that must be received by the shell before the shell terminates. The default is 1.
INPUTRC	The filename for the readline startup file. The default is .inputrc in the home directory.
MAIL	The name of a file. If MAILCHECK is not set, the user is notified whenever mail arrives in the file.
MAIL_WARNING	If this variable exists, the user is notified of any attempt to read a mail message that has already been read.
MAILPATH	A colon-separated list of pathnames to be checked for mail.
noclobber	If set, the shell will not overwrite an existing file when doing output redirection.
notify	If set, terminated background jobs are reported immediately instead of just before the next prompt.
OPTERR	If set to 1, error message generated by getops are displayed. The default is 1.

Variable Name	Description
PATH	The list of directories the shell uses to locate executable files named on the command line (see the "PATH" section that follows).
PROMPT_COMMAND	If set, this is a command that is executed prior to the prompt being displayed.
PS1	The text of the prompt string (see the "PS" section later in this chapter).
PS2	The text of the secondary prompt string (see "PS" section later in this chapter).
PS3	The text of the prompt for the select command.
PS4	The text of the prompt displayed during an execution trace.
TMOUT	If greater than zero, it is the number of seconds the shell will wait for user input after issuing a prompt. A timeout will cause the shell to terminate.

PATH

The PATH environment variable contains an ordered list of directory names. The names are separated by colons. The following is an example:

```
PATH=/sbin:/bin/::/usr/sbin:/usr/bin:/usr/X11R6/bin
```

Whenever a command is entered on the command line, each of these directories is searched until an executable file with the same name as the command is located. The directories are searched from left to right—in the previous example, the search would start in /sbin and, if not found, move on to /bin, and so on.

It is fairly common to add a new directory to the list of directories already defined. To add the new directory as the last one on the right, do the following:

```
PATH=$PATH:/home/newdir
```

To add it on the left and have it become the first directory searched, do the following:

```
PATH=/home/newdir:$PATH
```

It is possible to set up the PATH variable to also check the current local directory. The current directory is specified as a single dot, as shown in the following:

```
PATH=/usr/bin:/bin:.:/home/fred/bin
```

In this example, the shell will search /usr/bin and /bin, and then will search the current directory, before moving on to /home/fred/bin. If the same program resides in the current directory, as in /home/fred/bin, only the one in the current directory will be found.

> **Note:** If you are worried about security, you want to avoid the dot in the pathname. In particular, you want to make sure it isn't there for any of the superuser logins. This leaves the system vulnerable to a Trojan horse attack. Entering a command could execute a Trojan horse program in the current directory instead of the expected one in, say, /usr/bin. The program has root permission and could then do anything—like add a new user to /etc/passwd.

PS

The environment variables PS1 and PS2 contain the text of the prompt displayed to the user by the shell. PS1 is the primary prompt—it requests that the user start a new command. PS2 is the secondary prompt—it shows up on continuation lines of commands that are longer than one line.

These prompts contain more than just simple strings. Table 11.4 shows the special characters that can be used to construct informational prompts. Each of these characters will simply show up as itself unless it is preceded by a backslash.

Table 11.4   The Special Characters Used to Define Prompts

Character	Description
\d	The date in text format, as in "Tue Apr 13."
\h	The hostname.
\n	Start a new line.
\nnn	The character corresponding to the octal value nnn.
\s	The name of the shell program.
\t	The current time in HH:MM:SS format.
\u	The name of the current user.
\w	The pathname of current working directory.
\W	The simple name of the current working directory.
\!	The history number of this command.
\#	The command number of this command.
\$	If the effective UID is 0, a # character is displayed, otherwise a $ is displayed.

Character	Description
\ [	The start of a sequence of non-printable characters. It could be a terminal control sequence embedded in the prompt.
\ ]	The end of a sequence of non-printable characters.
\ \	A literal backslash character.

HISTORY

When the shell is running in its interactive mode, a list of the most recent commands are all available for execution. The environment variable, HISTSIZE, specifies the number of commands to be held in the history file. The file, normally in the home directory of the user, is named based on the environment variable HISTFILE.

Whenever the interactive shell first starts running, the history is initialized from the file. That is, many of the commands you issued during your last session (or a parallel session in another window) are available to you in this session.

Enter the built-in command history from the command line, and the shell lists its entire command history. You will see a numbered list of commands. If you have had a few sessions, the numbers will go beyond the maximum allowed (usually 1000) because the numbers are not reused—that is, command number 842 will remain number 842 as long as it is in the file. If you take a look at the top of the list (by piping history through more) you will notice that some of the older commands have been deleted.

There is more than one way to use the history information. The simplest and most direct method is probably to use the up-arrow key to move up through the list of commands and, once you have found the one to be repeated, just press return. This can be very handy instead of retyping a command line that is long and cumbersome.

It happens quite often that a command is entered and there is something wrong with the format—maybe a space was omitted or the wrong flag was used. You can retrieve the command, edit it, and submit the corrected version. With the bash shell, you can use the up arrow to move back through the previous commands to find the one you want to use again. You can either press Enter to resubmit it unchanged, or you can edit it on the line.

If you using a shell that doesn't include command history or, for some reason, you are unable to use the arrow keys, there is another approach. The built-in command fc can be used to directly edit and repair the most recently entered command. Entering fc on the command line will cause the command to appear as text in a text editor, so any corrections you want to make can be done easily. When you exit from the editor, the new command is issued.

There are still other ways to get at the history commands, as shown in Table 11.5. You may notice that there is more than one way to do most things. That is because personal preferences vary from person to person.

Table 11.5   Methods of Accessing the Command History

Command	Action
Arrow Keys	The up and down arrow keys can be used to move back and forth through the command history. Each previously entered command line is displayed and can be executed by pressing the return key.
fc	The previous command will be loaded into a text editor to be modified. When you exit the editor, the command will execute.
!string	Locates the most recent command starting with the string. For example, if you entered the find command with a complete set of arguments and you want to do it again, just enter !find. The shell will find the most recent invocation of find and use the same set of arguments.
!?string?	Locates the most recent command containing the string.
!-n	This is an offset to a previous command. If n is 1, it is the immediately previous command, if n is 2, it is the command before that, and so on.
!!	A synonym for !-1.
!n	Refers to a specific command, where n is the command number.
^str1^str2^	Repeats the most recent command, substituting str2 in the place of str1.

Invoking a Shell

There is more than one way to start the bash shell. The arguments passed to, and even the name under which it is invoked, will make a difference in how it operates.

The Login Shell

A *login* shell is one that is started with the -login option. Its purpose is to be the manager of an interactive session. This is the mode used by the system when starting a user's shell from the /etc/passwd file. A login shell assumes that nothing has been initialized and sets up the entire environment by following these steps:

1. If the system file /etc/profile exists, it is sourced. This file contains basic settings for PATH, LOGNAME, the ulimit, and other things that must be set.

2. If the .bash_profile file exists in the home directory of the user logging it, it is sourced. The commands in this file set some of the user-specific environment variables.

3. If .bash_profile does not exist, the shell looks for it under the name .bash_login.

4. If neither .bash_profile nor .bash_login exists, the shell looks for it under the name .profile. This is the name of the file used by the original, called sh, and, because bash is compatible with sh, the same set of configuration commands works for both.

5. If the file .bashrc exists in the home directory, it is normally sourced by .bash_profile or by .bash_login. It normally contains the alias and function definitions.

6. As the session ends and the shell is being shut down, the file .bash_logout is sourced if it exists.

The Non-Login Interactive Shell

It is possible for any program you run to spawn a new shell—in fact, you can do this yourself directly from the command line. A child shell inherits all of the exported settings from its parent, so there is no need to go through the entire definition sequence. All the shell does is source .bashrc. Even this action can be suppressed by starting the shell with the -norc option.

The Non-Interactive Shell

A shell of this type is spawned by one process to execute another one. For example, if you enter a command line with an ampersand at its end, a non-interactive shell is started to execute the command.

If the environment variable ENV has been set, it is expected to hold the name of a file that is to be sourced to set the appropriate environment. The filename of ENV must be the full pathname, because PATH is not used to look for it.

Bourne Compatibility

The bash shell program has two names in Linux—/bin/bash and /bin/sh. The name /bin/sh was, on UNIX, the name of the original shell. If /bin/sh is used to start the shell, it makes every effort to behave like the original shell. It only attempts to source the system file /etc/profile followed by the local file .profile. No other system files are used.

Some Special Command Line Constructions

In using the shell, there are some situations that arise that require some special capability of the shell. Built in to the shell are some rules about modifying and expanding some things on the command line.

Environment Variable Expansion

The value of an environment variable, as defined in the shell, can be used on the command line by preceding the variable name with a $ character. Take the following three commands:

```
echo PWD
echo $PWD
echo ${PWD}
```

The first command will simply display the three characters PWD, while the second one will display the pathname of the current directory. The third one is exactly the same as the second—the braces are optional. There are times when the braces are necessary. For example, if you have an environment variable named VERSION that is used to construct filenames with the version number embedded in them, there could be characters immediately after the variable name preventing the shell from figuring out where the variable name ends. If, for example, the VERSION number is set to 2.1 and the name of the file is code2.1b.c, the filename could be constructed in the following way:

```
ls -l code${VERSION}bc
```

The braces prevent the trailing letter b from being tagged directly onto the name VERSION, creating a new name: VERSIONb.

Command Expansion

If you want to execute a program and have its standard output assigned to an environment variable, you will need to instruct the shell to execute the program, not just use its name. For example, if you want to assign a list of the currently logged in users to an environment variable, the following won't work:

```
ULIST=who      **Wrong**
```

The result of this simple assignment will cause ULIST to contain the string who. Using a pair of grave accent marks (also called back tics) to enclose the command will cause the shell to execute the command and use its output, as in the following:

```
ULIST=`who`
```

This back tic quoting can also be used to enclose any arguments or options on the command line like the following:

```
ULIST=`who -q`
```

There is another syntax that is sometimes used to do the same thing—a dollar sign and parentheses. The previous example could just as well have been written this way:

```
ULIST=$(who -q)
```

Brace Expansion

It is possible to use braces to create a list of specific names. This comes in handy when there is a naming convention of some sort and you want to specify a specific list of names. For example, suppose you have a directory filled with files that all have names in the following format

```
ccNNNj.doc
```

where *NNN* is a three digit number. If you want to get the file size and date information on numbers 210, 399, and 410, you could enter the command as the following:

```
ls -l cc{210,399,410}j.doc
```

The shell expands the command line to the following:

```
ls -l cc210j.doc cc399j.doc cc410j.doc
```

This can also be used to create a family of directories, like the following:

```
mkdir /home/pramp/work/{current,previous,next,safety}
```

Tilde Expansion

A tilde alone, or a tilde immediately followed by a slash, is a synonym for the pathname of the home directory of the currently logged in user. From anywhere in the system you can list names of the files in your home directory in the following way:

```
ls ~
```

Probably the most common form is to address a subdirectory in the home directory, as in the following:

```
ls ~/result/workdir
```

The tilde can also be used to address the home directory of another user. A tilde followed immediately by the name of a user in the /etc/passwd file will expand to the name of that user's home directory. For example, the games login has /usr/games as its home directory, and the files in that directory can be listed in the following way:

```
ls ~games
```

Shell Functions

A shell function can be used to assign a name to a stored series of commands. A function is always executed in the context of the current shell. This makes functions quite efficient, and any environment variables that get set will remain after the function has completed. The following is an example of a function:

```
function newgen {
    rm -rf $HOME/holding/old
    mv $HOME/holding/backup $HOME/holding/previous
    mv $HOME/holding/newest $HOME/holding/backup
    mkdir $HOME/holding/newest
}
```

This function is designed to create a directory to hold the newest information from the process. Instead of deleting the previously held information, it is backed up for two generations by changing the names of directories. Only the oldest version is deleted.

The keyword `function` is not necessary. The name of the function can be designated by placing a pair of parentheses to the right of the name, as in the following:

```
newgen() {
    <commands>
}
```

The keyword `return` can be used anywhere inside a function to cause the function to immediately exit.

It is possible to override the name of program, or a built-in command, by assigning the same name to a function. If you have done this, and you want to execute the original command instead of your function, use the `command` keyword. For example, say you have redefined `ls` as the following:

```
ls() {
    dir -l
}
```

If the occasion arises that you need to execute the original `ls`, it can be done as the following:

```
command ls
```

Shell Aliases

An alias can be used to assign alternate names to commands. There are a couple of very good uses for this. First, if you come to Linux from another system and have the tendency to type `cls` when you mean `clear`, you can use an alias to have Linux recognize `cls`.

Just put the following line in your .bahsrc file (or any other file that is used for bash startup):

```
alias cls='clear'
```

Each time the command cls is entered, it will be immediately translated to clear. The second use for an alias is to define a set of default arguments for a command. For example, I like to have the ls command show hidden files and indicate which files are directories and which are executable. The alias is defined as the following:

```
alias ls='ls -AF'
```

Once defined, every time ls is typed on the command line, it is immediately translated to ls -AF. You can still use other arguments on the line, but the -AF will always be there.

If you need to delete an alias, use the keyword unalias. For example, to remove the ls definition created in the previous example, add the following:

```
unalias ls
```

Built-In Bash Commands

There are quite a few built in commands in the bash shell. Many of them have been discussed earlier in this chapter, but those not previously covered are described in this section.

help

This built-in command is for the purpose of helping with the built-in commands. If you just type help, a brief list of all the commands and their options is displayed. If you follow help with the name of a command, you will get more information.

bg and fg

The bg command can be used to place a running job in the background. This can be useful when you start something on the command line and then find that it is going to take longer than you thought, and you want the prompt back. Simply press Ctrl+Z (which temporarily suspends the job and prompts you for a command) and then enter **bg**. The suspended program is treated just as if it had been started using an & at the end of the line—it is assigned a process ID number and you will be notified when completed.

The fg command can be used to grab a job that you have running in the background and change it to an interactive job at the terminal. That is, it takes the background job and brings it to the foreground. To do this, you must supply fg with the ID number that was returned to you when the job began running, as in the following:

```
fg 2
```

The jobs command can be used to determine the names and ID numbers of any currently running background processes.

cd

This command is used to change the current directory. If a directory is named as an argument, it will become the current directory. If no directory is named, the home directory of the user becomes the current directory. If a directory is named that does not exist in the current directory, the environment variable $CDPATH may be defined holding a list of colon-separated directory names that cd will search to find the target directory.

echo

The echo command lists to standard out the text it finds on its command line. This output can be redirected, just like standard out from any other program, or it can be allowed to display on the screen. Normally, there is a newline at the end of the displayed string, but using the -n option will suppress it, as shown in the following:

```
/bin/echo -n
```

The arguments on the line are separated by spaces. If you supply more than one argument, the echo command has no way of determining how many spaces should go between them. The result is the following command

```
echo Now      is the time
```

which will display as

```
Now is the time
```

If you want to embed spaces, put either single or double quotes around the text, as shown in the following:

```
echo "Now      is the time"
```

The display now looks like

```
Now       is the time
```

> **Note:** If you find yourself in a situation where echo doesn't seem to work, you may have found a bug in your version of bash. However, there is a version of echo on disk that does work. Instead of just echo, use the form /bin/echo in your command and it should always work.

hash

When you enter the name of an executable file on the command line, the shell uses the PATH variable to look through directories until it can find it. To make this search more efficient, the shell assumes that if you used a command once, you are likely to use it again, so the shell remembers the complete pathname of any executable files found this way. The next time you enter the command, the shell goes directly to it without searching the path.

There are some circumstances where this is not such a good thing. For example, if you have written script in a working directory, and you move the script to a production location somewhere on the PATH, entering the name of the script will continue to execute the one in the working directory.

Entering the hash command with the -r causes the shell to forget everything it has remembered about file locations and start searching the path for them again. Entering hash with no arguments will cause the shell to list the pathnames of all the files it has remembered.

kill

This command will send a signal to one or more processes. The process to receive the signal is specified by its pid (process ID number). Any of the standard signals can be sent, but the default is kill (which is signal number 9). To send a kill signal to process number 842, enter the following:

```
kill 842
```

The actual signal can be specified as a number or as a name. The kill signal is number 9, and is the default, but if you wanted to send the termination signal (signal number 15) to the process, it could be done in two ways:

```
kill -s 15 842
```

or

```
kill -s SIGTERM 842
```

To list all the signal names and numbers, enter the following:

```
kill -l
```

There is a utility program described in Chapter 12, "Introduction to Shell Programming," that is capable of sending signals by the name of a process.

There is a utility program named killall that allows you to send signals to processes by using the processes' names instead of their id numbers. It is described in Chapter 12.

test

The test command is used to determine whether or not a specific condition exists. It can be used in functions, but it is most often found in scripts (see Chapter 12 for examples).

Most often, you will find it used in an `if` statement. `test` has an alias—it can also be called `[ ]`. For example, the following two conditional statements are identical:

```
if test $# -ne 2 ...
if [ $# -ne 2 ] ...
```

ulimit

If you run out of disk space, or if some program fails, it could be because you tried to exceed one of the system-imposed limits. Every user has a limit defined for each of ten specific things. They can all be displayed by using the `-a` command. The following is a typical `ulimit` display for the root login:

```
core file size (blocks)    1000000
data seg size (kbytes)     unlimited
file size (blocks)         unlimited
max memory size (kbytes)   unlimited
stack size (kbytes)        8192
cpu time (seconds)         unlimited
max user processes         261
pipe size (512 bytes)      8
open files                 256
virtual memory (kbytes)    2105343
```

Because this is the root login and has superuser powers, several of the settings have no limit. A core file is the file written to disk whenever a program aborts. The user processes are the maximum number of programs that can execute simultaneously. Data is buffered in pipes, and the pipe size determines the number of 512-byte buffers that are allocated for this user.

These limits are set to help balance the load on the computer—to prevent any one user from hogging all the resources. As you can see from this list, it is possible to have no limits imposed for some or all of the resources.

umask

Whenever a new file or directory is created, it is assigned the permissions and restrictions as defined by `umask`. If you enter the command `umask` with no arguments, three octal digits are displayed representing the permissions. Normally, the value is `022`.

The permissions for a file can be viewed by entering `ls` with the `-l` option. The files are listed one per line, and each line begins with a ten character permission indicator string. Actually, the first character of the ten is not a permission—it is an indicator of the file type (usually `d` to indicate a directory or `-` to indicate a regular file). The next nine characters represent the permissions. Each user category is assigned three of these characters—the first three represent permissions of the user that owns the file, the second three are the group permissions (the group to which the user belongs), and the last three are the permissions granted to anyone else.

Read permissions are indicated by an r, write permissions by a w, and execution permissions by an x. Any position containing a - character is a permission denied. The following is an example that assigns all permissions to both the user and the user's group, but denies read and write permission for everyone else:

```
-rwxrwx--x
```

Because there is an x in all three position, all three have execution permission. When a new file is created, the bit pattern for the permission is created by allowing all permissions except those specified by the umask value. For example, the normal umask value of 022 will cause the permissions to look like the following:

```
-rwxr-xr-x
```

Octal digits are used to represent the permission settings. An octal number is one that begins with a zero, and each digit represents three bits (the values 0 through 7). For example, the value 0111 represents the permission settings ---x--x--x, and 0711 represents -rwx--x--x.

> **Note:** If you run a program that creates a file, and the program doesn't do anything special about permissions, the umask value will be used to set the file permissions. However, the program can use a mask of its own to specify the permissions. When this happens, the only permissions granted will be the ones granted by both the program and umask.

Some Handy Command Line Utilities

There are some utility programs that are not actually a part of the shell, but they are used so often that they can be considered part of normal shell operations. There is a great deal of system documentation available, and there are ways to discover things about the type and content of files.

Documentation

Help is available online. There is the traditional documentation utility called man, and a newer utility called info. They both do basically the same thing—format disk files into a displayable or printable format.

info

This form of online documentation is much newer than man. This program has many more controls and has the ability to proceed from one page to another through links and list-like menus. The best way to learn about info is by using its tutorial. To start the tutorial, enter the following:

```
info info
```

Note: If the info utility does not find the requested name in its files, it invokes man to retrieve the page, and then info displays it. This means that if you get no response from info, you will get no response from man. However, there is another place to look—use the help command in case it happens to be a shell built-in.

man

The man utility has been around since UNIX began. There is a surprising amount of information to be found in the man documents. The documentation is normally kept in several different directories and the MANPATH environment variable is used to locate them. The documentation files are given the same names as the commands (or whatever) that they are documenting. This makes for easy lookup. For example, to find the description of the kill command, type the following:

```
man kill
```

Once the page has been displayed, you can use the navigation keys to move around the document. There are several single-letter commands. If there is something special you need to be able to do, type the letter H and a help screen will appear. To exit, press the letter Q.

To be able to use man, it is not necessary to set MANPATH. In fact, it would be best if you didn't set it unless there is something special you want to do. There is a file named /etc/man.config that contains the set of default pathnames. This same file contains some other configuration settings (like which program to use to decompress files).

There are a couple of options that come in quite handy when using man. If you don't know the exact name of something, you can type in just part of the name and use the -k option, as shown in the following:

```
man -k rcv
```

This command will list, one per line, a brief description of every entry that has the letters "rcv" either in the name or in the one-line description. There is also a situation where two things have the same name. For example, the kill example used earlier will retrieve information on the kill command, but there is also an entry in the man pages for the kill function call that can be made from a C program. To tell man that you would like to see every entry for a name, enter the command in the following way:

```
man -a kill
```

This will cause the appearance of the same text as before but, when you use the letter Q to exit, the next page will appear.

There are many more options. If you want the details on man, get it to tell you by entering the following:

```
man man
```

> **Note:** You will, from time to time, find an entry in man that has a disclaimer stating that this particular document is no longer maintained and that it could contain incomplete or erroneous information. When this happens, there is normally an updated version of the documentation that can be found by using info.

Changing Virtual Terminals

Using the same terminal, it is possible to have more than one active login session. In fact, it is possible to have one for each function key 1 through 12. The default is virtual terminal number 1. Each of these virtual terminals is completely independent of the others. With the virtual terminals, you can be simultaneously logged in as different users having different levels of access.

There are two ways to switch the display from one virtual terminal to another. The following command will switch to virtual terminal 3:

```
chvt 3
```

The same thing can be done by pressing Alt+F3 or possibility Ctrl+Alt+F3, depending on the system configuration.

You may find that your system is configured for something less than 12 virtual terminals. That's because there is a little overhead involved and a person seldom uses as many as that. However, if you would like to have more of them, it is only necessary to edit the /etc/inittab file and add them to the list. The login prompt is issued by a program named mingetty. There is one entry in inittab for each virtual terminal, so all you need to do is copy one of the existing entries and change the terminal number to the new one you want to add.

> **Note:** You should never attempt to switch virtual terminals while you are running X. It won't work, and it could lock up your terminal. Some Linux systems disable this capability during an X session, but some do not.

Finding Out Things About a File

There are several commands that can be used to tell you something about a disk file. The most obvious one is ls, which is normally used to simply list the names of the files.

However, the -l (ell) option causes the filenames to be listed one per line and be accompanied by some information about the file. The lines look like the following:

```
-rwxr-xr-x  1 maryg    devel     20480 Apr  9 17:22 sedit.tar
```

The name of the file is sedit.tar. It was created, or it was last modified on the afternoon of April 9th. Its total size is 20,480 bytes. The owner of the file is maryg, and she is a member of the devel group. There is only one hard link to the file.

The leading character in the permissions indicates the file type. The example shows a - as the leading character, which indicates that it is a normal file. If it were a d, it would indicate a directory. There are a couple of other types: c to indicate a character device and b to indicate a block device, but these are special hardware nodes and normally only appear in the /dev directory.

There are three sets of permissions defined, each one being assigned the three character sequence rwx. A missing character, indicated by the presence of -, indicates that particular permission is denied. If r is present, read permission is granted. If w is present, write permission is granted. If x is present, execute permission is granted. The leftmost three characters apply to the owner of the file, the middle three to the members of the owner's group, and the rightmost three apply to everyone else. Of course, the superuser has the power to override any restrictions.

The type command is built into the shell. It can be used to tell you what would happen if you entered a name as a command. If you use the following type option:

```
type -type cp
```

this will search for the file in the directories listed in the PATH variable and, if found, will simply display the word file because that's what cp is. It will also indicate whether the name is an alias, keyword, function, or builtin.

It happens occasionally that you are entering a command, but are not really sure of the location of the executable file—you know it is on your PATH, but where? The type command can find it for, for example

```
type -path cp
```

If the file exists on the PATH, its full pathname will be displayed.

The file command can be used to determine the type of contents found in a file. For example, if you come across a file named blogg and have no idea what it is, enter the following:

```
file blogg
```

You will get a displayed line of text describing what's in the file. If the file is a program, the description could look something like the following:

```
ELF 32-bit LSB executable, Intel 80386, dynamically linked
```

Or it could tell you that the name is a directory, ASCII text, or any one of dozens of other things. If the file command cannot determine the type, it assumes it is just raw binary data and displays the following:

```
data
```

The file command recognizes hundreds of file types, and new ones can be added easily. The file /usr/share/magic (or possibly /etc/magic) contains a list of the known file types, and instructions for recognizing them. Mostly the instructions consist of looking for special numbers (called magic numbers) that are always in the same place in files of the same type.

If you want to know just about everything there is to know about a file, use stat. For example, enter the following command:

```
stat /bin/grep
```

The displayed information looks like the following:

```
  File: "/bin/grep"
  Size: 69444          Filetype: Regular File
  Mode: (0755/-rwxr-xr-x)     Uid: (   0/    root) Gid: (   0/    root)
Device:  3,0   Inode: 16132     Links: 1
Access: Fri Apr 16 12:23:45 1999(00000.00:10:28)
Modify: Wed Sep  9 23:13:46 1998(00218.13:20:27)
Change: Thu Feb  4 05:10:27 1999(00071.06:23:46)
```

The first two lines display the filename, size, and type. The next line shows the mode (also called the permissions) as both rwx characters and as bits set in three octal digits. The file's owner is identified by both the user ID and username. The group is identified by both the group ID and the group name. The Device is the hardware device on which the file is stored. The Inode is the number of the node in the Linux file system that holds the name and disk address of the file.

Viewing ASCII Files

A file can be listed to the screen with the cat command. All you need to do is name the file on the command line, as shown in the following:

```
cat textfile
```

The text will scroll up the screen until the end of the file is found. However, if there is more than one screen full of text, everything except the last 24 lines will scroll off the screen so fast that you cannot see them. You can display one full screen of text at a time in the following manner:

```
more textfile
```

The screen will fill with text and wait for you to take action. If you press the Enter key, the text will scroll up one line. If you press the spacebar, it will scroll up one full screen. Pressing the letter Q will cause it to exit. At the bottom of the display is a percentage number that shows you how much of the text you have already viewed.

A viewer that allows you to go back and forth through the text is called less. The following is an example:

```
less textfile
```

Like more, a full screen of text is displayed. You can use the Page Up, Page Down, up arrow, and down arrow keys to scroll the text up and down on the screen. Also, the Enter key and the spacebar work the same way they do in more. If you prefer, you can also navigate forward in the text with the letters d (for down) and u (for up). To exit, press q. Whenever you use the man command, it is less that displays the text of the document.

Examining File Contents

The grep utility has the ability to look inside a collection of text files and find some string you have requested. The grep command will list the filename and the complete line for each place the string was found. Wildcards can be used to select the filenames, as shown in the following:

```
grep time *.c
```

This command will look through all files in the current directory that end with .c and display any lines that contain the four character sequence time. The search string can be literal characters, as in this example, or it can include special characters that make up a regular expression. Regular expressions are described in Chapter 12.

If you have some kind of binary file or a file of some unknown type, you can extract all of the character strings from it by using the strings command, as shown in the following:

```
strings /bin/grep
```

This will cause all the textual messages and object filenames to display. Any time there are four or more valid ASCII characters in a row, it is taken to be a string and displayed. Of course there are some coincidental strings that appear out of the binary code of the program—things like t3h?w and s8SR.

There are a pair of utilities that can be used if you want to look at the values of the bytes in a file. The od command will list the value of each byte as octal digits, and the hexdump command will list them as hexadecimal digits.

For example, if there is a file named fred that, as the cat command would show, contains the following line of text:

```
Use info to get more information.
```

using od to read the file results in the following:

```
0000000 071525 020145 067151 067546 072040 020157 062547 020164
0000020 067555 062562 064440 063156 071157 060555 064564 067157
0000040 005056
```

Using hexdump to read the file results in the following:

```
0000000 7355 2065 6e69 6f66 7420 206f 6567 2074
0000010 6f6d 6572 6920 666e 726f 616d 6974 6e6f
0000020 0a2e
```

Summary

A shell program prompting for a command line entry has been a part of UNIX since its beginning. Until X, it was just about the only way to access the system. Its usefulness has been increased over the years by the addition of a large collection of very useful utilities. Anything that can be done in Linux can be done from the command line. In fact, there are some commands that are so useful and so fundamental to the system that it will be a long time before any graphical interface can possibly catch up.

On Your Own

Look at the man page for your shell program and read the options that are available and how to set them. You will probably find some changes you would like to make. To do this, use the set command in your .bashrc file. For example, to be able to use vi commands to edit the command line, use the following:

```
set -o vi
```

Experiment with changing the mode of a file. Create a shell script and use chmod to change the permission settings so it becomes executable and you can run it.

Create a script that sets the value of one or more environment variables. Execute the script, and then check your environment for the changes. Then use the source command to execute the script and check your environment again.

Introduction to Shell Programming

A shell is a program that reads commands from the keyboard, or from a file, and takes whatever action is necessary to obey the command. There are hundreds of small utility programs designed to run from the command line and, as discussed in Chapter 11, "Using the Command Line Shell," there are some often-used commands built right into the shell program itself. You have your choice of using several different shells and, while they all do basically the same things, the command-line syntax will vary from one to another.

A shell program is a sequence of one or more commands stored in a file. This file is executable, and can be called a *shell procedure*, a *shell script*, or simply a *script*. The shell program has some special built-in commands that can be used in a shell script for iteration, conditional execution, and defining local variables.

In Linux, a shell script has the same status and can be executed in the same way a compiled and linked program can. For both of them, the permissions must be set to allow execution (more on this later), and all you need to do is enter the name of the file and it will run. The shell program—the one reading your input command—will look for the file along the PATH, and then will look at the file to determine what the file contains and, if it is a script, will take the actions necessary to have the commands interpreted.

As you read through this chapter, you will notice some things are used before they are described. Describing shell scripting is sort of like describing a merry-go-round—there is no clear beginning and end, you just have to jump on somewhere. Every attempt is made to make things as clear as possible, but, depending on your level of knowledge, you may need to peek ahead from time to time.

The Construction of a Shell Script

Because there are a number of shell programs, and because their syntax is different, it is necessary to know which shell program should be used to run the script. If, for example, you are using the C shell and the script you want to execute was written for the Bourne shell, it is very likely that the script simply won't work. There is a simple cure for this.

The various shell programs have agreed on a special construct on the first line that can be used to specify the shell, as shown in the following:

```
#!/bin/sh
```

In the case of **Linux**, /bin/sh is simply another name for /bin/bash, so a script with this first line will **always** be executed by the bash shell. Even if a user executes the script from within the C shell, the bash shell will be called on to execute the script. The opposite is also true—if you want to guarantee that a script is always executed by the C shell, the following should be its first line:

```
#!/bin/chsh
```

Note: The very first UNIX shell was the Bourne shell. It's full name on disk was /bin/sh. The Bourne shell is assumed to be present on every UNIX system. As time went by, a number of new shells were available, but most script writers continued to write using the Bourne syntax. Then an upgrade came. GNU created a new shell, fully compatible with the Bourne shell, called the *Bourne again* shell. It does everything Bourne does and a little extra besides. On your Linux system, it is named /bin/bash. However, there is also a link named /bin/sh, so either name can be used.

Any line—other than the special first line—that begins with an octothorpe (#) is considered to be a comment and is ignored. Blank lines will simply be skipped.

The following is a simple shell script that will display the hostname of the computer and list all the users currently logged in:

```
#!/bin/sh
hostname
who
exit 0
```

The last line specifies the value of the code to be returned when the script completes execution. This is not strictly necessary because the return code from a script is the same as the return code of the last command executed in the script, but it is good form to include it. In addition, the exit command can be used to shut down a script at any point—this is a handy device to report error conditions to the process executing the script. More on this later.

Before a script can be executed, it must be made executable. The chmod utility can be used to add the executable attribute to a script. For example, if the file holding your script is named wahoo, to make it executable by everyone, enter the following command:

```
chmod 777 wahoo
```

You can, of course, use whatever settings you want. The 777 settings (octal digits) give read, write, and execute permissions to everyone.

It is seldom desirable to give all permissions to everyone. You can modify the file permissions one or two at a time for specific users by using identifying letters. For example, to allow the file to be modified or deleted by other members of your group, enter

```
chmod g+w wahoo
```

Or, to allow execute permission for all users, enter

```
chmod a+x wahoo
```

Enter the following to remove execute and write permissions for members of your group:

```
chmod g-xw wahoo
```

The first letter specifies the user. The letter u represents the user that owns the file, g represents the other users in the owner's group, and o represents other users. The letter a can be used to change the permissions for all three. The permissions are r for read, w for write, and x for execute. A plus sign between them grants permissions, and a minus sign removes them.

The script can now be run. Simply enter the name of the executable file from the command line (or from another script, for that matter), and your shell program will take over. It will look at the file to determine what kind of executable it is and, because it is a text file, will look at the first line to find out which shell is to do the work. The shell program is launched and fed the commands from the file; the script executes.

Do you want to know what shell you are using? The following is a simple little one-line script that will show you:

```
#!/bin/sh
grep `whoami` /etc/passwd
exit 0
```

The backward tic marks around `whoami` instruct the shell program to execute whoami and use its output (your current login name) as part of the command line. For example, if you are logged in as root, the line will become

```
grep root /etc/passwd
```

The grep command searches through the /etc/passwd file and lists each occurrence of a line containing the word root. The output looks something like the following:

```
root:eUu0m43/Xx5aI:0:0:root:/root:/bin/bash
```

The /etc/passwd file stores all the login names. Each line is a list of comma-separated fields. From left to right, the fields are the username, the encrypted password, user ID number, group ID number, comment, the long directory, and, finally, the pathname of the shell.

Arguments

You can specify arguments that will be passed to a script in the same way as arguments would be passed to any other executable program. The following is a simple example:

```
#!/bin/sh
sort $1
exit 0
```

This script will execute the sort command using a file named on the command line. A script can be written to accept a number of arguments—the first argument is named $1, the second is $2, and so on. There are a couple of special values—the symbol $0 contains the name of the script being executed, and $# contains a count of the number of arguments (not including $0). For example, the following is a simple script that displays its own name and then displays the first three arguments on the command line:

```
#!/bin/sh
echo $0
echo $1 $2 $3
exit 0
```

If this script is stored in a file named doback, it can be executed with the following command:

```
doback one fred three four
```

The output will look like the following:

```
./doback
one fred three
```

If more than three arguments are supplied, the additional arguments are ignored because the script simply doesn't look any further. If less than three are supplied, the missing ones are simply blank. There are times when you need to write a script that will accept a variable number of arguments. There is a built-in bash trick to handle this. The following is a script that will display a numbered list of all the arguments supplied on the command line:

```
#!/bin/sh
ArgNumber=0
until [ $# = 0 ]
do
    ArgNumber=`expr $ArgNumber + 1`
    echo $ArgNumber $1
    shift
done
exit 0
```

There are some things in this example that have not been discussed yet (such as looping), but the point is that the shift command is used to move from one argument to another. It does so by changing the position of all the arguments. shift copies the contents of $2 into $1, and then copies the contents of $3 into $2, and so on, until it has copied all of them. There is one less argument than there was before the shift. The value $# is a constantly adjusted count of the number of arguments, and, when it reaches zero, there are no more arguments. In the example, the loop is executed continuously until the argument count is 0.

It seems that in Linux there are several ways to do everything. There is yet another way to get the arguments into your shell script. The for loop, described later in this chapter, has a special form that can be used to access the arguments directly.

Conditional Execution

You can specify that some commands execute only under certain conditions. For example, you may want to display an error message if a file is missing or if something else has gone wrong. A simple conditional if statement has the following syntax:

```
if <condition>
then
    <commands>
fi
```

The value of the condition is the exit code from the execution of another script or program. If the exit code is zero, the condition is false. If the exit code is non-zero, the condition is true. For the most part, the return of a zero exit code indicates success. A non-zero code is quite often an error code number. You may find cases where different non-zero code values represent differing degrees of success.

There is a special shell built-in named test that can be used to construct conditions. For example, a command that would list the contents of a text file, but would list nothing if the file does not exist, could look like the following:

```
#!/bin/sh
if test -r $1
then
    cat $1
fi
```

The -r option of test will result in true (non-zero) only if the file exists and is readable. There are a number of options available with test—you can determine whether the file is a directory, a socket, a zero-length file, writeable, executable, or even if it is owned by a specified user or group. Not only that, but test can compare one file to another, compare numeric values and strings, and even combine other conditionals with Boolean AND and OR. A list of all the options, and how to use this, can be found in Chapter 11.

As you may suspect, where there is an if, there is also an else. The following is the basic syntax:

```
if <condition>
then
```

```
    <commands>
else
    <commands>
fi
```

The following script replaces a text file with a sorted version of itself:

```
#!/bin/sh
if test -r $1
then
    echo "The file $1 does not exist"
    exit 1
fi
if sort $1 >temporary.work.file
then
    rm -f $1
    mv temporary.work.file $1
    echo "Done..."
else
    echo "Error. Unable to sort $1"
    exit 1
fi
exit 0
```

If the file does not exist, a message is displayed and a non-zero exit value is returned.

The sort utility is used to sort the text of the input file into a temporary working file. Because the sort utility is executed on an if statement, the exit code from sort will determine which of the two sets of code will execute. If, for some reason, the sort did not succeed, a non-zero value will be returned and an error message issued. Also, in the case of an error, this script will return a non-zero value to indicate an error to its caller, if any. If a success code is returned, the original file is deleted and the new file renamed to take its place.

There is another form of the if statement. This one allows for the selection of one of a several choices. The syntax of it looks like the following:

```
if <condition>
then
    <commands>
elif <condition>
then
    <commands>
elif <condition>
. . .
elif <condition>
then
    <commands>
else
    <commands>
fi
```

For example, say that you are giving a discount for volume purchase of some item. Anyone buying more than 100 items can get them for a unit price of $2.90, buying between 51 and 100 has a unit price of $3.10, from 11 to 50 has a unit price of $3.45, and 10 or less will be sold for $4.00 each. Given the number of items, the output of the following script is the unit price:

```
#!/bin/sh
if test $1 -gt 100
then
    price=2.90
elif test $1 -gt 50
then
    price=3.10
elif test $1 -gt 10
then
    price=3.45
else
    price=4.00
fi
echo $price
exit 0
```

The test command is built into the shell, and it has [and] as a synonym. A test can be written in the following way:

```
if [ $1 -gt 100 ]
```

which is exactly the same as

```
if test $1 -gt 100
```

Looping

There are three ways of looping. The while statement repeatedly executes as long as a conditional expression is true. The until statement executes as long as a conditional is false. The for statement will execute once for each member of a list. The break and continue commands can be used in any loop to exit from the middle of a loop.

while

As long as a conditional expression is true, a while loop will continue to execute. The basic syntax looks like the following:

```
while <condition>
do
    <commands>
done
```

The following example runs a counter from one to five and displays its value with each iteration:

```
#!/bin/sh
Counter=1
while [ $Counter -lt 5 ]
do
    echo $Counter
    Counter=`expr $Counter + 1`
done
exit 0
```

The expr utility, described later in this chapter, is used to increment the counter. Of course, any conditional expression can be used—it doesn't have to be a counter. The following example reads the name of a file from the keyboard and searches the entire disk for the file. The entire paths of any matching filenames are displayed:

```
#!/bin/sh
echo "Enter the name of a file to be found."
while read FileName
do
    find / -name "$FileName" -print
    echo "    Enter another, or Ctrl+D to exit."
done
exit 0
```

The built-in read command exits with a non-zero value whenever data has been entered, and it exits with a zero value whenever it encounters a Ctrl+D. The find command, as it is used here, searches for the named file beginning in the root directory, which means it will search through all directories of all mounted drives. Notice that on the find command, the name of the file is enclosed in quotes. This is so there will be no problem if the input name includes wild card characters—the find command works fine with wild cards, and so does this script.

> **Note:** Using Ctrl+D for the end of the input is pretty standard for all of Linux. In fact, this is pretty standard across all UNIX systems. The Ctrl+D character is the ASCII end-of-file mark, and you will find that many utilities will expect it as the command to cease processing. Whenever you are in some program that won't respond to "quit", try Ctrl+D.

until

As long as a conditional expression is false, the loop will continue to execute. This is just the opposite of the while loop described earlier. The basic syntax looks like the following:

```
until <condition>
do
    <commands>
done
```

It is a matter of preference which one you use, because anything that can be done with while can also be done with until. For example, the following is the loop counter example changed to use until instead of while:

```
#!/bin/sh
Counter=1
until [ $Counter -ge 5 ]
do
    echo $Counter
    Counter=`expr $Counter + 1`
done
exit 0
```

for

The for loop will execute once for each member of a list. The following is the basic syntax:

```
for <name> [ in <list> ]
do
    <commands>
done
```

The following script displays the names of the files and directories to be found in the current directory:

```
#!/bin/sh
Flist=`ls`
echo $Flist
for FileName in $Flist
do
    echo $FileName
done
exit 0
```

Note: Something nice happens when ls is used in a script to assign the list of filenames to a variable. The extra spaces, line feeds, and whatnot are all stripped out. The form of the list becomes one long line with the names separated by spaces.

As is implied by the syntax, the list is optional. If you do not supply a list, the list of arguments from the command line is assumed. The following code will list each command-line argument on a separate line:

```
#!/bin/sh
for Argument
do
    echo $Argument
done
exit 0
```

break and continue

While in the middle of a `for`, `while`, or `until` loop, it is possible to break out of the loop without halting execution of the script. There are two ways to do this: the `break` command simply jumps to the statement beyond the end of the loop, and the `continue` command jumps to the end of the loop and, depending on the condition, starts another iteration.

The following example will list all the filenames in the current directory, but if it finds and lists the filename "`loopuntil`", it immediately quits:

```
#!/bin/sh
Flist=`ls`
for FileName in $Flist
do
    echo $FileName
    if [ "$FileName" = "loopuntil" ]
    then
        break
    fi
done
exit 0
```

The other kind of loop escape abandons the only current iteration, not the entire loop. The following example displays all the values of a counter, except one:

```
#!/bin/sh
Counter=0
until [ $Counter -ge 5 ]
do
    Counter=`expr $Counter + 1`
    if [ $Counter -eq 3 ]
    then
        continue
    fi
    echo $Counter
done
exit 0
```

The counter values of 1, 2, 4, and 5 will all be displayed, but the `echo` statement is skipped whenever the value is 3.

case

The case statement is a multi-way branch—it selects which statements are to be executed by pattern matching using regular expressions. Its syntax looks like the following:

```
case <word> in
<pattern>)
    <commands>
    ;;
```

```
<pattern>)
    <commands>
    ;;
. . .
esac
```

> **Note:** If you think the syntax of the case statement looks a little odd, you are thinking straight. It's odd. This syntax has come down to programmers, unchanged, as part of the UNIX heritage. It appeared in this form in the original shell program and has never been modified. However weird it may be, it works just fine (as long as you hold your mouth right when you type it in).

The following is an example that examines filenames and takes action depending on how the names are formed:

```
#!/bin/sh
Flist=`ls`
for FileName in $Flist
do
    case $FileName in
    *.c)
        echo "Found a C source file: $FileName"
        ;;
    *00*)
        echo "Found a double-oh file: $FileName"
        ;;
    *)
        echo "Default: $FileName"
        ;;
    esac
done
exit 0
```

The case statement is executed once for each file in the current directory. The name of the file is tested against each of the possible choices, starting at the top and going down, until one is found to match. While it is possible to have names that would match with two or more expressions, only the first one encountered will be executed.

The selections are made by using regular expressions (described in more detail in the next section). In this example, the first case looks for any file that has .c as its final two characters. The second case looks for a file that includes the character pair 00 anywhere in it. The final case is the default—the single asterisk will match anything, so any file that does not match either of the other two will match this one.

Regular Expressions

A regular expression is a string of characters that lay out a pattern rule. The pattern rule can then be applied to other strings to determine whether or not there is a match—that is, whether or not the string being tested follows all the rules.

In a regular expression, there are some characters that are assigned special meanings. An asterisk (*), for example, is a wildcard that will match any number of any characters. The question mark (?) is a wildcard that will match any one character. The square brackets ([) and (]) can be used to specify a range or group of characters. The vertical bar (¦) acts as a logical OR between two regular expressions. Table 12.1 contains examples showing how these characters can be used to match names.

Table 12.1 Examples of Regular Expression Matching

Expression	Will match these...
a	atom, bat, amazon, extra
*a	extra, area, flicka
a*	apple, aardvark, amount
oo	loop, shoot, bookkeeper, loo
m?x	mix, max, mox
m??	mix, mad, moo, mrs
?amp	camp, ramp, damp
?am?	camp, lamb, same
[abcd]	a, b, c, d
[crd]amp	camp, ramp, damp
[b-d]ad	bad, cad, dad
[a-z][0-9]	a1, b4, m1
hm[13579]	hm1, hm5, hm9
C[oO][bB]	Cob, COB, CoB
h*n¦c*t	hitman, cement, horn, cleat

Note: There are some irregularities among regular expressions. There are a number of programs in Linux that use regular expressions, but not all of these programs are created equal. The rules for forming expressions vary somewhat from one application to the next. The examples in Table 12.1 will be valid for case statements in bash. They will also be valid for many other applications, but not for all.

Execution of Scripts and Programs

A script can execute another script in more than one way. Whenever one script executes another, the newly executed one is called the *child*, and the one that started the child is called the *parent*. The parent can wait for the child to terminate before continuing. Both the parent and the child can execute simultaneously, with the parent waiting for the child to terminate. A parent can cease execution and immediately turn control over to a child—which immediately takes the place of the parent.

> **Note:** This section discusses one script (the parent) executing another (the child). In every case, the parent and the child process can either be a script or an executable program written in C, FORTRAN, Assembly, or some other language that generates an executable file. When a command is entered, it is the job of the shell to determine what kind of program file it is and to take the necessary actions to run it.

Simple Execution

This is the most common method used by one script to execute another. Simply naming a script, just as you would on the command line, causes the script to execute. The parent script is suspended and waits until the child ceases execution before continuing.

Naming the child process in a conditional expression results in the exit code of the child becoming the value of the conditional—zero is interpreted as false and any non-zero value is interpreted as true. For example, the following script will display whether the exit code from showstatus is zero or non-zero:

```
#!/bin/sh
if [ showstatus ]
then
    echo "True is represented by any non-zero value"
else
    echo "False is represented by zero"
fi
exit 0
```

Spinning Off a Child Process

It is a very simple matter to spin off a background process. All you need to do is include an ampersand (&) at the end of its startup line. This can be done from inside a script the same as it can from the command line. The following code runs the find command and has its output redirected into a file:

```
find / -name "Xt*.c" -print >xtlist &
```

Because of the terminating ampersand, the find command will run as a background process, leaving the parent script free to do other things. In fact, the parent script could start a number of find commands and they would all execute simultaneously. The wait command can be used to pause the parent script until all the child processes have completed, as in the following:

```
#!/bin/sh
find / -name "Xt*.c" -print >xtist &
find / -name "fred" -print >fredlist &
echo Waiting...
wait
echo Done...
exit 0
```

In this example, both find statements start running, and the script continues on to the wait statement. The wait statement will cause the shell to wait until both the child processes have completed so that, when the script continues execution, the files xtlist and fredlist will exist and be filled with data.

By using the built-in wait command, it also is possible to wait for a specific child process to complete. Each new process has a unique ID number assigned to it by the system. This number can be used to determine whether a process is executing. The following example starts two child processes, but only waits for one of them to complete:

```
#!/bin/sh
find / -name "Xt*.c" -print >xtlist &
IdNumber=$!
find / -name "fred" -print >fredlist &
echo Waiting for $IdNumber
wait $IdNumber
echo Done...
exit 0
```

The special notation $! is the ID number of the most recently started background process. When this number is supplied to the wait command, the shell waits for only that one child process.

Replacing the Existing Process

There is a special command that will immediately halt the current process and start another one in its place. The following is an example:

```
exec unroll
```

This line of code will immediately halt the current script, load a script (or program) named unroll into its place in memory, and set it into execution.

> **Note:** The same end result can be achieved by executing the child process in the background and then having the parent process exit. Using the exec command is more efficient because there is no new process started. The same context is
>
> *continues*

used; it is just the executable program that changes. In fact, when you start a child process, the parent process first clones itself (this is called *forking*) and the exec command is issued for one of the clones. Going directly to exec saves this extra step.

Some Utilities That Can Be Useful in Scripts

There are literally hundreds of utilities supplied with Linux. This giant array of utility programs has been developed over the years—each one came about because somebody somewhere had a need. As many as there are, you can be pretty sure that one or more of them were written to solve the problem you may have right now.

There are certain utilities that seem to appear quite often in scripts. The following list by no means includes all the utilities available, but these are the ones that seem to appear often enough in scripts to make them worth mention. If you don't find what you need here, don't despair—there are more than 800 utility programs found the /bin and /usr/bin directories.

Note: There is a special command you can use to locate a utility without knowing its name. The apropos command compares what you type to the name and a one-line description of the command. All matching utilities are listed and you can refine your search from there. For example, if you want to find every command that has the word internet in its description, just enter apropos internet. Using apropos is the same as using man with the -k option.

at

Reads commands from a file and waits to execute the commands at the specified time. For example, the following statement will run the commands in the file named endofday at 4:30 p.m.:

```
at -f endofday 16:30
```

You can also specify the date by adding it after the time, as shown in the following:

```
at -f endofday 16:30 08/22/99
```

The batch utility performs the same function that at does, but, instead of executing right on schedule, it will wait until the load on the system is very low. For example, the following command will execute at the first moment after 4:00 a.m. that the load on the computer drops below 0.8:

```
batch -f endofday 04:00
```

The `atrun` utility can be used to change the load limit determining when `batch` will release its jobs for execution. For example, to change the level to 1.5, use the following:

```
atrun -1 1.5
```

> **Tip:** There are a couple of commands that can be used to monitor and control scheduled processes. The `atq` command will list all the pending jobs, and the `atrm` command can be used to delete them.

There is a security limitation to using `at` and `batch`. The superuser can always use them, but other user's permissions are controlled by having their names in a couple of files. If the file `/etc/at.allow` exists, a user's name must be in the file before he can use `at`. If the file `/etc/at.deny` exists, no user name in it can use `at`. If neither file exists, only the superuser can use `at`. To allow all users to use `at`, create an empty `/etc/at.deny` file.

awk

Linux has the GNU implementation of the POSIX standard `awk` programming language. It is a text processing language. The command line must specify the program to be run (either directly on the command line or in a file) and one or more files that will have `awk` processing applied to them. If you need some very sophisticated text processing, this could be just what you are looking for. Making it as flexible and complete as it is made it a bit complicated, though, so, if you are new to the `awk` language, plan on spending a bit of time getting it figured out. However, it will do some pretty fancy tricks and a lot of people depend on it.

> **Note:** The `awk` programming language has an odd name. It is actually a sort of acronym for the three guys that thought it up: Aho, Kernigan, and Weinberger. Also, on Linux, it has both the traditional name `awk` and the GNU name `gawk`, but the two are identical.

An `awk` program consists of one or more pattern or action pairs. The text in the input file is processed line-by-line looking for a pattern match. Whenever a match is found, the action is taken. The line can be processed as a whole, or each individual token on the line can be processed.

The following examples use a file named `awkdata` that contains these lines of text

```
6 11.34 Firewall
3 6.89 Speedo
5 4.72 Phydeaux
8 17.1 Longrun
2 4.55 Quickie
```

The data is about race cars. The numbers are a number of laps around the track and the total elapsed time in minutes for all the laps. The third column contains the name of the car making the laps. The following command will list the average time taken for each lap for each car:

```
gawk '{ print $3, $1 / $2 }' awkdata
```

Single quotes are used to enclose the program whenever it is specified on the command line. The action is specified between a pair of braces ({ and }). This example has no pattern to be matched so, by default, it matches and processes every line in the file. The input can be from more than one file—by naming more than one file, each is read in turn just as if the data had been included in a single file. This awk program defines that the action to be taken is to print the third column ($3), divide the first column ($1) by the second column ($2), and then print the results of the division. The output looks like the following:

```
Firewall 0.529101
Speedo 0.435414
Phydeaux 1.05932
Longrun 0.467836
Quickie 0.43956
```

The following command will perform the same action, but any car making less than four laps will not be included in the list:

```
gawk '$1 > 4 { print $3, $1 / $2 }' awkdata
```

This program consists of both the pattern to be matched and the action to be taken. The pattern comes first—before the opening brace ({) of the action. In this example, a match will occur only if the number in the first column is greater than four. The output looks like the following:

```
Firewall 0.529101
Phydeaux 1.05932
Longrun 0.467836
```

Instead of being specified on the command line, the program can be stored in a separate file. For example, if you create a file named awkprog1 containing the following awk program:

```
$1 > 4 { print $3, $1 / $2 }
```

the following command line will do exactly the same thing and will produce the same output:

```
gawk -f awkprog1 awkdata
```

The -f option specifies that the program is to be found in a file instead of on the command line. There can be more than one pattern/action pair in an awk program stored in the file. Processing proceeds by reading a line from the input data file and testing that line against each pattern in the program. When the pattern matches, the action is taken and the next line is read from the data input. This continues until all the text has been processed. For example, the file named awkprog2 contains the following:

```
$1 > 4 { print $3, $1 / $2 }
$1 <= 4 { print $3, "(Not enough laps)" }
```

This two-line program performs one action when the lap number is greater than 4, and another action when it is not greater than 4. The output looks like the following:

```
Firewall 0.529101
Speedo (Not enough laps)
Phydeaux 1.05932
Longrun 0.467836
Quickie (Not enough laps)
```

This is just the beginning of awk. There is a lot more to the language—it has functions, built-in arithmetic operators, variables, arrays, sorting, conditional execution, looping, and so on. It is a full-blown language.

Because of the way the language is designed, you can do quite a bit in a single line. It has become a sort of UNIX tradition over the years to create fancy awk one-liners that perform useful tasks. As you proceed through the world of Linux, you are bound to encounter some.

chvt

Using the same keyboard and display, a single user can be logged in to Linux a number of times. Each login has a virtual terminal for its display, only one of which can be active at any given time. The chvt command can switch the display from one virtual terminal to another. Given a number, this command will switch the active display from one virtual terminal to another one. For example, the following command will switch to virtual terminal number three:

```
chvt 3
```

The same thing can be done from the keyboard by holding down the Alt key while pressing the function key of the desired terminal number.

cksum

This utility will calculate and print a CRC (Cyclical Redundancy Check) value and the total number of bytes in a file. For example, in the following:

```
cksum automake
```

the file automake is read byte-by-byte to generate the CRC value and the byte count. The output looks like the following:

```
3477740872 172565 automake
```

The first number is the CRC value and the second is the number of bytes.

The CRC value can be tested to verify that the file has not changed since the last time cksum was run. The numbers can also be used to verify that two files are identical, or that a file was properly transmitted over a communications link.

clear

Clears the terminal screen. The screen is left blank with the prompt appearing in the upper-left corner.

cmp

This command does a binary comparison of two files. For a pair of text files, it will output the line number and the character count from the top of the file where the first difference was found. For example, in the following:

```
cmp oldlist newlist
```

if the files are the same, there is no output. If the files differ, the output will look something like the following:

```
oldlist newlist differ: char 144, line 6
```

There can be multiple differences, but cmp will only find one. If the two files are binary, cmp reports the count of bytes to the first one that differs.

compress and uncompress

This utility uses adaptive Lempel-Ziv coding to compress files. The compressed file is tagged with a .z extension. The uncompress utility can be used to restore files with the .z extension. Any kind of file can be compressed, but ASCII text, usually reduced by more than 50%, usually compresses best.

For example, say you have a file named fred to be compressed. Do the following:

```
compress fred
```

The file fred in the current directory is replaced by a smaller file named fred.z. The file named fred has been deleted. To restore the file to its original state, do the following:

```
uncompress fred
```

Notice that the .z extension is not specified. This command will restore the file named fred and delete fred.z. You can do this on entire directories of files by using wildcards. For example, to compress every file in a directory, enter the following:

```
compress *
```

Using the -r option will cause recursive action—that is, all the files in all the subdirectories will also be compressed.

> **Tip:** You may also want to look at gzip and zip. Both compress and gzip are commonly used in conjunction with tar to shrink files and pack them into a single file for distribution. The zip utility both compresses files and packs them into a single file.

cut

The cut utility can be used to extract characters from specific columns of a text file. For example, the following command will extract and output the first four characters from each line of the input file cutdata:

```
cut -c 1-4 cutdata
```

More than one range can be specified by separating each one with a comma. The following example will extract the first, third, and the fourth through the tenth characters from each line:

```
cut -c 1,3,4-10 cutdata
```

The -c option is for characters and -b is for bytes (which are the same unless Unicode is being used). There is also a -f option that works by field numbers in much the same way that awk does.

diff

This command reads through two text files and lists the differences between them. It also returns a exit code that indicates whether the files are different. It can be used in a script in the following way:

```
if diff filename1 filename2 >/dev/null
then
     echo The files are different
else
     echo The files are identical
fi
```

It is necessary to redirect the output to /dev/null because diff lists the text and the location of every line that is found to be different. If you run diff on a couple of files and examine the output, you will see some odd looking codes and numbers between the lines—these are commands that can be used by certain archiving software to combine a file with these conversion codes and produce the other file.

env

This command is used to view, set, and clear environment variables. To view the current variables, just enter the command without any arguments. To set an environment variable, use an equals sign to assign a value to a name, as shown in the following:

```
env LASTOUT=/home/px
```

This will set the environment variable LASTOUT to the pathname /home/px. For no reason other than tradition, environment variables are named using uppercase letters—this is not a requirement, but everyone seems to do it.

> **Note:** These environment variables are used by programs. Inside a running program, an environment variable is checked to determine a counter value or a file location. If you enter the env command without any arguments on the command line, you will see the list of pre-defined variables. Some of the system programs use these settings, so you should be careful about what gets changed or removed.

To remove an environment variable, use the -u option, as shown in the following:

```
env -u LASTOUT
```

You can remove the value of an environment variable, as shown in the following:

```
env LASTOUT=
```

Using the -u option removes the variable, while the second method leaves the name defined but with no value assigned to it.

expr

If you write many scripts, you will find places where expr is absolutely essential. It simply evaluates the expression supplied to it and writes the result to standard out.

It has the normal operators for add (+), subtract (-), multiply (*), divide (/), and remainder (%). There are no parentheses, but there are two precedence levels (*, /, and % come first, followed by + and -). For example, the evaluation of the following expression is 25 because the division occurs first:

```
expr 20 + 10 / 2
```

There are some Boolean operators that result in 1 for true and 0 for false. The operators are

```
    <
    <=
    =
    ==
    !=
    >=
    >
```

The equals (=) and the double equals (==) are the same. Every attempt is made by expr to convert the expression on both sides of the comparison operator to a numbers, and, if it succeeds, the numbers are used for the comparison. If either one of them can't be converted to a number, a string comparison is made. There is a slight collision with expr and the shell—the angle brackets are interpreted by the shell as input and output redirection. If you are going to use them, you will need to escape the brackets, as shown in the following:

```
expr $A \< 5
```

This is also true of other operators that are treated as special commands by the shell—in particular, the AND (&) and OR (¦) operators must be escaped. For some shells, the remainder (%) operator will also need to be escaped.

The OR operator (¦) results in the value of the first argument if it is not zero or null, otherwise it results in the value of the second argument. For example, the following results in 4:

```
expr 0 \¦ 4
```

The AND operator (&) results in the first argument if neither argument is null or 0. If either argument is null or 0, the result is 0. For example, the following results in 4:

```
expr 4 \& 25
```

And the following results in 0:

```
expr 4 \& 0
```

find

With the find command, you select the root of a directory to be searched, the name of the files or directories you want to find, and supply instructions about what should be done when they are found. For example, to search the entire file system for every file named furball.c and display the full path of all of them, use the following command:

```
find / -name furball.c -print
```

This command starts at the root directory (/) and looks in the directory and in all subdirectories for any file with a name matching the one following the -name option. For each file found, the -print command is executed to list its path.

You can use wildcards for the search. However, while the wildcard characters have meaning to the find command, they also have meaning to the shell, so you will need to put wildcard expressions in quotes so your command line won't be mis-translated before it is passed to find, as shown in the following:

```
find / -name "*.c" -print
```

This `find` command will list the pathname of every file ending with `.c`. You can limit the depth that the search will go down into the directory tree by using the `-maxdepth` option, as in the following:

```
find / -name furball.c -maxdepth 3 -print
```

This limits the search to the named directory and two directories directly beneath it. You can do a lot more than simply name the files—you can perform any action you would like on them by using the `-exec` option, as shown in the following:

```
find / -name "fred*.c" -exec rm {} \;
```

The `-exec` action option will execute the command line following it, right up to the trailing semicolon. The double braces (`{}`) are translated into the name of the current file being processed. The trailing semicolon must be preceded with the escape character (`\`) to keep the shell from processing it away. You can perform more than one action. The following example lists every file on the system that ends with `.c` and lists every line in each of the files that contain the characters `Xt`:

```
find / -name "*.c" -print -exec grep Xt {} \;
```

Of course, once an action fails (that is, it returns non-zero exit code), no other actions on the line are executed. The actions of the previous example can be reversed, and only the filenames that are found by `grep` to hold the string will be listed:

```
find / -name "*.c" -exec grep Xt {} \; -print
```

The `-print` option is not executed unless the `-exec` command returns a non-zero value which, in turn, is determined by the exit code from `grep`.

There are tests other than simply the name of the file. You can test for each file's modification date, whether the found file is newer than some other file, test the file type, file ownership, permissions, whether the user ID of the file is valid, and the size of the file.

fmt

This is a simple text line formatter. It can be handy if there is some kind of ragged text that needs to be printed. As input, it can take one or more text files.

Blank lines are left intact to separate paragraphs, while continuous lines of text are joined or broken as necessary to form the body of a paragraph. Any indentation at the beginning of a paragraph is maintained.

> **Note:** With word processors becoming more common, this command is not as useful as it once was. However, it is not uncommon to wind up with a file full of badly formed text that needs to be fixed up so it is easier to read. You can fiddle with the `fmt` options and improve the readability of almost any raw text file.

fold

This command accepts text as input and breaks it into shorter lines. It can happen that text is generated in great long lines, and this utility can be used to break it into usable chunks. For example, if the file named OneLongLine contains a list of names, and the names are in one long line, the following command will break the text into lines no longer than 80 characters each:

```
fold -w 80 OneLongLine
```

The output goes to standard out (which can be redirected to another file). The input can come from more than one file by simply including the filenames on the command line.

grep

The grep utility (named for *Get REgular Expression*) searches through one or more files to find matches for a regular expression. Some examples of regular expression matching can be found in Table 12.1. Table 12.2 lists the expression patterns recognized by grep.

Table 12.2   Basic Regular Expressions for grep

Expression	Matches
c	Any character c not otherwise defined matches itself.
\c	The special meaning of any character can be turned off by a preceding backslash.
^	The beginning of a line.
$	The end of the line.
.	Any single character.
[...]	Any one of the characters. The list can be individual characters. Using a hyphen represents a range of characters, as in a-z.
[^...]	Any character that is not in the list. Using a hyphen represents a range of characters, as in a-z.
r	Zero or more occurrences of the regular expression r.

Note: This is one of those programs that has been around for a long time. It is handy in all sorts of circumstances, but it is so convenient and necessary for programmers that, after a while, its use becomes almost automatic. In some form or other, it has been ported to every operating system of consequence. Like any utility that is this useful and has been around for this long, it has lots of options, as well some major variants. The grep that comes with Linux covers all the bases by having optional settings for everything.

There are a lot of option flags, but generally the grep command is followed immediately by the string being sought, and the string is followed by the list of filenames that are to be scanned. For example,

```
grep MinMax *.c
```

will search through all files with a .c extension and display (to standard out) any line that contains the string MinMax. Case counts—that is, this command will not locate minmax or Minmax. There are a couple of ways to get case insensitivity. The most straight-forward would be to tell grep to compare the strings without regard to case, as shown in the following:

```
grep -i minmax *.c
```

The next example shows another way to have the search include both upper and low case:

```
grep [Mm]in[mM]ax *.c
```

The square brackets tell grep to match any one of the characters in a list. In this example, a match will be made for either case of M. The square brackets can also be used to exclude things by including a caret as the first character in the list. For example,

```
grep t[^aeiou] *.doc
```

will find all lines containing the letter t not followed by a vowel. When used at the beginning of the regular expression, the caret has another meaning—it limits the range of the search to the beginning of each line. For example,

```
grep ^rsh .*
```

will search through any files that are named beginning with a period, and it will display any lines that begin with the three characters rsh. At the other end,

```
grep ing$ *aa*.h
```

will display all lines that end with ing in all files with a name containing aa and ending with .h. If you don't need to see the actual lines—you just need to find the list of file-names containing a string—you can suppress the normal line-by-line output by doing the following:

```
grep -l apple *.text
```

This will list the name of all files that end with .text and contain the word apple.

Instead of getting it from a file, the grep command can receive its input through a pipe. This can be particularly useful to filter the output from some other command. Let's say there is a directory that has more files than you can display with a simple ls command, but you need to find a file and all you know is that is has the letters "chat" somewhere in its name. The following command would list the filenames for you:

```
ls -l ¦ grep chat
```

There will come a time when you want to search for a character that grep normally assumes to be some sort of special character in the regular expression. Say, for example, you want to find the three-character string x*]. The last two characters both have special meanings, so, to be taken literally, they will need to be preceded by a backslash character, as in the following:

```
grep x\*\] *.text
```

If there is something in a text file, and you can define a pattern for it, grep can be commanded to locate it. For example, the fields in the /etc/passwd file are separated by colons, and the second field is the encrypted form of the password. If the field holds an asterisk, the account is disabled. If the field is blank, the account is enabled and has no password. The following command will display all the accounts that do not have passwords:

```
grep ^[^:]*:: /etc/passwd
```

Just a quick glance at this command can be confusing, but grep is being asked to do a somewhat complicated search, so the complication must be in the expression. It works like this: the leading caret requires that the match be at the beginning of the line. Inside the brackets, any character qualifies *except* a colon. An asterisk following the brackets means that the bracketed part can be repeated any number of times, so the scanning proceeds to the first non-colon character on the line. Then there are a pair of colons, which is exactly what will happen if the password is missing.

One thing that almost everyone does with grep is devise a shell script that can be used to do a search on the files in an entire directory tree. There are times when this is necessary and nothing else will do. This capability is not built into grep, but it can be done by combing grep with find. There is an example of doing this in the description of find earlier in this chapter.

groups

This command retrieves a list of group names. With no arguments, the output will be the names of all the groups. For the superuser, the output looks something like the following:

```
root bin daemon sys adm disk
```

A user name can be specified, as in the following:

```
groups wilbur
```

The list of groups for the named user will be displayed.

gzip and gunzip

These utilitiesuse Lempel-Ziv coding to compress and uncompress files. The compressed file is tagged with a .gz extension. The gunzip utility can be used to restore files with the

.gz extension. These utilities work with files from other operating systems (such as DOS, OS/2, and VMS), and, if adding the .gz extension makes the name too long, gzip will truncate it.

For example, say you have a file named fred to be compressed. Do the following:

```
gzip fred
```

The file fred in the current directory is replaced by a smaller file named fred.gz. The file named fred has been deleted. To restore the file to its original state, do the following:

```
gunzip fred
```

Notice that the .gz extension is not specified. This command will restore the file named fred and delete fred.gz. You can do this on entire directories of files by using wildcards. For example, to compress every file in a directory, enter the following:

```
gzip *
```

Using the -r option will cause recursive action—that is, all the files in all the subdirectories will also be compressed.

> **Note:** You may also want to look at compress and zip. Both compress and gzip are commonly used in conjunction with tar to shrink files and pack them into a single file for distribution. The zip utility both compresses files and packs them into a single file.

head

This command will copy the first few lines of a file to the standard output. The following will output the first ten lines of a file named show.text:

```
head show.text
```

The number of lines displayed can be specified to be something other than the default of ten by using the -n option. For example, the following command will list the first 16 lines:

```
head -n 16 show.text
```

There is a companion utility, named tail, that lists the last few lines of a file.

killall

This command will send a signal to all processes that were started by the specified command—that is, signals can be sent by the process name. For example, if there is a script or program by the name of scantree, and one or more instances of it have been started as background processes, they can all be sent a kill signal in the following way:

```
killall scantree
```

While `kill` is the default, the actual signal sent can be specified by name or number. For example, SIGTERM (signal number 15) can be sent in either of the following ways:

```
killall -15 scantree
```

```
killall -TERM scantree
```

To determine the names of the signals known to `killall`, enter the following:

```
killall -l
```

look

If a text file is already sorted, this utility will find the line that begins with a specific string and display it. If there is more than one line beginning with the specified string, all of them are displayed. The file must be sorted because, to work fast in large files, `look` uses a binary search to find the matching string.

nohup

Normally, running a process leaves it open to receive signals that could stop it from running. These signals can be blocked by running a process under the control of `nohup`. Also, `nohup` increases the priority of the process by 5, and opens a file named `nohup.out` to receive any output from the running program. It doesn't automatically put the process in the background, but that can be done by using the ampersand, as shown in the following:

```
nohup find / -name *.txt -print &
```

This will cause `find` to run in the background in such a way that `kill` cannot stop it, and the file `nohup.out` will end up containing the name of every file in the system that ends with `.txt`.

mkdir

`mkdir` creates a directory. The directory name can either be in the current directory, or on a specified path. For example,

```
mkdir newdir
```

will create a directory named `newdir` as a subdirectory of the current directory. The entire path can be specified in the following way:

```
mkdir /home/fred/newdir
```

All except the last directory in the path must already exist. For example, to create the entire directory path of the previous example, it will be necessary to create all three directories, as shown in the following:

```
mkdir /home
mkdir /home/fred
mkdir /home/fred/newdir
```

paste

paste combines the contents of text files by concatenating lines. The first lines of each file are pasted together end-to-end to create the first output line. This is then done with the second line, and then the third, and so on, until all the text in all the input files has been processed.

Normally, there is a tab inserted where the lines are joined, but the -d option can be used to specify the separation character. For example, a text file named mary1 contains the following lines:

```
Mary had
It's fleece was
```

And a file named mary2 contains

```
a little lamb
white as snow
```

Entering the following command will paste the two files together side-by-side using a single space as the delimiting character:

```
paste -d " " mary1 mary2
```

The final output will look like the following:

```
Mary had a little lamb
It's fleece was white as snow
```

pr

Whenever you need to print a text file but would like to reformat it first, you may be able to use the pr utility to get the results you want. It has the ability to put text into columns, single or double space the output, convert tabs to spaces, specify a header to be printed on each page, control the page length, set the margins, convert unprintable characters octal values, and set the page width.

The options are described in Table 12.3. If no options are specified, there is a heading on each page that includes the date and time, the name of the file, and the page number.

Table 12.3   Options of the pr Utility

Option	Action
-*<number>*	To get the output to appear in multiple columns, just use the digit of the number of columns as if it were an option letter. The default is 1.

continues

Table 12.3 Continued

Option	Action
-a	Print columns across instead of down.
-b	Make the length of the columns the same on the last page.
-c	Use a caret character to print control characters as a pair of characters, as in ^C for Ctrl+C. Other unprintable characters will appear in backslash octal notation.
-d	Double space.
-e<*width*>	Expand tabs to spaces. If you don't specify a tab width, the default is 8.
-f	Use formfeed instead of newlines to separate output pages.
-h<*header*>	Replace the header on the top of each page. The default is the filename.
-i<*width*>	Replace spaces with tabs. If width is not specified, a width of 8 is assumed.
-l<*length*>	The length of a page. The default is 66.
-m	Print all the files listed on the command line beside one another—one file per column.
-n	Number the lines.
-o<*width*>	The number of characters of width to add to the left margin.
-r	Do not output an error message if an input file cannot be read.
-s<*character*>	Separate columns with the specified character. The default is a space.
-t	Do not print the five lines of the header and trailer on each page.
-v	Print all unprintable characters in the octal backslash notation.
-w<*width*>	Specify the path width. The default is 72 characters.

printf

This utility can be used to format text for display. It is very much like the printf() function in the C programming language. Its first argument is a formatting string and the rest of the arguments are values to be plugged into the string. For example,

```
HOOPS=44
printf "The final count is %s hoops\n" $HOOPS
```

will produce the following output:

```
The final count is 44 hoops
```

rm

This command can be used to delete a file, a collection of files, or an entire directory tree along with every file in it. To delete a file, just name it on the command line, as shown in the following:

```
rm filename
```

If no path is named, the file is assumed to be in the local directory. To specify the exact location, the pathname can be used, as shown in the following:

```
rm /home/fred/filename
```

Wildcards can be used to delete groups of files. For example, to delete every file in the current directory that ends with .doc, use the following:

```
rm *.doc
```

If you want to delete a directory and everything it contains—including any subdirectories the files and the directories they contain—use a command like the following:

```
rm -r dirname
```

The contents of the directory named dirname, and everything inside dirname, will be deleted.

There are circumstances that will cause the rm command to display information or even prompt the user for a decision. Usually, inside a script, this is an unnecessary activity, so the prompts can be suppressed with the "force" option, as in the following:

```
rm -rf dirname
```

The -r option tells the command to remove things recursively, and the -f option suppresses any messages and forces rm to delete everything in the tree. Of course, if you don't have the appropriate permissions to delete a file or directory, it won't happen.

> **Caution:** There is potential disaster lurking in rm. The -r option will descend to all subdirectories, and the -f option will delete everything and won't even tell you that it's doing it. The worst case scenario is logging in as the superuser, changing to the root directory, and entering the command rm -rf *. This would wipe out everything on the disk drive, and on all the mounted volumes—Everything.

rmdir

This command will remove an empty directory. The syntax is as follows:

```
rmdir dirname
```

This utility is used in the recursive form of rm for deleting directories after each of the files has been deleted.

sed

This is a stream editor. That is, you can give it a set of instructions and have it apply them to a file by reading sequentially through the file and applying your instructions to each line. The editing instructions can be supplied on the command line or in a separate file.

The most common action to be performed is to replace one string with another. For example, to replace corn with grain, use the following command:

```
sed s/corn/grain/ textfile
```

This second string can be null—the following command will remove corn from the file altogether:

```
sed s/corn// textfile
```

Let's say you want to insert four spaces at the beginning of each line. The caret character matches the beginning of a line, so the command could be entered in the following way:

```
sed 's/^/    /' textfile
```

It is necessary to put the command in single quotes because it contains spaces and the shell would break it into separate arguments. There are some special characters that can follow the replacement command that have an effect on how it works. Take the following four cases:

```
s/oldstring/newstring/
s/oldstring/newstring/g
s/oldstring/newstring/p
s/oldstring/newstring/w filename
```

If no letter is specified on the end, the old string is replaced only the first time it occurs in a line. If g is specified, every occurrence on the line will be substituted. If p is specified, the line will be printed. The w option will write the line to the named file.

The following example will delete every line containing the word corn:

```
sed '/corn/d' textfile
```

> **Note:** After using sed for a while, you will find that using sed in a script is a lot easier than using it directly from the command line. The reason for this is that the editing commands can get to be a little arcane, and you will want to test them before you have them modify all your files. If it is in a script, you can debug it just as you would any other program.

The following sed command will double-space text:

```
sed 's/$/\
/' textfile
```

Here's how it works. The dollar character ($) selects the end of each line, and that's where you want to insert a newline character. The backslash is the escape character telling sed that the next character, no matter what it is, should be taken literally as part of the command string. The next character is a newline character so, through substitution, an extra newline character is appended on the end of each line. The text is double-spaced.

The following command will insert the text this goes here after every line in the input file:

```
sed 'a\
this goes here' textfile
```

You can extract a group of lines from a file. The following command will output lines 25 through 37 of the file, and then stop:

```
sed 25,37p textfile
```

The sed utility has been a part of UNIX for a long time. Some of its syntax may be strange, but it does simple editing very well and very efficiently.

sort

The sort utility works on text files and can do three different things. It can sort a file, merge two already-sorted files, and test a file to see whether it is sorted. If no option flag is specified, the input will be sorted. If -c is specified, the input is test for being sorted. If -m is specified, the input files are expected to be sorted and will be merged together to a single output.

Its most useful form is for sorting. For example, the following command will sort a file named intext and create a new sorted file named outtext:

```
sort intext >outtext
```

The entire line of text is the sort key—the characters are compared one by one until one line is found to be greater than the other. If you want to skip some leading characters on the line and have the comparison start at, say, character 12, you can do the following:

```
sort +12 intext >outtext
```

If you want to specify the key position being from column 5 through 9, use the following command:

```
sort +5 -10 intext >outtext
```

The options for the sort command are listed in Table 12.4.

Table 12.4   Options for the sort Command

Option	Means
-b	Skip leading blanks when looking for the key value for comparison.
-d	Ignore all characters except letters, digits, and blanks.
-f	Lowercase characters are converted to uppercase for the purposes of comparison.
-i	Ignore any characters outside the range of the printable ASCII characters.
-M	Sort the three-letter names of the months (Jan, Feb, and so on) in chronological order.
-n	The key is interpreted as a numeric value, and the value is used for the comparison. Number strings can include leading signs and a decimal point.
-o*<file>*	Name the output file.
-r	Reverse the order of the sort.
-t*<char>*	Specify the character used to separate one field from another.
-u	If two or more lines compare as being equal, output the first of the lines.

tail

tail copies the last few lines of a file to the standard output. The following example will output the last ten lines of a file named show.text:

```
tail show.text
```

The number of lines displayed can be specified to be something other than the default of ten by using the -n option. For example, the following command will list the last 16 lines:

```
tail -n 16 show.text
```

One common use for this utility is to list each line of a file as it is written. Say you have a program running that has opened a file named dostuff.log and, from time to time, writes a new entry to it. The tail command can be used to echo each line to standard out as it is written in the following way:

```
tail -f dostuff.log
```

With the -f option, the tail program does not terminate. It displays the last few lines of the file and waits forever for new lines to appear. To cause it to stop waiting, it is necessary to break out of the program (normally by pressing Control+Z, but sometimes Control+C will also work).

There is a companion utility, named head, that lists the first few lines of a file.

tar

This utility will store a number of files and directories into a single file. This is an old UNIX utility originally designed to read and write data on tape; the name derived from "tape archive." The output file normally ends with the characters .tar, and these files are often referred to as "tar files" or as "archives." Depending on the option flags used, the program can either read or write a tar file. Table 12.5 lists the options that can be used to create and maintain tar files.

Note: The tar format is often used in conjunction with the compress utility, or the gzip/ungzip utility pair, to create a package of files for distribution. To signify how the files have been packaged, the name either ends with .tar.Z for compress, or with either .tar.z or .tar.gz for gzip.

Table 12.5 The tar File and Directory Options

Option	Description
-A	Adds files to an existing tar file.
-c	Creates a new tar file.
-d	Compares a tar file to a set of files on disk.
--delete	Deletes a file from the tar file
-f <filename>	The name of the output tar file.
-k	When extracting files from a tar file, do not overwrite any existing files.
-r	Appends files to the end of the tar file.
-t	Lists the contents of the tar file.
-u	Only add files that are newer than the ones already in the tar file.
-v	Produces a verbose listing of the file processed.
-x	Extracts files from the tar file.
-z	Applies compression to the tar file using gzip and ungzip.
-Z	Applies compression to the tar file using compress and uncompress.

If no tar filename is specified, the tar command will assume standard input or output. The following example will create a tar file named fred.tar containing all the files in the current directory, and all the files in all its subdirectories:

```
tar -c * >fred.tar
```

It is also possible to specify the filename on the command line by using the `-f` option, as shown in the following:

```
tar -cf fred.tar *
```

Once the `tar` file is created, you can view its contents in the following way:

```
tar -t <fred.tar
```

The `-t` option lists the names of the files and directories in the `tar` file. The command can be made to be more verbose, as shown in the following:

```
tar -tvf fred.tar
```

The `-t` option is the command to list the contents, and the `-v` option is used to make the listing verbose. The listing includes information on each files permissions, owner, group, and the last date the file was modified.

To extract the files from the `tar` file, a command like the following can be used:

```
tar -xf fred.tar
```

If you would rather see the list of the filenames as they are being extracted, use the verbose option shown in the following:

```
tar -xvf fred.txt
```

The `tar` utility performs no file compression itself, but it can be told to call upon other utilities to do the compression for it. For example, to create a `tar` file and compress it with the `compress` utility, do the following:

```
tar -cZf fred.tar.Z
```

Once it is created, you can verify its contents by listing the filenames, as shown in the following:

```
tar -tvZf fred.tar.Z
```

The files can be extracted from the archive in the following way:

```
tar -xZf fred.tar.Z
```

In similar fashion, a `tar` file can be created and compressed using `gzip`, as shown in the following:

```
tar -czf fred.tar.z
```

The contents of the file can then be extracted in the following way:

```
tar -xzf fred.tar.z
```

tty

This utility prints the name of the terminal connected to standard input. For regular Linux logins, this will be /dev/ttyN, where N is the number of the current virtual terminal. A login made from some location other than the local display will display the name of its local connecting device.

uniq

The uniq utility removes consecutive duplicate lines from a file. Its most common use is to come along behind a sort operation and clean up the file.

The following example reads the lines of text in intext and, after deleting consecutive duplicates, writes the output to outtext:

```
uniq intext outtext
```

The contents of outtext includes only one of any duplicated lines. If the output file is not named, the output will go to standard out, and if neither file is named, the input comes from standard in and the output goes to standard out.

Using the following form will cause both of any duplicated lines to be deleted:

```
uniq -u intext outtext
```

The following form will cause one copy of each duplicated line to be sent to the output, but nothing else:

```
uniq -d intext outtext
```

users

This command will display the list of names of the users that are currently logged in. The names are output in a single list suitable for use on a for statement. If you need to know more that just the names, use the who command.

wall

This command can be used to send a message to every session logged in, for example,

```
wall It's time for recess. We're having cookies and milk.
```

If the following command is entered from the root on tty1, this message will display on the screen of everyone logged in (including the sender):

```
Broadcast message from root (tty1) Thu Sep 16 10:27:17 1999
It's time for recess. We're having cookies and milk.
```

For a user to receive a message, he must have messages enabled. To enable messages, enter the following:

```
mesg y
```

To disable messages, enter

```
mesg n
```

By default, messages are enabled.

wc

wc prints the number of lines, words, and bytes in a text file. Words are separated by white space (including tabs and the end of the line). The default form of the output is to print the three numbers followed by the filename, as shown in the following:

```
wc cardtext
```

The output from this command will look something like the following:

```
    82    511    2313 cardtext
```

This means the file contains 82 lines, 511 words, and 2313 characters. If you don't need all the information at once, it can be acquired one value at a time, as shown in Table 12.6.

Table 12.6   The wc Options

Option	Description
-c	Displays only the character count value
-l	Displays only the line count value
-w	Displays only the word count value

who

The who command lists information about currently logged in users. Entering the command with no options lists the name of each user, the login devices, and the time and date each logged in. The output looks like the following:

```
root      tty1     Apr  7 15:34
harvey    tty3     Apr  8 09:44
mcoop     ttyv9    Apr  8 10:19
```

Using the -i or -u option, the same information is displayed, but the elapsed time since logging in is also displayed, as in the following:

```
root      tty1     Apr  7 15:34    .
harvey    tty3     Apr  8 09:44 01:28
mcoop     ttyv9    Apr  8 10:19 00:53
```

Notice that the root login was more than 24 hours ago, so it appears as a single dot. The -H option can be used to put a heading on top of each column. For example, the following command combines two of the options:

```
who -iH
```

The output from this command looks like the following:

```
USER      LINE     LOGIN-TIME    FROM
root      tty1     Apr  7 15:34
harvey    tty3     Apr  8 09:44 01:28
mcoop     ttyv9    Apr  8 10:19 00:53
```

There is a special form of the who command that can be used to find out information about the current session, as shown in the following:

```
who am i
```

The output from this includes the name of the host as well as the other information, and looks like the following:

```
maxim.belugalake.com!root       tty1    Apr 7 15:34
```

The following is a short form that lists only the user names followed by a count of users:

```
who -q
```

The output looks like the following:

```
root harvey mcoop
# users=3
```

The who command can be used to determine which users allow themselves to receive messages. The default is for a user to receive messages, but a user can turn it off by using the mesg command, as shown in the following:

```
who -w
```

The output from this command looks like the following:

```
root      -     tty1    Apr  7 15:34
harvey    +     tty3    Apr  8 09:44
mcoop     ?     ttyv9   Apr  8 10:19
```

The minus sign indicates that the user allows messages, the plus sign indicates that the user prohibits messages, and the question mark means that the who command cannot find the terminal device.

zip and unzip

The zip command will compress a collection of files and store them into a single file. The unzip command will read a file created by zip and restore the files to their previous size.

> **Tip:** The format of the files is the same as the ones used in DOS and can be accessed directly with WINZIP, PKZIP, and PKUNZIP. However, some of the older versions may not be that compatible. If you run into trouble, get a newer version of PKZIP and PKUNZIP.

There are a lot of options to both zip and unzip, but they are easily accessible. Just type zip or unzip without any arguments and all the options will be displayed.

Summary

With the combination of the command line utilities and the shell script programming facilities, it is possible to write some very complex systems. There are many application systems today that are made more of shell scripts than of compiled programs. This is because of the concept of having a flexible scripting language along with a large number of small utility programs each designed to do one task. By combining them using files, pipes, return codes, and so on, it is possible to create very complex scripts.

On Your Own

Write a script that uses file and test to find out all there is to know about a file. You can find out exactly what kind of file it is, how old it is, how big it is, and so on.

Write a one-line script that uses find and head and can be used to list the first few lines of each qualifying file in an entire directory tree.

Use grep to locate lines with two words on them, but allow the words to occur in any order and to have other words between them. Hint: pipe the output of one grep into the input of another.

PART IV

Networking with Linux

TCP/IP Networking with Linux

The acronym TCP/IP refers to a large family of protocols that work together to communicate among computers all over the world. The technology of TCP/IP has been such a success that almost all networks are based on it. There are a few proprietary networks here and there that use other protocols, but most of those also support TCP/IP. Linux is no exception—all Linux networking is based on TCP/IP.

General TCP/IP Networking

Every computer connected via TCP/IP is called a *host*.

A host can be a *server*. A server waits for incoming requests from other hosts, obeys the commands, and may or may not respond with some data. For example, a printer server will send the incoming data to a printer, while a file server will return the contents of a file or the filenames in a directory.

A host can be a *client*. A client sends requests to a server for action to be performed. For example, a client could be running a Web browser and issue a request to a Web server to retrieve a Web page.

A host can be a *router* or a *gateway*. A router has the job of inspecting the destination addresses of incoming messages and forwarding them to the correct computer—either the final destination or a computer that connects to the destination. A gateway has the job of passing messages back and forth between two otherwise disconnected networks—often using different technology and/or protocols.

A host can be a *firewall*. A firewall is a computer, attached to a local network, that handles all incoming and outgoing traffic to other networks, including the Internet. Nothing private or irreplaceable is stored on the computer. To protect the local network from outside attack, restrictions can be placed on what sort of activities are allowed. For example, there may be an FTP directory on the firewall computer, or on a local host outside the firewall, but no outside FTP access is allowed to the other computers in the local network.

A host can be any combination of these things. A single computer can be a server for one service while acting as a client for another, and all the while it could be doing some routing.

The Internet uses Internet technology. Lowercase is used to refer to the technology, and uppercase is used to refer to the world-wide network made up of millions of computers.

The IP Address

Every host has a unique address. The IP (Internet Protocol) address is a 32-bit number. You are accustomed to seeing Internet addresses like amazon.com and www.linux.org, but these names are simply used to look up the actual addresses—just like you look up names in the phone book to find a person's number (more on the IP lookup process later in this chapter).

An IP address is normally displayed and written as four base-10 numbers representing the value of each of the four bytes. It is a little more intuitive to read an address written in the following way

97.129.44.202

than to read the same address written in the following form:

1,616,793,022

The dot format is especially useful because byte-by-byte masking can be done to define subnetworks and address categories.

You don't need to have an IP address before you dial up to an Internet provider. The provider has reserved a block of addresses and, when you log in, assigns one of them to you. You will use the address as long as you remain online. It is this address that the various servers and routers use to send messages back to you. When you log off, the address you were using goes back into the address pool to be assigned to another caller.

If you are going to be building a local network of your own, you will need to have some IP addresses. Fortunately there have been some set aside just for this purpose. You can use any address from 192.168.1.1 through 192.168.1.254. Although you can use the addresses freely in your own network, you need to make sure they don't go out over the Internet, because, the Internet being what it is, there is no predicting what will happen to your data packets. This range of addresses gives you enough space to build a network of over 250 computers, which is large enough for most purposes. If you are going to need more than 250 addresses, you may want to contact your ISP to get a larger block of addresses. If you accidentally use an address internally that matches that of some external host, you will not be able to send messages to the external host (all messages to it will be routed locally).

IP Address Classes and Masks

IP addresses are often allocated in blocks so an organization can use a set of contiguous addresses. This has the advantage that multiple-host operations (such as broadcasting a message) are much easier to execute. These networks come in different sizes, so address ranges have been divided into groups called *classes* as listed in Table 13.1.

Table 13.1   The IP Address Classes

Class Address	Initial Byte	Initial Bit value	Network Address	Local Address
A	0 to 127	0...	7 bits	24 bits
B	128 to 191	10...	14 bits	16 bits
C	192 to 223	110...	21 bits	8 bits
D	224 to 239	1110...	-	-
E	240 to 255	1111...	-	-

The number of leading 1 bits in the first byte of the address determines the address class and, since these are the high-order bits of the byte, they impose a numeric range for the first byte of each of the classes. All of addresses are 32 bits long, but they are divided up differently. A class A address only has 7 bits to define its network, so there can't be more than 128 networks with class A addresses. However, with the 24-bit local address, each of these class A networks can be very large. A class C address uses all of the first three bytes (three leading bits and the 21 bits that follow it) for the network address, so there can be a lot of these networks. But each network is limited to 254 unique addresses (the numbers 0 and 255 have special meanings as described later).

Class D and class E addresses are special. A class D address is used for multicasting. Simply put, several hosts can be configured to receive messages sent to a multicast address so a single packet can be sent out on a network and it will arrive at multiple destinations. Class E addresses are for experimentation and should be used with care— mostly these are used on local networks, but occasionally one may escape to the Internet.

Addresses can be masked to create subnets within a network. The mask is a 32-bit value, just like an IP address, and is written in the same way. For example, the mask 255.255.255.0 can be applied to a class C address to extract the network portion. As it turns out, these masks can be very handy in routing in subnetworking. In your local network, for example, if your computer is on a class B network that has the address 163.9.82.221, the network mask 255.255.0.0 would extract the address of the network: 163.9.0.0. You could also have a departmental router (or, there could be some other reason to create a subnet) and assign your department's network address as 163.9.82.0, which means every host in your department must use this address and change the last byte to a unique number. The subnet mask would be 255.255.255.0. This mask could be used by routers to determine the identity of the subnet and route messages accordingly.

The Port Number

While the IP address is sufficient to locate a computer, it is also necessary to locate a specific application on that computer. For example, if the incoming message is email, it needs to be sent to the mail reader. If the incoming message is a request from a Web page, it needs to be routed to the program that sends out Web pages.

There is an ID number, called the *port* number, that is sent with every message. It is necessary for the sender to know the port number as well as the address, so certain numbers are standard. These standard values are known as the *well known* port numbers. For example, every Web browser knows that the port number is 80 on every host with a Web server. There are also numbers assigned for email, FTP, and every other kind of Internet service.

While the default port number is 80 for the Web, it is possible to specify another port number. This would require that there be a program listening to the other port number. For example, if a computer has an experimental Web server on port 1099, a URL to address it could be written as follows:

```
http://www.belugalake.com:1099/index.html
```

Whenever a message is sent from a client to a server, the return address and return port number are included. The server uses these address numbers to form the address for returning the response. Whenever you start your Web browser or email reader, it requests an unused port number for the local machine. It uses that number as part of its return address and will listen for, and receive, any incoming messages addressed to that port. This is why it is possible to run several Internet programs simultaneously and the messages never get mixed.

The Domain Name System (DNS)

DNS is the phone book used to look up names to find their IP addresses. The phone book files are distributed—in fact, with the Internet being so large, this information is undoubtedly the most distributed database on Earth. The DNS system was designed to operate automatically, and it has been evolving over a long period of time and uses some ingenious algorithms. It is so robust that if you connect a brand new host to the Internet (using an IP address that has been assigned to you), that host is immediately available, by name, from any place in the world. If you change the name of a host, the new name can immediately be addressed from anywhere.

Names and addresses can be manually stored on your local computer in text files. In fact, this is the way the Internet began, and is still a common practice for small networks. As soon as the network grows beyond just a few computers, it starts getting to be a problem to maintain all the addresses on all the computers. It made sense to automate list maintenance—have one computer manage the list and have the other computers refer to it to look up addresses.

In earlier days of the Internet, there was one central location that held all the names and addresses. Every time there was a need to find the address for a name, this central database was queried and the address was returned. As the Internet expanded, it became less and less practical to have every address request go to the same place—there had to be some way to distribute the database, but, at the same time, have it be correct and up to date.

The basic information is still kept in one of several central repositories. There is one for each domain (.com, .org, .net, and so on). These are the Domain Name Servers. Just like in the earlier version of the Internet, whenever you want the address of a name in, say, the org domain (such as gnome.org or linux.org), the request is routed to the central org name server and the address is returned. But some other things happen.

The central repository doesn't keep the name of every host—just every domain name. For example, if you request the address of www.mizzen.homer.com, the domain name server will only know the address of homer.com. The request for the address is forwarded to homer.com to be resolved further. If homer.com does not know the address, it will pass the request on to mizzen.homer.com.

It is likely that your request for the address will be passed through several hosts on its way, and the response could also pass through several hosts on its way back to you. As the address information is returned, each host takes a peek at the name and address being resolved and adds the information to its list of known names and addresses. Now, if you or someone else, requests the address again, and the request comes to one of the hosts that took a peek, the host will respond with the address it grabbed earlier instead of sending the request on up to the top. The more often a name is used, the faster the lookups become.

The concept of the address tables is simple enough, but there are some bookkeeping things involved. The main problem is that addresses picked up this way can become stale (the address of the host could change or even disappear entirely). To solve this problem, the entries in the table are set to expire after a certain period of time causing any new requests for the address to get a fresh address from further up the hierarchy.

To keep addresses as fresh as possible, the computers that are directly connected to one another keep up a constant chatter among themselves sharing address information. This way, the hosts easily keep up with names and addresses that are one or two hops away. And it is surprising how much of the world is connected by one or two hops.

DNS and Routing

The trick is to use the 32-bit IP address to move a message from one place to another. The computers responsible for doing this maintain routing tables—this is a principal characteristic of a router. The routing tables are consulted for every incoming message to determine where the message should be sent next.

There are three possible results of a router looking for an address in the table. The destination host can be directly connected to the router, in which case the message is immediately passed on. The table entry can also hold the IP address of a directly connected computer that will accept the message and pass it on. The third possibility is that the destination IP address simply isn't in the table—in this case, the message is forwarded to the default IP address to be used for all "other" addresses. This default address is a router, normally higher up in the Internet hierarchy and should have access to more routing information.

These routing tables are maintained automatically. When a router is first set up, it is configured with one or more hardware connections, and it is given the address that will receive messages that have unknown addresses. The software takes it from there. The new router will broadcast a message to all of its directly connected hosts. These hosts will respond with their names and addresses, and with the names and address of any other computers they know about. The basic routing table has been established. This conversation among directly-connected hosts continues as long as their connections are maintained. This way, if a computer becomes disconnected from the network, its name and address will disappear from the routing tables after a short period of time. If the host is reconnected (or rebooted), its name and address will once again propagate through the system.

The routing tables are built and maintained from the information passing through. Each router forwarding a message appends its own name and address. By the time a message reaches its destination, there can be a long list of names and addresses included in the header. As each router adds its own name and address, it reads the names and addresses of those already in the list and uses the information to update its routing tables. This way, a router is able to learn the routing of remote computers.

Actually, the routing table doesn't need to contain the complete route to a remote host. All that is required is the address of the host that will forward the message appropriately (it is possible to specify an exact route, but that has nothing to do with normal routing). For example, if a message is passing through and it shows that it originated with a host named fred and went through the routers sam, pete, and harvey to get here, there is a bit of information that can be added to the table. The host named harvey must be directly connected to this host. Also, to send a message to fred, sam, or pete, just send it to harvey and it will be forwarded. The more messages that are sent, the more comprehensive the routing tables.

It often happens that there is more than one way to get from point A to point B on the Internet. That's where the metrics come in. Along with the routing information, there is a count of the number of hops (a count of the intermediate routers) it takes to get from one place to another. A router will always choose the route with the lowest number of hops, but it keeps the other one in its tables in case the shortest one fails.

What you have just read is a very simplified view of routing. There is a good deal of bookkeeping and confirmation that goes on as the routers constantly chat among themselves. Also, there is a lot of different software out there that has its own procedures for maintaining routing tables, but the protocols passing between them are standard, so they all seem to play together nicely.

Special IP Addresses

There are some IP address that are set aside for special purposes.

The *loopback* address is 127.0.0.1. Any message sent to this address will not be sent over the network. It will turn around and come back to the local host, just as if it had come from the network. This is mostly used by programmers and system administrators for debugging applications—the client and server can both be running on the same machine.

Every computer on the Internet must have a unique IP address assigned to it. So, if you would like to have a local network of your own, you will need some unique addresses. But there is no need to use worldwide–unique numbers because there is a block of addresses that have been set aside just for local networks. The addresses 192.168.1.1 through 192.168.1.254 can be used by the hosts for your local network and, barring an error of some sort, will never interfere with outside Internet traffic.

The value of 255 (all ones) has special meaning in an address. The address 255.255.255.255 will broadcast a message to every host on your local network. This can be used, for example, to distribute local messages or to find out which computers are attached to the network and are up and running. Assuming the hosts on your local network use the addresses 192.168.1.xxx, you can also broadcast to them all by using 192.168.1.255.

The value of 0 also has special meaning in an address. The address 0.0.0.0 addresses the current host on local network. In effect, it is the same as the loopback address.

The Files

There is a collection of files that hold the names and addresses used for communications. Some of the files are edited directly, and some are modified using utility programs. The majority of these configuration settings were made when you installed Linux, so you may not have to do anything to them, but if you decide to change something or you need to troubleshoot your network, these are the places to look.

The `/etc/protocols` File

This file defines the set of low-level protocols. Unless you are doing something very special (like adding a whole new protocol) you will never need to edit this file, but it is important to TCP/IP communications.

Every packet of data sent or received over the Internet is encapsulated in a protocol wrapper. The sender must know how to wrap the data, and the receiver must know how to unwrap it. The two hosts agree on a group of ID numbers that are used as tags to identify the protocol when the message arrives. These ID numbers are kept in the /etc/ protocols file that looks like the following:

```
ip     0     IP     # internet protocol, pseudo protocol number
icmp   1     ICMP   # internet control message protocol
igmp   2     IGMP   # internet group multicast protocol
ggp    3     GGP    # gateway-gateway protocol
tcp    6     TCP    # transmission control protocol
pup    12    PUP    # PARC universal packet protocol
udp    17    UDP    # user datagram protocol
raw    255   RAW    # RAW IP interface
```

The first column is the name of the protocol, and the second is its ID number. There can be one or more aliases following the number—in most cases there is an uppercase form of the name, but it can be anything. From the entries in the table, you can see that there is more to TCP/IP than just TCP and IP. Some of the protocols (icmp, igmp, and ggp) are used by Internet hosts to communicate addresses and routing information.

Almost all messages sent over the Internet use either TCP or UDP. The two are similar enough, but there is one major difference. The UDP protocol is connectionless—that is, it sends out messages without verifying that they are ever received on the other end. The TCP protocol is connected—that is, the sender expects each packet to evoke a response when it is successfully received.

The /etc/services File

When a host receives a message from the Internet, the message must be routed to the program for which it is intended. This is done by using the entries in the /etc/services file. The file contains an entry for many services. Having an entry in this list does not mean the service is running, it only means that if it were running, this would be its port number and protocol. The file looks like the following:

```
tcpmux      1/tcp        # rfc-1078
echo        7/tcp
echo        7/udp
discard     9/tcp sink null
discard     9/udp sink null
systat      11/tcp users
daytime     13/tcp
daytime     13/udp
netstat     15/tcp
qotd        17/tcp quote
chargen     19/tcp ttytst source
chargen     19/udp ttytst source
ftp-data    20/tcp
ftp         21/tcp
```

```
telnet      23/tcp
smtp        25/tcp mail
time        37/tcp timserver
time        37/udp timserver
rlp         39/udp resource       # resource location
name        42/udp nameserver
whois       43/tcp nicname        # usually to sri-nic
domain      53/tcp
domain      53/udp
mtp         57/tcp                # deprecated
bootps      67/udp                # bootp server
bootpc      68/udp                # bootp client
tftp        69/udp
gopher      70/tcp                # gopher server
rje         77/tcp
finger      79/tcp
http        80/tcp
link        87/tcp ttylink
kerberos    88/udp kdc            # Kerberos authentication-udp
kerberos    88/tcp kdc            # Kerberos authentication-tcp
linuxconf   98/tcp                # added by linuxconf RPM
hostnames   101/tcp hostname      # usually to sri-nic
pop-3       110/tcp               # PostOffice V.3
pop         110/tcp               # PostOffice V.3
snmp        161/udp
snmp-trap   162/udp
login       513/tcp               # BSD rlogind(8)
who         513/udp whod          # BSD rwhod(8)
pcnfs       640/udp               # PC-NFS DOS Authentication
nfs         2049/udp              # NFS File Service
dos         7000/tcp msdos
```

This file is not complete because there are hundreds of protocols and new ones are being devised all the time. Most of the numbers in this table fall into the category of being *well known* port numbers. For example, the World Wide Web, based on the http protocol, is expected to have its server waiting on port 80. Any incoming TCP message with a port number of 80 will directed to the Web server. Some of the services can operate in both UDP and TCP mode—for example, the simple echo protocol listens to port 7 for both incoming TCP and UDP messages. A protocol can have more than one name. For example, port 42 is used by the name protocol, also called the nameserver protocol. The FTP protocol requires two port numbers—it uses 20 to transmit and receive data while it uses 21 to send and receive control and configuration information.

The /etc/hosts File

Several Linux utility programs require an IP address. After you use these utilities a bit, you will find that you need a better way to enter addresses than typing in four numbers with periods—they are hard to remember and it's easy to make errors. This is a better way. If you put the names and addresses in the file named /etc/hosts, the utilities will translate the name of a host into its IP address.

The following is an example of a host's file:

```
127.0.0.1          localhost
192.168.1.10       arlin
192.168.1.3        rimshot herbert winbox
192.168.1.1        cygnus louise cygnus.localdomain.com
```

The first address is the special loopback address. This entry should be in every host's file. Having the loopback address defined this way allows software to use the standard name localhost to address the machine on which it's running.

This is the host's file for a computer name arlin, and the name and address of the local host is in the table. This has about the same effect as the loopback address because messages sent to this address will come right back. The last two entries contain the addresses of two computers on the local network.

Some of the entries have more than one name. The first name in the list is required, but you can define as many aliases for a host as you would like. Any names after the first one are considered aliases because, whenever the host's file is used to translate an IP address to a name, the first name in the list is used. The last entry in the table shows that it is possible to use periods to enter a complete domain name.

> **Note:** The contents of the /etc/hosts file is only available to software on the local computer. It is sort of a privately held address book. For a network to operate properly, each computer on the network will need an /etc/hosts file containing the names and addresses of the others.

The /etc/hosts.allow and /etc/hosts.deny Files

These two files are for security. If you want to grant access to only a specific list of hosts or prevent access for a specific lists of hosts, you can do that with these files. The process goes as follows:

1. The /etc/hosts.allow file is checked and permission is granted if the host is specifically granted permission for the requested access.

2. The /etc/hosts.deny file is checked and permission is denied if the host is specifically prohibited permission for the requested access.

3. Permission has not been specifically granted nor denied, so it is granted by default.

Monitoring Your Network

There are several utilities included with Linux that can be used to gather information about the condition of your network. Most of these utilities have existed for a long time because TCP/IP and UNIX sort of grew up together. There are many more utilities than the ones listed here, but the others mostly deal with specialized services such as news and mail.

The arp Utility

The Address Resolution Protocol (ARP) defines a way that a host on a local network can broadcast the information about its address and receive information about the address of other hosts. This protocol was originally designed to supply the information needed for each host to be able to translate an IP address into an Ethernet hardware address, but the design is flexible enough that it also works for token rings and other types of networks.

The Linux kernel maintains a list of address resolutions in a memory cache. This cache can be viewed and modified using the arp utility. To display a listing of the cache, enter arp with no arguments, as shown in the following:

```
arp
```

The output will contain one line per cache member. The following example output shows the cached addresses for two hosts:

```
Address              HWtype  HWaddress           Flags Mask   Iface
cygnus.athome.com    ether   00:10:4B:22:10:6A   C            eth0
rimshot.athome.com   ether   00:50:4E:03:BD:6D   C            eth0
```

The first column is the domain name of the host, and the second column is the type of connection (in this case, Ethernet). The HWaddress column is the Ethernet hardware address. For this host to send a message to rimshot, it is necessary to send an Ethernet packet to the hardware address. The letter C indicates the entry has been dynamically acquired and is complete. The last column contains the name of the interface as it appears in ifconfig.

The cache also stores the IP address as well as the name of each host. To display the IP addresses, request a numeric display, as shown in the following:

```
arp -n
```

The format of the output is the same, except the names of the hosts are replaced by the IP addresses, as shown in the following:

```
Address              HWtype  HWaddress           Flags Mask   Iface
192.168.1.1          ether   00:10:4B:22:10:6A   C            eth0
192.168.1.3          ether   00:50:4E:03:BD:6D   C            eth0
```

This cache is very dynamic and can change from one moment to the next. If, for example, there is no communication with another host for a period of time, it will be dropped from the cache. Under normal circumstances, the cache is maintained automatically, but it is possible to use the arp command to modify the cache. For example, a host can be removed from the list with the following command:

```
arp -d rimshot
```

With arp, as with most utilities, a host can be identified by either its name or its numeric IP address—anyplace you can use one, you can use the other. Hosts can be added to the cache also. For example, the following command will add a new host name and its hardware address:

```
arp -s clamage 00:51:4E:5A:AD:03
```

An entry manually added to the cache is not considered dynamic information and will not be removed. It will be listed in the output with its flag set to P for permanent.

The host Utility

This utility uses the domain name service to look up host names and return information about them and about how the network is organized. By using domain and host names with the host utility, it is possible to discover the connection pathways for an entire domain or sub-domain.

To find the basic address information about a host, just enter the domain name of the host on the command line, as shown in the following:

```
host belugalake.com
```

The response will vary depending on what information is available, but a typical response to this command includes the IP address of the host and the address of one or more of its email addresses, as shown in the following:

```
belugalake.com has address 208.151.161.66
belugalake.com mail is handled (pri=10) by ix.netcorps.com
```

Many hosts handle their own mail, but it is common (especially on hosts with heavy traffic) to have one or more other systems handling email. Continuing with the same example, information on the email system can be gathered by using the name of the mail handler, as shown in the following:

```
host ix.netcorps.com
```

The display shows the IP address of the email handler and also points out that it handles its own mail, as in the following:

```
ix.netcorps.com has address 207.1.125.106
ix.netcorps.com mail is handled (pri=10) by ix.netcorps.com
```

You can get a list of all the names and addresses within a domain:

```
host -l linux.org
```

In a large domain, this could be a very long list. In some domains, because of security concerns, the query will be refused. The displayed list contains the domain name and a description of its purpose. The following are some examples taken from a much longer list produced by the previous command:

```
linux.org name server ns.invlogic.com
nl.linux.org name server terra.geo.uu.nl
```

```
news.linux.org has address 198.182.196.57
europa.linux.org has address 198.182.196.49
```

There are two kinds of entries in the list. The last two lines contain the IP address of simple hosts. The entry for linux.org, on the first line, displays the name of a name server. The second line also displays a name server implying that nl.linux.org is the root of a subdomain of linux.org. You can discover the names and addresses of the hosts in the subdomain by entering this command:

```
host -l nl.linux.org
```

This command will display the addresses and name servers of the hosts in the subdomain.

It is possible to use host with the -t option to get other information. For example, to match the name of the hosts with their nicknames, enter a command like this:

```
host -l -t cname linux.org
```

A search will be made through the linux.org domain, and a list like the following will be displayed:

```
irc.linux.org is a nickname for irc.linpeople.org
irc.us.linux.org is a nickname for irc.us.linpeople.org
agora.linux.org is a nickname for agora.linpeople.org
```

Table 13.2 lists the data selection options available. These options are used as an argument to the -t option and can be used in combination with both -l and -v. The -v option changes the format of the output by including much more detailed information.

Table 13.2   Values for the -t Option on the host Utility

Value	Retrieves
a	Dotted IP address.
ns	An authoritative name server for the domain.
mx	A mail exchanger host. If there is more than one, a preference value is supplied (lower numbers are selected first).
cname	The alias name, or names, assigned to a host.
soa	The start of a zone authority information for a domain.
rp	The person responsible for the domain name.
ptr	A domain name pointer.
hinfo	Host information (such as the operating system and type of CPU).

The `ifconfig` Utility

The `ifconfig` utility can be used to display the currently active network configuration and status using the following:

```
ifconfig
```

The data displayed depends on the configuration of your system. The following is the output from a system with a single network adapter and no dial-up capability:

```
lo        Link encap:Local Loopback
          inet addr:127.0.0.1  Bcast:127.255.255.255  Mask:255.0.0.0
          UP BROADCAST LOOPBACK RUNNING  MTU:3584  Metric:1
          RX packets:460 errors:0 dropped:0 overruns:0 frame:0
          TX packets:460 errors:0 dropped:0 overruns:0 carrier:0
          collisions:0

eth0      Link encap:Ethernet   HWaddr 00:60:08:34:93:12
          inet addr:192.81.82.10  Bcast:192.81.82.255  Mask:255.255.255.0
          UP BROADCAST RUNNING MULTICAST  MTU:1500  Metric:1
          RX packets:362 errors:0 dropped:0 overruns:0 frame:0
          TX packets:67 errors:0 dropped:0 overruns:0 carrier:0
          collisions:0
          Interrupt:10 Base address:0x6900
```

There are two network entries for this computer. The first one, labeled `lo`, is the loopback address described earlier. The second one, labeled `eth0`, is an Ethernet connection. Along with the IP addresses and basic configuration descriptions are the current statistics on received (`RX`) and transmitted (`TX`) packets. The number of packets is shown followed by a list of exceptional occurrences. The count of the number of collisions on an Ethernet can be indicative of the amount of traffic. It is normal for Ethernet collisions to occur (it is a part of the standard Ethernet protocol), but the higher the number the less efficient the network is running.

The value of the `MTU` (Maximum Transmission Unit) is the largest single block of data that can be carried over the connection. The Ethernet has a standard size limitation of 1500 bytes. This is not a hindrance to the TCP/IP protocol because the software uses the MTU number to split packets into as parts as are needed to fit within the limitations.

The first line of the `eth0` entry shows the hardware address of the network adapter card as being `00:60:08:34:93:12`. This address is built into the card and cannot be changed. Part of the job of the communications software is to translate IP addresses into hardware addresses. It is possible to have more than one Ethernet card installed on a single computer (`eth1`, `eth2`, and so on), and each card will have its own IP address and hardware address.

The addresses can be changed using `ifconfig`. For example, the IP address of this host on the Ethernet can be changed with the following two commands:

```
ifconfig eth0 192.168.1.10
ifconfig eth0 broadcast 192.168.1.255
```

The first command changes the address of this host, and the second changes the broadcast address.

> **Note:** These settings are fundamental. Configuration settings at this low level are seldom changed. They are only read by Linux when it boots, so if you make a change, you should reboot your computer. A reboot isn't always necessary, but it will guarantee that the new settings take effect.

The `netstat` Utility

This utility will display information about all the sockets on your local host. To view all the socket information, just enter the following command without any arguments:

```
netstat
```

The output looks like the following:

```
Active Internet connections (w/o servers)
Proto Recv-Q Send-Q Local Address           Foreign Address         State
tcp        0    336 hom-3-2.xyz.net:4132    www.linux.org:www       ESTABLISHED
tcp        0    335 hom-3-2.xyz.net:4131    www.linux.org:www       ESTABLISHED
tcp        0      0 hom-3-2.xyz.net:4130    www.linux.org:www       ESTABLISHED
tcp        0      0 hom-3-2.xyz.net:4062    www.linux.org:www       ESTABLISHED
tcp        1      0 arlin.athome.com:www    arlin.athome.com:3999   TIME_WAIT
udp        0      0 hom-3-2.xyz.net:domain  *:*
udp        0      0 arlin.athom:netbios-dgm *:*
udp        0      0 arlin.athome:netbios-ns *:*
udp        0      0 arlin.athome.com:domain *:*
udp        0      0 localhost:domain        *:*
Active UNIX domain sockets (w/o servers)
Proto RefCnt Flags       Type       State         I-Node Path
unix  2      [ ]         STREAM                   109207 /dev/log
unix  2      [ ]         STREAM     CONNECTED     109206
unix  2      [ ]         STREAM                   107117 /tmp/.ICE-unix/481
unix  2      [ ]         STREAM     CONNECTED     107116
unix  2      [ N ]       STREAM                   107078 /tmp/.X11-unix/X0
unix  2      [ N ]       STREAM     CONNECTED     107077
unix  2      [ ]         STREAM     CONNECTED     98121
unix  2      [ ]         STREAM     CONNECTED     98120
unix  2      [ W ]       STREAM     CONNECTED     98119
unix  2      [ ]         STREAM     CONNECTED     98118
```

This list was originally much longer because at the time the list was generated, the X11 graphical interface was running and uses a large number of sockets.

The top section of the listing shows all the active Internet socket connections, and the bottom lists all the active local socket connections. The column labeled Proto is the protocol being used. In this example, both the UDP and TCP protocols are used to communicate with the Internet. The UDP entries are the connections with the ISP, and the TCP entries were created by the Netscape browser loading the home page of www.linux.org. The name of the ISP is xyz.net, which supplied the local host with the address it associated with the domain name hom-3-2.xyz.net.

The Send-Q heading is the number of bytes that have been sent to the remote host but not yet acknowledged. The TCP/IP stack retains this information until it is acknowledged because if an error occurs, it will have to be sent again. The Recv-Q is the number of bytes that have arrived from the remote host but have not yet been successfully passed on to the application (Netscape).

A socket that connects to the Internet has two ends. For the Internet, one end is at the local address and one is at the foreign address. In this example, the local end of the socket is identified by the local host name—that is, the temporarily assigned domain name hom-3-2.xyz.net. When the local host established the connection with the foreign host, it supplied the return address and a port number. The port number is displayed with the local address name, separated from it by a colon. The foreign host also shows the domain name as its address, and the name following the colon is the service it is providing—in this example it is www.

The rightmost column, the one with State as its heading, displays the current Internet connection. The UDP protocol is connectionless (that is, messages are simply transmitted without acknowledgment), so it has no state. The TCP protocol is a connected protocol that defines a series of acknowledgement sequences and re-transmission operations so that each end of the connection must be aware of what the other end is doing. To do this, the TCP protocol moves predictably from one state to another.

The second part of the listing is normally much larger than the first because it lists every local socket. The unix protocol is used for local sockets. The RefCnt shows the number of processes connected to the socket; this is normally 2 with a process at each end. It can be 1 if a process has opened a socket, but there is no process on the other end yet, or if it is a one-way datagram (connectionless) socket.

The i-node and path name are the locations of the local sockets. Because local sockets are built using the Linux filesystem, every socket must have an i-node number. There may or may not be a directory entry for the i-node. This is the difference between named and unnamed sockets.

The same basic information that you can get from `ifconfig` is available, in a different format, with the following command:

```
netstat -i
```

The output is columns of figures containing counts of receive and transmit errors, drops, and overruns for all of the active interfaces. It is also possible to display the current routing table using the following command:

```
netstat -r
```

The `nslookup` Utility

The `nslookup` utility will query the domain name server, or servers, for the IP address assigned to a host name. For example, to find the address of `www.linux.org`, simply enter the following:

```
nslookup www.linux.org
```

The resulting display lists both the name server that was queried and the resulting address, as shown in the following:

```
Server:   origin.xyz.net
Address:  207.14.89.2

Non-authoritative answer:
Name:     www.linux.org
Address:  198.182.196.56
```

The output begins with the name and address of the name server and ends with the name and address of the targeted host. In this case, the name was acquired from a non-authorized source, which means the address information was acquired by retrieving the information from a server that copied it from another host. There is a slight possibility that the address could be wrong. This can happen if the original host has changed its address and the information has not had time to propagate through the system. These instances are relatively rare, but the efficiency advantages of distributing the addresses are very large.

The utility can be used in interactive mode by entering the command name without any arguments. Normally the default name server, or servers, are used to resolve addresses, but any domain name server on the Internet can be used, as shown in the following:

```
nslookup - border-ai.invlogic.com
```

Using the minus sign as the first argument tags the following domain name as that of the name server to be used to resolve addresses. The `nslookup` utility will then use a > prompt for you to enter the domain name, as shown in the following:

```
> www.gnome.org
Server:   border-ai.invlogic.com
Address:  205.134.175.254
```

```
Non-authoritative answer:
Name:    gnome.labs.redhat.com
Address:  199.183.24.235
Aliases:  www.gnome.org

>
```

The requested name server is queried for the address of www.gnome.org, and the answer returns contain the address and the actual name of the server. It turns out that the domain name used to find the address is actually an alias. The nslookup utility then prompts for another name. To end the session, enter exit.

The ping Utility

The ping utility is meant to be used to determine whether or not there is a connection between the local host and some other host. You can use an IP address to specify the remote host in the following way:

```
ping 208.151.161.66
```

If you have a name server, or if you have set up the configuration files to contain the name, you can use a domain name, as shown in the following:

```
ping www.belugalake.com
```

In either case, you will get a response if the remote host is running and is connected to the Internet. This is often the first step in configuring a network. If you can get a remote host to respond to a ping, there is nothing wrong with the physical connection, and TCP/IP is installed and running on both machines. All you need to do now is configure the server and client software you want to use.

The route Utility

After the ifconfig utility, described earlier in this chapter, is used to set up the routing table, the route utility can be used to view it and modify table entries. The routing table can be listed by simply entering the command with no arguments, as shown in the following:

```
route
```

The output will look something like the following:

```
Kernel IP routing table
Destination     Gateway         Genmask         Flags Metric Ref    Use Iface
hom-2.xyz.net   *               255.255.255.255 UH    0      0        0 ppp0
192.168.1.0     *               255.255.255.0   U     0      0       52 eth0
127.0.0.0       *               255.0.0.0       U     0      0        7 lo
default         hom-2.xyz.net   0.0.0.0         UG    0      0        9 ppp0
```

This routing table shows an active PPP Internet connection along with an Ethernet connection and the standard loopback address.

The following command will add the address of a host to the table:

```
route add -host 208.151.161.66 dev ppp0
```

When you add a host or a network to the table, the data is validated by contacting the named host—if contact cannot be made, nothing will not be added to the table. In this example, the host address is to be found through the ppp0 connection. If the host were located on the local Ethernet, the device would be eth0. To remove the entry you just added, enter the following:

```
route del -host 208.151.161.66
```

When a network is added to the routing table, you may also want to specify a network mask, as shown in the following:

```
route add -net 208.151.161.0 netmask 255.255.255.0 dev eth0
```

If the network mask is not specified, a mask suitable for the class of the IP address is automatically inserted. The dev option is normally not required because the route utility will attempt to determine the device by inspecting the existing connections.

The tcpdump Utility

The tcpdump utility monitors a TCP/IP connection and displays information from incoming and outgoing packet headers. You can specify which interface is to be monitored, which packets are to monitored, and some control over the display format. For example, to monitor all the traffic coming and going over the Ethernet, enter the following:

```
tcpdump -i eth0
```

Even on a relatively quiet network, there is a lot of traffic, so you will probably want to reduce the display to include only those packets that interest you. Normally, the TCP/IP stack will only accept incoming packets bound for the local host and ignore those addressed to another computer on the network (unless, of course, the local host is a router). When the tcpdump utility is run, it puts the TCP/IP stack in *promiscuous* mode. This mode causes all packets, from any host to any other host, to be accepted and made available for display. If you want to see only the traffic to and from the local host, you can use the -P option to prevent promiscuous mode, or you can specify the name of a host in the following way:

```
tcpdump -i eth0 host arlin
```

In this example, only packets issued from or addressed to arlin will be monitored. The host name can be the local host, or it can be any host on the local network. You can monitor only data being sent from arlin in the following way:

```
tcpdump -i eth0 src host arlin
```

You can monitor only packets sent to arlin in the following way:

```
tcpdump -i eth0 dst host arlin
```

You can monitor packets that have passed through a specific gateway by specifying its name, as shown in the following:

```
tcpdump -i eth0 gateway cygnus
```

If you want to monitor either TCP or UDP packets that are addressed to a specific port, you can specify the port number, as shown in the following:

```
tcpdump -i ppp0 host arlin and port 80
```

This command will display the headers from every packet to and from arlin that are addressed to port number 80 (which is the port number for Web servers) or have a return port number of 80. If you want to list only the ones sent to port 80, use dst port. And if you want to display only those with a return port number of 80, use src port. The two conditions must both be true because of the and operator used to join them—conditions can also be joined by or, and then the packet will be displayed if either condition is true.

There are a number of other options that can be used to filter the packets. You can specify specific protocols and packet sizes; you can even monitor packets that contain specific data at some location within the packet. To be able to use the more detailed filtering methods, you will need to be familiar with the form and content of the networking protocols you want to monitor, and then check the man page for tcpdump to find a set of options that will do what you want. There are a lot of options.

The traceroute Utility

The traceroute utility lists the host at every hop that was used to send a packet from your local host to a remote host. This is done by specifying the interface and the host name, as shown in the following:

```
traceroute -i ppp0 www.linux.org
```

This command will analyze a route from the local host to www.linux.org over the dialup link ppp0. Because of the dynamic nature of the Internet, the routes can vary from one minute to the next. The following is an example of the output from this command:

```
 1  hom-3.xyz.net (207.14.89.7)  123.376 ms  119.529 ms  119.904 ms
 2  hom.xyz.net (207.14.89.5)  119.878 ms  119.837 ms  119.896 ms
 3  198.70.247.77 (198.70.247.77)  139.906 ms  129.795 ms  159.887 ms
 4  kiwi.arctic.net (198.51.13.1)  149.883 ms  139.832 ms  149.931 ms
 5  198.70.254.5 (198.70.254.5)  179.830 ms  129.845 ms  139.896 ms
 6  12.127.194.101 (12.127.194.101)  219.878 ms  189.835 ms  219.928 ms
 7  br1-a3110s1.sffca.ip.att.net (12.127.1.142)  239.869 ms  239.802 ms  239.943 ms
 8  gr1-a3120s1.sffca.ip.att.net (192.205.35.253)  259.844 ms  229.813 ms  260.240 ms
 9  att-gw.sf.uu.net (192.205.32.22)  259.533 ms  239.776 ms  279.897 ms
10  114.ATM2-0.XR1.SFO1.ALTER.NET (146.188.148.218)  249.889 ms  269.831 ms  239.886 ms
11  287.ATM1-0.TR1.SCL1.ALTER.NET (146.188.147.154)  349.905 ms  259.779 ms  259.924 ms
12  107.ATM6-0.TR1.DCA1.ALTER.NET (146.188.136.221)  289.882 ms  *  320.064 ms
13  199.ATM7-0.XR1.TC01.ALTER.NET (146.188.161.165)  309.877 ms  309.779 ms  289.894 ms
14  193.ATM9-0-0.GW2.TC01.ALTER.NET (146.188.160.57)  309.894 ms  *  310.078 ms
15  uu-peer.pos-4-oc12-core.ai.net (205.134.160.2)  299.850 ms  299.787 ms  309.888 ms
16  border-ai.invlogic.com (205.134.175.254)  329.897 ms  359.814 ms  329.899 ms
17  router.invlogic.com (198.182.196.1)  409.903 ms  369.839 ms  409.870 ms
18  www.linux.org (198.182.196.56)  369.872 ms  489.813 ms  409.878 ms
```

This route consists of 17 hops from one host to another. The first host listed is the originating host, and the last one is the final destination host. Each line starts with the name of the host, if it is available—if not, the IP address is used as lines 3, 5 and 6. Each host along the route is tested three times, and the three round-trip times for the packets are displayed in milliseconds.

The traceroute utility analyzes the route by sending UDP packets with small time-to-live settings and then listening for the reply that states the time has been exceeded. The time-to-live setting limits the life of the packet to a specific number of hops. The first packet is sent with a time-to-live of 1 that, when decremented at the first hop, becomes zero and returns a message to the sender. The second packet is sent with a time-to-live value of 2, which expires at the second host along the route, and a message is returned to the sender. This process is continued until the entire route has been traversed—one host at a time.

The maximum number of hops defaults to 30, but you can set the limit to other values by using the -m option. If a host fails to respond, an asterisk is displayed marking the failed attempt, so you may see some entries in the list preceded by one or two asterisks. You may occasionally see one of the lines that just contains three asterisks, as in the following:

```
18 * * *
```

This is the result of a host along the route returning a message without all the information or failing to return a message.

The usernet Utility

If you are running X, you can use this utility to control the network interfaces. The window, shown in Figure 13.1, has column of buttons—one for each interface—that can be used to enable or disable the interface. An interface that is enabled is displayed in green in the right column. A disabled interface is displayed in red, and one that is changing from one state to the next is displayed in yellow.

Figure 13.1
Enable and disable network interfaces.

> **Note:** Depending on which distribution you are using, and what parts of the distribution have been installed, there are other network configuration tools available. The utility named `netcfg` (Network Configurator) from Red Hat can be used to view and modify the contents of the files discussed in this chapter. There is also `linuxconf` (Linux Configuration) from the Gnome project that does the same thing. They both use X for a GUI interface, and are easy to use (once you understand the contents of the files). Both of these are GNU open source and freely available.

Summary

Every host on the Internet has a unique 32-bit IP address. Every process on a host that can send or receive Internet messages has a port number. Messages sent are addressed by both the IP address and port number of the recipient. A server is a process that waits for a command or query to arrive so it can formulate a response and transmit the answer to the client that sent the message.

There is a one-to-one mapping from a domain name to an IP address, but one IP address can be assigned to several domain names. The name is for human use and can be translated into its numeric counterpart either by being hard-coded into a table or determined by using a name server.

There is quite a collection of utilities that can help you set up and maintain your network. If you have all of the correct names and addresses, networking is really easy to set up—it's as if Linux were born to communicate. In most cases, almost everything you need will have been set up during the Linux installation.

Getting Online with Modems

This chapter describes how to attach a modem to your computer and use it to connect to the Internet, enable dialup users to log in, and receive faxes.

This is all done with a communications link with a modem. While a serial link can be used as a direct connection between two computers, it is seldom done these days because of the low cost networking facilities now available. That leaves serial communications with the job of communicating remotely through modems.

This chapter explains one manual and three automatic ways to connect to the Internet. To configure your system, you should start with the manual method—it is tedious to log on this way but, if something is wrong, you can immediately see where the problem lies. After you have these basics out of the way, you can proceed to configure the automatic method (or methods) you would like to use.

Toward the end of the chapter is an explanation of how to set up your modem to answer incoming calls.

Serial Communication

A modem is a serial device. That is, it connects to a serial port on your computer, and the computer sends and receives data by streaming it one bit at a time. Originally, modems also used some kind of serial communications across the telephone lines, but, to get the higher speeds available today, the method of transmission and reception over a phone line can be quite complex. This doesn't really matter to Linux, because the connection between a computer and its modem is the same as it has always been. In fact, modern modems are easier to use because they can automatically adjust to a number of situations, including baud rate.

Getting an ISP

To be able to successfully dial out, you need to have someone you can call—someone with a modem ready to receive your call. An Internet Service Provider (ISP) has, among other things, a bank of modems that can grant you access to the Internet. There are probably several ISPs in your area.

When you are online through an ISP, your computer becomes a host on the Internet just the same as any other host. Each host has its own IP address, so your computer will also need one. The address assignment can be either static or dynamic. It is possible for the ISP to assign you a permanent IP address (a static address), but it is more likely that your address will be dynamic (assigned when you dial in).

ISPs maintain a pool of IP addresses and select a dynamic address for you when you dial in. Fortunately, the protocols employed to make the connections make this assignment process completely automatic. The point is that you will not know your own IP address until you are logged in.

Connecting a Modem

There two basic kinds of modems. One plugs directly into the bus of your computer (an internal modem), and the other sits on the table and connects to a serial port on your computer with a special cable (an external modem). They both do the same thing, and they both have their advantages. An internal modem costs less (because there is no box and power supply), and doesn't take up any space on your desk. An external modem has a row of lights on its face that can be used to determine what activity, if any, is in progress. Also, an external modem is insulated from any peculiarities of the hardware or the operating system.

> **Note:** There are some internal modems, called *winmodems*, that were designed to work with Windows and will not work with Linux. These modems are also sometimes called *soft* modems, because a number of essential modem functions are implemented in software and are not a part of the modem at all. Unfortunately, not all winmodems are labeled as such. If you buy an internal modem, you should either be familiar with it or make sure it can be returned if it does not meet your needs.

Internal modems are a little more difficult to configure than external modems. This is because an external modem connects to a serial port. Each of the serial ports has its own pre-defined hardware settings, and Linux already knows how to talk to them. An internal modem may require that you set the IRQ and port address (of course, some internal modems simply take over the IRQ and address of one of the two serial ports).

Finding and Configuring the Port

Once the modem is physically connected to the computer, the next step is to tell Linux which port it's on and how to talk to it. There are four serial port device nodes in the /dev directory:

```
$ ls -l /dev/ttyS*
crw-r--r--  1 root      root      4,  64 May  5 1998 /dev/ttyS0
crw-r--r--  1 root      root      4,  65 May  5 1998 /dev/ttyS1
crw-r--r--  1 root      root      4,  66 May  5 1998 /dev/ttyS2
crw-r--r--  1 root      root      4,  67 May  5 1998 /dev/ttyS3
```

Note: The numbers 0 through 3 correspond to DOS COM ports 1 through 4. The port /dev/ttyS0 is COM1, /dev/ttyS1 is COM2, and so on.

In Linux, a device node is a special filename that is used to connect to a hardware device. It works like a file in that you can write to it and read from it, but, instead of the data being stored in a file on the disk, the data goes to the hardware device. There are two numbers associated with each node: the major number and the minor number. The *major number* specifies which device driver is to be used to control the device, and the *minor number* specifies which hardware is being addressed.

The device nodes /dev/ttyS0 through /dev/ttyS3 have device drivers that specifically know how to talk to modems through a serial port. To point the Linux software to the right node, you need to add a link to give another name that is connected to your modem. For example, if your modem is connected to /dev/ttyS0, do this:

```
ln -s /dev/ttyS0 /dev/modem
```

This link makes life a little easier. Some Linux software, by default, will look for the node /dev/modem, which you have made into an alias for the actual node. If something happens and you have to change your modem port, there is no need to reconfigure all your software and scripts. All you have to change is the link.

The next thing to do is to configure the port. If your modem speed is less than 38400 (four times 9600), and if you are using one of the standard serial port IRQ/address pairs, there is nothing else to do. However, if you need to change some things, you can do so with setserial. To view the current port settings, enter the following:

```
setserial -a /dev/modem
```

The output will look something like the following:

```
/dev/modem, Line 1, UART: 16550A, Port: 0x02f8, IRQ: 3
        Baud_base: 115200, close_delay: 50, divisor: 0
        closing_wait: 3000, closing_wait2: infinite
        Flags: spd_normal skip_test
```

This example has an IRQ of 3 and uses port 2F8. The baud base is the fastest speed available on this particular serial port (it is almost always 115200). Notice that there is no baud rate—that number is assigned at the time an application opens the port. Most programs open the port requesting a baud rate of 38400, but you can use setserial to set up for a higher baud rate. The following command will configure the port so that any request for 38400 will result in the actual baud rate being 57600:

```
setserial /dev/modem spd_hi
```

You can even fix it so a request for 38400 will result in the baud rate being 115200:

```
seserial /dev/modem spd_vhi
```

It is also possible to use setserial to set the IRQ and port numbers. The default settings are shown in Table 14.1.

Table 14.1 Default Settings for Serial Ports

Device Name	Port Address	IRQ
/dev/ttyS0 (COM1)	3F8	4
/dev/ttyS1 (COM2)	2F8	3
/dev/ttyS2 (COM3)	3E8	4
/dev/ttyS3 (COM4)	2E8	3

The serial port settings can be changed by using setserial, as in the following:

```
setserial /dev/modem port 0x3A8 irq 10
```

Note: When Linux boots, it initializes the serial ports to the default values. If you want to make these changes and have them be permanent, it will be necessary to execute your setserial command every time the system boots. Probably the most reasonable thing to do is add the command to the bottom of the /dev/rc.d/rc.local file or create a script named /etc/rc.d/rc.serial and have it executed from /etc/rc.d/rc.

Talking to the Modem

The next thing you want to do is verify that the modem is connected and is willing to talk to you. There are several ways you can do this, but one of the simplest is to use a program called minicom. Just enter the following from the command line:

```
minicom
```

You will be warned about not having a configuration file, but that doesn't matter at this point—the defaults work just fine for what you want to do. If everything is working as planned, minicom has opened the modem port and is waiting for your instructions. As shown on the screen, press Ctrl+A and then Z to display the list of commands. Select the command M, which is to initialize the modem. The program will tell you that you are online (which only means you are connected to a serial port) and ask you whether you really want to initialize the modem. Click Yes and, after a few seconds, you will see OK displayed on the screen. That OK comes from the modem.

Being inside minicom, you are now in the position of being able to talk directly to the modem and see its responses. You can command your modem to dial a number, if you wish, by typing in something like the following:

ATDT5559023

You can even dial your ISP directly from here. When a connection is made, the word login: will appear. After you type in your login name there will be a password: prompt. Assuming the ISP is expecting to make a point-to-point (PPP) connection, you will get a string of plain text containing the IP address of the ISP and the IP address being assigned to you for the duration of your session. Then you will get some garbage on the screen— the ISP starts talking to you in PPP protocol, which minicom knows nothing about.

> **Note:** While the prompts "password:" and "login:" are fairly standard, you may find other words such as "PASS:" and "Username:." There are some that use the company name or the name of the computer as part of the prompt.
>
> Also, you may see no words at all on a system that uses CHAP (Challenge-Handshake Authentication Protocol) and PAP (Password Authentication Protocol). In the end, the connection still uses the PPP protocol, but these protocols are used to establish the connection. CHAP and PAP set up a sequence of queries and responses across the link to identify and verify the caller. CHAP is usually tried first, because it has a higher level of security, and PAP is only tried if CHAP doesn't seem to have been implemented by the caller. If your ISP uses one or both of these protocols, that information should be included with the other information that was supplied to you along with the ISP's phone number.

By the way, if you want to see the initialization string that was sent to set up the modem by minicom, select the M command a second time. The outgoing command string will be echoed by the modem and appear on the display.

The minicom program provides very low-level control for your modem. It can be useful for special communication circumstances, but those circumstances are becoming more rare every day because almost everything is done using TCP/IP on the Internet now. But, if you wind up in a situation where you absolutely must use low-level access or need something like Kermit to transmit files, minicom supplies it.

Connecting with PPP to the Outside World

Point-to-point (PPP) protocol is used by almost every ISP. It is simple, fast, and accurate. It was designed to be used as a direct connection between a pair of computers connected by a serial line. It operates on what is known as a *peer-to-peer* basis—that is, once a connection is established, there is no difference between the called computer and the calling computer. And it is an Internet protocol standard, which means different kinds of computers can use it to talk to one another.

The Linux PPP is in two parts. There is code in the kernel and there is a daemon called pppd. The code in the kernel establishes the path that is used to pass messages between the modem and the applications. The pppd daemon assumes the responsibility for negotiating the connections. The negotiation includes various forms of authentication and information gathering—for one thing, pppd retrieves one or more IP addresses from the host that was called.

You may or may not already have PPP installed. If not, you will need to install it and, because PPP requires kernel support, you will need to make a new kernel.

You can tell whether PPP has been installed by using the insmod, rmmod, and lsmod utilities. PPP is a loadable module; that is, it can be linked and unlinked with the kernel on demand. The lsmod utility has no arguments, so just enter it from the command line, as shown in the following:

```
lsmod
```

The output is a list of all the modules that are currently loaded, looking something like the following:

```
Module       Pages    Used by
slip           2              1 (autoclean)
slhc           2      [slip]  1 (autoclean)
3c59x          4              1 (autoclean)
aic7xxx       23              0
```

This is a list of all the currently loaded modules. The bottom two entries in the list are typical for a network adapter and a SCSI controller. The first row designates that the SLIP protocol is currently loaded and the second row is a loaded module that is used by the SLIP protocol. The number of pages for each module has to do with the amount of memory required by the module. If an autoclean module is not used for a certain period of time (usually about a minute), it will be automatically unloaded. The utility insmod can be used to load modules. To determine whether you have PPP installed on your system, you can attempt to load it with the following command:

```
insmod -k ppp
```

When you enter this command, one of two things will happen. If PPP is not installed on your system, you will get a response that looks like the following:

```
insmod: ppp: no module by than name found
```

On the other hand, if PPP is installed, entering lsmod will include a new line that looks like the following:

```
ppp                5            0 (autoclean)
```

The -k option on insmod loads it as an autoclean module that allows the kernel to remove it if you don't actually use it. If you don't use the -k option, it will stay loaded until you unload it, which can be done with the following command:

```
rmmod ppp
```

If PPP is not already installed on your computer, you can install it by changing to the directory with the .rpm files (either on a CD-ROM or downloaded from the Internet) and entering the following command:

```
rpm -ivh ppp*.rpm
```

This will install the PPP software, but it may not be instantly usable. Because some loadable modules depend on the presence of other loadable modules, after installing new modules you may need to set the dependencies. This is done using the following command:

```
depmod -a
```

This builds a file listing all the modules and their inter-dependencies. This information is used when the kernel loads modules. After doing this, go back and try insmod and lsmod again to see whether PPP has been installed.

If it still has not been installed, you will need to remake the kernel. The process for creating a new kernel is described in detail in Chapter 25, "Kernel Hacking." When setting the kernel options, be sure to click Yes to point-to-point protocol. Also, be sure to enable the loadable module support and remake the modules, because PPP is implemented as a module. By the way, it isn't necessary right now, but if you want to completely automate connecting and disconnecting your modem, as described later in this chapter, you will need SLIP. It may be simpler to install it now because the same process used to install PPP is used to install SLIP.

After the software is installed, you will need to change the permission settings of /usr/sbin/pppd. The program must run with root permissions so, for other users to be able to run it, you need to set its permissions in the following way:

```
chmod u+s /usr/sbin/pppd
```

This will cause pppd to execute with root privileges, regardless of which user starts it.

Dialing the Internet

The daemon pppd is does not start running until a connection to the Internet has been made. There is more than one way to establish the connection once you have your system configured. To get your initial configuration set up, it would be wise to start by going through the process of manual dialing. This process goes step by step and will show you how to get your system configured for one or more of the automatic connection methods that follow.

Dialing Manually

There is a program named dip that enables you to manually establish a connection to the Internet. It can be used to dial to your ISP and start the pppd daemon on the port. It can also be made to take its arguments from a script, but, for now, it is better to do it by hand so you can discover any of parts that are not working. To make a manual connection, enter the following:

```
dip -t
```

The -t option is for test mode—it will allow you to test your dialing and connecting capabilities. The test mode is an interactive session, and dip will prompt for each line of input from you, as shown in the following:

```
DIP>
```

Because you are going to be using your keyboard to both talk to dip and to talk to the remote computer, you need to be able to switch between terminal mode and dip mode. Start with the following sequence of commands:

```
DIP> port /dev/modem
DIP> speed 38400
DIP> dial 5552389
DIP> term
```

The first two commands set the device name and the baud rate, and the third line dials the number. The fourth line changes the mode of operation of dip. In this mode, the incoming data from the remote host will be displayed onscreen, and anything you type in from the keyboard will be sent to the remote host. You may or may not get a welcome message from your ISP (mostly they don't bother, because these messages are normally thrown away anyway). You will, however, get a prompt for your login name and password:

```
login: arthur
passwd:
PPP session from (207.14.89.182) to (207.14.89.6) beginning ...
```

The text shown here is immediately followed by what appears to be some garbage characters. It usually has a lot of right braces (}) in it. What you are seeing is the protocol stream issued by the remote PPP server. Every few seconds you will see the characters repeat themselves in a continuing attempt to make contact. If, after a fairly short period of time, no connection is made, the PPP server will simply drop the connection.

The server is trying to make a connection, so you need to switch to PPP mode on your end before a response can be made. To get out of terminal mode, and back into dip command mode, press Ctrl+].

This is a manual process. You have intercepted the two IP addresses that were sent from the server, so you will need to enter them before moving on to PPP, as shown in the following:

```
DIP> get $locip 207.14.89.182
DIP> get $rmtip 207.14.89.6
DIP> mode PPP
```

This command causes the daemon pppd to start running and an Internet connection to be established. There are some things you can do to check to make sure. For one, you can look at the routing by entering the following command:

```
netstat -r -n
```

The output will look something like the following:

```
Kernel IP routing table
Destination     Gateway         Genmask          Flags   MSS Window  irtt Iface
207.14.89.8     0.0.0.0         255.255.255.255  UH      1500 0         0 ppp0
192.168.1.0     0.0.0.0         255.255.255.0    U       1500 0         0 eth0
127.0.0.0       0.0.0.0         255.0.0.0        U       3584 0         0 lo
0.0.0.0         207.14.89.8     0.0.0.0          UG      1500 0         0 ppp0
```

> **Note:** If the destination 0.0.0.0 has some gateway address other than the one from the ISP, you will not have normal communications over the Internet. If, during Linux installation, a gateway address was specified, it will always be used instead of the Internet. This entry is only useful if you are accessing the Internet through another computer on your local network. You can use the route command to remove it.

You can also use ifconfig to get information about the connection. The following is an example of the output of ifconfig on a system that has an Ethernet connection and is also currently running a PPP session:

```
lo        Link encap:Local Loopback
          inet addr:127.0.0.1  Bcast:127.255.255.255  Mask:255.0.0.0
          UP BROADCAST LOOPBACK RUNNING  MTU:3584  Metric:1
          RX packets:115 errors:0 dropped:0 overruns:0 frame:0
```

```
         TX packets:115 errors:0 dropped:0 overruns:0 carrier:0
         collisions:0

eth0     Link encap:Ethernet  HWaddr 00:60:08:34:93:12
         inet addr:192.168.1.10  Bcast:192.168.1.255  Mask:255.255.255.0
         UP BROADCAST RUNNING MULTICAST  MTU:1500  Metric:1
         RX packets:2936 errors:0 dropped:0 overruns:0 frame:0
         TX packets:1771 errors:0 dropped:0 overruns:0 carrier:0
         collisions:0
         Interrupt:10 Base address:0x6900

ppp0     Link encap:Point-to-Point Protocol
         inet addr:207.14.89.107  P-t-P:207.14.89.8  Mask:255.255.255.0
         UP POINTOPOINT RUNNING  MTU:1500  Metric:1
         RX packets:186 errors:0 dropped:0 overruns:0 frame:0
         TX packets:225 errors:0 dropped:0 overruns:0 carrier:0
         collisions:0
         Memory:22ae038-22aec04
```

The first two members of the list are for the loopback address and an Ethernet, respectively. The entry labeled ppp0 is the point-to-point connection that was established by using dip.

The real test is when you connect to something out on the Internet. The simplest way to do this is by using ping to detect the presence of a remote host. Select an IP address that you know exists and ping it with the following code:

```
ping 208.151.161.66
```

The command continuously sends short messages that will be echoed by the remote computer if connection was successful. To disconnect from the Internet, enter the following:

```
dip -k /dev/modem
```

If you want to use names instead of numbers to address things on the Internet (and who doesn't), you will have to tell your system where it can find the domain nameserver (DNS). This nameserver is like an Internet phone book—it accepts the names of Internet hosts and returns IP addresses for them. The DNS address(es) are kept in a file named /etc/resolv.conf. In the following example, the domain name of the ISP is xyz.net, and it has both a primary and secondary nameserver:

```
search xyz.net
nameserver 207.14.89.2
nameserver 198.51.13.3
```

There is more than one nameserver listed, so if one is unreachable, there is a backup available. Your computer will query each nameserver in the list, beginning with the first one. If you have a nameserver on your local network, it can also be included in the list.

In fact, it would make sense to list your local nameserver first because of the speed of the connection.

There is a quicker way to resolve addresses, but it is decidedly manual. Before checking with any of the nameservers, the /etc/hosts file is checked. If the sought-after name is found in the file, no nameserver will be queried.

> **Note:** You may not find the address of the nameserver as you go through the information provided by your ISP. If not, you should take a look at the ISP's Web site; a lot of ISPs post the information there. If not, you will have to contact the ISP to get the address. Most people contact the Internet through Windows, which automatically acquires the address of a nameserver, so some ISPs don't bother to publish the information.

You can now access things on the network by name. The following command causes ping to request the IP address before it starts sending and receiving messages:

```
ping belugalake.com
```

This ping statement is the same as the previous one except that the nameserver is first queried for the IP address. You are now connected to the Internet and can access anything on it.

Establishing Connect and Disconnect Commands

Because you are now able to contact the Internet manually, you may want to configure an easier way. One way to do this is to configure a couple of commands that enable you to establish and drop a connection whenever you want. A connection can be made by using the command ppp-on, and the connection can be dropped by entering ppp-off.

Create a new directory named **/etc/ppp/scripts**. Copy the following three example scripts to the documentation directories for PPP:

```
cp /usr/doc/ppp*/scripts/ppp-on /etc/ppp/scripts
cp /usr/doc/ppp*/scripts/ppp-off /etc/ppp/scripts
cp /usr/doc/ppp*/scripts/ppp-on-dialer /etc/ppp/scripts
```

ppp-on and ppp-off are the scripts executed from the command line to establish and break connections. The ppp-on-dialer script is used by ppp-on. Make sure the scripts are executable, and, so the names of the scripts can be found by the PATH variable, you can either add this directory to your path, or you can add links to names in a directory already on your path, as shown in the following:

```
ln -s /etc/ppp/scripts/ppp-on /usr/sbin/ppp-on
ln -s /etc/ppp/scripts/ppp-off /usr/sbin/ppp-off
```

The ppp-on Script

You will need to make some changes to the ppp-on script. The purpose of this script is to start the pppd daemon, with the correct settings, and have it make the connection. Initially, the script looks like the following:

```
#!/bin/sh

#

# Script to initiate a ppp connection. This is the first part of the

# pair of scripts. This is not a secure pair of scripts as the codes
# are visible with the 'ps' command. However, it is simple.
#
# These are the parameters. Change as needed.
TELEPHONE=555-1212     # The telephone number for the connection
ACCOUNT=george         # The account name for logon (as in 'George Burns')
PASSWORD=gracie        # The password for this account (and 'Gracie Allen')
LOCAL_IP=0.0.0.0     # Local IP address if known. Dynamic = 0.0.0.0
REMOTE_IP=0.0.0.0    # Remote IP address if desired. Normally 0.0.0.0
NETMASK=255.255.255.0   # The proper netmask if needed
#
# Export them so that they will be available at 'ppp-on-dialer' time.
export TELEPHONE ACCOUNT PASSWORD
#
# This is the location of the script which dials the phone and logs
# in.  Please use the absolute filename as the $PATH variable is not
# used on the connect option.  (To do so on a 'root' account would be
# a security hole so don't ask.)
#
DIALER_SCRIPT=/etc/ppp/ppp-on-dialer
#
# Initiate the connection
#
# I put most of the common options on this command. Please, don't
# forget the 'lock' option or some programs such as mgetty will not
# work. The asyncmap and escape will permit the PPP link to work with
# a telnet or rlogin connection. You are welcome to make any changes
# as desired. Don't use the 'defaultroute' option if you currently
# have a default route to an ethernet gateway.
#
exec /usr/sbin/pppd debug lock modem crtscts /dev/ttyS0 38400 \
        asyncmap 20A0000 escape FF kdebug 0 $LOCAL_IP:$REMOTE_IP \
        noipdefault netmask $NETMASK defaultroute connect $DIALER_SCRIPT
```

You will need to edit the file to include the telephone number of your ISP, along with your login name and password. The exec command at the bottom uses the environment variables set earlier in the script, and throws in a few values of its own. There are quite a few arguments on the argument list, and you may want to change some of them if you have any problems. Be sure to check that the device node and requested speed are correct. You can change /dev/ttyS0 to /dev/modem, and change 38400 to the speed you established earlier during setup. Make sure that the DIALER_SCRIPT is set to the full pathname of ppp-on-dialer.

The ppp-on-dialer Script

The following script dials the number of the ISP, logs in, grabs the IP address of the ISP and the IP address assigned to your local computer, and uses this information to update the routing tables. All this is done by a program called chat.

```
#!/bin/sh
#
# This is part 2 of the ppp-on script. It will perform the connection
# protocol for the desired connection.
#
exec chat -v  \
        TIMEOUT         3   \
        ABORT           '\nBUSY\r'   \
        ABORT           '\nNO ANSWER\r'   \
        ABORT           '\nRINGING\r\n\r\nRINGING\r'   \
        ''              \rAT   \
        'OK-+++\c-OK'   ATH0   \
        TIMEOUT         30   \
        OK              ATDT$TELEPHONE   \
        CONNECT         ''   \
        ogin:--ogin:    $ACCOUNT \
        assword:        $PASSWORD
```

You may not need to modify this script, but if you have some special situation with the login procedure for your ISP, you can check the man page for chat and see how to set it up. The arguments to chat come in pairs. There are a lot more options than the ones used in this script, but these work in most cases. You can supply the commands either in a file or, as in this case, directly on the command line. There are two timers set in this script:

```
TIMEOUT 3
```

and

```
TIMEOUT         30
```

A TIMEOUT command defines the maximum amount of time allowed for the command that follows it. The first timeout is set to 3 seconds, because if there is no immediate response from the modem, something is wrong. Where no timeout is specified, the default is 45 seconds. The next three commands define the responses from the modem that will cause the command to abort:

```
ABORT           '\nBUSY\r'
ABORT           '\nNO ANSWER\r'
ABORT           '\nRINGING\r\n\r\nRINGING\r'
```

The next line is an "expect" and "response" pair:

```
' '              \rAT
```

The quoted string with nothing in it means that nothing is expected from the modem so, without waiting, the AT command is sent to the modem. The AT command should cause the response that is being waited for by the following command:

```
'OK-+++\c-OK'   ATH0
```

This entry is waiting for an OK to return from the modem. If chat doesn't get the OK, it will send three plus signs followed by a carriage return, and then wait for the OK again. You can string as many of these together as you want by putting minus signs between them. Once an OK has been received, and after the timeout has been set to 30 seconds, the following command waits for an OK before dialing the number:

```
OK              ATDT$TELEPHONE
```

After the number is dialed and the connection made with the modem on the far end, the modem will announce its success by responding with the word CONNECT (usually followed by the baud rate). The following statement waits for the CONNECT:

```
CONNECT         ' '
```

When the CONNECT is received, the statement does nothing, so the following statement starts waiting for the login prompt:

```
ogin:--ogin:   $ACCOUNT
```

It is good policy to skip the first letter because the prompt is sometimes capitalized and sometime not, and you must have an exact match on the string. Or you may need to change it to something else entirely if your ISP uses a different prompt.

As in the previous example, the minus sign will cause chat to try more than once. The final step is to field the password prompt (once again, without the first letter):

```
assword:       $PASSWORD
```

The connection has been made, and you can crank up your Internet software.

The ppp-off Script

The ppp-off script is used to break the connection. It will probably not need any modification. Not only does this script break the connection, it also cleans up the running process and clears the lock files. The following is the ppp-off script as it comes with the PPP software:

```
#!/bin/sh

##########################################################################
#
```

```
# Determine the device to be terminated.
#
if [ "$1" = "" ]; then
        DEVICE=ppp0
else
        DEVICE=$1
fi


######################################################################
#
# If the ppp0 pid file is present then the program is running. Stop it.
if [ -r /var/run/$DEVICE.pid ]; then
        kill -INT `cat /var/run/$DEVICE.pid`
#
# If the kill did not work then there is no process running for this
# pid. It may also mean that the lock file will be left. You may wish
# to delete the lock file at the same time.
        if [ ! "$?" = "0" ]; then
                rm -f /var/run/$DEVICE.pid
                echo "ERROR: Removed stale pid file"
                exit 1
        fi
#
# Success. Let pppd clean up its own junk.
        echo "PPP link to $DEVICE terminated."
        exit 0
fi
#
# The ppp process is not running for ppp0
echo "ERROR: PPP link is not active on $DEVICE"
exit 1
```

If you have more than one dialout connection, you can specify which one. For example, to specify dropping connection number three:

```
ppp-off ppp3
```

The default is ppp0, which is the also the default name used to establish connections.

Network Configurator

If you are running Red Hat and using X Windows, there is a utility that will enable you to configure an automatic Internet connection. To do this, you must have superuser permissions, so log in as **root**. From the main menu, under Administration, select Network Configuration. A window appears with a row of buttons across the top. The Names button will display information about domains other than this one, if any are listed. The Routing and Hosts buttons display windows enabling you to edit the routing table and list of host names. Select the Interfaces button so the displayed window looks something like Figure 14.1.

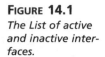

FIGURE 14.1
The List of active and inactive interfaces.

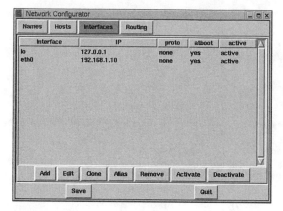

Any previously defined addresses will be displayed in the window. In this example, there is the loopback address and the Ethernet address. The buttons across the bottom can be used to edit the entries. You want to add a new entry, so select the Add button at the bottom of the window, causing the dialog box in Figure 14.2 to appear. Select PPP and then OK.

FIGURE 14.2
The available interface types.

The window in Figure 14.3 appears and prompts for the phone number of the ISP, along with your login name and password. Enter the requested data and select Customize to bring up the window displayed in Figure 14.4.

FIGURE 14.3
Necessary ISP contact information.

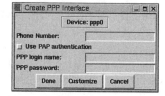

The line speed is the speed at which your computer will talk to the modem. For the modem to deliver maximum performance, the speed setting must be at least as fast as your maximum modem speed, but it can be set faster. Setting the hardware flow control option will prevent data overruns by toggling the flow of data on and off as necessary.

FIGURE **14.4**

*Modem settings
of PPP.*

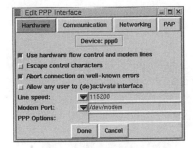

Selecting the Communications button will bring up the dialog box shown in Figure 14.5. The Init string is sent to the modem each time a connection is going to be made. Its purpose is to initialize the modem to a known condition. If you have a standard modem, there is probably no need to change the modem initialization string or the dial command, but some modems may require something special for initialization. This can happen if you also use your modem for faxes, and the fax software fails to clean up behind itself. Historically, modems have been known to get themselves into states that required special initialization to get them out, but that is not so much the case any more. If you have any problems, check your modem's manual for a more robust initialization.

FIGURE **14.5**

*The command
sequence for
logging in.*

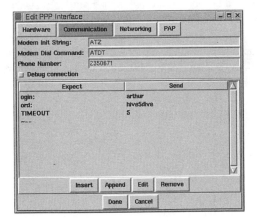

The Expect and Send lists in Figure 14.5 define the conversation for logging your computer into the remote computer. The log in process starts at the top of the list and works its way down—it sits and waits for an incoming string to match the one on the left, and then returns the one on the right. The example in the figure shows the login and password prompts and their responses. At the end, there is a five second timeout because, if nothing is wrong, the remote PPP software should respond immediately.

Select the Done button and save the new configuration. The window in Figure 14.1 will have a new line showing the PPP interface. It will be displayed as inactive until you actually dial in and make a connection.

To connect to the Internet, select the Activate button at the bottom of the window. If the connection fails for some reason, a message will be displayed. If the connection succeeds, the software says nothing—if you hear your modem dial and connect, and nothing else seems to happen, you are connected. To disconnect, select Deactivate.

Using `diald` for Automatic Dialing

The `diald` daemon will perform demand dialing. That is, whenever an application requests an IP address that is not on your local network, `diald` will automatically make an Internet connection. You can use this for programs that you start yourself, and it can be set up, using `cron`, to do things like automatically dial in and check for mail. It sets itself up as if it were a fully operational Internet connection, so when it receives a message that should be sent to the Internet, it dials, makes the connection, and forwards the message to the ISP. The daemon then monitors all traffic over the connection and, whenever it determines that the link is idle, it drops the connection.

You may not have a copy. Check to see if `diald` is on your Linux CD-ROM and, if not, you will have to go and get your own copy. Among other places, there is an `rpm` file on the FTP site `sunsite.unc.edu`. You may find it necessary to get the source code of `diald` and install it from scratch, as described later in this section. You will find the source code at `sunsite.unc.edu` the `/pub/linux/distributions/` directory. There are directories there for several Linux distributions, so select the one that matches yours.

To install the files, use the `rpm` utility on the downloaded file, as shown in the following:

```
rpm -Uvh diald-01.16.4-1.i386.rpm
```

At this point, `diald` is installed, but it is not configured. There are some files and directories that need to be created.

For `diald` to run, you must have both PPP and SLIP installed. This is true, even if you are not making any SLIP connections. SLIP is used as a sort of proxy by `diald` to monitor the traffic flow in and out of the Internet. And you must have the `chat` program to do the actual dialing.

The `connect` File

There is an example `connect` file in the `/usr/doc/diald-0.16.4-1` directory. Copy the file to `/etc/ppp/connect`.

Many things in the connect file can stay as they are, but there are some that must be changed. The following is what the distributed connect file looks like:

```
#!/bin/sh

#-------------------------------------------------------------------
# For the RPM I've added a few lines to report the connect speed.
# See /usr/lib/diald for the original connect script. -- Dave Cook
#-------------------------------------------------------------------

# Copyright (c) 1996, Eric Schenk.
#
# This script is intended to give an example of a connection script that
# uses the "message" facility of diald to communicate progress through
# the dialing process to a diald monitoring program
# such as dctrl or diald-top.
# It also reports progress to the system logs. This can be useful if you
# are seeing failed attempts to connect and you want to know when and why
# they are failing.
#
# This script requires the use of chat-1.9 or greater for full
# functionality. It should work with older versions of chat,
# but it will not be able to report the reason for a connection failure.

# Configuration parameters

# The initialization string for your modem

MODEM_INIT="ATZ&C1&D2%C0"

# The phone number to dial
PHONE_NUMBER="5551212"

# The chat sequence to recognize that the remote system
# is asking for your user name.
USER_CHAT_SEQ="ogin:--ogin:--ogin:--ogin:--ogin:--ogin:--ogin:"

# The string to send in response to the request for your user name.
USER_NAME="USER"

# The chat sequence to recognize that the remote system
# is asking for your password.
PASSWD_CHAT_SEQ="word:"

# The string to send in response to the request for your password.
PASSWORD="PASSWORD"

# The prompt the remote system will give once you are logged in
```

```
# If you do not define this, the script will assume that
# there is no command to be issued to start up the remote protocol.
PROMPT="annex:"
# The command to issue to start up the remote protocol
PROTOCOL_START="ppp"

# The string to wait for to see that the protocol on the remote
# end started OK. If this is empty, no check will be performed.
START_ACK="Switching to PPP."

# Pass a message on to diald and the system logs.
function message () {
[ $FIFO ] && echo "message $*" >$FIFO
logger -p local2.info -t connect "$*"
}

# Initialize the modem. Usually this just resets it.
message "Initializing Modem"
chat TIMEOUT 5 "" $MODEM_INIT TIMEOUT 45 OK ""
if [ $? != 0 ]; then
    message "Failed to initialize modem"
    exit 1
fi

>/var/log/connect

# Dial the remote system.

message "Dialing $PHONE_NUMBER"
chat -r /var/log/connect \
        REPORT CONNECT \
        TIMEOUT 45 \
        ABORT "NO CARRIER" \
        ABORT BUSY \
        ABORT "NO DIALTONE" \
        ABORT ERROR \
        "" ATDT$PHONE_NUMBER \
        CONNECT ""
case $? in
    0) message "$(cat /var/log/connect)";;
    1) message "Chat Error"; exit 1;;
    2) message "Chat Script Error"; exit 1;;
    3) message "Chat Timeout"; exit 1;;
    4) message "No Carrier"; exit 1;;
    5) message "Busy"; exit 1;;
    6) message "No DialTone"; exit 1;;
    7) message "Modem Error"; exit 1;;
    *)
esac

# We're connected try to log in.
```

```
message "Loggin in"
chat \
        TIMEOUT 5 \
        $USER_CHAT_SEQ \\q$USER_NAME \
        TIMEOUT 45 \
        $PASSWD_CHAT_SEQ $PASSWORD
if [ $? != 0 ]; then
    message "Failed to log in"
    exit 1
fi

# We logged in, try to start up the protocol (provided that the
# user has specified how to do this)

if [ $PROMPT ]; then
    message "Starting Comm Protocol"
    chat TIMEOUT 15 $PROMPT $PROTOCOL_START
    if [ $? != 0 ]; then
        message "Prompt not received"
        exit 1
    fi
fi

if [ $START_ACK ]; then
    chat TIMEOUT 15 $START_ACK ""
    if [ $? != 0 ]; then
        message "Failed to start Protocol"
        exit 1
    fi
fi

# Success!
message "Protocol started"
```

The script will be used by diald to set the parameters that are passed to chat (the program that does the actual dialing). You may want to take a look at MODEM_INIT and make sure it is valid for your modem. You will need to change PHONE_NUMBER to the number of your ISP. The chat response definitions defined by USER_CHAT_SEQ and PASSWD_CHAT_SEQ will only need to change if your ISP uses something other than login: and password: as the login sequence. You will certainly have to change USER_NAME and PASSWORD to your login name and your password.

In most cases, you will want to omit PROMPT, PROTOCOL_START, and START_ACK. There are some systems that prompt for the service or protocol once you have logged in. If the PROMPT string is defined, your computer will wait until that string arrives and, once it does, the PROTOCOL_START string will be returned. If there is a PROMPT and PROTOCOL_START, there may also need to be a START_ACK defined as a check for the confirmation string coming from the remote host—in the example file it is used to skip past the remote computer announcing the start of the selected protocol.

The rest of the connect script contains chat and other commands that use the preset variable strings to attempt to dial the remote host. Because this file is a script, you will need to use chmod to make it executable, as shown in the following:

```
chmod 755 /etc/ppp/connect
```

The diald.conf File

There is an example diald.conf file in the /usr/doc/diald-0.16.4-1 directory. Copy the file to /etc/diald.conf.

The content of the file looks something like the following:

```
fifo /etc/diald/diald.ctl
mode ppp

connect "sh /etc/ppp/connect"
device /dev/modem
speed 115200

modem
lock
crtscts
local 127.0.0.2
remote 127.0.0.3
dynamic
defaultroute
pppd-options asyncmap 0
include /usr/lib/diald/standard.filter
```

Most of these entries can be left as they are. The first line specifies the name of a file that will be created and used by diald, so make sure the directory exists by entering the following:

```
mkdir /etc/diald
```

You may need to change the name of the device to the port you are actually using. The connect command names the script that is executed to make the actual connection. The local and remote addresses can be set to loopback addresses. The include statement at the end refers to a set of filtering commands that are used to determine the protocol type of an incoming message and decides what to do with it.

The diald.init Script

To start and stop the diald daemon, there is a script named diald.init. To start the daemon running, enter the following:

```
diald.init start
```

You can stop it by entering the following:

```
diald.init stop
```

The diald program should start running, as you can verify with the following:

```
ps xw ¦ grep diald
```

Nothing will happen until some program tries to access the Internet. The daemon will field the request, make the connection, and pass on the message. It will stay connected until there is an appropriate length of time with no activity on the line, at which time it will drop the connection.

If you want to have diald started whenever you boot Linux, you will need to place a startup command in the rc files. First, edit the diald.init script and remove the requirement for an argument on the command line. Your file should look something like the following:

```
#!/bin/sh

#  Source function library
. /etc/rc.d/init.d/functions

#  Source networking configuration
. /etc/sysconfig/network

#  Check whether the diald files exist
#  networking is not disabled
[ ${NETWORKING} = "no" ] && exit 0
[ -f /usr/sbin/diald ] ¦¦ exit 0
[ -f /etc/diald.conf ] ¦¦ exit 0

# Start the daemon
echo -n "Starting diald: "
daemon diald
echo
exit 0
```

Name this script **/etc/rc.d/init.d/diald.init** and make links to it from each of the run levels that you use. Run level 3 is the most common, so the link can be created in the following way:

```
ln -s /etc/rc.d/init.d/diald.init /etc/rc.d/rc3.d/S98diald
```

If you use other run levels, you may want to add links for them. Because the initialization scripts are executed in the order they appear in the directory, it has become standard to specify the order by using a prefix on each name. Using the prefix S98 causes diald to be one of the last actions taken.

Installing `diald` from Source Code

It is possible to get a tar file containing the source code and compile diald yourself.

Among other places, you can get a copy from the FTP site sunsite.unc.edu in the pub/Linux/system/network/serial directory. As this is being written, the latest version is 0.16, so the filename is `diald-0.16.tar.gz`. You can also get the latest version from the `diald` home page, `http://www.loonie.net/~eschenk/diald.html`, where you will also find a FAQ and all the latest information.

Change to a directory that is to be the parent directory of the source code for `diald`. Enter the following two commands:

```
gunzip diald-0.16.tar.gz
tar -xvf diald-0.16.tar
```

The first command will uncompress the file, the second will create the subdirectory and fill it with the source code, some documentation, and a makefile. For this version, the directory is named `diald-0.16`.

There are some default filenames and locations that must be compiled into the program. They are all defined in `config.h`. More than likely, you will not need to make any changes because all the pathnames are pretty standard.

The software is compiled and installed with the following three commands:

```
make depend
make
make install
```

Dialing in from the Outside World

Several users can be logged in to Linux simultaneously. There are virtual terminals enabling several local logins by the same person. It is also possible to attach a dumb terminal to a serial port and use it to log in. Additionally, it is possible for a remote user to dial in by calling the modem. To enable logins through your modem, you need to configure Linux so it will answer the phone and then issue a prompt for a login name and password. The program that does this is called `mgetty`.

The program responsible for handling non-modem serial ports is called `getty`. This program has been handling dumb terminal logins since the beginning of UNIX. The `getty` program sits listening to a port waiting for some kind of action. If you press a key on the keyboard of the connected terminal, the `getty` will respond with a login prompt. To handle the virtual terminals, there is a special `getty` program named `mingetty`. To respond to modem ports, there is a special version of `getty` named `mgetty`. An `mgetty` sits listening to the modem and, when the phone rings, it answers the call and monitors the modem for a connection. If another modem connects to this one, a login prompt is issued. If there is not another modem, it will try to receive a fax. If a fax is received, it will be stored on disk and you will be notified. If the call fails, you will be notified of that too.

Among the most useful capabilities of `mgetty` is its ability to stay out of the way when you use the modem to dial out. As long as you maintain the connection, the `mgetty` remains dormant so that incoming data will be passed on to your application. When you are finished, mgetty detects the dropped modem and returns to monitoring the modem port for an incoming call.

An mgetty is normally started when the computer boots. It connects to the modem and waits for a ring to come from it. It then answers the ring with an ATA command and waits for a CONNECT message from the modem. If the incoming call is from a fax machine, the fax is saved in a directory named /var/spool/fax/incoming. If the incoming call is from another modem, mgetty displays the login prompt and starts a program named /bin/login to take it from there. This is the same /bin/login program used by the regular getty, so the login session is the same remotely as it is locally.

The `inittab` File

The program that starts all other Linux programs is /sbin/init. At boot time, it configures the entire system. To do this, it reads a file named /etc/inittab for its instructions. Among other things, it executes the appropriate startup scripts in the /etc/rc.d directory and starts all the getty programs for all the ports. Each of the Linux virtual terminals must have a mingetty. There must also be a getty for any serial ports connected directly to a dumb terminal or another computer. It can also be instructed to start the mgetty program on your modem port.

The following is a typical inittab file, without an mgetty:

```
#
# inittab       This file describes how the INIT process should set up
#               the system in a certain run-level.
#
# Author:       Miquel van Smoorenburg, <miquels@drinkel.nl.mugnet.org>
#               Modified for RHS Linux by Marc Ewing and Donnie Barnes
#

# Default runlevel. The runlevels used by RHS are:
#   0 - halt (Do NOT set initdefault to this)
#   1 - Single user mode
#   2 - Multiuser, without NFS (The same as 3, if you do not have networking)
#   3 - Full multiuser mode
#   4 - unused
#   5 - X11
#   6 - reboot (Do NOT set initdefault to this)
#
id:3:initdefault:

# System initialization.
si::sysinit:/etc/rc.d/rc.sysinit

l0:0:wait:/etc/rc.d/rc 0
l1:1:wait:/etc/rc.d/rc 1
l2:2:wait:/etc/rc.d/rc 2
l3:3:wait:/etc/rc.d/rc 3
```

```
l4:4:wait:/etc/rc.d/rc 4
l5:5:wait:/etc/rc.d/rc 5
l6:6:wait:/etc/rc.d/rc 6

# Things to run in every runlevel.
ud::once:/sbin/update

# Trap CTRL-ALT-DELETE
ca::ctrlaltdel:/sbin/shutdown -t3 -r now

# When our UPS tells us power has failed, assume we have a few minutes
# of power left.  Schedule a shutdown for 2 minutes from now.
# This does, of course, assume you have power installed and your
# UPS connected and working correctly.
pf::powerfail:/sbin/shutdown -f -h +2 "Power Failure; System Shutting Down"

# If power was restored before the shutdown kicked in, cancel it.
pr:12345:powerokwait:/sbin/shutdown -c "Power Restored; Shutdown Cancelled"


# Run gettys in standard runlevels
1:12345:respawn:/sbin/mingetty tty1
2:2345:respawn:/sbin/mingetty tty2
3:2345:respawn:/sbin/mingetty tty3
4:2345:respawn:/sbin/mingetty tty4
5:2345:respawn:/sbin/mingetty tty5
6:2345:respawn:/sbin/mingetty tty6

# Run xdm in runlevel 5
x:5:respawn:/usr/bin/X11/xdm -nodaemon
```

This file is used by /sbin/init to perform the most fundamental setup tasks. Each entry in the file is a colon-separated list of arguments that control the actions taken by init.

At the top of the file is a brief description of the run levels. Whenever init runs, it sets everything up for one of the run levels. The following line in inittab determines the default run level:

```
id:3:initdefault;
```

If init was invoked with a run level as its argument (which is done when changing from one run level to another), this value is ignored. If there were no run level specified, init will use the one named as the default. You can determine the current and previous run levels used on your computer with the following command:

```
runlevel
```

The output shows the previous run level (if any) and the current run level, as shown in the following:

```
N 3
```

This output means that there has not been any other run level since the computer was booted, and the current run level is 3. To change the run level, you must have superuser privileges. The runlevel can be changed with a command like the following:

```
telinit -t 10 2
```

This command will wait ten seconds and then switch to run level 2. The default wait is five seconds.

Some of the things you are familiar with change the run level. Issuing the shutdown command or pressing Ctrl+Alt+Del is a switch to run level 0. Issuing the reboot command is a switch to run level 6.

The `inittab` Entry

Each entry in the inittab, other that the first one that sets the default run level, is a sequence of four fields separated by colons. The following is an example of an entry for a mingetty that controls the login of a virtual terminal:

```
2:2345:respawn:/sbin/mingetty tty2
```

The first thing on the line is the ID of the entry. It must be unique, and it can only be two characters long.

The second field specifies the run levels for which this action will be executed. If no run level is specified, the action will take place for all run levels. In this example, the mingetty will be run for levels 2, 3, 4, and 5.

The third field is the action. In this example, the action is respawn, which means that the program should be restarted again if it should halt for any reason. This works particularly well for getty programs, because it guarantees that the login port will always recover no matter what happens. There are several of these action keywords (such as once that means the process should not be restarted, and wait that means that init should wait until the program finishes), but, for getty programs you should always use respawn. For example, if someone tries to log in and fails to enter the correct password, you want the getty to restart and issue another login prompt.

The fourth field is everything else on the line. It is the command to be issued by init to execute the command. It is the name of a program or a script and any arguments that are to be passed to it.

An `mgetty` Entry

To set up an mgetty that will answer your modem and prompt for a login, add a line like the following to /etc/inittab:

```
md:3:respawn:/sbin/mgetty -s 38400 -m '"" ATH0 OK ATZ OK' modem
```

This entry will initialize the modem and set its speed to 38400. The initialization string, enclosed in single quotes, is a sequence of expect/respond pairs that are used on a call to chat, as described earlier in this chapter. The first thing expected is the empty string " ", so the ATH0 command to hang up the phone is issued immediately. After the modem responds with OK, the ATZ initialization sequence is issued, and another OK is expected.

You may need to experiment with your modem initialization sequence. Any edits you make to inittab will only take effect when there is a reboot or a run level change that causes the program to start running. This example is set to execute only in run level 3, so switching to run level 2 will halt mgetty, and switching back to 3 will start it again. To restart your mgetty when you have changed the parameters, be logged in as root and enter the following command:

```
telinit 2
```

After the new run level is established and the mgetty has been halted, enter the following command:

```
telinit 3
```

The mgetty will be started again. If everything goes as it should, your modem will be initialized and mgetty will be waiting for a phone call.

A simpler way to do the same thing is to enter the following command:

```
telinit q
```

This causes a switch out of the current run level and then right back into it again. The result is the same as switching to another run level and then switching back.

> **Note:** If you are going to be using mgetty at home to receive faxes and allow remote logins, there is not much else you will need to do. If, however, you plan to have a more robust installation, such as a bank of modems receiving calls, you will want to look closely at the configuration options for mgetty. There are some options that can be set on the command line, but there is a lot of configuration that can be done by compiling your own version. In fact, there are some options that cannot be set any other way.

Summary

It seems that anything you wish to do with Linux can be done in several different ways. This chapter presented four ways to connect with the Internet. The manual one using dip works, but it would be very tedious to use—there is just too much data entry required. The one that works from X requires that you open a window and activate a connection, but it does give you manual control of when you connect and disconnect. The one that works from the command line is quick and simple, and it gives you manual control over connects and disconnects. The completely automatic one is a bit more difficult to configure, but you will not have to be concerned about whether or not you are connected—it all happens on an "as needed" basis.

On Your Own

As an experiment, try using `diald` for two or three days, and then switch to the `ppp-on` and `-off` scripts. You will find both methods have advantages and disadvantages, and you will probably prefer one over the other.

After you have made your connection to the Internet, run the `tcpdump -i ppp0` command to view information about every packet sent and received. Check the man page for `tcpdump` to find other display options.

There are three programs available for transferring files to and from a remote computer. They work very much alike, but each one has its special features. You should experiment with each one to discover your preferences for the sort of things you do. Just enter the program name on the command line and a prompt will appear. The simplest one is `tftp` (trivial file transfer protocol). The traditional UNIX version is `ftp` (file transfer protocol). The traditional program has a number of features and a new interface in `ncftp`.

FTP Server Fundamentals

FTP (File Transfer Protocol) is an Internet protocol that can be used to copy files from one place to another.

FTP is an important protocol. It is used by virtually everyone to copy files from one computer to another. All of Linux can be copied to your computer by using FTP. Web browsers—even with the file transfer capabilities of HTTP built into them—all are capable of executing FTP file transfers.

FTP is quite mature. It handles file transfers smoothly and flawlessly. The implementations on both the client and server sides have matured over the years, so the system is both flexible and stable. Setting up a server is very simple (in fact, most default Linux installations include a simple server), but, if you are going to operate an FTP site that has a lot of people doing different things or if you expect to have a lot of traffic, you will need to examine the configuration options to determine how to make it work best for you.

A Dual Connection Protocol

An FTP session maintains two connections between the client and the server. One connection is used to send and receive control and command information, the other connection is used to transmit the actual data as shown in Figure 15.1. This dual connection has the advantage that commands and acknowledgments can be passed back and forth without interrupting the flow of data.

The FTP session is always initiated by the client. The user interface supplies the control process with the information needed to make the connection (the Internet address, login name, and password). The client's control process establishes a connection with the server's control process, and the client's data process connects with the server's data process.

The FTP server processes can handle several FTP clients simultaneously. Normally, to keep system load at a reasonable level, there is a limit to the number of simultaneous connections allowed.

FIGURE 15.1

The FTP server and client.

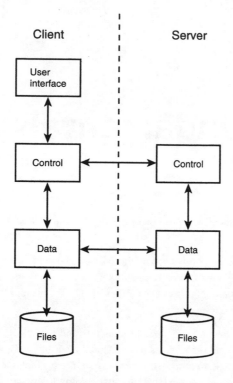

The user interface on the client side completely controls the session. By entering commands, the user can do any of the following:

- Copy one or more remote files to the local host.
- Copy one or more local files to the remote host.
- Append a local file to a file on the remote host.
- Change to another directory on the remote host.
- List the files in the current remote directory.
- Create and delete remote directories.
- Rename and delete remote files.

Configuring the FTP Server

A remote user connects to the server by logging in using FTP client software. This login starts the Linux FTP server daemon named ftpd. Each FTP session has its own ftpd daemon and, so there are no FTP sessions currently active, there are no ftpd daemons running.

There are several files that control the capabilities of an FTP session. The Linux installation should have set everything up for standard FTP sessions so, unless you have some special situation to take care of, the default server configuration may be all you need.

The /etc/services File

You should not have to do anything with this file because the port numbers and protocol are standard. However, if you want to experiment, you can use different numbers—your FTP server will only be accessible to those clients that know the numbers.

An FTP server connects with clients on two ports. The control processes use port 21 and the data transfer processes use port 20. These are the Internet standard ports, and they are specified in the file /etc/services. Both of these are TCP connections. There is a one-line entry in the file for each port number:

```
ftp-data        20/tcp
ftp             21/tcp
```

The /etc/passwd File

For a client to log in to FTP, the client must have a username in the /etc/passwd file. The contents of the entry in the file are used to validate the user's name and password, and to set the default directory on the server. Your system can be configured to prevent it but, normally, any user that can log on to the system directly (even root) can also log on as FTP. Among other requirements, the home directory of the user must exist.

There must be a shell program associated with the login. Many logins are used for special purpose (such as running a specific application program or shutting down the computer) so these logins would be inappropriate for an FTP session. The shell program is specified as the last parameter on /etc/passwd line. The following is the format of each line in the file:

```
fred:cFDkthZsG:500:500:/home/fred:/bin/bash
```

The different fields in the line are separated by colons. The username is fred. There is an encrypted password. The group ID is 500 and the user ID is 500. The home directory is /home/fred. The shell program is /bin/bash. The file /etc/shells contains a list of all the shells on the system—the ftpd daemon uses the file to make the verification.

There is a special case. An anonymous login is one that does not require a password. To allow anonymous logins, create an entry in the file that looks like the following:

```
ftp*:14:50:FTP User:/home/ftp:
```

If you do not want to allow anonymous logins, remove the ftp entry (because it may have been inserted automatically during installation). To log in as an anonymous user, the remote client sends anonymous as the login name and, traditionally, an email address as the password. There can be no real validation on the password because an anonymous login allows anyone to enter the system, but it is considered impolite to use anything other than your email address.

The /etc/ftpusers File

This file contains a list of users that are prohibited from logging in as FTP. Even if the username is in the /etc/passwd file and has a valid shell, if the name is also in this file, the user cannot initiate an FTP session.

As a safety measure, you may want to list users with Superuser powers and users that login for special purposes. A Superuser could log in and accidentally destroy critical operating system files.

The /etc/ftpaccess File

This file is read by ftpd when it starts up. It contains all the configuration settings. A typical file looks like the following:

```
class    all    real,guest,anonymous   *
email root@localhost
loginfails 5

readme   README*    login
readme   README*    cwd=*

message /welcome.msg          login
message .message              cwd=*

compress        yes           all
tar             yes           all
chmod           no            guest,anonymous
delete          no            guest,anonymous
overwrite       no            guest,anonymous
rename          no            guest,anonymous

log transfers anonymous,real inbound,outbound
shutdown /etc/shutmsg
passwd-check rfc822 warn
```

There are a lot of settings available. A large number of them deal with security and safety precautions. It can become quite complicated to assign a set of permissions to one group of users and a different set to another group. The following is a description of the commands that can be included in the file /etc/ftpaccess.

Many of the commands have <types> as a parameter. This refers to the types of users to which the command will apply. If the user is one with a regular login account (that is, the username appears in the /etc/passwd file), the keyword for the type is real. If the user logs in to a guest account (as defined on the groupname command described next), the keyword for the type is guest. An anonymous FTP user's type is anonymous. More than one type name can be used by separating the names with commas. For example, if you want a command to apply to all three types, for the <types> parameter use real,guest,anonymous.

alias *<name>* *<directory>*

This command assigns the *<name>* to the *<directory>*. A user can use the cd command to make *<name>* the current directory and the actual current directory will be <directory>. Also see cdpath.

autogroup *<groupname>* *<class>* [*<class>* ...]

If an anonymous user logs in, and that user is a member of class named *<class>*, the group ID of the user is switched to that of the *<groupname>*. The *<groupname>* can be any of those listed in /etc/group.

banner *<filename>*

This command causes the text of the named file to be displayed to a caller before login. The *<filename>* is an absolute path name relative to the system root directory, not the FTP directory.

It's best not to use this if you are making FTP files available for general use because it confuses some client FTP software.

cdpath *<directory>*

This command defines a directory in the cdpath, very much like the CDPATH environment variable use for shell access. You can specify multiple directories by using multiple cdpath commands. Any time the user enters a cd command, the named directory will be sought in the current directory and then in each of the cdpath directories. Also see alias.

chmod <yes¦no> *<types>*

This command allows or disallows the ability to modify file permissions. The *<types>* specifies the users affected by the command and is a comma-separated list of one or more of the keywords real, anonymous, and guest.

class *<class>* *<types>* *<aglob>* [*<aglob>* ...]

This command defines a class of users. There can be several classes defined, and several users can be in each class. A user can only be in one class, so, if the same user is in more than one class, all but the first entry is ignored. If a user is not part of a class, access will be denied.

The *<types>* is a comma-separated list specifying the types of users. The *<aglob>* is a domain name or an IP address, either of which may contain wildcard characters.

This option can be used to configure permissions individually, giving some users more access privileges than others.

compress <yes¦no> <class> [<class> ...]

For the named class or classes, this command enables or disables O_COMPRESS capabilities as specified in the file /etc/ftpconversions. Wildcards can be used in the class names. Also see tar.

delete <yes¦no> <types>

This command allows or disallows the ability to delete files. The <types> parameter specifies the users effected by the command.

deny <aglob> <file>

This command denies access to any user logging in from the host name <aglob>. When access is denied, the text of the <file> is displayed to the user. Hosts without working name servers can be denied by using !nameserved as the <aglob>.

email <address>

This command specifies an email address to be used to send messages to the FTP administrator.

guestgroup <groupname> [<groupname> ...]

If a real user (one with a user name in the /etc/passwd file) logs in and is a member of one of the named groups, the session is set up as if it were anonymous FTP. The <groupname> can be any of those listed in /etc/group.

For this to work properly, the user's home directory should be set up to be the FTP root directory. It is also useful to have a default working directory. This is done using a special notation in the /etc/passwd file. Because the named directory will appear as the root directory to the user, access is limited to that directory.

For example, a group name and number is defined in the /etc/group file like the following:

```
remlogger:x:500
```

The line added to the /etc/ftpaccess file looks like the following:

```
guestgroup remlogger
```

The username is defined in the /etc/passwd file something like the following:

```
tony:jKEoOsX:503:500:Tony D:/home/tony/./transfer:/bin/bash
```

> **Note:** These are text files and can be edited directly, but the number of fields in the /etc/passwd file makes it easy for mistakes to happen, so you may want to use the useradd utility to create or modify entries.

The user's home directory becomes the root directory. In this example, there is a period in the path name used to instruct FTP to change directories when the user logs in. On login, the directory /home/tony will become the root directory and be referred to simply as /. Also, on login, FTP will make /home/tony/transfer the current directory, but, because of the location of the root directory, it will show up as the directory named /transfer.

Although it usually works out better to have a separate login for regular user account logins, this one can also be used as a normal login and the bash shell will be executed. If you want to prevent normal logins, you can replace or delete /bin/bash. If you replace it with /bin/false, the entry can be easily spotted as being a dummy.

limit <class> <n> <times> <file>

There can be no more than <n> users of <class> logged in at any one time. An attempt to exceed the limit will cause the text in <file> to be displayed.

The <times> can be used to limit the hours of access for members of the class. It is entered as a day-of-the-week specification followed by two 24-hour clock values separated with a hyphen. There are no spaces in the format. The word any does not limit the access days. The work wk limits access to Monday through Friday. The word never denies access. You can also use one or more two-letter names of the days of the week to specify access is allowed on only those days. The following are some examples:

```
any0900-1800
wk0430-0900
mowefr2000-2200
any1900-0530
```

The first one will limit access to the hours between 9:00 a.m. and 6:00 p.m., but on any day. The second one allows access only between 4:30 a.m. and 9:00 a.m. Monday through Friday. The third one limits access to the two hour period from 8:00 p.m. to 10:00 p.m. on Monday, Wednesday, and Friday. The last one allows overnight access any day from 7:00 p.m. until 5:30 a.m. the next morning.

log commands <types>

This command causes individual user commands to be logged to the file /var/log/messages. The <types> field refers to the user types that will have their commands logged.

log transfers <types> <direction>

This command causes file transfers to the logged to the file /var/log/xferlog. The direction of the file transfers can be either incoming or outgoing, or it can be both by separating them with a comma. The <types> field specifies to the user types that will have their transfers logged.

loginfails *<number>*

This command causes the connection to be broken after a specified *<number>* of failed logins. The default is 5.

message *<filename>* *<when>* [*<class>* ...]

This command displays the text in *<filename>* either when the user logs in or changes to a specific directory. The *<when>* parameter is either login, to display the message to every user logging in, or cwd=*<directory>*, to display the message when the user changes to the *<directory>*. You can include several message commands to display different messages for different directories. During any one session, each message will only be displayed once to avoid annoying the user.

If a *<class>* is specified, the message will only be displayed for members of the class.

The text in *<filename>* has some special formatting capabilities in the form of "magic cookies" that can be embedded in the text and will be expanded with data from the FTP server. As shown in Table 15.1, each cookie is a two-character sequence of a percent sign and a letter.

Table 15.1   The Magic Cookies of the Message Text

Magic Cookie	Description
%C	The name of the current working directory.
%E	The email address of the FTP administrator. The address is defined in /etc/ftpaccess with the email command.
%F	The amount of free space available in the current working directory.
%L	Name of the local host.
%M	The maximum allowed number of users of this class.
%N	The current number of uses of this class.
%R	Name of the remote host.
%T	The server's local date and time in a 25 character format. Example: Sun Jun 27 21:40:32 1999.
%u	The username that has been validated via ASP (Authentication Server Protocol).
%U	The username supplied at login time.

noretrieve <*filename*> [<*filename*> ...]

This command denies the ability for any user to retrieve any of the named files. The file-names can be absolute (which specifies exactly one file) or relative (which specifies several files of the same name in different directories). Wildcards cannot be used.

overwrite <*yes¦no*> <*types*>

This command allows or disallows the ability to overwrite an existing file by transferring a new file by the same name. The <*types*> specifies the types of users affected by the command.

passwd-check <*level*> <*action*>

This command specifies the level of password validation, and the action to be taken if the validation fails. If the <*level*> parameter is none, no password validation is required for the user to log in. If the <*level*> parameter is trivial, the password must contain an at-sign character (as would be expected from a user entering an email address as the password). If the <*level*> parameter is rfc822, the password must be a valid Internet address as defined in the standards document RFC822. The <*action*> is either warn (which warns the user, but allows the login to continue) or enforce (which notifies the user and then breaks the connection).

path-filter <*types*> <*file*> <*allowed*> [<*disallowed*> ...]

For the specified <*types*>, the files that can be downloaded are limited to those that match the regular expression <*allowed*>. Optionally, there can also be one or more <*disallowed*> expressions to prevent downloads of files. The <*file*> parameter is the name of a file that contains the text of a message to be displayed to a user whenever a download is disallowed. The message is also displayed if the filename is invalid.

The regular expression is made up from the standard set of characters used by grep and other utilities. For example, using [a-z]*$ for <*allowed*> will limit downloads to only filenames beginning with a lowercase letter. Using ^\. for <*disallowed*> will prevent the user from downloading any file beginning with a period.

private <*yes¦no*>

If yes, after a user logs in, the FTP SITE command is available, allowing the user to enter a username and password to change the login. After the change, the user becomes a member of one of the groups listed in /etc/ftpgroups. An example entry in the /etc/ftpgroups file looks like the following:

tagname:PuVRIfmmQ:*groupname*

The *tagname* is an arbitrary alpha-numeric name to be used on the SITE command. Following the tag name, separated from it by a colon, is a password encrypted just like the ones in /etc/passwd. The *groupname* is a valid group listed in /etc/group.

readme *<filename>* *<when>* [*<class>* ...]

This command notifies the user that the file *<filename>* exists, along with the date and time of its latest modification. The *<when>* parameter can be login, to display the message when the user first logs in, or it can be cwd=*<directory>* to display the message whenever the user changes to the named *<directory>*. This is often used to notify users of the presence of some kind of index file and to specify the last time a directory's contents were updated.

If a *<class>* is specified, the message will only be displayed for members of the class.

rename *<yes¦no>* *<types>*

This command allows or disallows the ability to rename files. The *<types>* specifies the users affected by the command.

shutdown *<filename>*

If the named file exists, it will be checked regularly by the ftpd daemon to see if the local host is going to be shut down soon. If a shutdown is planned soon, FTP will deny any new connections and will notify the users logged in. Finally, if some users remain logged in, the connections will be cleanly dropped before the shutdown time comes.

The file can be automatically created by the program ftpshut described later in this chapter.

tar *<yes¦no>* *<class>* [*<class>* ...]

For the named class or classes, this command enables or disables O_TAR capabilities as specified in the file /etc/ftpconversions. Wildcards can be used in the class names. Also see compress.

umask *<yes¦no>* *<types>*

This command allows or disallows the ability to use the umask command to change the file permissions for newly created files. The *<types>* specifies the user types that will be allowed or disallowed to use umask.

upload *<root>* *<directory>* *<yes¦no>* *<owner>* *<group>* *<mode>* [dirs¦nodirs]

This command specifies upload access to one or more directories. The *<root>* is the path to the root directory of the user's FTP account (for example, /home/ftp). If a real user has a private FTP directory, there must be an upload command using that directory as the *<root>* to limit uploads.

The *<directory>* parameter is the name of the directory within the root directory. A wild-card expression can be used to specify several directories. If *<yes¦no>* is yes, upload are allowed into the directory—if it is no, uploads are prohibited.

Each file uploaded will be owned by *<owner>* and *<group>* and will have its permissions set by *<mode>*. The *<owner>* and the *<group>* are specified by name. The value of *<mode>* is in the octal format used as the argument to chmod. For example, 0666 grants read and write permissions to everyone.

Specifying dirs or nodirs either permits or prohibits the user from creating new subdirectories, respectively.

virtual *<IP>* *<setting>* *<path>*

This command enables the capabilities of a virtual FTP server with the specified IP address. The keyword used for *<setting>* determines the meaning of *<path>*. If *<setting>* is root, the *<path>* is the path name of the root directory of the file system to be used by the virtual FTP server. If *<setting>* is banner, the *<path>* is the name of a file holding text that will be displayed to the user. If *<setting>* is logfile, the *<path>* is the name of the FTP log file.

Controlling and Monitoring the FTP Service

FTP service is quite stable and, once it is set up and running, seldom needs attention. However, there are circumstances where it needs to be shut down and, because file transfers can consume a lot of resources, you may need to monitor the level of usage.

Checking the Current Load

There is a simple utility program named ftpcount that displays the number of FTP currently active. Just enter the following command:

```
ftpcount
```

A line will be displayed for each service class:

```
Service class all              - 0 Users (no maximum)
Service class longdep          - 2 Users (no maximum)
```

This indicates that there are no users logged in to the class named all, but there are two users logged in to the longdep class. Neither of these groups are configured to limit access to a maximum number of concurrent users.

Checking the Current Sessions

A list of the currently logged in users can be displayed by using ftpwho. Enter the following command with no options:

```
ftpwho
```

There will be one line for each logged in user. Because each logged in user has a copy of ftpd running, a list of the ftpd processes is also a list of the login sessions. The output of ftpwho is the same as from ps ax ¦ grep ftpd. Each line includes the process ID of the daemon, the amount of CPU time consumed, the name of the user, and the current activity of the user.

Shutting Down and Restarting the FTP Service

The program named ftpshut can be used to halt FTP. The command operates on a timer and can also be used to notify the users that FTP is going down.

To shut down FTP immediately and without warning, enter the word now for the time, as shown in the following:

```
ftpshut now
```

To shut down FTP in 10 minutes, use a plus sign to designate a duration, as shown in the following:

```
ftpshut +10
```

The third way to determine the shutdown time is to specify the time in a four-digit hour and minute format, as shown in the following:

```
ftpshut 1045
```

This command will shut down FTP at 10:45 a.m. Any time specified this way must be in the same day—the only way to span midnight is to specify the time as a number of minutes.

Before FTP is actually shut down, new logins are prohibited. Also, prior to the shutdown, current sessions are logged off. The default is to prohibit logins for 10 minutes prior to shutdown and to log off active users 5 minutes before shutdown. These will occur immediately if the shutdown time is initialized to something less than their time. You can adjust the times in the following way:

```
 ftpshut -l 30 -d 15 1400
```

This command will prohibit any logins after 13:30, log off any existing sessions at 13:45, and shutdown FTP at 14:00.

There is one more argument available on the command line. It is possible to specify the text of the warning message that will be displayed to the users, as in the following:

```
ftpshut -l 30 -d 15 1400 "FTP is shutting down"
```

The text can be any length, because it will be reformatted into lines with a maximum length of 75 characters each. Also, you can have special information included in the formatted output by using the following special characters:

%C	The name of the user's working directory
%d	The scheduled time that the current connections will be closed
%E	The email address of the FTP system administrator
%F	The amount of free space in the user's current working directory
%L	Name of the local host
%M	The maximum number of concurrent users allowed in this class
%N	The number of users of this class that are currently logged in
%r	The scheduled time new logins will be disallowed
%R	Name of the remote host
%S	The scheduled shutdown time
%T	Local time in the standard 25-character format
%U	The name of the logged in user

The ftpshut creates a file that holds all of the shutdown settings. The presence of this file causes FTP to shut down and remain shut down. To restart FTP, simply delete the file. The filename is specified by the shutdown command in the /etc/ftpaccess file (normally named /etc/shutmsg), as described earlier in this chapter. The file contains all the time settings and the warning text, as shown in the following:

```
1999 05 28 14 06 0010 0005
This is text of the warning message.
```

The first four fields specify the date and time of the shutdown. New users will not be allowed to log in 10 minutes before shutdown, and existing users will be logged off 5 minutes before.

Granting and Denying Service

The /etc/ftphosts file can be used to limit access to the FTP system. It can contain a number of allow and deny commands, both of which limit FTP access.

The allow command can be used to limit the remote hosts that can be used by a certain username, as shown in the following:

```
allow fred hcab
```

This line allows fred to log in from a host named hcab, but from nowhere else. There can be more than one host specified for a username by using wildcard names and/or a list of names. The following is an example:

```
allow fred *.athome.com *.xyz.net
```

This will allow logins by `fred` from any host in the `athome.com` domain or in the `xyz.net` domain, but from nowhere else.

The `deny` command has the same syntax, but will specifically deny the user access from the specified host, as shown in the following:

```
deny fred *.athome.com *.xyz.net
```

This will allow `fred` to log in from anywhere *except* the `athome.com` domain and the `xyz.net` domain.

Automating File Conversions

FTP can be configured to convert files from one format to another as part of the file transfer process. Files can be tarred and zipped, or they can be un-tarred and unzipped. This is all under the control of the file named `/etc/ftpconversions`. A typical file looks like the following:

```
:.Z:   :  :/bin/compress -d -c %s:T_REG¦T_ASCII:O_UNCOMPRESS:UNCOMPRESS
:    :  :.Z:/bin/compress -c %s:T_REG:O_COMPRESS:COMPRESS
:.gz:  :  :/bin/gzip -cd %s:T_REG¦T_ASCII:O_UNCOMPRESS:GUNZIP
:    :  :.gz:/bin/gzip -9 -c %s:T_REG:O_COMPRESS:GZIP
:    :  :.tar:/bin/tar -c -f - %s:T_REG¦T_DIR:O_TAR:TAR
:    :  :.tar.Z:/bin/tar -c -Z -f - %s:T_REG¦T_DIR:O_COMPRESS¦O_TAR:TAR+COMPRESS
:    :  :.tar.gz:/bin/tar -c -z -f - %s:T_REG¦T_DIR:O_COMPRESS¦O_TAR:TAR+GZIP
```

Each line is a list of fields separated by colons. When a field is missing, it must have at least one space as a place holder. Each line begins with a space and a colon because the format defines the first parameter as a prefix file extension to be stripped off, but this has never actually been used and is normally not even implemented by `ftpd`. Likewise, the third field is a prefix to be added to the filename but, again, it is always empty.

The second and fourth fields define the name conversions. The second field is the file suffix that is expected to be on an incoming file. The input suffix is stripped off during processing and replaced by the third field, which is the output suffix. For example, according to this example file, if a file by the name of `fred.doc.Z` is converted, it will be uncompressed into `fred.doc`.

The next field is the complete command used to convert the file from one state to another. The command is written to use standard input to receive incoming data, and a `%s` entry in the command line will become the name of the output file.

You can specify one or more file types that any particular conversion routine can process. Any regular file can be processed for the type `T_REG`. The `T_ASCII` setting specifies ASCII files. If `T_DIR` is specified, the command is capable of processing entire directories. A vertical bar can be used to combine two types.

The next field specifies the type of action. It is O_COMPRESS if the file is to be compressed and O_UNCOMPRESS if the file is to be uncompressed. If a collection of files is going to be combined into a single file, it is O_TAR. If a file is to be split into multiple files, it is O_UNTAR. If more than one action is to take place, a vertical bar can be used to combine two types.

The rightmost field is a description of the action being taken.

The FTP Log File

The FTP log file is named xferlog. It can be located in different places, but on Linux it is normally found in /var/log. A new log file is started each day with the old log files being renamed. The file from the previous day will be named xferlog.1, the one for the day before that is named xferlog.2, and so on.

Every line in the log file has the same format. It is a string of fields separated by spaces. The fields have the format and the order shown in Table 15.2.

Table 15.2   A Log Entry Is an Ordered Sequence of Fields

Field Name	Description
CurrentTime	The time the log entry was made is in the standard 25-character format. Example: Sun Jun 27 21:40:32 1999. This field contains embedded characters (the delimiter for the rest of the entry) but it is always exactly 25 characters long.
TransferTime	The number of seconds it required to transfer the file.
RemoteHost	The name of the client host.
FileSize	The number of bytes in the transferred file.
FileName	The name of the transferred file.
TransferType	A single character flag. It is either a for ASCII transfer or b for binary transfer.
SpecialActionFlag	One or more character flags indicating any special action taken. The letter C indicates the file was compressed. The letter U indicates the file was uncompressed. The letter T indicates the file was made into a tar file. If no action was taken, the - character is used as a placeholder.
Direction	The letter o is for an outgoing transfer, i is for incoming.

continues

Table 15.2 Continued

Field Name	Description
AccessMode	A single letter indicating how the user can be logged in. The letter a represents an anonymous login. The letter g represents a guest login (defined by the guest-group command in /etc/ftpaccess). The letter r represents a real user—a user that has normal access to the computer and has logged in using FTP.
UserName	The local username. For an anonymous login, the identity string used for the password will be used.
ServiceName	The name of the service being invoked. This is almost always ftp.
AuthenticationMethod	The digit 0 indicates that no authentication was used. If 1, the user name has been validated using ASP (Authentication Server Protocol).
AuthenticatedUserID	The user ID returned from the authentication. If there is no ID, an * character is displayed.

Note: The log file can be used to analyze the kind of activity that has been taking place over a period of time by writing simple scripts to read and process the log files. Also, by using the tail command with the -f option, it is possible to keep a running monitor on FTP activities. By piping the output of tail into the input of a formatting program, you can extract and display only the data in which you are interested.

Using FTP Client Software

There are two FTP client programs supplied with Linux. The one named ftp is the traditional program that operates from the command line—you enter a command an it obeys and scrolls up information on the action it took. The program ncftp also operates from the command line, but is a bit more visually oriented—it uses the full screen to display names and status information.

Both programs operate on the same fundamental principle. You use the program to log in to the remote computer, and then you can browse around to copy, delete, or change the names of files and directories. It is quite obvious that the commands in ncftp were based on the commands found in the older ftp program. There are some functional differences, and some of the commands found in one are not found in the other. You can find out more about ncftp, and get the latest version, at http://www.ncftp.com.

Both ftp and ncftp have built-in help text. To get a list of the commands, just enter **help**. To get help on a specific command, enter the word **help** followed by the name of the command. The following are the command names listed by the help command of ncftp:

```
!            create    lcd       mkdir     pls       rename    set
bookmark     debug     lls       mode      predir    quit      site
bookmarks    dir       lookup    mput      prefs     quote     type
cat          echo      lpage     open      put       rhelp     version
cd           get       lpwd      page      pwd       rm
close        help      ls        pdir      redir     rmdir
```

And the following are the command names listed by the help command in ftp:

```
!            debug        mdir       sendport    site
$            dir          mget       put         size
account      disconnect   mkdir      pwd         status
append       exit         mls        quit        struct
ascii        form         mode       quote       system
bell         get          modtime    recv        sunique
binary       glob         mput       reget       tenex
bye          hash         newer      rstatus     tick
case         help         nmap       rhelp       trace
cd           idle         nlist      rename      type
cdup         image        ntrans     reset       user
chmod        lcd          open       restart     umask
close        ls           prompt     rmdir       verbose
cr           macdef       passive    runique     ?
delete       mdelete      proxy      send
```

An FTP Session

The most common FTP activity is logging on to a remote site and retrieving one or more files. This is an example of using ftp to connect to a remote system, locate a file, and retrieve a copy of it. Enter **ftp** from the command line and the program will start running. It prompts you from the command line, as shown in the following:

```
ftp>
```

You can then start a remote session by naming the remote host on an open command. The command, and the response from it, look like the following:

```
ftp> open ftp.us.kernel.org
Connected to ftp.us.kernel.com.
220 ubu.NWS.ORST.EDU FTP server (Version wu-2.5.0(1) Sun Jun 13 21:36:26 PDT
1999) ready.
Name (ftp.us.kernel.org:arthur):
```

That last line is a prompt for the login name. If you have an account on the remote system, you can enter its name. If your remote account name is the same as your local account name, it becomes the default and you can just press Return. Or, if the server allows anonymous logins, you can log in in the following way:

```
Name (ftp.us.kernel.org:arthur): anonymous
331 Guest login ok, send your complete e-mail address as password.
Password:
```

Again, the last line is a prompt. If you are logging in to an account, you will need to know its password. For anonymous logins, just enter your email address. The password is not echoed and the result from entering it looks like the following:

```
Password:
230 Anonymous access granted, restrictions apply.
Remote system type is UNIX
Using binary mode to transfer files.
ftp>
```

The regular prompt returns, and you are ready to explore the remote system and download some files. To take a look at the contents of the current directory, use the ls command, as shown in the following:

```
ftp> ls
200 PORT command successful.
150 Opening ASCII mode data connection for file list.
total 0
drwxr-xr-x   2 root     root         1024 Apr 15 08:03 bin
drwxr-xr-x   2 root     root         1024 Apr 15 08:03 etc
drwxr-xr-x   2 root     root         1024 Feb 21 17:19 mirrors
drwxr-xr-x   4 root     root         1024 May  5 09:23 pub
228 Transfer complete.
```

The directory contains no files, but it does contain four subdirectories. The cd command is used to change to a subdirectory, as shown in the following:

```
ftp> cd pub
250 CWD command successful
```

By using successive cd and ls commands, you can navigate through the FTP site to find the file or files that you want get. For example, you find the file you want with the ls command, as shown in the following:

```
-rw-r--r--   1 root     ftp        151205 May 28 00:30 syslinux-1.44.zip
```

To retrieve this file, use the get command, as shown in the following:

```
ftp> get syslinux-1.44.zip
local syslinux-1.44.zip remote: syslinux-1.44.zip
200 PORT command successful.
150 Opening BINARY mode data connection for syslinux-1.44.zip (151205 bytes).
226 Transfer complete
151205 bytes received in 46.1 secs (3.2 Kbytes/sec)
```

You can then close the connection in the following way:

```
ftp> close
```

And you can exit the ftp program in the following way:

```
ftp> quit
```

> **Note:** The ftp program mentioned twice that the file transfer was being done in binary mode. This is because using the wrong transfer mode can scramble your data. If you are transferring data to and from systems that store files in the same format, there is no problem. Linux and UNIX files all have the same internal formats, so files can be transferred freely from one to the other. DOS and Windows, however, have a different internal format for text files (they have an extra character at the end of each line of text) so the transfer mode should be set to ASCII by entering the command ascii.
>
> But be careful that you use the ASCII mode only to transfer text files. Setting the ASCII option to transfer binary data will quite likely scramble the data in a binary file in such a way that it usually cannot be retrieved.

Summary

The FTP protocol and FTP software are very mature because they have been used for many years to transfer files across an Internet. The open source movement owes much of its success to the fact that FTP can be used to copy files easily from one place to another. Because a typical FTP server is available to anyone on the Internet, there are many configuration settings that control access and security. While there is a large number of options that can be set, it is convenient that almost all of them are in the same file.

On Your Own

Log in to your own account as an FTP client. This can be used to test the basic FTP installation. You don't need to log in from a remote host—you can do this on the local host by using the open command with the local host name.

Install your own set of messages that are displayed to the user when he or she logs in, logs out, and when a file is not found.

Establish two FTP accounts that use the same directory as their root. Limit one of the accounts so that it can only download files, and permit the other account to also upload and delete files. This will give you a user account and an administrative account.

Create a subdirectory in your FTP directories that can only be used to upload files. This can be done by using a separate login or by setting permissions.

Linux Web Servers

There is no doubt that if any one object is responsible for what the Internet is today, it is Web browsers. The word "Internet" is synonymous to most people with what is actually the World Wide Web, or, more accurately, their browsers. And, of course, browsers would be useless without Web servers.

The popularity of large Web sites brimming with flashy images and sound effects can distract people from some of the less extravagant uses for a Web server—internal memo boards, departmental servers, and general places for co-workers or communities to share knowledge and cooperate on projects.

Which Web Server Is for You? Apache Versus NCSA Versus Netscape

Different requirements usually lead to choosing different products—but in this case the choice is almost always the same—Apache.

The NCSA server is the oldest of all three. It is no longer developed and contains no priority functionality that is not provided by Apache, so there is very little reason to use it.

Netscape provides a variety of commercial Web servers for a variety of platforms. The lowest version of their Web server, the FastTrack Web Server, has been ported to Linux—but good luck in finding it. At the time of this writing, I can find no information about if it is contained on Caldera's OpenLinux 2.2 CD-ROM, and Netscape's site contains nothing but press releases regarding Linux.

Netscape servers do provide an easy, HTML-based setup and configuration. There are GUI-based configuration tools for Apache, but they are not as easy to use as Netscape's.

According to the Netcraft Webserver Survey (http://www.netcraft.com/survey/), Apache has been the most popular Web server on the Internet for a long time, with over 50 percent of the sites surveyed by Netcraft using it. Apache is free, extremely powerful and extendable, and comes with just about any Linux distribution (including Caldera).

Installing the Web Server

Most distributions will offer to install the Apache Web server during installation. In RPM-using distributions, you can check whether or not Apache is installed by typing the following:

```
# rpm -q apache
```

If Apache is not installed on your system, you probably have an rpm file (or whatever package management software your distribution uses) on your distribution CD-ROM. You should consider checking for any updates or newer versions on your distribution's Web site. You can also download the source code or precompiled binaries from the Apache Web site at http://www.apache.org.

Software installation is covered in Chapter 9, "Administrative Tasks."

Configuring Your Web Server

Depending on the version of Apache you have installed, it may have one or three configuration files you can edit. Their location, will vary, depending on your installtion method. Red Hat's rpm will install them in /etc/http/conf/. If you have installed from a recent source code package without modifications, they will be in /usr/local/apache/conf. Other locations are /etc/httpd/apache/conf or /etc/apache/conf, though these are not as popular.

Some Web Server Basics

Practically anyone who has used the Internet recently is familiar with how a Web browser works—you type in a URL, and a HTML file and several images get downloaded to your machine.

Actually, the Web browser is sending an HTTP request to port 80 on the Web server. The Web server receives this request and sends the requested files and information back to the browser.

All the data files transferred by the Web server must be in directories that are predefined in the configuration files. The top level of the directory files is called the *Document Root*. The Web server usually also has default index files, normally called index.html. If the Document Root is defined to /usr/local/web/, a Web browser requesting http://www.yourserver.com/ will actually be getting the local file /usr/local/web/index.html.

GUI-Based Configuration Tools

Although Apache doesn't come with any GUI-Based configuration tools, there are third-party products for managing Apache. The linuxconf package can provide some functionality, as can the Comanche project (http://comanche.com.dtu.dk/comanche/).

Figure 16.1 shows Comanche running on a fairly standard Apache installation. The top server shows a tree-based configuration of the Web server and its directories. Double-clicking a directory name will bring up a new window with options specific to that directory. The bottom part shows the process ID numbers for the currently running server.

FIGURE 16.1
Comanche window open with some standard directories.

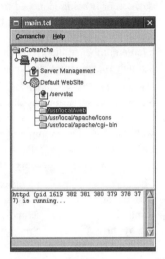

Text File-Based Configuration

Older versions of Apache used three separate configuration files—httpd.conf for the Web server daemon configuration, access.conf for access and directory control, and srm.conf for resource configuration. To avoid confusion, all of these files have been combined into httpd.conf in more recent versions of Apache.

These files are well documented, and Apache comes with very good documentation. This section will cover the more pressing issues for getting your server up and running.

This section will also refer to the three separate configuration files. If your configuration is all contained within one single file, just ignore the filename heading.

The format of these files is similar to that of most UNIX text configuration files: lines beginning with a hash mark (#) are comments. Other lines contain a key and a value, separated by a whitespace.

httpd.conf

This file contains configuration information for the Web server daemon (httpd). This information includes what port numbers or IP addresses to listen to, what permissions the daemon runs with, how many daemons to spawn, and information about virtual hosts.

Table 16.1 lists some of the more important directives defined in this file.

Table 16.1 Common `httpd.conf` Directives

Directive	Description
ServerType standalone	The `ServerType` directive tells the `httpd` daemon whether it is running as a dedicated, standalone daemon or is being launched from `inetd`. Most servers will run as standalone. If you are going to run a low-powered server that is not meant to serve a large number of hits, you can consider running it through `inetd`. However, this is not advised.
Port 80	Port number 80 is the standard HTTP port. Running the server on any other port will require potential viewers to enter that port along with the URL. For example, if your server is running on port 1080, the URL will be `http://www.yourserver.com:1080`. You may want to run on a different port for security reasons, or because there already is another server using port 80 on this machine. Also, unless initially run by the Superuser, no program can bind to a port number lower than 1024. If you are installing without `root` privileges, you may need to use a higher port number.
HostnameLookups off	Apache will keep a log of visitors to your site. With `HostnameLookups` turned off, Apache will register the IP address, not the hostname. This is probably a better idea if you want higher performance. DNS hostname lookups can take a while.
User nobody Group nogroup	These directives determine which user and group the `httpd` daemon runs as. This is necessary for security reasons, because the httpd server is normally used by remote users to read information off your server, and, if CGI scripts are used, can also be used to write data to your server. You might want to setup a dedicated user and group (normally both are named `httpd`) for the Web server to run as. Don't forget to change ownership and permissions on the rest of your system to prevent this user from accessing anything but Web server data.
ServerRoot @@ServerRoot@@	This directive specifies the root location for the server's configuration and log files. In older versions of Apache, it was neccessary to manually change this value in the source code to produce the desired effect.

access.conf

This file contains access information on a per-directory basis. Definitions on what exactly is allowed to happen in each directory are located here.

Definitions for each directory must begin with a *<directory name>* line, and end with a *</directory>*. For example, the first few lines of this file may contain the following lines, which set up restrictive permissions as the default:

```
<Directory />
Options None
AllowOverride None
</Directory>
```

Here are a few of the directives which may appear inside each directory definition.

```
Options Indexes FollowSymLinks
```

The `Options` directive may be followed by any of the following keywords:

- `Indexes` will allow the Web server to generate an index of the files contained within this directory, if no index document is found.

- `Includes` allows server-side includes.

- `FollowSymLinks` will allow the server to follow symbolic links.

  Note: This may allow the server to exit the Web server directory and gain access to other protions of the filesystem.

- `ExecCGI` enables CGI scriptexecution from this directory.

- `MultiViews` enables content-based negotiation multiple document views. This is useful for multiple language documents—the desired language may be negotiated on connect and the correct document retrieved.

- `None` disables all options.

- `All` enables all options, except for `MultiViews`, which must be set manually.

The following directives are used to allow or deny access to the Web server. The `from` keyword may be followed by an IP address or hostname.

```
order allow,deny
allow  from all
deny      from none
```

Partial names are allowed. For example, the following will allow accesses only from `mydomain.com`:

```
order deny,allow
deny from all
allow from .mydomain.com
```

The following is an example of the document entry for a Document Root directory:

```
<Directory @@ServerRoot@@/htdocs>

Options Indexes FollowSymLinks
order allow,deny
allow from all

</Directory>
```

`srm.conf`

This file contains directives defining the directories and files used by the Web server, as well as defining resources that determine how requests from Web browsers are handled.

Table 16.2 lists some of the important directives set within this file.

Table 16.2   Common `srm.conf` directives

Directive	Description
DocumentRoot @@ServerRoot@@/htdocs	This directive defines where the Document Root is. It is quite often set to one directory below the directory where the server files are installed, but is also quite often in its own dedicated directory, such as /usr/local/web. Under Red Hat systems, it is usually set as /home/httpd/html.
UserDir public_html	If you want to allow users on your system to have their own personal Web sites, this directive gives the directory name users must create inside their own home directory. A request to http://www.yourdomain.com/~user will then translate to the ~user/public_html directory.
DirectoryIndex index.html, Welcome.html	If no filename is specified by the browser request, the files defined by this directive are searched for in the order in which they are entered. If they are not found, and the Indexes option was set in the access.conf file, an index of all files will be generated.
FancyIndexing on	With FancyIndexing turned off, directory indexes will contain only a bulleted list of filenames. Turning this directive on, however, will cause the index to contain more information, such as file sizes, descriptions, and icons corresponding to the file type. Note that descriptions and icons can also be set from within the srm.conf file—see the next few entries.

Directive	Description
AddIconByEncoding (CMP,/ icons/compressed.gif) x-compress x-gzip AddIconByType (TXT, /icons/text.gif) text/* AddIcon /icons/binary. gif .bin .exe	These directives are used to define specific icons for specific files. Icons can be assigned by MIME encoding, by file type, or simply by filename or extension. Note that the icons pointed to in these examples are icons included with the Apache package.
AddDescription "GZIP compressed document" .gz	This directive will add a description based on filename or extension. This description will be shown if a directory index list is created and if the FancyIndexing directive is on.
IndexIgnore .??* *~ *#	The files defined by this directive will not be included in directory indexes.
DefaultType text/plain	If the Web server is unable to determine the file type, it will use the type defined here.
Alias /icons/ /usr/local/ apache/icons/	The Alias directive is used to create directory name aliases. This is useful when you want to keep many files of the same type (for example, icons) in a separate directory, not within the Document Root. In this example, a request to http://www. yourdomain.com/icons/ will lead to the /usr/local/apache/icons directory. Without this directive, the request would lead to a directory named icons below the Document Root directory— assuming the Document root is /usr/local/web/, this would be /usr/local/web/icons/.
ScriptAlias /cgi-bin/ @@ServerRoot@@/cgi-bin/	This directive works like the Alias directive, except that CGI scripts are allowed to run from within these aliases.

Tuning Your Web Server

There are many little things you can do to get more performance out of your Web server, including increasing or decreasing the amount of running processes, checking the log files often, changing the permissions, and so on.

Turning Off Hostname Resolving

As stated before, the Apache Web server will keep a log of all accesses to your Web site. Connecting hosts are only identified by their IP address, so Apache has to do a reverse-DNS lookup to find the hostname. This process may take anywhere from a split second to several seconds, during which time the remote host has to wait, so access to your site seems slow.

Worse yet, DNS lookup is usually a locking operation, meaning other httpd processes may need to wait for each other to use it. This can slow down the system incredibly.

It is recommended that you leave hostname resolving turned off. If you ever need to look up a specific hostname, you can do so manually by using the nslookup command. Many log file analyzers contain options to automatically do name lookups for final reports.

Hostname resolving may be neccesary for security reasons. You might want to block connecting hosts based on names rather than IP addresses. In this case, name resolving must be left on.

To turn off hostname lookups, make sure the directive HostnameLookups is set to off in the httpd.conf file.

The Server Pool

Apache will try to maintain a server pool, ready to answer many simultaneous accesses. It does this by checking how many httpd processes are waiting for requests, and increasing or decreasing the size of the pool according to the load and predetermined configuration settings in the httpd.conf file. The following is an example of the directives that should be set (or modified) in httpd.conf:

```
StartServers 10
MinSpareServers 10
MaxSpareServers 20
```

The StartServers directive determines how many processes Apache will run as soon as it starts. Apache will periodically check how many of these processes are busy, and will make sure that there are at least as many spare ones as defined in MinSpareServers, and no more than the amount defined in MaxSpareServers.

The Server Status Handler

Apache contains a built-in handler that will let you view the server status online. You need to add (or uncomment) the following section in the access.conf file:

```
<Location /server-status>
SetHandler server-status
order deny,allow
deny from all
allow from your.ip.address # Change to your actual IP address
</Location>
```

This will allow you to access the URL http://www.yourdomain.com/server-status/ and get information about your currently running server. This information includes the version of Apache, the time and date when the server was started, total accesses, total traffic, httpd process status, and more. The following is an excerpt from such a request:

```
Apache Server Status for www.yourdomain.com

Server Version: Apache/1.3.6 (Unix)
Server Built: Mar 24 1999 10:13:55

Current Time: Saturday, 31-Jul-1999 21:52:32 CDT
Restart Time: Saturday, 06-Jul-1999 16:34:18 CDT
Parent Server Generation: 0
Server uptime: 25 days, 58 minutes 14 seconds
Total accesses: 181315 - Total Traffic: 912318 kB
CPU Usage: u.06 s.01 cu0 cs0 - .002% CPU load
1.93932 requests/sec - 10.39979 kB/second - 5.0316742 kB/request
1 requests currently being processed, 7 idle servers
```

Apache Log Files

Log files are your friends. You can tell how many accesses your Web server is receiving by typing the following:

```
# tail -f /var/log/httpd/access_log
```

You may need to type in a different directory name. This command will display the last 10 lines of the log file, and will continue appending until interrupted. The rate at which your Web server writes to its log file will indicate the amount of accesses you are getting.

Even if you are not trying to fine-tune your server, you should look through the log files occasionally. Run tail -f on the logfiles and stare at the lines. Zen is an important part of Linux.

Adding Virtual Hosts

Virtual Hosting allows you to host more than one Web site on the same machine, which is usually a better solution than getting a new, dedicated machine for every Web site you intend to host. This means, of course, that all the Web sites will be sharing resources, so this solution may not be appropriate in all cases.

There are two methods for virtual hosting: IP Address-based and Name-based.

IP Address-Based Virtual Hosting

This method is the more reliable one, because it doesn't require any special features on the browser side. It does require that your machine have a separate IP address for each Web site you intend to host. This can be achieved either by installing additional network cards or by using IP Aliasing.

This section assumes the machine has two IP Addresses, 192.168.0.1, which resolves to www.domain1.com, and 192.168.0.2, which resolves to www.domain2.com.

There are two methods of setting up IP-based virtual hosts: multiple daemons or single daemons.

Multiple Daemons

Although setting up the configuration files for this method is a lot simpler, it requires a completely separate installation of Apache for each virtual host. This will probably mean you have to install from the source-code package, because you will have to change some of the predefined directories.

After this is done, however, all you have to do is add the Listen directive to the httpd.conf file. For example, the httpd.conf file for www.domain1.com will contain the following:

```
Listen 192.168.0.1:80
```

Single Daemon

This method requires only one installation of Apache, but requires more configuration of the httpd.conf file. The VirtualHost directive is used to define the values for each of the virtual hosts. You can set up different document root directories, server administrators, and log files for each host. The following is an example of the section of the httpd.conf file required to set up two virtual hosts—www.domain1.com and www.domain2.com.

```
<VirtualHost 192.168.0.1>
ServerAdmin webmaster@domain1.com
DocumentRoot /usr/local/web/domain1
ServerName www.domain1.com
ErrorLog logs/domain1_error_log
TransferLog logs/domain1_access_log
</VirtualHost>

<VirtualHost 192.168.0.2>
ServerAdmin webmaster@domain2.com
DocumentRoot /usr/local/web/domain2
ServerName www.domain2.com
ErrorLog logs/domain2_error_log
TransferLog logs/domain2_error_log
</VirtualHost>
```

Name-Based Virtual Hosting

While more reliable, IP-Based Virtual Hosting may not always be available. For example, additional IP addresses may not be readily available. The HTTP/1.1 protocol supports methods for the server to know what address the browser is requesting, making it possible for more than one server to share an IP address.

Setting up Name-Based Virtual Hosting is very similar to setting up Single-Daemon IP-Based Virtual Hosting. The biggest difference is that you must use the NameVirtualHost directive in the httpd.conf file. In this method, too, different Document Root directories, server administrators, and log files can be specified.

The following is an example of the section in the httpd.conf file needed to set up name-based virtual hosts. This example assumes that both www.domain1.com and www.domain2.com resolve to 192.168.0.1.

```
NameVirtualHost 192.168.0.1

<VirtualHost 192.168.0.1>
ServerAdmin webmaster@domain1.com
DocumentRoot /usr/local/web/domain1
ServerName www.domain1.com
ErrorLog logs/domain1_error_log
TransferLog logs/domain1_access_log
</VirtualHost>

<VirtualHost 192.168.0.1>
ServerAdmin webmaster@domain2.com
DocumentRoot /usr/local/web/domain2
ServerName www.domain2.com
ErrorLog logs/domain2_error_log
TransferLog logs/domain2_error_log
</VirtualHost>
```

Summary

With more and more of them popping up by the second, Web sites have turned into one of the most important components of every network, and a large number of all the public Web sites on the Internet are running under Linux. Practically any Linux distribution comes with everything you need to set up anything from a small, departmental-internal Web site, to a large millions-of-hits-per-month site. Or both. Installing the Apache rpm package under Red Hat will leave you with a Web server all ready to go—just add content. And with virtual hosting, you need not stop at just one server.

While there are smaller, faster, and more commercially oriented servers than Apache, none of them provide a solution as easy to implement and complete as Apache.

Web sites have become the de facto measure of the size of the Internet. Sooner or later everyone will have one—so go set yours up right now.

On Your Own

After your server is installed, try accessing it from various machines and looking at the information your log files provide. Using the tail -f command, you can get a continuously updated display of your logs in real-time. Try accessing pages to see how the log file displays them. Try accessing pages that do not exist, and check how both the access and error log report them.

Try making your own custom "Page Not Found" messages. If you are brave and know some Perl (or even simple shell scripting), you can try making some simple CGI files. In fact, try to make a custom CGI "Page Not Found" program that offers suggestions.

You can try using Telnet to access port number 80 on your machine and talk directly to your server.

Or you can try building your own home page on your own little corner of the Internet. Even though setting up Web servers is a serious, and sometimes important function, don't forget that you can also have a lot of fun with them.

DNS and Other Network Services

inetd Considerations

inetd's role on your system is similar to that of a receptionist. It answers network calls made to your machine and routes them to the appropriate program. inetd is usually used for network services that do not need to have their own daemon waiting for calls. You can also use inetd to selectively screen calls based on their source, so inetd can also enhance system security.

Unfortunately, most systems come with a wide open inetd configuration file, enabling many services you probably don't want or need. If your system is connected to the Internet, even if only through occasional dialup, you should check your inetd configuration as soon as possible.

The /etc/services file

The /etc/services file should come with your system, and there is usually no need to edit it.

Every TCP/IP network protocol or service has a corresponding port number. For example, the port number for HTTP service is 80. To retrieve Web pages from the server, your Web browser accesses port number 80.

The /etc/services file contains a list of services and their port number. Each line in the file contains a service name, port number, whether this is a TCP or UDP service, and, optionally, aliases and comments. The line for HTTP service should look like the following:

```
http      80/tcp
```

This file can be edited with any text editor. Applications that require modifications to this file should contain instructions within their documentation.

The `inetd` Configuration File—`/etc/inetd.conf`

Continuing on the receptionist analogy, the `inetd.conf` file is like an internal phone list. It contains a list of services and the corresponding daemon that controls each. The `inetd` daemon routes calls based on this list.

If you want to enable anything from Telnet sessions and FTP transfers to POP3 mail and the finger service, `inetd.conf` is the place to look.

The line enabling Telnet sessions should look like the following:

```
telnet  stream  tcp     nowait  root    /usr/sbin/in.telnetd  in.telnetd
```

The important sections in this line are the service name (`telnet`), the daemon path (`/usr/sbin/in.telnetd`), and the arguments to send to the daemon. If there are no arguments, as in the previous example, the daemon's name is supplied again.

The line in your file may look like like the following:

```
telnet  stream  tcp     nowait  root    /usr/sbin/tcpd  in.telnetd
```

This means that your system is configured to use TCP-WRAPPERS, an enhanced security package described later in this chapter. In this case, the daemon name will *always* be `tcpd`, and the arguments section will contain the real daemon name.

Once again, if your machine is connected to a network and system security is of any importance, you should go through your `inetd.conf` file as soon as possible and comment out the services that are not absolutely required. If TCP-WRAPPERS are installed, make sure they are configured, too.

Specific `inetd` Services

The following is a list of services that should already exist in your `/etc/inetd.conf` file. Disabled services will be commented out by having a hash (#) at the beginning of the line. You can comment out services by commenting them out, or enable services by removing the hash mark.

`echo, discard, daytime, chargen`

These services are mainly used for testing. They can be safely disabled without losing any system usability.

`ftp`

The `ftp` protocol allows users to remotely access files on your system. Unless you have set up an anonymous FTP server, users will need to use their passwords to access their files.

Unless `ftp` is needed, you should disable this feature.

For more information about setting up an FTP server, refer to Chapter 15, "FTP Server Fundamentals."

telnet

telnet allows people to log on to the machine from remote locations. Although not particularly secure, most Linux machines have this service enabled.

If possible, try and use TCP-WRAPPERS to restrict access to your system.

gopher

The gopher protocol was rendered practically obsolete by HTTP. It is safe to assume most people will not be using this service, but some distributions have it enabled, nonetheless.

shell, login, exec

These services can allow remote logins and remote file execution on your machine *without password authentication*. This should only be allowed from trusted machines. You should definitely read the manual pages for the corresponding daemons (rshd, rexecd, and rlogind), and the TCP-WRAPPERS section.

smtp

The Simple Mail Transport Protocol is used to deliver Internet email. This service will probably be disabled, because the SMTP server usually uses a standalone daemon. Your system is most likely to have the Sendmail daemon installed. It is described later in this chapter.

pop

Also appearing as pop-2 and pop-3, the Post Office Protocol is used by remote users to retrieve email from the system. Virtually all modern email clients use the pop-3 protocol, so you can safely disable pop-2.

You will need to have pop server software installed on your system for pop mail to work. This is not automatically installed by all distributions.

finger

The finger command can allow remote users to retrieve information about users on your system. For example, if your machine is connected to the Internet, a user on any other machine connected to the Internet can type the following:

```
$ finger john@your.machine.com
```

They will be presented with various information about the user named john.

Worse, anyone from across the Internet can receive a list of people currently logged on by typing the following:

```
$ finger @your.machine.com
```

If this is undesirable, you can disable this service. You will still be able to run the finger command locally.

You might want to look into some of the alternate `finger` commands available, such as `cfinger`. These will allow you to restrict the amount of information released to unknown remote users.

auth

Also known as `ident`, this service is used by remote machines to verify the authenticity of a user on your system. This is used to prevent malicious users from using your machine name illegally.

TCP-WRAPPERS

The TCP-WRAPPERS package is used to restrict accesses to certain services based on from where the call is coming. You can allow or deny access based on an IP address or hostname. TCP-WRAPPERS is controlled by two configuration files: `/etc/hosts.allow` for granting access and `/etc/hosts.deny` for denying access. If they do not exist or are empty, TCP-WRAPPERS will allow all hosts to access all services.

Each line in the `hosts.allow` and `hosts.deny` files contains a service name and a list of addresses that are allowed to access them. Addresses may be complete or partial hostnames or IP addresses. Partial names act as wildcards. For example, using `.mydomain.com` will allow any hostname ending with `.mydomain.com` to access that service. However, `mydomain.com`, without the period, will only match `mydomain.com`.

There are also several keywords that can be used instead of addresses or service names. For example, to grant access from all hosts to all services, enter the following line in the `/etc/hosts.allow` file:

```
ALL:            ALL
```

Having that same line in `/etc/hosts.deny` will deny all hosts access to all services.

If you want to grant `telnet` access to all hosts at `mydomain.com` and all hosts whose IP addresses start with `192.168.1`, enter the following line:

```
in.telnetd:      .mydomain.com, 192.168.1.
```

Configuring DNS

For any computer network to function, each machine on the network needs to have a unique address. On TCP/IP-based networks, such as the Internet and most UNIX-based networks, each machine has its own unique IP address for this purpose. To reach a specific machine, you have to know its IP address, which is a group of four numbers separated by a dot (.). This can be confusing even on small networks.

Because it is much easier to remember words than strings of numbers, a way to relate between names and numbers had to be implemented. In the early days of the Internet, each machine on the network had a local file containing this list of machine names and their addresses. However, as the Internet (and local networks) grew, this became impractical. This is where DNS comes in.

Whenever anyone types a hostname in any Internet application, the application sends a query to a DNS server to get the corresponding IP address. This is called *name resolving*. The application then uses the IP address to connect to the remote host.

DNS can also translate an IP address into a network name. This is called *reverse resolving*.

This section covers simplistic configurations of both client and server setup. You should read the manual page for the DNS daemon, named ("man named"), as well as the DNS-HOWTO file. There are also several books dedicated to the DNS service.

Local (Client) DNS settings

If your machine is networked and needs to access other machines, you will need to set up name resolving. Please note that you need to set this up even if your machine is a DNS server.

The /etc/hosts file

Although technically not a part of the DNS services, this file is used to resolve hostnames—in fact, it is used to resolve hosts before the DNS services have been loaded. Since the hosts in this file are usually searched before DNS, you can use it for faster results with hosts you access more than others.

Each line of the /etc/hosts file contains an IP address, and then a list of names corresponding to that address. You can have as many names corresponding to an address as you like.

The following is an example for a short /etc/hosts file:

```
127.0.0.1        localhost loghost localhost.localdomain
192.168.1.1      thishost thishost.mydomain.com
192.168.1.10     ftp ftp.mydomain.com
www www.mydomain.com
```

> **Note:** The IP address 127.0.0.1 always refers to the local host.

You probably already have an /etc/hosts file on your machine.

/etc/resolv.conf

The /etc/resolv.conf file contains your domain name and the IP address to one or more DNS servers:

```
search mydomain.com
nameserver 192.168.1.25
nameserver 192.168.1.26
```

The search option is your default search domain. It will be appended to all queries not containing a domain name. For example, a query for www will automatically query for www.mydomain.com.

You can have as many nameserver lines as you want. If a query to the first one fails, the query will be sent to the next one.

If you are running a DNS server on your machine and would like to use it for queries, enter the local machine IP address in the /etc/resolv.conf file:

```
nameserver 127.0.0.1
```

DNS Server Setup

You must have the DNS server installed to function as a DNS server. Some distributions do not install this function by default, because most workstations and servers do not need to run their own DNS servers. On Red Hat systems, make sure you have the bind package installed.

DNS server configuration consists of a main configuration file (/etc/named.boot), which contains pointers to other data files. The other files are the root DNS servers file, named.ca, and database files for each domain for which the server is acting as DNS server.

All files except for /etc/named.boot are usually placed in a specific directory. This would also be specified in named.boot. Usual places include /etc/namedb/ and /var/named/.

A bare-bones version of /etc/named.boot has probably been installed by your distribution, along with a named.ca file, providing you have installed the BIND package.

You should never edit or modify the named.ca file. It contains a list of root nameservers from around the world, and is used by your DNS server to resolve names that aren't part of your own domains.

The following is an example named.boot file:

```
;
; named.boot file for my main DNS server.
; This server is the primary DNS server for mydomain.com.
; It is also acting as secondary for our business partners, otherdomain.com.
; I have also set it up to secondary emaildomain.com, because most
; people here access that domain, and this will speed up DNS lookups.
;
directory                                       /var/named
cache                       .                   named.ca
;
; Primary domains
;                   Domain/Network              DB filename
primary             0.0.127.in-addr.arpa        named.local
primary             mydomain.com                db.mydomain.com
```

```
;
; Secondary domains
;                       Domain name            Primary server IP
secondary               otherdomain.com    192.168.10.10
zone.otherdomain.com
secondary               emaildomain.com    192.168.55.1
zone.emaildomain.com
```

As you can see, set up of this file is quite simple. The first two lines (which will probably already be in your pre-existing file) tell the DNS server what directory contains the data files (/var/named) and the name of the cache file (named.ca).

Lines starting with the keyword primary indicate that you are the primary DNS server for the following domain name. The first parameter is the domain or network name, and the second is the database file containing the definitions for this domain.

As stated earlier, DNS can also translate IP addresses into network names, or do *remote resolving*. As with regular translation, this will require its own database, and is referred to, per the previous example, as a reverse string of the IP address followed by in-addr.arpa. For example, the IP network 192.168.1.0 would be referred to as 1.168.192.in-addr.arpa.

Lines starting with the keyword secondary mean that you are actually copying the domain name database from a remote server. The first parameter is the domain name. The second is the IP address of the primary DNS for that domain—you will be transferring the information from that server. The last parameter is the filename in which your DNS server will save this information.

Domain Database File

Each domain's address translation tables are located in its file.

The following is an example of the domain database file for mydomain.com:

```
; Domain Database File for mydomain.com
; This file contains the name=IP address table.
;
; First, definitions for the entire domain, or for the hostname 'mydomain.com'.
; The $ORIGIN is redundant with newer versions of BIND.
$ORIGIN com.
; Each Domain Definition file should start with an SOA (Start Of Authority) record.
; This contains the contact for this domain, the file's serial number, refresh time,
; retry time, expiration time, and minimum TTL (in seconds).
;
; The contact for mydomain.com is root@mydomain.com
mydomain IN     SOA     mydomain.com. root.mydomain.com. (
                        1999041501   ;The serial number MUST be increased
                                     ;whenever this file is edited.
                        14400        ;Refresh time. Secondary DNS servers will
                                     ;attempt to re-poll this domain's
                                     ;information at this interval.
```

```
                       7200                    ;Retry: secondary servers will retry
                                               ;at this interval if not successful.
                       5184000      ;Expires: how long before this information
            ;expires.
                       3600 )       ; Minimum TTL: secondaries will not try
                                               ; to refresh sooner than this.
                                               ;
                                               ; END of SOA record
                                               ;
            IN      A     192.168.1.1          ; The A keyword indicates
                                                    ; an ADDRESS.
                                               ; This line means that the IP
                                               ; address for 'mydomain.com' is
                                               ; 192.168.1.1

            IN      NS    dns.mydomain.com.    ; The NS keyword is used to
                                               ; pint to DNS servers.
                                               ; This line means the DNS server
                                               ; for 'mydomain.com' is
                                               ; dns.mydomain.com. Note that
                                               ; the hostname 'dns.mydomain.com'
                                               ; must be defined below.
                                               ; You can have more than one
                                               ; NS records.
            IN      MX    10 mydomain.com.     ; The MX keyword stands for
                                               ; Mail Exchange. It indicates
                                               ; which host serves as Email
                                               ; server for this domain. The
                                               ; number before the hostname
                                               ; indicates priority. The lower
                                               ; the number, the higher the
                                               ; priority.
            IN      MX    100 m.mydomain.com.  ; This mail host has a lower
                                               ; priority.
;
; Definitions for hostnames within 'mydomain.com'.
$ORIGIN mydomain.com.
boxer       IN      A     192.168.1.10                ; The host 'boxer.mydomain.com'
                                                      ; is 192.168.1.10
m           IN      CNAME boxer.mydomain.com.              ; The CNAME keyword indicates an
                                                      ; alias. The host 'm.mydomain.com'
                                                      ; is the same as
                                                      ; 'boxer.mydomain.com'.
dns         IN      A     192.168.1.15                ; The host 'dns.mydomain.com' is
                                                      ; 192.168.1.15
chihuahua   IN      A     192.168.1.25                   ; The hostname
                                                      ; 'chihuahua.mydomain.com is
                                                      ; 192.168.1.25
www         IN      CNAME chihuahua.mydomain.com.     ; The two hosts are the same
ftp         IN      CNAME chihuahua.mydomain.com.     ; as chihuahua.mydomain.com.
```

As you can see, each line contains one keyword describing a hostname.

There are a few important notes about these files.

Fully qualified hostnames *must* end with a trailing period (.) when used as an address, such as in CNAME records.

Whenever you modify one of these files, *always* update the serial number, or the rest of the world might never see the changes. A good way of remembering this is setting the serial number to the current date using the yyyymmddcc format. The two trailing control digits can be used if you make more than one update per day.

Reverse DNS Database File

Much like straight-DNS lookups, Reverse DNS files start with an SOA record.

Reverse DNS files usually use the PTR keyword extensively. This is the opposite of an A keyword, as it assigns an address to a name.

The following is an example file for the 192.168.1.0 network:

```
@       IN      SOA     mydomain.com. root.mydomain.com.  (
                                1999041501   ; Serial
                                14400        ; Refresh
                                7200                  ; Rerty
                                5184000      ; Expires
                                3600 )       ; Miminum TTL
                IN      NS      dns.mydomain.com.
;
$ORIGIN 1.168.192.in-addr.arpa.
1                       IN      PTR     mydomain.com.            ; 192.168.1.1 = mydomain.com
10                      IN      PTR     boxer.mydomain.com.
15                      IN      PTR     dns.mydomain.com.
25                      IN      PTR     chihuahua.mydomain.com.
```

Once again, make sure you update the serial number when you update this file, and remember the trailing periods with hostnames.

DNS Utilities—nslookup

The nslookup utility lets you manually look up hostnames. This is useful for debugging network problems, and for making sure your DNS is set up correctly.

To look up a hostname, type the following:

```
$ nslookup mydomain.com
Server: localhost
Address: 127.0.0.1

Name:   mydomain.com
Address: 192.168.1.1
```

A hostname that is aliased using the CNAME keyword will produce slightly different output:

```
$ nslookup www.mydomain.com
Server: localhost
Address: 127.0.0.1

Name:    chihuahua.mydomain.com
Address: 192.168.1.25
Aliases: www.mydomain.com
```

If you are looking up hosts in your own domain (or whatever is defined as your search domain in /etc/resolv.conf), you only need to type in the hostname:

```
$ nslookup www
```

You can also look up hostnames based on keywords. For example, to find the mail exchangers for mydomain.com, you would type utility the following:

```
$ nslookup -type=MX mydomain.com
Server:  localhost
Address:  127.0.0.1

mydomain.com         preference = 10, mail exchanger = m.mydomain.com
mydomain.com         preference = 0, mail exchanger = mydomain.com
mydomain.com         nameserver = dns.mydomain.com
m.mydomain.com        internet address = 192.168.1.10
mydomain.com         internet address = 192.168.1.1
dns.mydomain.com       internet address = 192.168.1.15
```

Using sendmail (the Basics)

The sendmail daemon is a Mail Transport Agent (MTA). It is used to receive and send email. It is not used to compose and read email—other, friendlier applications are used for that.

sendmail is one of the least-friendly-to-configure applications in the known universe. Comprehensive sendmail books can be used as boat anchors. This section will concentrate more on what sendmail does and how to interact with it, than how to configure it to do anything unusual.

sendmail is certainly capable of an amazing range of features, but most of them are not required by most users. sendmail is also well known for its security holes. There are other MTA packages for Linux that are more secure and easier to configure. I would personally recommend the Qmail package (http://www.qmail.org).

How sendmail Works

The sendmail daemon is constantly running, listening to port 25 on your system. MTAs communicate with each other through port 25, the SMTP (Simple Mail Transfer Protocol) port. When sendmail receives a piece of mail, it determines whether the recipient is local, based on its configuration files. Non-local recipients are sent on or rejected, again, based on the configuration files. A local recipient's mail is placed in the recipient's mail file. Local addresses can include regular users, aliases, and more.

sendmail is also invoked by email reading applications. They will send their data to sendmail locally. sendmail then goes through the same delivery process.

sendmail Configuration

Your distribution should have installed a default sendmail configuration file, which will generally accept deliveries to your local machine and allow you to send mail from it. It is also likely to allow anyone to use your host as a relay.

The main sendmail configuration file is /etc/sendmail.cf. You can check to make sure this file has been installed.

If it isn't there, make sure sendmail is, in fact, installed. On Red Hat systems, you can type the following:

```
# rpm -q sendmail
```

Next, make sure sendmail does get started when the system starts up. On Red Hat systems, type the following:

```
# chkconfig --list sendmail
```

You can make sure sendmail is running by using the ps utility, as shown in the following:

```
# ps auxw|grep sendmail
root     3398  0.0  1.4  1432   932 ?  S    17:59   0:00 sendmail: accepting
connections on port 25
```

You can also make sure that sendmail is accepting connections by telnetting directly into your system's port 25, as shown in the following:

```
# telnet localhost 25
Trying 127.0.0.1...
Connected to mydomain.com.
Escape character is '^]'.
220 localhost.localdomain ESMTP Sendmail 8.8.9/8.8.9; Wed,  7 Jul 1999 18:12:43 -
0500
quit
221 localhost.localdomain closing connection
```

You can try this from a remote server to see if sendmail is accepting remote connections.

The Mail Queue

Email that can't be sent immediately is placed in the mail queue. sendmail will retry sending the emails in the mail queue at intervals defined by the command line when sendmail was launched. If you look through the system's init scripts, you may see a line such as the following:

```
/usr/sbin/sendmail -bd -q1h
```

The `-bd` option tells `sendmail` to launch as a daemon. The `-q` option, or rather the parameters following it, tell `sendmail` how often to try to flush the queue. The parameters are `<number>` followed by m for minutes, h for hours, or d for days.

You can check what is in the mail queue by typing the following:

```
# mailq
```

You can manually flush the mail queue, too. This is extremely useful for debugging, as you will see what errors `sendmail` received.

```
# sendmail -q -v
```

Note that, if you have many pieces of mail that are trying to go to hosts which are currently down, this may run for a long time.

Aliases

If you would like to set up an email address on your system without creating a user, or would like to create a small mailing list, or would like to use an external program to process email messages, you need to set up an alias.

Contained in the `/etc/aliases` file, the simplest alias is one for a nonexistent user. For example, if you want the user sjohnson to get all the email addressed to Webmaster, enter the following into `/etc/aliases`:

```
webmaster:        sjohnson
```

If you want more than one user to receive email for that address, simply add them on the same line:

```
webmaster:        sjohnson, kellyb, rickyd
```

You can use external addresses, too:

```
webmaster:        sjohnson, kelly@somewhereelse.com
```

This is useful if you'd like to forward mail to someone who no longer has an account on your system.

After changing the aliases file, you should run the `newaliases` command to update `sendmail`'s database.

Files Used by `sendmail`

`sendmail` includes several files and executable programs and requires a number of directories to exist on your server to function correctly.

sendmail

The sendmail daemon executable might not be installed anywhere in the system's path. Although sometimes found in /usr/sbin/, it might be in /usr/lib/.

newaliases

The newaliases executable should be in the search path, but if it's not, try looking for it in the same directory in which sendmail is located.

mailq

The mail queue viewing utility might not be installed on your system. If it's not, you can type the following:

```
# sendmail -bp
```

This will produce the same results.

/etc/sendmail.cf

This is sendmail's main configuration file. It is usually heavily commented, but still unreadable.

/var/spool/mqueue/

This is the physical location of the mail queue.

/var/spool/mail/

This directory contains users' mail files. Each user's mail file can actually contain many email messages. This can cause these files to become rather large—quotas are very useful on this directory. Please note that these are actually mail spool files—while some email readers will work directly on this file, others will copy messages out of the spool directory and into the users' home directories.

In the interest of security, you should make sure this directory has the *sticky* bit set—this means that only a file's owner (or the Superuser) can write to a file. You can do this by typing the following:

```
# chmod 1777 /var/spool/mail
```

Also, make sure all files in this directory are only readable and writable by their owners by typing the following:

```
# chmod 600 /var/spool/mail/*
```

As another security concern, you should create an empty mail file for new users, and make sure they're owned by, and only accessible to, the new user. For example, if you've just created a new user named john, type the following:

```
# touch /var/spool/mail/john
# chown john /var/spool/mail/john
# chmod 600 /var/spool/mail/john
```

Setting Up POP

The Post Office Protocol, or POP, can be used by remote users to download their mail from the system without logging in.

POP server installation is quite simple and straightforward. First of all, you must make sure the pop server is installed.

The POP daemon might not be installed by default. On Red Hat systems, the POP daemons are installed alongside the IMAP daemons, so the package name is actually imap, and not pop:

```
# rpm -q imap
```

If not installed, you have to install the packages yourself before the POP service will be available.

Once the daemon is installed, you need to enable the POP service in /etc/inetd.conf. The POP line in inetd.conf might be commented out, as shown in the following:

```
#pop-2   stream  tcp     nowait  root    /usr/sbin/ipop2d ipop2d
#pop-3   stream  tcp     nowait  root    /usr/sbin/ipop3d ipop3d
```

Uncomment these lines by removing the # at the beginning.

If there are no POP lines in your /etc/inetd.conf, you can use the previous examples. Be sure you are pointing to the correct path—if you didn't install the POP daemons into /usr/sbin/, or if the executables have a different name, be sure you enter them correctly.

Note that you are enabling both POP3, and the obsolete POP2. Because this does not take up additional system resources, it doesn't do any harm.

Once you have saved the changes to /etc/inetd.conf, you must restart the inetd daemon. You can do this by issuing the following command:

```
# killall -HUP inetd
```

or by typing the following:

```
# ps aux ¦ grep inetd
```

and sending a kill -HUP to the appropriate PID.

You can be sure the POP daemon is accepting connections by telnetting directly into port 110:

```
# telnet localhost 110
Trying 127.0.0.1...
Connected to localhost.
Escape character is '^]'.
+OK POP3 localhost v6.50 server ready
```

Configuring IMAP

IMAP is similar to POP in that both protocols allow users remote access to their email. The difference is that IMAP allows users to maintain mail folders on your system, rather than downloading all their email to their own machine.

IMAP configuration is very similar to POP configuration. You must first make sure the IMAP daemon is installed on your system. On Red Hat systems, IMAP and POP are both part of the same package, so if you have the one, you have the other.

You must then make sure IMAP is enabled in /etc/inetd.conf. The line in /etc/inetd.conf should look like the following:

```
imap    stream tcp     nowait root    /usr/sbin/imapd imapd
```

If you have modified /etc/inetd.conf, you must restart the inetd daemon by sending it the HUP signal:

```
# killall -HUP inetd
```

You can check whether imapd is accepting connections by telnettting directly into port 143:

```
# telnet localhost 143
Trying 127.0.0.1...
Connected to localhost.
Echaracter is '^]'.
* OK localhost IMAP4rev1 v11.241 server ready
```

Summary

As this chapter shows, Linux cannot only be completely integrated as a member of a network, a Linux server can function as a vital member of a network, providing network information services to other servers and workstations. Functioning as a mail server, using POP and IMAP, Linux can provide an email solution for an entire organization. Web and FTP servers can allow users to share files and ideas. And Linux is very scalable—all of these services can be run on an old 486-based computer that has been discarded, or on a large, multi-processor–based machine, as your network grows and evolves.

On Your Own

The `inetd` daemon is a gateway to many interesting services. Consider looking through your `/etc/inetd.conf` file and reading the manual pages for services with which you are not familiar.

Try running `nslookup` on different hosts and domain names with different command-line switches and check the different results.

Look at the content of a mail spool file. Watch it grow in real time by issuing the following command:

```
# tail -f /var/spool/mail/username
```

Then send mail to that user. Note the different headers created by mail sent from different hosts or different locations.

Check what types of email retreival different mail readers support.

Peter Norton

Network Troubleshooting with Linux

Introduction

This chapter is all about the software tools you can use to monitor your network state and activities.

There are three problems that can occur with a network. It can be

- *Down*—This means there are one or more hosts on the network that cannot communicate with the others.
- *Slow*—The network is working, but it is taking a long time to move data from one place to another.
- *Hacked*—Someone (or something) broke through the security and has done something they shouldn't have.

The first condition can often be diagnosed easily if the network was up and suddenly went down. Something changed somewhere, and all you have to do is find it. As often as not, this is caused somewhere in the wiring, but it can also be caused by hardware failure or a router crash. There are a lot of possible causes. It could even be case number two—the network could be running so slowly it only seems to be down.

The second condition comes mostly from increased usage. Networks grow by having more and more computers added to them. They also grow as users and their software begin to make more use of network applications. There are two things you can do—you can install new hardware to get faster throughput, and you can examine your network configuration and monitor data flowing through the network. Once you get a picture of how the data is flowing, and you can see where the bottlenecks are, you may find a solution as simple as changing the routing by moving a few cables around. Or you may need to defend the rest of the network from a busy area by adding a new router.

The third condition is one that you can hope will never happen, but is becoming more and more common. If your local network is connected to the outside world in any way, you need to put up some defenses against attack.

Troubleshooting Guidelines

Every network is different. With the thousands of software and configuration options available, there is no standard sequence of steps that can be taken to locate and fix trouble. Finding trouble on a network is doing detective work. Pay close attention to the clues—even the ones that seem insignificant—and try to figure out what situation could cause all the symptoms. The clues may point you to entirely different parts of the network, but even this misdirection can be clue—it could be that a problem in one place caused a problem in another.

It takes detective work to track down network problems. Finding trouble is more of an art than a science, and some people seem to be naturally better at it than others. As time goes along and you experience different kinds of network failures, you will begin to get a feel for what you need to do to "round up the usual suspects."

The more suspects you can eliminate, the better off you are. For example, if two computers simply refuse to communicate with each other, check them both to see if they can talk to other computers on the network—if one can and the other can't, you have a prime suspect.

Many of the tools you will need to find network problems are described in Chapter 13, "TCP/IP Networking with Linux." For example, the ping utility that sends a simple message and gets a simple response can be enormously helpful. If you get ping to work, you know that not only is the hardware okay, but so is the basic configuration of the network. Also, if you have a partial network failure, you can use ping to find out which hosts are reachable and which ones are not.

The most important thing, though, is to be prepared ahead of time. There are some things you can do to give yourself a head start:

- *Know your network's configuration.*—Don't wait until it breaks and try to figure out how it is *supposed* to work. Study the system while it's working to see how it does what it does.

- *Keep tabs on the hardware.*—You should know where and how the cables are run, what adapter cards are used, and so on. This is particularly important when different vendors or different networking technologies are combined.

- *Be familiar with the software used to send and receive messages across your network.*—This includes those that come as part of Linux and those from other sources. You should have a pretty good understanding of how all of the servers and clients are set up and how they do their jobs. If your network includes operating systems other than Linux, you will need to know about the software they are using also.

Networks are enormously complex, with all the software and all the possible configuration settings. Add to this the fact that they are never static—something is always being changed or added. Even the smallest of networks can present seemingly unsolvable puzzlers, but the more you know about how it all works, the better your odds of keeping it under control.

Is a Wire Stopped Up?

There are lots of wires involved in networking. If a cable gets pulled out or pulled apart, the network is cut off at that point and no amount of debugging any configuration checking will fix it. If part of the network is down—and down completely—the primary suspect is a cable. If the cables seem to be connected properly (between a computer on the network and one that can't connect), check for a pinched wire or a wire that has been partially pulled away from the connector on the end.

Even if you can't see a problem with a wire, it would be prudent to try replacing it with one that you know is good. If this fixes it, good. If not, you have narrowed the possibilities.

There are also power cords. It is amazing how often some part of the network has been disable by being denied electricity. Power plugs can sometimes just fall out of sockets by themselves, but usually they are unplugged to make room for an electric eraser or something.

The most vicious kind of wire problem is the one that has an intermittent connection. If you find you can move a wire and the connection restores itself, replace the wire immediately. Don't leave it there hoping it won't disconnect again—I can tell you, it will happen again. Every time.

Peeking at the Status

There is a lot of information about the network status and configuration held in the kernel. This information is readily accessible through some utilities and the /proc pseudo directory.

A primary tool for determining the current network configuration and its level of activity is ifconfig, which is described in more detail in Chapter 13. Just entering ifconfig on the command line, with no arguments, will supply you with quite a bit of information about your network. It tells you what network interfaces are up and (supposedly) running and the number of packets transmitted and received by each one of them. There are also counts of the errors.

The pseudo directory /proc/net provides you access to current information. To look at the current values of some counters, you can enter the following command:

```
cat /proc/net/dev
```

The following is an example of output that detected an error:

```
Inter-|   Receive                      |  Transmit
 face |packets errs drop fifo frame|packets errs drop fifo colls carrier
   lo:   5975    0    0    0    0     5975    0    0    0     0    0
 eth0: 199299    0    0    0    0    15068    0    0    0     0   39
```

The output consists of a number of counters—input counters on the left and output counters on the right. On a perfect network, all counts will be zero except the transmitted and received packet counts. Non-zero values don't necessarily indicate problems, because they can be caused by moments of peak usage. If, however, you are dealing with a slow network situation, these numbers are a critical clue. In this example, notice that the right-most counter for the Ethernet (eth0) is a non-zero value. That means that, at some time in the past, there were 39 attempts to transmit data across the Ethernet, but there was some physical problem with the connection. This could indicate that a wire is disconnected, an interface card has gone bad, or the Internet card address is not correct.

If you have some kind of intermittent problem, you can keep a constant watch on the network activity with a script such as the following:

```
while [ true ]
do
    cat /proc/net/dev
    sleep 3
done
```

Interrupts and Addresses

There is information in the /proc pseudo directory that can be useful in diagnosing an ailing network adapter card. During initial installation of the card, or during the installation of some other device after the card has been installed, the system could have been configured with two devices attempting to share the same interrupt or I/O address.

The following command will display a list of the assigned interrupts:

```
cat /proc/interrupts
```

The output looks like the following:

```
 0:   78688830    timer
 1:     482742    keyboard
 2:          0    cascade
 3:   69915654 +  serial
 8:          1 +  rtc
 9:         14    aic7xxx
10:     217692    eth0
12:    2732471    PS/2 Mouse
13:          1    math error
14:    2254719 +  ide0
15:       3534 +  ide1
```

This listing shows the interrupt numbers on the left and the device name on the right. The number in the center is a count of the number of interrupts that have occurred. Looking at this list, it is apparent that interrupt 10 has been assigned to the Ethernet card (named eth0, just as it is in ifconfig) and, because no other device has interrupt 10, there are no conflicts.

To see the list of I/O addresses, enter the following command:

```
cat /proc/ioports
```

The output looks like the following:

```
0000-001f : dma1
0020-003f : pic1
0040-005f : timer
0060-006f : keyboard
0070-007f : rtc
0080-009f : dma page reg
00a0-00bf : pic2
00c0-00df : dma2
00f0-00ff : npu
0170-0177 : ide1
01f0-01f7 : ide0
02f8-02ff : serial(auto)
0376-0376 : ide1
03c0-03df : vga+
03f0-03f5 : floppy
03f6-03f6 : ide0
03f7-03f7 : floppy DIR
03f8-03ff : serial(auto)
6400-64be : aic7xxx
6900-691f : 3c905 Boomerang 100baseTx
f000-f007 : IDE DMA
f008-f00f : IDE DMA
```

The left column is the range of addresses used by the device named in the right column. In this example, the network adapter card is named 3c905 Boomerang 100baseTx and uses the addresses 6900 through 691f. The listing is ordered by the addresses, and these addresses don't overlap any of the others, so this is not a problem.

Check On the Server Setup

A server daemon, usually started at boot time by a script in /etc/rc.d, could require certain environment variables to be set and certain command line options. You can verify that it was started correctly by retrieving the information from the /proc directory. There is a numbered subdirectory for every executing process.

Use the ps command to find the process ID number of the daemon in question, and that number will be the name of the directory. For example, if the process ID number is 280, the information about it will be in the directory /proc/280. To see the command line that started the process, enter the following:

```
cat /proc/280/cmdline;echo
```

The reason for the echo command on the end is to add a newline character—without it, the command line becomes part of the next line's prompt. To see the environment variables that were set when the process started, enter the following:

```
cat /proc/280/environ;echo
```

Using Simple Tools

There are a number of utility programs supplied with Linux that can be used to examine the network. A lot of them are described in Chapter 13, along with the discussion of TCP/IP installation and configuration.

The `tcpdchk` Utility

This utility does a quick check of the TCP setup and reports any possible problems. This actually has more to do with security and permissions than it does with correct operation, although it will also find some fundamental errors such as an executable file that is missing, inappropriate wild-card expressions, name and address conflicts, invalid arguments to executables, non-existent groups, and more.

You can run the utility by running it from the command line with no arguments. Just enter the name from the command line and, if nothing is reported, there is nothing wrong. It doesn't necessarily mean the configuration is complete, it just means that nothing is blatantly wrong.

You can use the -a flag to have it report accesses being permitted without the keyword ALLOW being specified. The -v option will generate a display of all the access rules.

It examines the contents of /etc/inetd.conf and reports anything suspicious. It also analyzes the contents of /etc/hosts.allow and /etc/hosts.deny and compares the settings to settings in other network files.

The `tcpdmatch` Utility

Using tcpdmatch you can determine how your system will react to an access request from some other host. It will test how the names on the command line match with the entries in /etc/hosts.allow and /etc/hosts.deny. For example, you can simulate a request to access your FTP server coming from a remote host named rimshot.belugalake.com, as shown in the following:

```
tcpdmatch in.ftpd rimshot.belugalake.com
```

This command does not actually invoke the FTP server (in fact, it doesn't even check to see if it exists), but it does check to see if your system would permit or deny access. The output could look something like the following:

```
warning: can't verify hostname: gethostbyname(rimshot.belugalake.com) failed
client:   hostname paranoid
client:   address  208.151.161.66
server:   process  in.ftpd
access:   granted
```

This output indicates that the host does not appear in `/etc/hosts.allow` or `/etc/hosts.deny`, but was granted access anyway. If it had found a match in one of the access files, the output could look something like the following:

```
warning: can't verify hostname: gethostbyname(rimshot.belugalake.com) failed
client:   hostname paranoid
client:   address  208.151.161.66
server:   process  in.ftpd
matched:  /etc/hosts.deny line 9
access:   denied
```

The dig Utility

You can gather up information about your Domain Name Server by using `dig` (domain information groper). The `dig` utility is like a `ping` that specializes in name servers. It sends out a query to the DNS server and, if it gets a response, displays the details of the information in the response.

It can be used from the command line for relatively simply inquiries. It can also be instructed to read its instructions from a file for complicated inquiries.

A Simple Example

The simplest form of the `dig` command is just to specify a domain name, as shown in the following:

```
dig belugalake.com
```

The response from the DNS server is formatted to look like the following:

```
; <<>> DiG 8.1 <<>> belugalake.com
;; res options: init recurs defnam dnsrch
;; got answer:
;; ->>HEADER<<- opcode: QUERY, status: NOERROR, id: 6
;; flags: qr rd ra; QUERY: 1, ANSWER: 1, AUTHORITY: 2, ADDITIONAL: 2
;; QUERY SECTION:
;;       belugalake.com, type = A, class = IN

;; ANSWER SECTION:
belugalake.com.         23h44m3s IN A  208.151.161.66

;; AUTHORITY SECTION:
belugalake.com.         23h44m3s IN NS  ns1.netcorps.com.
belugalake.com.         23h44m3s IN NS  ns2.netcorps.com.

;; ADDITIONAL SECTION:
ns1.netcorps.com.       1d9h46m24s IN A  207.1.125.101
ns2.netcorps.com.       1d9h46m24s IN A  207.1.125.102

;; Total query time: 177 msec
;; FROM: arlin.athome.com to SERVER: default -- 207.14.89.2
;; WHEN: Thu Jul 15 13:15:17 1999
;; MSG SIZE  sent: 32  rcvd: 128
```

The output is divided into sections with blank lines between them.

The first section displays local information—that is, things that were known before the query was sent out—and status information about the return. The first line displays the version number of dig and the domain name that is the subject of the query. If NOERROR is not present, the query simply didn't work. The optional flag settings are displayed (in this instance, they are the defaults). The line following the QUERY SECTION line, is a repeat of the query options. Type A means it is a request for the network address, and class IN means it should be an Internet IP address.

The ANSWER SECTION displays the basic information that came back with the response. The domain name is displayed, along with the IP address retrieved from the DNS server. The type and class settings are shown again.

There is a duration included with each of these entries. Every address held in the domain system will, after a period of time, be considered stale and will be deleted. The next query will cause the system to re-acquire the address information from an authoritative server.

The AUTHORITY SECTION contains the name that was the target of the query. The IN indicates that it is an Internet server. The NS indicates that the information to the right is the domain name of an authoritative server. As you can see from this example, there are two authoritative servers for this domain.

The ADDITIONAL SECTION has one entry for each of the authoritative servers—the names are listed on the left and the IP address on the right.

In the last section, the Total query time is the elapsed time between the time the query was sent and the response was received. It is possible to specify a server on the command line, but this command used the default address of 207.14.89.2. The last line is the total number of bytes transmitted and received.

Some Useful Options

The dig command has quite a few options. What follows is a description of some of the most useful ones, but, if you don't find what you need here, and if you have a special situation, read the man page. And for even more information, see RFC 1035.

There must always be a domain specified as the target of the query. By default, dig expects a name, but it is possible to use the -x option to specify an IP address, as shown in the following:

```
dig -x 208.151.161.66
```

This will change the type of query (because it is now a reverse-address resolution request), and the resulting displayed output changes a little—because the format of the response is slightly different—but the basic information displayed is the same.

It is possible to specify the name server to be queried by placing an at sign (@) in front of it, as shown in the following:

```
dig @ns1.netcorps.com belugalake.com
```

The name server can also be specified by address:

```
dig @207.1.125.101 belugalake.com
```

You can specify the type of query made by specifying the query type and the network class. The type comes first, followed by the class. For example,

```
dig belugalake.com a in
```

This specifies the type as a and the class is in (the defaults). Note how the type and class are positioned on the line—they follow the domain name, and the type comes before the class. Table 18.1 lists the types and Table 18.2 lists the classes.

Table 18.1   Query Types for dig

Type	Description
a	Query for the network address of the domain. This is the default.
any	Query for any and all information available for the specified domain.
mx	Query for information on the mail exchanger for the domain.
ns	Query for name servers of the domain.
soa	Retrieve information on the zone of authority for the domain.
hinfo	Query for host information instead of domain information.
axfr	Query for zone transfer information. This must be asked of an authoritative server.

Table 18.2   Query Network Classes for dig

Class	Description
in	Use only information from the internet class domain.
any	Use all class information.

Batched dig Queries

It is sometimes convenient to put the arguments to the dig command in a file. By doing this, it is possible to have dig wait after each query before starting on the next one. For example,

```
dig -f digfile -T 5
```

will read a line of the file digfile and use it as if it had appeared on the command line. After executing one line of the file, dig will pause five seconds before starting on the next one.

If you want to run the script in a timed loop to monitor some changing situation, you can enter the command in the following way:

```
arl% while [ true ]
> do
> dig -f digfile -T 10
> done
```

This command will loop continuously, executing each command in the file at 10-second intervals.

Network Security

With networking come security problems. System attacks can come from anywhere at any time, but there are some things you can do to prevent them from happening. No system is perfect, but if yours is hard to get into, the attacker may just move on to another opportunity.

Some Specific Things You Can Do

There are some specific things you can do to help secure your Linux system from network attacks and to inspect your system to look for evidence of an attack. This list is by no means complete, but it does prevent your system from being one of the "easy" ones.

Keep Your Eye on the /etc/passwd File

This file is the doorway into your system, and you need to examine the lock from time to time. Check it for any account names that may have been added to it. Check the user ID numbers with an eye to any account that has a UID of 0 (the Superuser). Make sure all the accounts have passwords.

Look for accounts that don't have passwords. It is possible to install software that sets up a user account and to give that account a default password—these should be changed.

Once you have inspected the file, make a backup of it that can be compared to the working file for changes—this makes future inspection very simple. You can even automate the comparison and have it notify you if it finds something. You can't really trust the modification date on the file because it can be altered.

You may want to disable the TFTP (Trivial File Transfer Protocol), because it can often be used by an intruder to get a copy of the /etc/passwd file. If you want to continue using the TFTP service, experiment with it to see if you are vulnerable.

Use Strong Passwords

Don't use passwords that can be easily guessed. An intruder may just steal a copy of the /etc/passwd file and crack it at his leisure. The words chosen should not be any proper name or any word that could appear in any dictionary. It is best to include upper- and lowercase letters, digits, and punctuation. This makes the passwords hard to crack, but it also makes them hard to remember. One trick is to derive the password from the sounds in a sentence. For example, the sentence "What is the plural of Mother Goose?" could represent the password `wit2?omg`.

Examine the `cron` and `at` Files

The `cron` and `at` utilities are used to schedule a job to be run at some future time. It is possible for one of the files to hold a batch job that will open a back door for an intruder. Examine these files and make sure you know what they all do. The files for `cron` are stored in `/var/spool/cron`, and the files for at are stored in `/var/spool/at`.

Anonymous FTP Configuration

If you are configuring to allow anonymous FTP, you need to examine the configuration and make sure the limitations are in place. The anonymous FTP root directory, and its subdirectories, should not be owned by `ftp`. Make sure the file and directory permissions limit access to only the public files.

Check for `setuid` Programs

A program can be set to execute with Superuser permissions if it is owned by `root` and uses a call to the function `setuid()`. An intruder may break in to your system and, with `root` permissions, leave a copy of such a program on your system. This will allow him or her to come back in later (maybe through an authorized log in) and use this program for quick and easy access to `root` permissions. The program left could be a modified version of `/bin/sh` or any other utility.

You can find the programs that may have this ability with the `find` command, as shown in the following:

```
find / -user root -mount -perm -4000 -print
find / -group kmem -mount -perm -2000 -print
```

In this example, `find` commands start searching at the `root` but will ignore any mounted filesystems. Files that are owned by the right user (or are members of the right group) and have their permissions set accordingly are listed in the output.

If you run this command on a fresh system, you can determine the list of files that normally appear in the list. Saving the output from this "clean" run will help you detect any new or modified files.

Check for Replacement of System Programs

Your system is supplied with a number of executable programs (and system libraries) that require special permissions to perform their functions. An intruder can simply replace these programs with versions that, whenever executed, take some mischievous action along with their regular task. This way, the intruder can keep a back door open— or perform any other activity—while remaining undetected. Any program that is executed with the proper permissions is a candidate for this, but some programs that are popular for this kind of attack are su, login, telnet, netstat, ifconfig, ls, find, du, df, and sync. Almost all of these, at one time are another, will be executed by a Superuser.

Most often, the changed code will cause a change in the executable file size, but there are instances when the code was tuned to make the size of the new and old executables the same. However, there is almost no way that a modified program will retain both the same size and generate the same cyclical redundancy checksum value. To take advantage of this fact, use a script to run the cksum or md5sum utility on the binaries, and keep a copy of the output. Of the two, md5sum is probably superior. If you really want to be secure, use them both—nothing will sneak past that! Later, by executing the same script, a comparison will detect the presence of a modified program.

By the way, be sure to keep your copies of cksum and md5sum privately held so they can't be modified. An intruder could replace these program so he or she knows the names of modified programs and produces the expected result for them.

Track Changes to the /etc/rc.d/inet.d/ Scripts

This directory contains the scripts that are executed when the system boots. Every one of these scripts are run with permissions sufficient to do anything an intruder would want to do. A quick edit can be made to insert a line or change the argument list of an existing startup command, and your system will be made vulnerable every time it boots.

To prevent this from happening, you can set up a mechanism to track changes made to these scripts. The files are all ASCII text, so they are easy to change, but it is also easy to detect any changes. If you duplicate the contents of a clean version of the files to some secure location, you will be able to run diff on the scripts to locate any unexpected changes. You will, of course, need to create new secure copies every time a legitimate change is made to the files.

Check the Network Configuration Files

The network configuration files are text files that are subject to quick and simple edits that can open the system to attack. A simple text edit can award full access permissions to a remote user. These files need to be read by many users, but should have write privileges restricted to the system, or network, administrator.

The following are the files that should be examined for changes or creation:

```
~/.rhosts
/etc/hosts.allow
/etc/hosts.deny
/etc/ftpaccess
/etc/ftphosts
/etc/protocols
/etc/services
/etc/uucp/config
```

The first three are probably the most important. Each user can edit his or her own .rhosts file. In a script, the find command can be used to locate any new .rhosts files and to compare the existing files against a known "clean," previously captured file. When one of these files has been changed, check for entries that include the names of unknown hosts and entries that use a + option. The `.rhosts` files should be monitored for all accounts, but they are especially sensitive for `root`, `uucp`, `ftp`, and any other accounts that have special access privileges.

Check `sendmail` Configuration

In the past, `sendmail` has been used in different ways to attack systems, but the current version of the program seems to have plugged all the holes. However, you need to check the `/etc/aliases` file to see that mail is being rerouted to the right places.

Check Log Files

Check the log files for connections that were made from unknown locations. There can also be other unusual entries in the log file that indicate some unusual activities have been taking place. Take some time now to familiarize yourself with the log files and their contents, so you will be able to examine them quickly to spot anything out of the ordinary.

Logging can be thwarted. An intruder with `root` permissions will often edit the log files to hide the fact that he or she has been there. You might consider configuring your system to write your log files to some other name and location.

Check Your Trustworthy Neighbors

Usually, permissions are relaxed a bit among computers on the same local network. To check security for one computer, you will need to check security for all of them, because if an intruder gets `root` access to one of them, access will be granted to all of them. Also, if you find evidence of intrusion on one computer, you need to look for evidence on the others.

Check the `/etc/exports` File

You can inspect the file directly, or you can use the `showmount` utility. Whenever possible, filesystems should be exported as read-only. You should not include a `localhosts` entry in the file, nor should any host export files to itself. Always use the full domain name for hosts.

SATAN

SATAN (Security Administrators Tool for Analyzing Networks) is software that can be used to scan the hosts on your network to probe for points of vulnerability. It does the same sort of things that crackers do to infiltrate systems but, instead of exploiting your system's vulnerabilities, SATAN reports them.

It examines and reports flaws in the servers for NFS, NIS, `finger`, `ftp`, `rexd`, and others. The flaws can be in the form of a bug or, most often, a poorly constructed configuration file.

There is also an educational benefit to SATAN. Along with the software is a tutorial that explains the types of vulnerabilities that can be exploited, and what can be done to secure them. It could be as simple as making a correction to a configuration file, or as complicated as installing a bug fix from a vendor. In some cases, to be secure, it may be necessary to disable a service.

The software is written in Perl5 and in C. Perl5 is available via anonymous `ftp` from `ftp.netlabs.com`. The output is HTML, so it requires a Web browser as its interface such as Netscape, Mosaic, or Lynx.

Keeping SATAN Under Control

There are some dangers and inconveniences that come with SATAN. An unauthorized person can use SATAN to analyze your network to find its weaknesses. The code and documentation of SATAN can be studied by crackers because it describes all of the hows and wheres of breaking into a system. (A *cracker* is the term used to refer to a mischievous and destructive hacker.) There are some systems that have intruder alarms in place, and executing SATAN on a network could cause it to reach out to a connected network and set off these alarms. Also, if you are connected to the Internet and are not working behind a firewall (or, if your firewall allows direct IP addressing over the Internet), a SATAN scan could include some hosts on the Internet.

There are some safety measures built in. SATAN doesn't expand its search indefinitely—there are some proximity settings that keep it from going beyond a certain number of hops away. It is also possible to supply SATAN with a list of hosts to be scanned (and it will scan no others) or a list of hosts not to be scanned (and it will scan all of the others).

> **Note:** You need to be very careful to keep SATAN reigned in, so that it only scans the computers in your local network. With legislation being what it is, it is quite possible that some of the actions performed by SATAN could be considered illegal if performed on someone else's system without his or her permission.

Getting Your Own SATAN

This is one program you want to compile for yourself. It is just too easy for someone to insert code that does something malicious. The program runs with `root` permissions and explores your entire network. There has already been one binary version of SATAN for Linux that added a new login entry to `/etc/passwd` and wrote security information (with world-readable permissions) to a remote location on the Internet. This was caused by using a version of SATAN that had been modified to attack the system—the real SATAN only reports on what it finds.

To get a copy of SATAN, you can use anonymous FTP. The official anonymous FTP site is `ftp.win.tue.nl/pub/security`.

There are a number of FTP sites around the world that can be used, and you can find a list of them at one of the following Web sites:

- `http://wzv.win.tue.nl/satan`
- `http://www.fish.com/satan/`
- `http://www.cs.ruu.nl/cert-uu/satan.html`

You can also get a copy via email by sending a message addressed to `mail-server@cs.ruu.nl` with the following message body:

```
begin
pathname@your.domain.name
send SECURITY/satan-1.1.x.MD5
send SECURITY/satan-1.1.1.README
send SECURITY/satan-1.1.1.tar.Z
send SECURITY/satan-1.1.1.tar.Z.asc
end
```

The pathname in this example should be replaced with the email address to receive the software.

TripWire

For purposes of security, this utility can be used to keep track of the status of the files in your system. It runs as a daemon that constantly watches what is going on and notifies the system administrator of anything suspicious. It will report whenever a new file appears in a secured directory, and it can be set to report the manner in which certain files are modified.

At installation, there is a default set of security procedures it will follow. Over time, to reduce the number of false alarms, you can make adjustments to the configuration settings that control what it considers to be a suspicious situation.

The information from TripWire cannot only be used to prevent an intruder from getting in, but, by keeping records of the intruder's activities, it also logs information that can possibly be use to identify the intruder.

The Website for TripWire is `http://www.visualcomputing.com`.

There are commercial versions of TripWire that can be purchased through the Web site, and there are free versions for specific versions of Linux.

Summary

A network is a combination of a lot of different parts, and any one of them can cause problems. Because of the interaction of all the different parts of a network, a small event can have large consequences. It is just as important to protect a network from mischievous activities as it is to properly connect and configure it. There is no way to simultaneously connect your network to the outside world and have it completely safe from attack, but there are some steps you can take that will make your system difficult to crack. Then, hopefully, an attacker will not consider it worth his or her while to break in.

This chapter has discussed security measures that can be taken by a host that is accessible from the outside world. Even more security can be achieved by not connecting your computer to the network—connect it to a firewall instead. A *firewall* is a host through which all outside data passes. This gives you a single point of tight security. Of course, you also need to pay attention to each individual host or, if the firewall is breached, your entire local network is wide open.

On Your Own

Set up some services on your system (many are installed during a normal default installation) and find out what client software you need to use to access them from the local host. Using the same set of client software programs, try to access the services from a remote host.

Keep a notebook that contains information about your network. Keep the notebook with you and add little tidbits to it as you come across them. Whenever there is a problem, it can be very handy to have all the addressing and naming information at your fingertips instead of having to dig it all out from scratch. There is so much information that you will never have it all, but any head start is a help.

PART V

Integrating Linux with Other Systems

Sharing and Printing Files with Samba

In this chapter, you will look at the Samba software package for Linux. Samba was created in 1992 by Andrew Tridgell to allow Linux workstations to share resources with Windows workstations on a Microsoft network. Samba is now maintained by a team of volunteer developers and allows Linux workstations to fully interact with Windows 3.11, 95, 98, and NT workstations using Microsoft's Common Internet File System (CIFS). CIFS is Microsoft's new standard for PC network communication, based on its older System Message Block (SMB) protocol. Samba implements all of the four basic CIFS services:

- File and print sharing
- Authentication and authorization
- Name resolution
- Service announcement (browsing)

Samba uses two separate daemons to implement these services. The smbd daemon controls file and print sharing, along with authentication and authorization. The nmbd daemon controls name resolution and browsing functions on the network. Samba enables a Linux workstation to become a fully functional member of a Microsoft network to include sharing drives and printers, browsing workgroups, and participating as a client in Windows NT domains.

Compiling Samba

Most distributions of Linux include a version of the Samba software. Some install it automatically during the Linux installation. If you do not have the Samba software, or want to obtain the most current version, it is available for download at the Samba Web site at http://samba.org/samba. The current release at the time of this writing is version 2.0.4b. You can download pre-compiled binary packages for many of the common Linux distributions. The RPM distribution format is available for Red Hat, Caldera, and TurboLinux users, while Debian Linux users can download the DEB format. There is also a generic binary distribution file that uses the .tar.gz format for Linux distributions that do not support specialized install packages.

Because Samba is distributed under the GNU General Public License, the source code is freely available to modify and recompile. The current source package available for download is always samba-latest.tar.gz. If you are not happy with the way your particular Linux distribution built and installed Samba, you can do it yourself. To do this you should perform the following steps:

1. Download the current Samba source distribution from http://samba.org/samba/ftp/samba-latest.tar.gz.

2. Unpack the source code into a work directory:

   tar -zxvf samba-latest.tar.gz

3. Run the configure program from the newly created samba-2.0.4b/source directory. This creates a makefile specific for your system to use in the final compile. The configure program performs tests on your Linux system to determine various settings required by the makefile, such as availability of libraries and headers, location of compilers, and shell characteristics. When it is finished, it should produce several files specific to your Linux installation necessary for the final compile.

4. Examine the makefile. The new makefile contains several variables that will determine the placement of the binaries, log files, and the configuration file necessary for Samba to run properly. The default install location of the package is /usr/local/samba. If you want to change the install location, you can use the -prefix= option when performing the configure in step 3. This option points the makefile variables to a different location. Other default file locations can be changed using other configure options. You can type configure -help to list all of the configure options, and then change the default directories to your liking before compiling.

5. Run the GNU make utility from the samba-2.0.4b/source directory. This will build the binaries based on the configuration determined by the configure program and the makefile. The binaries will be placed in the samba-2.0.4b/bin directory.

Installing Samba

After you have the proper distribution of the binaries (or have built your own from the source), you can install Samba. If you are using one of the Samba distributions that is built for the RPM package installer, log in as **root** and type the following:

rpm -Uv samba-2.0.4b.i386.rpm.

This will install the Samba software in the default location for your Linux distribution. If you compiled the binaries from the source code, you can run

```
make install
```

from the `samba-2.0.4b/source` directory as the root user to install Samba in the directories specified in `makefile`. Once the software is installed, all of the programs listed in Table 19.1 should be available to use.

Table 19.1 Samba Installed Programs

File	Description
addtosmbpass	AWK script for adding multiple userids to smbpasswd
convert_smbpasswd	Converts old Samba 1.19 password files to 2.0
make_printerdef	Creates printer definition files for shared printers
make_smbcodepage	Creates codepages used for internationalization
nmbd	Controls browsing and name resolution
nmblookup	Resolves CIFS names to IP addresses
rpcclient	Uses RPC to run processes on remote devices
smbclient	An FTP-like program to access remote CIFS shares
smbd	Files and prints services, and authenticates clients
smbpasswd	Creates and modifies CIFS userids and passwords
smbstatus	Shows current access status on the Samba server
smbtar	Copies a CIFS share to a Linux tape drive
swat	Samba Web Administration Tool
testparm	Tests the Samba configuration file
testprns	Tests the Samba printer definitions

The `smbd` and `nmbd` daemons must be running to handle service requests from the network. There are two methods of starting these daemons:

- Add `smbd` and `nmbd` as part of an `init` start-up script to start them at system boot time.
- Add services to the `/etc/inetd.conf` file to allow the `inetd` process to spawn `smbd` and `nmbd` as necessary.

By placing `smbd` and `nmbd` in an `init` start-up script, Linux will automatically start the daemons when it boots. This method is the preferred way of starting Samba; since the daemons are already running, the response time to service network requests is faster. Listing 19.1 shows a standard Samba start-up script in the `init` run level 3 directory from a Red Hat 5.2 Linux workstation. This file is actually a symlink to the real file in the `/etc/init.d` directory, where all startup scripts are located. As all good startup scripts should, it first checks to make sure that its resources, a network connection and a Samba configuration file, are available before trying to start the daemons. To manually start the processes using this script, you would type **smb start**, and to stop them you would type **smb stop**.

Listing 19.1   Sample Samba Startup Script

```
1    #!/bin/sh
2    #
3    # chkconfig: 345 91 35
4    # description: Starts and stops the Samba smbd and nmbd daemons
5    #                    used to provide SMB network services.
6
7    # Source function library.
8    . /etc/rc.d/init.d/functions
9
10   # Source networking configuration.
11   . /etc/sysconfig/network
12
13   # Check that networking is up.
14   [ ${NETWORKING} = "no" ] && exit 0
15
16   # Check that smb.conf exists.
17   [ -f /etc/smb.conf ] || exit 0
18
19   # See how we were called.
20   case "$1" in
21     start)
22          echo -n "Starting SMB services: "
23          daemon smbd -D
24          daemon nmbd -D
25          echo
26          touch /var/lock/subsys/smb
27          ;;
28     stop)
29          echo -n "Shutting down SMB services: "
30          killproc smbd
31          killproc nmbd
32          rm -f /var/lock/subsys/smb
33          echo ""
34          ;;
35     status)
36          status smbd
37          status nmbd
38          ;;
39     restart)
40          echo -n "Restarting SMB services: "
41          $0 stop
42          $0 start
43          echo "done."
44          ;;
45     *)
46          echo "Usage: smb {start|stop|restart|status}"
```

```
47          exit 1
48   esac
```

The second method is more commonly used on servers that are tight on memory. The inetd process monitors all IP traffic and will spawn processes when needed. By configuring the inetd.conf file to support smbd and nmbd, inetd can automatically spawn them when it detects CIFS traffic for the server. This method does not require that smbd and nmbd run continuously, thus saving some processor and memory power. However, the penalty for this is in response time, because the daemons need to be restarted on every connection. This trade-off leans towards using startup scripts whenever possible. A normal inetd.conf entry to support smbd and nmbd would look like the following:

```
netbios-ssn        stream  tcp  nowait root  /usr/local/samba/bin/smbd  smbd
netbios-ns         dgram   udp  wait    root  /usr/local/samba/bin/nmbd  nmbd
```

For inetd to recognize the CIFS IP services, you also should ensure that the following lines are in the /etc/services file:

```
netbios-ns         137/tcp              # NETBIOS Name Service
netbios-ns         137/udp
netbios-dgm        138/tcp              # NETBIOS Datagram Service
netbios-dgm        138/udp
netbios-ssn        139/tcp              # NETBIOS session service
netbios-ssn        139/udp
```

Most Linux distributions that include Samba start the smbd and nmbd daemons automatically by using the init start-up script method.

Configuring Samba on Linux

After the Samba binaries are installed, it is time to configure your Samba server to work properly on your network. All of the configuration variables for Samba are contained in a single configuration file—smb.conf. The location of this file varies in different Linux distributions. The default location used as a result of building the source code is the /usr/local/samba/lib directory. Many Linux distributions place it in the /etc directory, along with configuration files from other software packages. If you do not know where the configuration file is located on your Linux system, you could search for it using the following command:

```
find / -name smb.conf -print
```

The smb.conf configuration file is a text file that looks suspiciously like an ordinary Windows .ini file, complete with section headings in square brackets. There is a reason for that. One of the goals of the Samba developers was to make Samba as easy as possible for a typical Windows network administrator to configure. Changing the server configuration is as simple as editing the text file with your favorite Linux text editor and restarting the server daemons. All lines in the configuration file that start with either a pound sign (#) or a semi-colon (;) are considered comments and are not processed by the server.

The smb.conf file contains separate sections defining the characteristics of each individual file area or printer shared, as well as three special sections. The [global] section defines parameters that affect the operation of the whole server. The [homes] section defines parameters for individual users' home shares. The [printers] section defines parameters for any printers shared by the server. Next you'll look at an example smb.conf file up-close.

The [global] Section

First, look at the global section line by line:

```
[global]
workgroup = MYGROUP
server string = Samba Server
```

The workgroup parameter determines the server's network, workgroup, or domain that it will try to join. If workgroup is set to a domain name, the server tries to locate a domain controller for the domain and join the domain as a client. If MYGROUP is not a domain, the server will attempt to locate and join the workgroup named MYGROUP by using standard CIFS methods. The server string parameter sets the description of the server that is broadcast to other nodes in the workgroup. The actual server network name used on the network is taken from the Linux hostname.

```
hosts allow = 192.168.1. 192.168.2. 127.
```

The hosts allow parameter allows you to restrict access to the Samba server based on IP addresses. Only addresses in the ranges listed will be allowed to establish connections. In the example shown, all hosts on the 192.168.1.x and 192.168.2.x subnets, as well as hosts on the 127.x.x.x subnet (the internal loopback address) will be allowed to connect to shares on this Samba server. If your network is connected to the Internet, this parameter is extremely useful by helping to keep unwanted hackers away from your server. This parameter is intended to supplement the normal userid/password method of protecting shares by adding a second layer of security.

```
load printers = yes
printcap name = /etc/printcap
;    printcap name = lpstat
printing = bsd
```

The global printer parameters determine how (or if) Samba will share any local printers on the server. The load printers parameter automatically reads the /etc/printcap file and advertises each configured printer by its Linux name if set to yes. Alternatively, you can advertise a subset of printers by using the printcap name parameter and pointing it to your own copy of the printcap file with just the printers you want advertised. As another option, you can let Samba find your printers by using the lpstat command if it is available on your Linux distribution. The `printing` parameter tells Samba how printer status information is interpreted on your Linux distribution.

```
guest account = pcguest
```

By default, Samba will allow guest access to shares using the `nobody` Linux userid (if the share allows guest access). If you want to set up a different userid for guest access, you can tell Samba about it using the `guest account` parameter. Make sure that the userid is a valid Linux userid or guest access won't work. Also, some older Linux distributions assign the `nobody` userid a UID of `-1` (or `65535`). This is now a well-known security hole, and Samba will report it to you as the `trapdoor userid` error. Changing the `nobody` UID to another value solves this problem.

```
log file = /usr/local/samba/var/log.%m
max log size = 50
```

By default, Samba will place the log file in the directory specified by the `makefile` when it was compiled. You can override this location by using the `log file` parameter. The variable `%m` can be used as well. The `%m` variable will expand to the hostname of the device connecting to Samba. Other variables are available to use in the `smb.conf` file, and can be seen in the `smb.conf` man pages. This configuration will produce a separate log file for each device that connects to the server. You can also limit the size of the log file using the `max log size` parameter. Samba will start a new log file when the file reaches 5MB by default. The parameter units are in kilobytes.

```
security = user
;    password server = <NT-Server-Name>
encrypt passwords = yes
smb password file = /usr/local/samba/private/smbpasswd
```

These are very important parameters. They control how the Samba server authenticates potential users. User authentication can be done in several different ways. With the `security` parameter set to `user` (the default in Samba 2.0), the Samba server will try to validate the requesting user by an existing Linux userid. If it is found, the user then has access to shares as determined by the standard Linux file permissions for that Linux userid (unless specifically restricted by the share section). With the `security` parameter set to `server`, the Samba server attempts to locate the server defined by the `password server` parameter and passes the username and password information to that server for validation. By setting the `security` parameter to `domain`, Samba will try to find a domain controller to validate the userid and password.

In the past, Microsoft clients would transmit their passwords across the network in plain text format. Now with security being a large concern, things have changed. With Windows 95 OSR2, 98, and NT 4.0, Service Pack 3, the default logon method, uses encrypted passwords. This complicates things considerably. For Samba to be able to authenticate a password that has been encrypted, it must have access to the encrypted version of the password. There are two ways to accomplish this. The easiest method (from Samba's point of view) is to set the `security` parameter to `server` and let another server validate the password. For this to work, you must also set the `encrypt passwords` parameter to `yes`, and make sure the `password server` parameter is set to the name of an NT server that can validate the user passwords. Samba will then forward the encrypted password to the password server and receive the response, whether the user is validated or not. If you are not fortunate enough to have a separate password server handy, Samba must maintain an encrypted password database itself.

For Samba to maintain its own encrypted password file, extra administration work is required. First, in the `smb.conf` file, the `security` parameter should be set to `user`, and the `encrypt passwords` parameter set to `yes`. Then a separate Samba password file must be created. The default location for the password file specified in the `makefile` for the source code is `/usr/local/samba/private/smbpasswd`. If you do not know where your Samba password file should be or want to change its location, the `smb password file` parameter will allow you to specify a different location. The `smbpasswd` utility can then be used to add users to the password file and set their CIFS passwords. You must use the `-a` option to add new userids to the file. Make sure that the `smbpasswd` userids match valid Linux userids, or `smbpaswd` will not add them to the password file. After this is done, clients that use encrypted passwords can connect to the Samba server and have access to shares as defined in the configuration file.

Finally, a third option for the security parameter is available to use. Security level `share` is a holdover from the old Windows for Workgroups days. A share can be connected to by using just a share password while not actually logging into the server. Samba supports this option, but has to perform some strange maneuvers to attempt to match a Linux userid with a supplied password. The details on how Samba attempts to match a userid to the password are explained in the `smb.conf` man pages and gets very involved.

```
;    include = /usr/local/samba/lib/smb.conf.%m
socket options = IPTOS_LOWDELAY TCP_NODELAY
;    interfaces = 192.168.12.2/24 192.168.13.2/24
```

The `include` parameter allows additional configuration parameters to be set by the server. The previous example shows how to customize parameters for individual devices. The `%m` variable expands to the name of the connecting device, thus different parameters are included for each device. The `socket options` parameter allows you to fine-tune Samba's network settings to the behavior of your network. Many standard IP parameters are available to try. Multiple values can be separated by spaces. Common values are `IPTOS_LOWDELAY` and `TCP_NODELAY`, which can improve response times on LANs. A list of all possible values is available on the `smb.conf` man page. If you are running Samba on a server with multiple network cards, the `interfaces` parameter must be set to help Samba sort out what networks are available on which interfaces. Without this parameter, Samba will find the primary interface but won't search for any others after that.

```
local master = no
;    os level = 33
;    domain master = yes
;    preferred master = yes
```

These parameters control how the Samba server behaves if it is set up to participate in a workgroup. Samba will follow the normal master browser negotiations when joining any workgroup. When a new device joins a workgroup, an election is held between the work-group devices to determine a new master browser. If you do not want the Samba server to be elected the master browser for the workgroup, set the local master parameter to no. If you just want to lessen its chances of being elected master browser, set the os level parameter to a lower value. The default value is 32, which makes Samba have an equal chance as an NT server of being the master browser. If you prefer that the Samba server always be the master browser, setting the preferred master parameter to yes forces a new election with the Samba server's OS level set to a high value, thereby almost ensuring that it will win the election. If multiple Samba servers are in the same workgroup with this parameter set, they will continually force new elections and fight for the master browser title, so be careful when using this parameter. The domain master parameter allows Samba to act as the domain master browser for its workgroup. It will then collect and maintain browser lists from other workgroups on the local network.

```
;    domain logons = yes
;    logon script = %m.bat
;    logon script = %U.bat
;    logon path = \\%L\Profiles\%U
```

These parameters control how Samba behaves if it is participating in a Windows NT domain. The domain logons parameter allows Samba to service Windows 95 and 98 domain client logons. Windows NT domain client logons require a Primary Domain Controller (PDC). At the time of this writing, the production Samba code release does not replicate the PDC functionality (but the development team is working on it). The logon script parameter allows Samba to download a logon script to clients when it validates a Windows 95 or 98 domain client logon. The location of the scripts are relative to the [netlogon] share, which by default is the directory /usr/local/samba/netlogon. The script files must be DOS style ASCII text files (cr/lf line endings) so the worksta-tions can execute them. As shown in the example, you can use the %m variable to cus-tomize scripts by device name, or use the %U variable to customize them by username. The logon path parameter is used to set the directory where roaming profiles for Windows 95 and 98 clients are stored. Again, this can be customized either by device or username. The %L parameter is replaced by the CIFS hostname that the client used to call the Samba server.

```
;    wins support = yes
;    wins server = w.x.y.z
;    wins proxy = yes
dns proxy = no
```

These parameters control the Windows Internet Name Service (WINS) support for Samba. A Samba server can act as a WINS server for a local subnet. This should not be necessary unless you have a multi-subnetted network. Only one server per subnet should act as the WINS server. The wins support parameter tells Samba to act as the WINS server for the subnet. Clients can obtain IP addresses for CIFS names by asking the

WINS server. If you already have a WINS server on your subnet, the wins server parameter tells Samba who it is and allows Samba to communicate with it. If you have some older clients on your subnet that do not implement WINS, you can have Samba proxy their queries to the WINS server by setting the wins proxy parameter to yes. The dns proxy parameter allows Samba to use standard DNS lookups to verify CIFS names while acting as a WINS server. If you do not have a DNS server on your network, make sure that this parameter is set to no.

These are the main global parameters needed by Samba to be functional in a Microsoft Network. There are many other less frequently used options that can be used to fine-tune the server. You can examine these options by reading the smb.conf man page. The next sections define how the Samba server shares resources on the network.

The [homes] Section

The [homes] section allows you to configure default shares for all of your users in one place. By default, each userid share will be mapped to the home directory of the userid on the Linux server, with the share name being set to the userid. As expected, there are some parameters that can fine-tune the behavior of the [homes] section.

```
[homes]
   comment = Home Directories
   path = /data/%S
   browseable = no
   writable = yes
```

As in the [global] section, the comment parameter further identifies the service to other devices on the network. If you do not want to use the Linux home directories as the Samba home directories for users, you can specify a different location with the path parameter. You can use the %S variable (which expands to the name of the share) so that each user connects to their own home directory. If you do not want to advertise the home shares on the network for security reasons, you can set the browseable parameter to no. The individual home directories will not be seen in the Network Neighborhood of network clients. If you allow users to have read/write access to their home directories, make sure you set the writable parameter to yes.

The [printers] Section

The [printers] section allows you to fine-tune printers that are being shared by Samba on the network. Settings in this section apply to all printers shared by Samba.

```
[printers]
   comment = All Printers
   path = /usr/spool/samba
   writable = no
   printable = yes
   browseable = no
   guest ok = no
```

Again, as in the [global] section, the comment parameter identifies the service to other devices on the network. The path parameter points to the directory where Samba will create the print spool files. The Linux permissions for this directory should be writable for everyone, and the sticky bit should be set. You may set the writable parameter to no to prevent unauthorized use of this directory. If you do set the writable parameter to no, the printable parameter becomes very important. It allows users to submit spool files to the directory specified without having write access to the directory (remember, you set writable to no). If clients don't have permission to write to the spool directory, they will not be able to submit print jobs. By using the browseable parameter, you can prevent printers from appearing on Network Neighborhood browse lists. If you prefer that they be advertised, you can set this parameter to yes. If the guest ok parameter is set to yes, clients can map to the printer without having to supply a userid and password.

The Share Sections

Apart from shares defined in the [homes] section, other individual shares that are available on the Samba server must have a separate section in the smb.conf file. The share name will be used as the heading name, and any parameters that are needed for the share apart from the global parameters should be included in the share section. An example share configuration would look like the following:

```
[katiedir]
   comment = Katie's shared disk area
   path = /data/katie
   valid users = katie jessica haley riley
   public = no
   writable = yes
```

This example demonstrates how to set up a share that can be accessed by more than one user. The location of the share is determined by the path parameter. The valid users parameter sets the users who will be allowed access to the share. Multiple users are listed with a space between the userids. Without the valid users parameter set, all Linux userids will have access to the share. All users who will access the share should have read and write permission to the share directory by Linux (be members of a group that has write privileges). As shown by the writable parameter, all of the listed users will have write access to the share. If the writable parameter is set to no, users will have read-only access to the share (including the owner of the share), even if the Linux permissions would allow them write access.

Printer shares can be customized in the same way that disk shares are by using a share section for the individual printer.

```
[franksprn]
   comment = Frank's shared printer on the server
   valid users = frank melanie alex
   path = /home/frank/spool
   printer = franks_printer
   public = no
```

```
writable = no
printable = yes
```

This section defines a printer share that only userids frank, melanie, and alex can access from the network. They all must have write permission to the /home/frank/spool directory for them to be able to print from the shared printer.

The SWAT Utility

There is a graphical utility that has been added to the Samba software suite to assist administrators in configuring the smb.conf file. The Samba Web Administration Tool (SWAT) is a Web-based utility that assists in the configuration of the smb.conf file using easy to use forms. The SWAT utility has been a standard part of Samba since version 2.0.0. Using the source code makefile install, the default location for SWAT is /usr/local/samba/bin/swat, with files used for the Web page located in directory /usr/local/samba/swat.

SWAT is launched via the inetd process in Linux. To run SWAT, first you must make an entry in the /etc/services file so Linux knows what TCP port to which it will listen. You can select any available TCP port to use, although there currently is a bug if you select a port higher than 1024. The current swat documentation uses TCP port 901 as an example, so that's what you will use. The entry in /etc/services should look like the following:

```
swat 901/tcp
```

Next, an entry must be made in the /etc/inetd.conf file so the inetd process knows what to spawn when it receives a request to connect to the SWAT port:

```
swat stream tcp nowait.400 root /usr/local/samba/bin/swat swat
```

You must restart the inetd process to read the new configurations. To do this type kill -HUP PID, where PID is the process ID of the inetd process. Once inetd has been restarted, you can use your favorite Web browser and connect to your Samba server using the port defined in the /etc/services file (http://198.168.1.1:901/, for example). Before connecting, SWAT will query you for a userid and password. Be careful, as these values are sent across the network in plain text format. Once you have logged into the SWAT utility, it should produce the home Web page shown in Figure 19.1. From the home page you can then view, add, delete, or modify all of the parameters in the smb.conf file. SWAT will also allow you to start and restart the smbd and nmbd daemons if you've modified the smb.conf file.

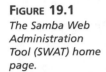

FIGURE 19.1
The Samba Web Administration Tool (SWAT) home page.

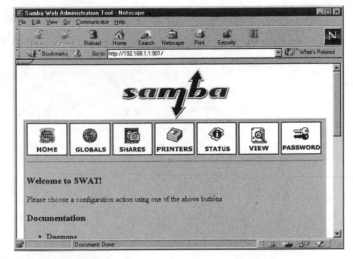

The `testparm` and `testprns` Utilities

Another useful utility for Samba administrators is the `testparm` program. This program tests the `smb.conf` file for configuration errors and inconsistencies. It will not, however, test for logical errors, such as shares that were configured with wrong access privileges, although the information it gives might help you locate those kinds of problems. The following is the format of `testparm`:

```
testparm [configfilename] [hostname hostIP]
```

where *configfilename* defaults to the standard `smb.conf` file, but can be changed if you want to test a different configuration file. If you want to see what access a particular host would have on the server, you can use the hostname and hostIP parameters. The `testparm` program lists the values of all the server parameters as set by the `smb.conf` configuration file tested.

The last configuration utility discussed is the `testprns` program. This tests the printers defined in the `smb.conf` file. It can verify if the printer exists in the `/etc/printcap` file, or in an optionally supplied printcap file. The following is the format of `testprn`:

```
testprn printername [printcap name]
```

where *printername* is the name of the printer you want to test, and *printcap* name is the location of the Linux printcap file you want to test. The default location is `/etc/printcap`. This is a good utility to use if you create a separate printcap file for Samba and want to test its validity.

Configuring Samba on Windows NT

Now that you have a Samba server up and running, you might want to have clients connect to it. The Samba server behaves as a normal device in a Microsoft CIFS network. Connecting to it is similar to connecting to other CIFS devices on the network.

For a Windows NT 4.0 workstation to connect to a Samba server, it must be configured as a client for a Microsoft Network. There are three different protocols that can be used in Microsoft CIFS networks—NetBEUI, IPX, and TCP/IP. At this time, Samba only supports Microsoft networks that use the TCP/IP protocol. Thus, all clients that need to connect to the Samba server must have TCP/IP configured properly, as well as having the normal Client for Microsoft Networks software installed.

To configure networking on a Windows NT workstation, you must first bring up the Network Configuration window by clicking Start, Settings, Control Panel, and then selecting the Network icon. Figure 19.2 shows a sample Network configuration window.

FIGURE 19.2
Network Configuration window for Windows NT workstation.

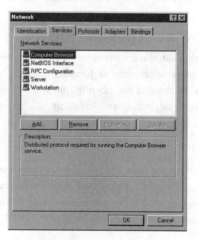

The following steps will help you configure your Network settings to allow the workstation to connect to the Samba server.

1. *Configure the network adapter.*—Start by selecting the Adapter tab. If you do not have your adapter card configured, you can add it by clicking the Add button and either selecting your card from the list of available cards or clicking the Have Disk button and using the driver disk that came with your card.

2. *Configure the Identification of your PC.*—Each device in a network workgroup must have a unique network name. It is also convenient to join the same workgroup or domain that your Samba server is in (that way the server appears in your Network Neighborhood), but it is not necessary. To change either of these settings click the Change button and type in the new values.

3. *Configure the TCP/IP protocol.*—You can do this by selecting the Protocols tab. If the TCP/IP protocol is not installed, click the Add button and select TCP/IP Protocol from the list of network protocols. Once the TCP/IP protocol is installed, it must be configured properly for your PC to communicate on the network. By selecting TCP/IP Protocol and clicking the Properties button, you can view and change the TCP/IP settings for the workstation. The IP address must be valid for your local network. If you are running Samba on a test network, you can use the public IP address range 192.168.*x*.*x* for your devices, where *x*.*x* can be replaced with any number from 1 to 254 (as long as no two devices have the same IP address). If you use this system, set the Subnet Mask to 255.255.0.0. If you are on an existing network, set the IP address and Subnet Mask to values appropriate for your network. If you are on a routed subnetwork, you may have to set the Default Gateway value to point to your router. Always check with your local network administrator if in doubt.

4. *Configure the Microsoft Network services.*—These services are usually installed by default on a Windows NT 4.0 workstation. Figure 19.2 shows the services that are required to connect the workstation to a Microsoft network. The Computer Browser, NetBIOS Interface, RPC Configuration, Server (if you want to share files from this workstation), and Workstation services should be available. If any of these services are missing, click the Add button and select the missing service from the list.

After the workstation is properly configured, you should be able to see the Samba server by clicking the Network Neighborhood icon. You can map drive and printer shares from it. If you can see the server but cannot map any shares, there may be a userid or password problem. The userid that the Windows NT workstation uses to connect with is the same as the userid that was used to log into the workstation. Also, remember that after Service Pack 3, Windows NT 4.0 uses encrypted passwords by default. If this is the case, the Samba server must be set to use encrypted passwords. If you prefer, you can override the encrypted password default on the workstation by adding a Registry value to an existing Registry key. This is not recommended if you are on a large network, or especially if you connect to the Samba server across the Internet, because your password will be sent as plain text. Also, modifying the registry is dangerous, so please remember to back up your registry before attempting to modify it—accidents can happen! The following is the Windows NT registry entry that enables clear text passwords:

```
[KHEY_LOCAL_MACHINE\SYSTEM\CurrentControlSet\Services\Rdr\Parameters]
:EnablePlainTextPassword"=dword:00000001
```

By using this Registry entry, the Windows NT workstation will send plain text passwords, and will connect to the Samba server without having to configure Samba to use encrypted passwords.

Configuring Samba on Windows 95/98

You can also connect to the Samba server using Windows 95 or 98 workstations. For these devices to connect to Samba, they must be configured to support Microsoft Networks, as well as have the TCP/IP protocol configured. These components can be configured using the Network Configuration window. This can be started by clicking Start, Settings, Control Panel, and selecting the Networks icon. Figure 19.3 shows a sample Windows 95 network configuration page. If you are missing any of the necessary components, you can add them by following these steps.

1. *Configure the Network adapter.*—Click Add, and select Adapter. Select your network card from the list, or click Have Disk to use the driver disk that came with your network card. This step may not be necessary, because Windows 95 and 98 will try to autodetect network adapters as they are added to the workstation.

2. *Configure TCP/IP.*—Click Add, Protocol. Select Microsoft from the manufacturers list and then click TCP/IP. Once the TCP/IP protocol is added to the services, you can configure your IP settings by selecting TCP/IP and clicking the Properties button. You can set the IP address as described in the previous section. Be sure that no two devices on your network have the same IP address, and that the Subnet Mask and default gateway are set accordingly.

3. *Configure the client for Microsoft Networks.*—Click Add, Client. Select Microsoft from the manufacturers list, and then click Microsoft Client for Microsoft Networks.

4. *Configure the identification of your workstation.*—Click the Identification tab. Each device in a workgroup must have a unique Computer Name. It is also convenient to join the same workgroup or domain that your Samba server is in, but not necessary.

After the network configuration is complete, you should be able to see the Samba server in the Network Neighborhood of the workstation. Double-clicking the server's icon will show what shares are available. Again, if you can see the server but cannot access any shares, there may be a userid or password problem. Windows 95 and 98 workstations will use the userid and password that you logged in to the workstation with for network connections. Make sure that they are valid on the Samba server. Also, remember that Windows 95 OSR2 and 98 use encrypted passwords, so Samba should be configured accordingly. Alternatively, you can add a Registry value to an existing Registry key on the workstations to allow clear text passwords. This is not recommended if you are on a corporate network or the Internet, because your password will be transmitted as plain text. Modifying the Registry is dangerous, so be sure to back up your Registry before attempting any changes. The following is the Registry setting to allow Windows 95 and 98 workstations to use clear text passwords:

```
[HKEY_LOCAL_MACHINE\System\CurrentControlSet\Services\VxD\VNETSUP]
"EnablePlainTextPassword"=dword:00000001
```

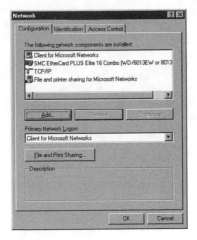

FIGURE 19.3
Network configuration window for Windows 95/98 workstation.

Using Samba

Now that you have a fully functional Samba server with clients connecting to shares and printers, you probably want to know how to monitor all the new activity.

Samba maintains detailed log files of all connections to shares. The default location for the log files is the /usr/local/samba/var directory. Some distributions of Linux use the /var/log/samba directory instead. The two main log files for Samba are log.smb and log.nmb. These files document the current status of the smbd and nmbd processes, as well as connection attempts to shares. If you used the option to create separate log files for each device, the log.smb log file will be split into individual log files for each device that accesses the server (log.meshach, log.shadrach, and so on).

The smbstatus utility can be used to monitor the status of current Samba connections. It will show current connections, as well as currently locked files and the current memory status of the server. This allows you to monitor connections to shares on the Samba server. An example smbstatus output is shown in Listing 19.2.

Listing 19.2   Output of smbstatus

```
1    meshach:~>smbstatus
2    Samba version 2.0.4b
3    Service     uid     gid     pid      machine
4    -------------------------------------------------
5    katiedir    jessica users   16642    shadrach (192.168.1.6)
➥Wed Jun 23 06:04:27 1999
6    katiedir    katie   users   15902    meshach  (192.168.1.5)
➥Tue Jun 22 09:55:54 1999
7
```

continues

Listing 19.2 Continued

```
8   Locked files:
9   Pid     DenyMode    R/W       Oplock          Name
10  --------------------------------------------------------
11  16642   DENY_NONE   RDWR      EXCLUSIVE+BATCH  /data/katie/newdoc.doc
➥  Wed Jun 23 07:44:59 1999
12  16642   DENY_NONE   RDWR      NONE            /data/katie/~WRL0004.tmp
➥  Wed Jun 23 07:02:49 1999
13
14  Share mode memory usage (bytes):
15    1048272(99%) free + 216(0%) used + 88(0%) overhead = 1048576(100%)
total
```

The `smbclient` utility can be used to connect to other network shares from your Samba server. This program uses an FTP-like interface when connecting to the remote share that allows you to browse, send, and receive files from the share. The following is the format of the `smbclient` command:

```
smbclient service <password> [options]
```

The `service` parameter is the name of the share to which you want to connect, using the standard CIFS naming conventions. Remember though, that a backslash (\) in Linux is an escape character, so to produce a single backslash you must type two of them (\\). Using that format, to connect to resource `\\shadrach\katiedir`, you would need to type `smbclient \\\\shadrach\\katiedir`. By default, `smbclient` will attempt to connect to the share using the userid with which you are logged in to Linux. If you want to connect as a different userid, you must use the `-U` option, which allows you to specify the userid on the command line. If Samba cannot find the device on the network, you can help it out by specifying the IP address using the `-I` option. Listing 19.3 is an output from a normal `smbclient` session with a Windows 95 workstation as the host.

Listing 19.3 Output from `smbclient` Session

```
1   meshach:~>smbclient \\\\test\\share -U jessica
2   Added interface ip=192.168.1.1 bcast=192.168.255.255 nmask=255.255.0.0
3   Got a positive name query response from 192.168.1.5 ( 192.168.1.5 )
4   Password:
5   smb: \> dir
6     .                              D       0  Thu Jun 17 07:39:58 1999
7     ..                             D       0  Thu Jun 17 07:39:58 1999
8     gladiato.mid                   A    4264  Wed Dec 23 07:10:16 1998
9     highd_wp.pdf                   A  435628  Tue Aug 11 07:31:04 1998
10    idglans.pdf                    A  154577  Tue Aug 11 09:26:14 1998
11    bookmark.htm                   A    2778  Thu Feb  4 07:51:42 1999
12    cfarc_wp.pdf                   A  584511  Tue Aug 11 10:08:14 1998
13    color.gz                       A 1369436  Wed Oct 21 07:37:46 1998
14
```

```
15                65505 blocks of size 32768. 19790 blocks available
16   smb: \> get idglans.pdf
17   getting file idglans.pdf of size 154577 as idglans.pdf (224.634 kb/s)
(average 224.634 kb/s)
18   smb: \> quit
19   meshach:~>
```

Line 1 shows connecting to a network device named test and a share named share (not too imaginative) using the userid jessica. In line 2, Samba performs a network broadcast to find the IP address of the host test. It is found at IP address 192.168.1.5 (see line 3). In line 4, smbclient queries the user for a password to send to the remote host. In line 5, a directory listing of the remote share is requested, and is shown in lines 6–15. In line 16, a file is requested from the share, and is downloaded to the local Samba server. Line 18 shows the termination of the session.

Printing Using Samba

Much like file sharing, printer sharing is based on the normal CIFS naming standard. Samba printer names are taken from the /etc/printcap file by default. Thus, a printer named frankprn on Samba server shadrach would be connected by using the CIFS name \\shadrach\frankprn. If the printer was set as being browseable, it should appear in the client's Network Neighborhood and could be connected to by double-clicking the printer icon and following the printer wizard's instructions. Alternatively, you can use the Add Printers Wizard in Windows 95, 98, or NT 4.0 to connect to a shared printer. Figure 19.4 shows how you would enter the CIFS name of the printer in the printer wizard to connect to the printer share. Also, you could click the Microsoft Windows Network line to expand the network tree and locate the printer via browsing.

FIGURE 19.4

Connecting to a Samba printer by using Windows NT's Add Printer Wizard.

Summary

This chapter discussed Samba, the software package that allows Linux workstations to inter-operate on Microsoft networks with Windows 3.11, 95, 98, and NT workstations. Most Linux distributions come with a version of Samba, so installation is often easy. You can configure Samba by editing entries in the smb.conf file. File and printer shares are configured individually to match the specific requirements for each share. Shares can be configured for either single or multiuser access. Samba also supports encrypted passwords that are being used by newer Microsoft clients. Connecting to a Samba server is as easy as connecting to other devices in Microsoft networks. The Samba server can be either a member of a workgroup or a client in an NT domain, and thus can be visible in a Network Neighborhood browse list. Samba also allows a Linux workstation to act as a client on the network and connect to shares located on remote devices. Finally, using Samba as a printer server was discussed by showing examples of connecting to a Linux printer from a Windows workstation.

On Your Own

Install and configure a Samba server on your Linux distribution, and set up several shares to use. Make one share available to just one user on the system, and not browseable. Make another share available to several users on the system, but for read only access. Make a third share available for read/write access for several users, and make it browseable. If you have a printer, make that shareable on the network for several users. Get comfortable with creating shared resources with multiple access permissions for multiple users. Now you are ready to turn your server loose on your network and amaze your customers.

Using NFS on Linux

The Network File System (NFS) originated with Sun Microsystems. It provides access to filesystems shared across a network. It is transparent because once a remote filesystem has been mounted locally, it looks and acts just like a local filesystem. Like other Internet networking protocols, NFS is designed to be independent from any hardware, operating system, or filesystem.

To give NFS its system independence, Sun uses Remote Procedure Calls (RPC) and an eXternal Data Representation (XDR). A *remote procedure* is a software function on one computer (the server) that can be executed by a call from another computer (the client). The XDR is a standard way of representing data—the sender converts all outgoing data from its local format to the standard format, and the receiver converts the standard format into data suitable for its local machine.

There is a special protocol, called the MOUNT protocol, that allows clients to establish connections with a remote file tree and logically attach to a point in the local file tree. The mounting process is subject to a named set of privileged clients.

The NFS system and its protocols are defined as Internet RFCs. The original RFC is 1094 and was published in 1989. The latest is version 3 of NFS and is described in RFC 1813.

> **Note:** If you want to include Microsoft Windows in your NFS network, you will need to buy commercial software (listed later in this chapter), because Windows doesn't include NFS software. Another option is to use Samba. This is a Linux utility that understands and speaks the Windows SMB protocol and can be used to share files and printers. And a mixed network is possible—you can run Samba and NFS simultaneously.

Introduction to NFS

NFS is a client/server system. The server supplies access to its local filesystem by receiving queries and commands, and then takes the requested actions and responds. The client makes the remote filesystem look like a local one by querying and commanding the server to take action and then formatting the returned data as it would be formatted for the local filesystem.

Big Client and Little Server

For NFS, there is a lot more in the software of an NFS client than there is in an NFS server.

The server side only has to have access to its local filesystem, know how to package data in XDS format, and wait for an RPC function call. The function call can send data to be written to a file, request a list of names from a directory, request that a file be created, and so on—all of the chores the server has to deal with in its native filesystem.

The client software has a bit of a translation problem. The data coming to the client has to be reformatted from the form supplied by the server into something that matches the data format of the local client. If the local filesystem has some facility or characteristic not included in the XDS format, some sort of action must be taken to fill in the missing information. Also, if some sort of error occurs, it is the client that must try to recover and/or report the mishap to the application program accessing the files.

The server and client have a stateless relationship. That is, the server doesn't retain any information about the current activities of any client. Each command that comes to the server is complete—the server doesn't have to know anything about the client to execute the request, because all the required information is included with every call. This even includes the user's authentication. There's some advantage to the stateless connection—either the client or the server can crash and, when the system comes back up, both ends can pick up where they left off without have to try to recover a link and restore some kind of status. This is particularly handy for the server, because there could be any number of simultaneous client sessions in progress, but the server just has to think about one thing at a time.

Data Modification

There are commands sent from the client to write to files. These operations are synchronous. That means, when the RPC function call returns control back to the client, the server has completed writing the data to disk. The client can assume the data has been flushed to the disk and that the directory, along with its time stamps and sizes, has been updated.

This is an important characteristic of the stateless server. Because the client can trust all reports of successful completion, there is no need for the client to verify the data.

Authentication and Permissions

NFS is built on RPC function calls, and every function has a parameter that can be used to pass authentication parameters. This means that each individual capability can be awarded or denied to a user. Of course, the system can be configured so that no authentication is required.

Even though NFS works with operating systems that have different kinds of filesystems, it uses the same sort of file descriptive information that is used in Linux. There are user and group ID numbers assigned to the files. Each RPC function call passes the user and group ID of the caller, and this is verified against the permissions. The result is that the user has the same permissions and limitations as on the local system. The user and group ID numbers (not the names) are used, so if this level of security and validation is important to you, be sure to use consistent numbering on all the systems on your network. Also, filesystems that do not include ID numbers need to provide some kind of mapping to user and group ID numbers.

Authentication can be made much more strict by using DES and Kerberos. Using DES, encrypted authentication parameters are included with the RPC calls. Using Kerberos, the authentication arguments are also encrypted using DES, but the keys used are exchanged via Kerberos for authentication.

Configuring NFS

To share your files with other computers, you will need to configure the NFS server system. If you want to access NFS files being shared by another computer, you will need to configure the NFS client software. If you want both, configure both.

The `/etc/fstab` File

The `/etc/fstab` file is used to configure the client side of NFS to automatically mount local and remote filesystems. At boot time, the filesystems listed in the file are automatically mounted. The file contains a list of filesystems that are to be mounted and the options to use when mounting them. This file contains more than the NFS filesystems— it contains all of the filesystems to be mounted. The following is a typical example of the contents of `/etc/fstab` without NFS configured:

```
/dev/hda1                 /                ext2     defaults      1 1
/dev/hda6                 /home            ext2     defaults      1 2
/dev/hda5                 /usr             ext2     defaults      1 2
/dev/hda7                 swap             swap     defaults      0 0
/dev/fd0                  /mnt/floppy      ext2     noauto        0 0
/dev/cdrom                /mnt/cdrom       iso9660  noauto,ro     0 0
none                      /proc            proc     defaults      0 0
```

The first column contains the name of the device to be mounted, and the second contains the Linux directory for the mount. For example, the hard drive `/dev/hda6` will be mounted so that it becomes accessible as the directory `/home`. The third column describes the type of filesystem being mounted. The file types are listed in Table 20.1.

Table 20.1   Filesystem Types That Can Be Mounted by Linux

Type	Description
coherent	The filesystem for Mark William's Coherent UNIX.
ext	The Linux extended filesystem. It has been replaced by ext2.
ext2	The second version of the Linux-extended filesystem. This is the filesystem currently created for a Linux installation.
ffs	The Amiga filesystem.
hpfs	The Hewlett-Packard HPFS filesystem.
iso9660	The ISO 9660 standard filesystem used by CD-ROMs.
minix	The filesystem of the Minix operating system. This was the first filesystem used by Linux.
msdos	The Microsoft DOS filesystem.
ncp	NetWare's remote filesystem protocol.
nfs	The NFS filesystem. It doesn't matter what the actual type of filesystem is on the remote computer; it is always accessed locally as an NFS file.
proc	The filesystem of the pseudo filesystem defined as the /proc directory. This filesystem acts as an interface to the Linux kernel.
smb	A remote filesystem protocol designed by Microsoft for LanManager. It can be used for access to Windows 9x or NT.
swap	The filesystem used by Linux as a swap area.
sysv	The filesystem of UNIX System V.
ufs	A filesystem used by several UNIX systems, including SunOS and Solaris.
umsdos	This is the UMS-DOS filesystem, which can be used to install Linux inside a DOS partition.
vfat	A Linux filesystem that is compatible with Windows 95, 98, and NT long filenames in the FAT filesystem.
xenix	The SCO Xenix filesystem.
xmsdos	The name of an older version of vfat.
xia	The Xia filesystem has been replaced by ext2.

If the disk is being accessed over the network with NFS, the file type is always nfs. The NFS software on each system is responsible for presenting and accepting information in the standard NFS format, so it all appears the same to the client.

To add an NFS file mount to /etc/fstab, use the server and directory name in the first column in place of the device. The second column is the name of the directory you want to be the mount point. This is followed by a comma-separated list of options. Different filesystems have different sets of options available—the ones for NFS are listed in Table 20.2.

Table 20.2   The /etc/fstab Options for NFS Filesystems

Option	Description
acdirmax=<secs>	The maximum number of seconds that information about a remote directory should be cached locally. The default is 60 seconds.
acdirmin=<secs>	The minimum number of seconds that information about a remote directory should be cached locally. The default is 30 seconds.
acregmax=<secs>	The maximum number of seconds that information about a remote file should be cached locally. The default is 60 seconds.
acregmin=<secs>	The minimum number of seconds that information about a remote file should be cached locally. The default is 3.
actimeo=<num>	Using this parameter will set acregmin, acregmax, acdirmin, and acdirmax to the specified value.
bg	If the initial NFS mount times out, the subsequent retries will be in the background. Once any mount on a particular server has been switched to background, all future mounts for that server will start as background mounts. The default is fg.
fg	If the initial NFS mount times out, subsequent retries will be in the foreground. This is the default behavior.
hard	If an NFS file operation times out (timeo reaches its limit), a server-not-responding message is sent to the console. This is the default behavior.
intr	Allows signals to interrupt file operations on the NFS-mounted filesystem. If interrupted, the errno value EINTR will be returned to the calling program. By default, signals cannot interrupt NFS file operations.
mounthost=<name>	The name of the host running mountd.
mountport=<num>	The port number of the mountd daemon. This is normally defined on the server in the /etc/services file as port number 635.

continues

Table 20.2   Continued

Option	Description
mountprog=<num>	Use this number as the RPC program number for the connection to the mount daemon on the server. The default value is 100005, which is the standard RPC mountd program number.
mountvers=<num>	Use this as the RPC version number. The default is 1.
namlen=<num>	If the NFS server does not support the version 2 facility of variable filename lengths, this will specify the maximum number of characters in a filename. The default is 255.
nfsprog=<num>	Use this number as the RPC program number for the connection to the NFS daemon on the server. The default value is 100003, which is the standard RPC NFS daemon number.
nfsvers=<num>	This is the is the RPC version number for the connection to the NFS daemon on the server. The default is 2.
noac	Disables all file and directory attribute caching.
nocto	Suppresses the retrieval of new attributes when creating a file.
port=<num>	The port number of the NFS server on the remote host. By default, this value is set to 0 causing a query of the remote hosts port mapper to determine the NFS port. If this doesn't work, the standard NFS port number of 2049 is used.
posix	The filesystem is to be mounted using POSIX semantics, which includes support for the pathconf command. For this to work, the server must also support version 2 of NFS.
retrans=<num>	The maximum number of retries on a transmission. The retry wait time is set by timeo. The default is 3.
retry=<minutes>	The number of minutes to retry the mount of an NFS filesystem before giving up. The default is 10,000 minutes (which is almost a week).
rsize=<bytes>	The number of bytes NFS will read from a server in a single block. The default, subject to change, is 1024.
soft	If an NFS file operation times out (timeo reaches its limit) a report of an I/O error is sent to the calling program. The default is to continue retries indefinitely.

Option	Description
tcp	Use the TCP protocol to communicate with the remote NFS server. The default is UDP, and many servers cannot use TCP.
timeo=<tenths>	The number of tenths of a second to wait for an RPC timeout to cause a retransmission of the RPC call. The default is seven-tenths of a second. With each timeout, the number is doubled for the next try. This process continues until either the number of retries exceeds the maximum set by retrans, or the timeout duration reaches 60 seconds.
udp	Uses the UDP protocol to communicate with the remote NFS server. This is the default.
wsize=<bytes>	The number of bytes NFS will write to a server in a single block. The default, subject to change, is 1,024.

Each entry that does not have a value associated with it—the Boolean settings—has an inverse that begins with no. For example, the option nohard will suppress the action of sending messages to the console.

In practice, unless you have a special situation, you won't need but three or four of the options listed in the table. A typical entry looks like the following:

```
arlin:/home/ftp/pub    /home/arpub    nfs rsize=8192,wsize=8192,intr
```

The remote host is named arlin. The remote directory /home/ftp/pub is to be mounted as the local directory /home/arpub. The local directory /home/arpub must already exist and is usually empty (because anything in it will be hidden). The type of filesystem is nfs. Three parameters are set by listing them, separated by commas.

It has been found that, as a general rule, setting rsize=8192 and wsize=8192 improves efficiency. Most systems get better throughput at 8192.

If the remote system is slow, or you connect to it through a slow link, you can benefit from adjusting the value of timeo upward. If increasing the value causes fewer timeouts to occur, it will reduce the traffic on the network, which will increase the efficiency of the overall operation.

There are some options (noac, acregmin, acregmax, acdirmin, and acdirmax) that deal with NFS caching information about the remote filesystem. If NFS caches data about files and directories, the system runs much faster because it doesn't have to query the server every time it needs the information. On the other hand, if there is some kind of change to a file or directory on the remote server, the client will not know about it until the cache has timed out and a new request for information has been made. If you are going to be working with fairly static filesystems, you can afford to use the caching to

speed things up. However, if the remote filesystem is being changed often, you may want
to reduce (or delete) the caching.

The /etc/exports File

The /etc/exports file is used by the NFS server to specify which directories are to be
made publicly available and what restrictions are to apply. The format of the file allows
for any directory to be exported to one or more host, and allows the access capabilities to
be set specifically for each host.

Each line in the file defines the exporting of one directory. The line begins with the name
of the exported directory. This is followed by the name of one or more hosts. Each host
name is followed by its options enclosed in parentheses. The following is an example:

```
/home/ftp/pub     rimshot(rw,all_squash) arlin(ro)
```

In this example, the directory /home/ftp/pub is available to a host named rimshot—the
access is for both read and write, and the user and group ID numbers are automatically
mapped to the anonymous user. The same directory is also available to a host named
arlin, but only for read access. All of the options are described in Table 20.3 and Table
20.4.

The name of the host can be the entire domain name, as shown in the following:

```
/home/ftp/pub     markus.belugalake.com(rw)
```

Also, in naming the host, you can use the characters * and ? for wildcards. For example,
if you want to define access for all the hosts at a specific domain, you would enter the
following:

```
/home/ftp/pub     *.belugalake.com(rw)
```

If you want to export a directory to a group name defined in the /etc/group file, the
name is preceded with an @ character, as shown in the following this:

```
/home/ftp/pub     @groupname(rw)
```

It is also possible to export a directory to every host. This is done by not specifying a
host but just specifying the options. For example, if you want to make the directory
/usr/upload available as a read-only directory on any host, create an entry like the following:

```
/usr/upload     (ro,noaccess)
```

Table 20.3   The Options Used to Specify NFS Access

Option	Description
insecure	Turns off the secure option that requires that NFS clients con-nect on an Internet port number less than 1024.

Option	Description
link_absolute	Makes no changes to the symbolic pathnames. This is the default.
link_relative	Translates the absolute symbolic pathnames to relative pathnames by prepending the appropriate number of ../ characters in front of the directory name. The default is link_absolute.
noaccess	The subdirectories of the exported directory are not accessible. The client will not even be shown the names of the subdirectories.
ro	Prohibits writing to the filesystem. The default is rw.
rw	Allows both read and writing. This is the default.
secure	This option requires that NFS clients connect on an Internet port number less that 1024. This is on by default.

As a security measure, you may want to squash some user and/or group IDs. To *squash* a user ID is to translate it to the group and user ID numbers of the anonymous user. Because file security in a Linux system is based on permission granted to specific user and group ID numbers, it may be necessary to squash incoming IDs to prevent coincidental ID numbers from awarding unintended permissions. Table 20.4 lists the options that can be used in the /etc/exports file to squash user permissions.

Whenever an ID is to be squashed, it is converted to the value found for the user named nobody in the /etc/passwd file. If it is not found in the file, the value 65534 is used for both the user ID and group ID numbers. Alternatively, you can specify the values to be used by specifying them on the anonuid and anongid options.

Table 20.4   Options Controlling NFS User and Group ID Mapping

Option	Description
root_squash	All requests from a remote user and group ID of 0 are mapped to the user and group ID numbers of the anonymous user.
no_root_squash	Disables root squashing. This allows remote root access (that is, user ID and group ID of 0).
squash_uids=<*list*>	Specifies a list of user ID numbers that are to be squashed. The list is a series of comma-separated numbers, each of which can be a range, such as 0,5-12,80,23.
squash_gids=<*list*>	Specifies a list of group ID numbers that are to be squashed. The syntax of the list is the same as for squash_uids.

continues

Table 20.4 Continued

Option	Description
anonuid=<num>	If the NFS server cannot find an entry for nobody in the /etc/passwd file, the user ID is set to this value. The default is 65534.
anongid=<num>	If the NFS server cannot find an entry for nobody in the /etc/passwd file, the group ID is set to this value. The default is 65534.
all_squash	All user and group ID numbers are mapped to the anonymous user.
map_daemon	This enables dynamic mapping of the user ID and group ID numbers between the server and client. For this to happen, the daemon rpc.ugidd must be running on the client. Even with this dynamic mapping, squashing will still take place.
map_static=<file>	Enables static mapping and specifies the name of the file containing the static ID mapping table.
map_nis=<hostname>	The NIS (Network Information Service) can be used to map user and group ID numbers. When the server receives a (so far unmapped) ID number, the NIS server is queried for the name of the local login to be used.

The /etc/netgroup File

The /etc/netgroup file is used by the NFS server to look up groups that are named (by using @) in the /etc/exports file. You will need this file only when you need to control access for individual users and well as hosts and domains. Each line of the file has the following format:

```
groupname (host,user,domain) [(host,user,domain)...]
```

For example, to grant read-only permissions for bert and ernie to the /etc directory, put an entry like the following in the /etc/netgroup file:

```
readetc (,bert,) (arlin,ernie,)
```

The netgroup named readetc will recognize any user named bert, but will only recognize ernie on the host arlin. The permissions are set in the /etc/exports file this way:

```
/etc    @readetc(ro)
```

All of the fields are optional. If no host name is included, all hosts are included. If no username is included, all users are assumed. If no domain name is included, the local domain is assumed. The following example is a netgroup named miglet that includes any

user named `fred`, the entire `belugalake.com` domain, and `sam` anywhere in the
`frammis.puffin.com` domain:

```
miglet (,fred,) (,,belugalake.com) (,sam,frammis.puffin.com)
```

The Programs of NFS

There are two daemon programs that run on the server:

- `rpc.mountd` This daemon waits for client requests for access to local directories.
  When a mount request is received, it is validated against the entries in
  `/etc/exports` and, if it is valid, adds an appropriate entry to `/etc/rmtab`. When an
  unmout request is received, the entry is removed from `/etc/rmtab`.

- `rpc.nfsd` This daemon waits for client requests to transfer information to or
  from the local filesystem.

The daemons are normally started at boot time by the `/etc/rc.d/init.d/nfs` script. This
script can also be run manually to stop and start the NFS system. To stop NFS, you will
need to log in as root and enter the following:

```
/etc/rc.d/init.d/nfs stop
```

You can start it again with the following:

```
/etc/rc.d/init.d/nfs start
```

The following command can be used to check whether the NFS daemons are currently
running:

```
/etc/rc.d/init.d/nfs status
```

The two daemons are RPC processes. This means that incoming connections to them
first arrive at the RPC daemon and are redirected to the appropriate NFS daemon. To
check the status of the programs supplying RPC functions, enter the following:

```
rpcinfo -p
```

The display will look something like the following:

```
   program vers proto  port      100000   2   tcp   111  rpcbind   100000   2
 udp   111   rpcbind
   100005   1    udp    635   mountd
   100005   2    udp    635   mountd
   100005   1    tcp    635   mountd
   100005   2    tcp    635   mountd
   100003   2    udp   2049   nfs
   100003   2    tcp   2049   nfs
```

The program number in the first column is the RPC number that identifies the program.
The second column is the version number, and the third column is the name of the connection protocol. The program `rpcbind` is the RPC daemon that is will receive messages

and pass them on to the appropriate daemon. In the version of Linux that produced this listing, there are mounted processes for each connection protocol (UDP and TCP) and for each version (1 and 2). There are two nfs processes—one for UDP and one for TCP. Of course, RPC is used for more than just NFS, so you may find other processes in the list.

Mounting and Unmouting Filesystems

As described earlier, it is possible to have filesystems automatically mounted by placing an entry for it in /etc/fstab, but filesystems can also be mounted and unmounted manually. The mount and umount commands work with all filesystems, whether or not they are NFS.

A list of all the currently mounted filesystems is stored in /etc/mtab.

The mount Utility

There are ways to use the mount command so it will read and use the information found in /etc/fstab. The following command is used at boot time to mount everything in the file except the elements specified as noauto:

```
mount -a
```

The -t option can be used to mount only certain filesystem types. For example, to mount only the NFS filesystems, use the following command:

```
mount -a -t nfs
```

If you want to mount only one file named in /etc/fstab, it is only necessary to name either the device or the mounting point. For example, to mount the CD-ROM and the floppy disk, enter the following:

```
mount /mnt/cdrom
mount /dev/fd0
```

If you want, you can have the mount command ignore the /etc/fstab file by specifying all the necessary information on the command line. The same values and options used in /etc/fstab are used on the mount command line. The following is an example:

```
mount -t nfs -o rw arlin:/usr/bin /home/fred/bin
```

This command will mount the remote NFS directory named /usr/bin as the local directory /home/fred/bin. Normally, only the root login can mount and unmount filesystems, but this limitation can be overridden with the user option, as shown in the following:

```
mount -t nfs -o rw,user arlin:/usr/bin /home/fred/bin
```

The umount Utility

To unmount all filesystems listed in /etc/fstab, enter the following:

```
umount -a
```

Filesystems that are busy (such has having a file open or being the current working directory for a shell) will not unmount. To unmount all the NFS filesystems in /etc/fstab, enter the following:

```
umount -a -t nfs
```

To unmount a specific filesystem, it is only necessary to name the device, the remote directory, or the local mounting point. For example, to unmount the floppy disk and CD-ROM, enter the following:

```
umount /mnt/cdrom
umount /dev/fd0
```

The usermount Utility

If you are running X, there is the graphical program named usermount that can be used to monitor and control the mounting of filesystems. It uses the /etc/fstab file to create a window that can be used to mount or unmount the filesystems. As shown in Figure 20.1, it can be used to mount or unmount all the different types of filesystems.

FIGURE 20.1
The usermount *utility to mount and unmount filesystems.*

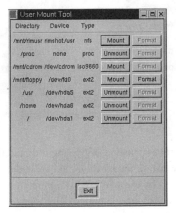

Commercial NFS Systems

Because Windows operating systems are not supplied with NFS server or client software, if you want to use them in an NFS network, it will be necessary to buy the software for them. There are a number of companies that make NFS systems for various Windows operating systems.

Xlink Technology (http://www.xlink.com) has a wide variety of NFS software for Windows 95, 98, and NT. Xlink is probably best known for its PC NFS products, but there is also an X server and an NFS gateway that both run on NT. There are light versions of PC-NFS for Windows 95 and 98.

Hummingbird (http://www.hummingbird.com) has a line of NFS software that can be used on Windows NT, 95, and 98, as well as VMS, various flavors of UNIX, Macintosh, IBM mainframes, and across the Internet. You can buy different combinations of capabilities to get what you need. Also, there is X server software that runs on these platforms.

NetManage (http://www.netmanage.com) sells a variety of networking software, including NFS for NT. The software is called InterDrive and can be configured separately for each NT user. The standard Windows GUI interface can be used to establish and break NFS connections.

Wick Hill in the UK sells an NFS implementation for NT. The company can be found at http://www.wickhill.com. The software can be configured to share both files and printers, and also provides a programming interface to the RPC function calls.

There is an implementation of NFS named Distinct that is for Windows NT and for the 16-bit Windows 3.x system. It includes software to share files and printers, and there is installation software that configures NFS. You can find information about it at http://www.distinct.com/nfs/nfs31.htm.

An NFS client for Windows 95 and NT is available from InterDrive. You can find a full description of it at http://www.components.mikrolog.fi/Tuotteet/ FTP_Software/idrive40.html.

Summary

The NFS system is a simple and robust method of sharing files and filesystems among computers. There is no daemon software required on the clientside, and the two NFS server daemons are normally started by the /etc/rc.d/init.d/nfs script when the system boots. Once NFS is properly configured, a remote filesystem will appear to the rest of the system as if it were physically attached to the local system.

On Your Own

Mutually share the home directories on two Linux systems in such a way that no one, other than the users involved, has access to the files.

If your network has a gateway with more than one name, you may want to list it in /etc/netgroup under each of its names. This will make it possible for you to reduce the number of entries in /etc/exports that refer to the gateway.

Emulating DOS and Windows

The reason a person would like to emulate Microsoft DOS and Windows (or any other operating system, for that matter) is because there are some application programs that run on DOS or Windows, and it would be very handy to have them run on Linux. This can be done, but there are limitations. Some, but not all, programs can be run by using a software emulator. If a DOS program behaves itself—that is, if it uses the standard system calls and interrupts for DOS execution—there is no problem. On the other hand, whether or not a Windows program will execute inside an emulator box is a matter of trial and error—some will, some won't, and you can't know until you try.

DOS Emulation

The purpose of DOS is to load a program into memory, set it into execution, and then, while it is running, act as the interface between the program and the hardware. Along with providing drivers to communicate with the hardware, DOS also loads a program named COMMAND.COM that is used to communicate with the user during the times when no other program is running. A DOS emulator running under Linux does these same things for DOS programs.

DOSEMU (DOS Emulator) can be run from the console or inside an X Window. It actually doesn't emulate DOS as much as it emulates the machine and environment in which DOS can run. You will find that, without loading your own version of DOS, most of the standard commands are missing. That said, even without an actual version of DOS loaded, the emulator will run many DOS programs by supplying them with access to the video BIOS, drive, keyboard, serial ports, and printer ports. There are simulated CMOS configuration settings, a clock, and memory management. However, if you or your program want (or need) the full DOS environment, you will need to use DOS along with the emulator.

Because of slowness and other problems, many DOS application developers have found it necessary to go around the operating system and address the hardware directly. While DOSEMU can handle a lot of these situations, it cannot handle them all. This is especially true for programs that have special methods of addressing "upper" memory (the DOS name for RAM addresses larger than 640KB) and utilities that implement RAM disks. If you have what is known as a *well-behaved* DOS program, you have a good chance of getting it to work.

> **Note:** This DOS emulation software is quite mature, but it is still in development because of the complexity involved. The day may never come that every DOS program can be run by the emulator. Because of the trial-and-error method required to emulate an undocumented system, sudden discoveries have caused some versions of the DOS emulator to be quite different from their predecessors. Even the names and formats of the configuration files have changed. As of this writing, the latest version is 3.9.6.

Starting DOSEMU

The DOS emulator is an executable program named /usr/bin/dos. There many options that can be used to configure it at startup, but there are four commands that will execute it:

- dos   Entering this command from any prompt will start the program running using your current terminal, virtual terminal, or X terminal.

- dosexec   This command can be used, followed by the name of a DOS executable file (that is, an .EXE), to cause the executable to immediately run and, on completion, return you to the Linux prompt.

- xtermdos   If you are running an X session, this script will look for the most suitable version of an X terminal to use and then open a window with dos running in it.

- xdos   If you are running an X session, this will start DOS running in its own window. This is the same as entering dos -L.

There are a number of command line options (available in the man page for dos) that can be used with each of these commands to solve special problems, but most situations are better handled by setting values in the configuration files.

The /var/lib/dosemu/globals.conf File

This file contains the basic configuration and setup information required at the startup of DOSEMU. When the emulator starts to run, it reads and interprets the instructions and settings in this file. Unless you know what you are doing, you should not change this file. This file concerns itself with very fundamental settings and operations, such as setting the version numbers, responding to the various emulator command line options, and determining the type of display, mouse, and user.

You should make your configuration settings in /etc/dosemu.conf, which is executed by being included in globals.conf. There is also a check for the existence of ~/.dosemurc and, if found, it is also executed. These two files allow for some settings to be made system-wide and also have some settings for each user.

The /etc/dosemu.conf File

This file contains the editable configuration settings for DOSEMU. It is a list of keywords and the values that are assigned to them. The names all begin with $_, and the assigned values are strings, numbers, or Boolean values. A string value is enclosed in quotes, a number is enclosed in parentheses, and a Boolean value is either on or off enclosed in parentheses.

The default file supplied with the installation contains the complete list of keywords and their default values. The file is commented quite well and anyone familiar with DOS operations should be able to make the appropriate settings.

There are settings for all sorts of things, but most of them will not be needed except in rare cases. You can set the emulation to a specific CPU, clock speed, and memory layout with the following keywords:

```
$_cpu = (80386)        # CPU emulation, valid values:  80[345]86
$_cpuspeed = (0)       # 0 = calibrated by dosemu, else given (e.g.166.666)
$_xms = (1024)         # in Kbyte
$_ems = (1024)         # in Kbyte
$_ems_frame = (0xe000)
$_dosmem = (640)       # in Kbyte, < 640
$_hardware_ram = "" # list of segment values/ranges such as
               # "0xc8000 range 0xcc000,0xcffff"
```

It is possible to circumvent the parent Linux system to some extent. By adjusting the hog level, you can control how much CPU time is allotted to the emulator, and there could be situations where you want the emulator to take control direct of the interrupts:

```
$_hogthreshold = (1)     # 0 == all CPU power to DOSEMU
$_irqpassing = ""    # list of IRQ number (2-15) to pass to DOS such as
               # "3 8 10"
```

There are a number of settings for the hardware terminal and keyboard:

```
$_term_char_set = ""    # Global code page and character set selection.
             # "" == automatic, else: ibm, latin, latin1, latin2
$_term_color = (on) # terminal with color support
$_term_updfreq = (4)    # time between refreshes (units: 20 == 1 second)
$_escchar = (30)    # 30 == Ctrl-^, special-sequence prefix
$_rawkeyboard = (0) # bypass normal keyboard input, maybe dangerous
$_layout = "us"     # one of: finnish(-latin1), de(-latin1), be, it, us
             # uk, dk(-latin1), keyb-no, no-latin1, dvorak, po
             # sg(-latin1), fr(-latin1), sf(-latin1), es(-latin1)
             # sw, hu(-latin2), hu-cwi, keyb-user
$_keybint = (on)     # emulate PCish keyboard interrupt
$_video = "vga"     # one of: plainvga, vga, ega, mda, mga, cga
$_console = (0)      # use 'console' video
$_graphics = (0)     # use the cards BIOS to set graphics
$_videoportaccess = (1) # allow videoportaccess when 'graphics' enabled
$_vbios_seg = (0xc000)  # set the address of your VBIOS (e.g. 0xe000)
$_vbios_size = (0x10000)# set the size of your BIOS (e.g. 0x8000)
$_vmemsize = (1024) # size of regen buffer
 $_chipset = ""      # one of: plainvga, trident, et4000, diamond, avance
             # cirrus, matrox, wdvga, paradise
$_dualmon = (0)      # if you have one vga _plus_ one hgc (2 monitors)
```

If you run the emulator inside as an X window, these are the settings that control the display and keyboard:

```
$_X_updfreq = (5)    # time between refreshes (units: 20 == 1 second)
$_X_title = "DOS in a BOX"  # Title in the top bar of the window
$_X_icon_name = "xdos"  # Text for icon, when minimized
$_X_keycode = (off)      # on == translate keyboard via dosemu keytables
$_X_blinkrate = (8) # blink rate for the cursor
$_X_font = ""          # basename from /usr/X11R6/lib/X11/fonts/misc/*
                # (without extension) e.g. "vga"
$_X_mitshm = (on)    # Use shared memory extensions
$_X_sharecmap = (off)    # share the colormap with other applications
$_X_fixed_aspect = (on) # Set fixed aspect for resize the graphics window
$_X_aspect_43 = (on)     # Always use an aspect ratio of 4:3 for graphics
$_X_lin_filt = (off)     # Use linear filtering for >15 bpp interpolation
$_X_bilin_filt = (off)   # Use bi-linear filtering for >15 bpp interpolation
$_X_mode13fact = (2)     # initial size factor for video mode 0x13 (320x200)
$_X_winsize = ""     # "x,y" of initial windows size (defaults to float)
$_X_gamma = (1.0)    # gamma correction
 $_X_vgaemu_memsize = (1024) # size (in Kbytes) of emulated vga frame buffer
$_X_lfb = (on)   # use linear frame buffer in VESA modes
$_X_pm_interface = (on) # use protected mode interface for VESA modes
$_X_mgrab_key = ""   # KeySym name to activate mouse grab, empty == off
$_X_vesamode = ""    # "xres,yres ... xres,yres"
                # List of vesamodes to add. The list has to contain
                # SPACE separated "xres,yres" pairs
```

You can tell the emulator the type and location of your floppy disks. There are two ways to set up the DOS filesystem. You can use an use an image file in the /var/lib/dosemu directory—this file contains DOS-like subdirectories, COMMAND.COM, and other directions that can be used to make it a complete DOS environment. An alternative approach is to specify a disk drive, or a drive partition, into which you have installed a version of DOS. Any name of the form /dev/... is taken to be a hardware drive, any other name is taken to be an image file in /var/lib/dosemu. Also, you can name as many of these as you want inside the same set of quotes (separated by spaces)—the first one will be C:, the second D:, and so on.

```
$_vbootfloppy = ""  # if you want to boot from a virtual floppy:
                # file name of the floppy image under /var/lib/dosemu
                # e.g. "floppyimage" disables $_hdimage
                #      "floppyimage +hd" does _not_ disable $_hdimage
$_floppy_a ="threeinch" # or "fiveinch" or empty, if not existing
$_floppy_b = ""     # ditto for B:
$_hdimage = "hdimage.first" # list of hdimages under /var/lib/dosemu
                # or disk drive devices under /dev.
```

If you have an application that talks directly to the serial ports, it will be necessary to map the COM names to the devices in the /dev directory. Also, there are some DOS programs that use a mouse.

```
$_com1 = ""    # e.g. "/dev/mouse" or "/dev/cua0"
$_com2 = ""    # e.g. "/dev/modem" or "/dev/cua1"
```

```
$_com3 = ""       # dito                    "/dev/cua2"
$_com4 = ""       # dito                    "/dev/cua3"
$_mouse = ""          # one of: microsoft, mousesystems, logitech, mmseries
             # mouseman, hitachi, busmouse, ps2
$_mouse_dev = ""      # one of: com1, com2, com3, com4 or /dev/mouse
$_mouse_flags = ""    # list of none or one or more of:
             # "emulate3buttons cleardtr"
$_mouse_baud = (0)    # baudrate, 0 == don't set
```

The /etc/printcap file lists the printers by name, and you can use this name to give
DOS access to the printer. The printer you name will appear as LPT1 to DOS. You can
specify other printer names in the same quoted string, and they will be LPT2 and LPT3:

```
$_printer = "lp"     # list of (/etc/printcap) printer names to appear as
             # LPT1, LPT2, LPT3 (not all are needed, empty for none)
$_printer_timeout = (20)# idle time in seconds before spooling out
$_ports = ""         # list of portnumbers such as "0x1ce 0x1cf 0x238"
             # or "0x1ce range 0x280,0x29f 310"
             # or "range 0x1a0,(0x1a0+15)"
```

Sound is turned off by default, but you can turn it on by supplying the correct set of values for it:

```
$_sound = (off)      # sound support on/off
$_sb_base = (0x220)
$_sb_irq = (5)
$_sb_dma = (1)
$_sb_dsp = "/dev/dsp"
$_sb_mixer = "/dev/mixer"
$_mpu_base = "0x330"
```

Note: Depending on your version of Linux, your version of the DOS emulator,
and which sound card you are using, you may not succeed with sound. It's as if,
in the parade of Linux development, sound is bringing up the rear. It will eventually all be here, but it isn't here yet.

DOS Tools

If you don't need full DOS emulation—if all you want to do is access DOS files and
directories, there are the mtools. These utilities can be used to manipulate DOS files and
to copy DOS files back and forth between DOS and Linux filesystems.

Note: Access to DOS filesystems is also possible by using mount and umount and
specifying the desired filesystem type. The mtools work directly on DOS filesystems without being mounted. Mounting a DOS filesystem provides Linux-like
access to the files, while mtools provides a set of DOS-like tools for manipulating the files and the filesystem itself.

The mtools set of utilities has been around for quite a while. There is a mailing list for support and news. For more information, and to get the latest version, the Web site is located at http://mtools.linux.lu/.

The /etc/mtools.conf File

The /etc/mtools.conf configuration file allows you to map drive letters to disk drives. This way, you can address specific disk drives and partitions by using a letter, just as in DOS. For example, you can map the floppy disk drives to letters as shown in the following:

```
drive a: file="/dev/fd0" exclusive
drive b: file="/dev/fd1" exclusive
```

The word exclusive at the end of the command ensures exclusive access to the drive. You can map a hard disk drive to C: in the following manner:

```
drive c: file="/dev/hdb1"
```

It is possible to directly address a DOSEMU disk image by mapping it to a letter, as shown in the following:

```
dirve m: file="/bar/lib/dosemu/diskimage.first"
```

Any letter can be mapped to any drive that is in a DOS format and has a device node in the /dev directory.

There are some variable names listed in Table 22.1 that can be set to either 1 or 0. They can be set directly in this file with an equals sign, as shown in the following:

```
MTOOLS_SKIP_CHECK=1
```

Alternatively, they can be set in the Linux environment as global environment variables from the command line or in a script, such as the following:

```
export MTOOLS_SKIP_CHECK=1
```

Table 22.1 Option Flags for mtools

Option	Description
MTOOLS_DOTTED_DIR	If set to 1, the mdir command uses a dot instead of spaces to display filenames. The default is 0.
MTOOLS_FAT_COMPATIBILITY	If set to 1, there are not FAT size checks. Some disks have an oversized FAT table and will be rejected on a size check. The default is 0.
MTOOLS_LOWER_CASE	If set to 1, short filenames are displayed as all uppercase. The default is 0.
MTOOLS_NAME_NUMERIC_TAIL	If set to 1, numeric tails (~1) are generated for

Option	Description
	all long filenames. If set to 0, numeric tails are generated only in a name collision. The default is 1.
MTOOLS_NO_VFAT	If set to 1, there will be no VFAT entries generated for mixed-case filenames that fit within the 8.3 size constraints. The default is 0.
MTOOLS_SKIP_CHECK	If set to 1, most sanity checks are skipped. Normally, this should only be set if there are complaints about reading some older Atari disks. The default is 0.
MTOOLS_TWENTY_FOUR_HOUR_CLOCK	If set to 1, twenty-four–hour clock notation is used. If set to 0, the AM and PM notations are used. The default is 0.

The Commands

There are several commands you can use to access and manipulate the files. These are similar to the DOS commands, except they all begin with the letter m.

The slashes can be either direction on the command line. That is, the names C:\UTIL\TEMP and C:/UTIL/TEMP are the same. The backslash character has a special meaning to a Linux shell, so you need to quote them—"C:\UTIL\TEMP", or escaped. C:\\UTIL\\TEMP.

The mattrib Command

This command is used to set file attributes. Each attribute is a bit that can be cleared or set. Each of the four attributes is represented by a single letter:

- a   Archive—Used by backup programs to detect modified files.
- r   Read-only—It cannot be modified or deleted.
- s   System—An operating system file.
- h   Hidden—The filename normally is not displayed by DIR.

Each of these four bits can be turned off by using a minus sign, or turned on with a plus sign. For example, enter the following to turn on the read-only bit:

```
mattrib +r a:\readme.txt
```

Using a -/ option will cause the command to recurse to files in the subdirectories.

The `mbadblocks` Command

To test a floppy disk and mark its bad blocks, enter the following:

```
mbadblocks a:
```

The `mcd` Command

This is the command to change the default directory and/or change the current drive. Entering the command by itself causes the name of the current directory to be displayed. For example, the following command will make the current directory the one named \TMP on the C: drive:

```
mcd c:\tmp
```

There may or may not be a current drive and directory stored in the .mcwd file in your home directory. If nothing is in the file, there is no current mtools directory. Also, if the data stored in the file is six hours old, it is ignored.

The `mcopy` Command

To copy a file from one place to another, name the source and destination files, as shown in the following:

```
mcopy <source> <destination>
```

The source and the destination can be either a DOS or Linux file or directory. A drive letter is always used to indicate a DOS file or directory. Multiple files can be copied into a directory by entering the following:

```
mcopy <source> [<source> ...] <destination>
```

In this case, the sources are all copied into the destination directory, but they can all be on different drives anywhere on Linux or DOS file systems. There are a few options:

- -/ One or more of the sources is a directory, and the copy is to include all of its files and subdirectories.
- -b Optimize for exceptionally large copies.
- -m Preserve the file modification time.
- -n Linux files can be overwritten without warning.
- -o DOS files can be overwritten without warning.
- -p Preserve the attributes of the copied files.
- -Q Do not copy any more files if one of the file copies fails.
- -t For copying text from DOS to Linux. Translates carriage-return/line-feed pairs into line-feed characters.

The `mdel` Command

To delete a DOS file or files, enter the following:

```
mdel <filename> [<filename> ...]
```

This command will delete a file with the read-only bit set, but it will prompt for confirmation.

The `mdeltree` Command

To delete a DOS directory and all the files and subdirectories within it, enter the following:

```
mdeltree <directory> [<directory> ...]
```

The `mdir` Command

This command displays the contents of a DOS directory. The directory can be specified or, if not, the directory last set by `mcd` will be used. The following are the command line options:

- `-/` Recursively show the contents of all subdirectories.
- `-w` Wide output. Show only the names, but organize them into columns so more names will show on the screen.
- `-a` Include hidden files in the list.
- `-f` Do not display the amount of free space on file systems where it has to be calculated.
- `-X` List the full path names but no other information. Recurse through all the subdirectories.

The `mdu` Command

This command displays the number of clusters being used by a directory and all its contents. The `minfo` command can be used to determine the cluster size.

By default, `mdu` lists all the subdirectories and the number of clusters for each. Using the `-a` option will cause it to also list all the files. Using the `-s` options causes it to list only the final total.

The `mformat` Command

The `mformat` command formats a floppy disk with a DOS file system. You can format a 1.44mb 3 1/2 inch floppy in the A: drive by entering the following command:

```
mformat -h 2 -s 18 -t 80 a:
```

The command specifies there are 2 heads, 18 sectors per track, and a total of 80 tracks.

If you don't know the values for these options, you can use `minfo`. The first line it displays is the correct argument list for `mformat`.

The `minfo` Command

The `minfo` command displays information about a DOS file system. The output includes the sector size, cluster size, boot sectors, number heads, number of bad tracks, and so on. It works with both floppies and hard disks. Enter the command and the drive letter, as shown in the following:

```
minfo c:
```

The `mlabel` Command

This utility will display the current label of a disk:

```
mlabel -s c:
```

It can write a new label to a disk in the following way:

```
mlabel c:newlabel
```

It can also erase the label, as shown in the following:

```
mlabel -c c:
```

The `mmd` Command

This command creates a subdirectory in the current directory, or along the specified path, as shown in the following example:

```
mmd c:/appdir/newdir
```

The `mmove` Command

The `mmove` command moves or renames a DOS file or directory. It can be used to move the file or directory to another location, or simply to rename it without moving it. The complete pathname can be specified, but the source and the destination must both be in the same filesystem, as shown in the following example:

```
mmove c:/doc/sourcedir c:/holding/destdir
```

If the destination does not have a full path specified, the directory of the source is assumed, and the file or directory is simply renamed.

The `mrd` Command

`mrd` removes a directory, as shown in the following example. The directory must be empty.

```
mrd a:/workdir
```

The `mren` Command

This is the same as the `mmove` command with one exception—if the destination name does not have a full path specified, the source directory is assumed.

The `mtoolstest` Command

Entering this command with no arguments will display all of the drive letter mappings and environment settings. The output looks like the following:

```
drive A:
    #fn=2 mode=128
    file="/dev/fd0" fat_bits=0
    tracks=0 heads=0 sectors=0 hidden=0
    offset=0x0
    partition=0
    exclusive

drive C:
    #fn=2 mode=0
    file="/dev/hdb1" fat_bits=0
    tracks=0 heads=0 sectors=0 hidden=0
    offset=0x0
    partition=0

drive N:
    #fn=2 mode=0
    file="/var/lib/dosemu/hdimage" fat_bits=0
    tracks=0 heads=0 sectors=0 hidden=0
    offset=0x2280
    partition=0
mtools_fat_compatibility=0
mtools_skip_check=0
mtools_lower_case=0
```

The output also includes two large tables of hexadecimal values. The one labeled fucase is used to map lowercase characters to uppercase characters. The one labeled tounix is use to translate DOS characters to Linux characters.

The `mtype` Command

This command lists the named file or files onscreen, as shown in the following:

```
mtype c:/autoexec.bat
```

Unless the drive is specified, A: is assumed.

Windows Emulation

Creating an emulation of Microsoft Windows is a very difficult chore because of vast areas of Windows that are unknown. Writing an operating environment that is compatible with Windows is particularly difficult because Windows is not compatible with itself—there are programs that will run under one version of Windows that will not run under another one (or will act very differently). Upgrading to a new version of an application can cause other seemingly unrelated applications to fail. There are constant patch releases to the Windows operating systems, some of which are not compatible with existing applications.

The Windows API is vast and largely unexplored. The documented functions do not always perform as advertised. And, no matter how much digging and experimenting is done, there are still plenty of undocumented system calls.

Applications make things difficult too. There is a tradition of application developers—being limited by non-working or unavailable API calls—going around the operating system to get something done. It is also common for an application to take advantage of, or make special arrangements for, bugs in the operating system and its system calls. All this has to be taken into account when trying to get an application to execute in an emulator. An emulator has to be bug-for-bug compatible.

WINE

WINE (WINdows Emulation) is an implementation of the Windows API for Linux. It is layer code that translates between the application and the internals of Linux. The project started in 1993.

There are two ways to use WINE to run a Windows application. You can load and run the executable files, just as you would on a Windows system. The WINE Windows emulator will load and execute code for both 16-bit (Windows 3.x) and 32-bit (Windows 95, 98, and NT) versions. A second option, if you have the source code, is to recompile the application and link it to the WINE libraries—this gives you a Windows program that is capable of taking full and direct advantage of the Linux features. In either case, the WINE graphics use the underlying X Windows System.

The WINE software is not finished, and probably will not be finished for a long time because the job is so large. However, the bugs and limitations are becoming fewer every day, and there are more reports of some of the larger applications successfully being executed. There is one large game maker that said 90 percent of their Windows games run under WINE on Linux.

There are a lot of individuals working on WINE because it's an easy project to fall into. It will happen that someone uses a particular Windows program and would like to be able run it on Linux. An effort is made to load it with WINE and it almost works, but there are some little things wrong here and there. It's open source, so they jump in start fixing it. With all the people working on it, there is a new version every couple of weeks.

There is one company, Corel, that has thrown a lot of its resources into WINE. They already have a version of WordPerfect and some other applications running with it, but they want to use it to get their entire Windows product line to run on Linux with WINE.

WINE Information

The home Web site for WINE is http://www.winehq.com.

To keep up with the release status of WINE, and to receive announcements about programs that it successfully runs, you can subscribe to the news group named comp. emulators.ms-window.wine.

If you would like to use WINE just to run one or two applications, you may be in luck. You can find out about specific applications by visiting http://www.winehq.com/Apps/query.cgi.

You will find a query form that you fill out and you will be shown a list of people who have attempted to run the application and their degree of success. There are some other Web sites that maintain lists of applications that have been successfully (and unsuccessfully) run on WINE:

http://www.progsoc.uts.edu.au/~wildfire/
http://www.winehq.com/apps.cgi

Loading and Running WINE

When WINE is loaded, it takes up about 125MB of drive space. It requires use of the X library libxml, and the X Windows System must be running. The Linux program named wine will then accept the name of a Windows program on its command line, as shown in the following:

```
wine winprog
```

Or you can specify the full filename, and the full pathname in either Linux or Windows format, as shown in the following:

```
wine winprog.exe
wine c:\\winbin\\winprog.exe
wine /home/winbin/winprog.exe
```

While WINE does not necessarily require the presence of a DOS partition on your drive, some of your applications might. If nothing else, during installation many applications write files to \windows and \windows\system directories. While it is necessary to have a DOS partition for some applications now, there are plans to eliminate this requirement in a future version of WINE. If you elect not to use a DOS partition, you will need to create directories named /windows and /windows/system.

The configuration file is named /usr/local/etc/wine.conf. If you want, you can specify a different name during configuration. Also, you can create a file named .winerc in your home directory, which is in the same format and serves the same purpose.

There is a version of this file distributed with WINE, and you should use it as a starter for your file. In the following example, the disk drives are defined by drive letters. The types of drives recognized by WINE are floppy, hd, cdrom, and network. DOS and Window drives all have 8-digit hexadecimal serial numbers. You can specify any Linux-accessible disk as being a particular type of Windows drive—there are three kinds of filesystems that can be simulated. Specifying the file type as msdos, dos, or fat means the type is FAT16. If the type is specified as win95 or vfat, it is a FAT32 drive. The unix file type should only be used if programs have been compiled and linked using the Winelib libraries.

The following is an example of a file layout that can be used as a beginning to set up your own. This file, or one like, is supplied with WINE:

```
[Drive A]
Path=/mnt/fd0
Type=floppy
Label=Floppy
Serial=87654321
Device=/dev/fd0

[Drive C]
Path=/c
Type=hd
Label=MS-DOS
Filesystem=win95

[Drive D]
Path=/cdrom
Type=cdrom
Label=CD-Rom
Filesystem=win95

[Drive E]
Path=/tmp
Type=hd
Label=Tmp Drive
Filesystem=win95

[Drive F]
Path=${HOME}
Type=network
Label=Home
Filesystem=win95

[wine]
Windows=c:\windows
System=c:\windows\system
Temp=e:\
Path=c:\windows;c:\windows\system;e:\;e:\test;f:\
SymbolTableFile=./wine.sym

# <wineconf>

[DllDefaults]
EXTRA_LD_LIBRARY_PATH=${HOME}/wine/cvs/lib
DefaultLoadOrder = native, elfdll, so, builtin

[DllPairs]
kernel  = kernel32
gdi     = gdi32
user    = user32
```

```
commdlg = comdlg32
commctrl= comctl32
ver     = version
shell   = shell32
lzexpand= lz32
mmsystem= winmm
msvideo = msvfw32
winsock = wsock32

[DllOverrides]
kernel32, gdi32, user32 = builtin
kernel, gdi, user       = builtin
toolhelp                = builtin
comdlg32, commdlg       = elfdll, builtin, native
version, ver            = elfdll, builtin, native
shell32, shell          = builtin, native
lz32, lzexpand          = builtin, native
commctrl, comctl32      = builtin, native
wsock32, winsock        = builtin
advapi32, crtdll, ntdll = builtin, native
mpr, winspool           = builtin, native
ddraw, dinput, dsound   = builtin, native
winmm, mmsystem         = builtin
msvideo, msvfw32        = builtin, native
mcicda.drv, mciseq.drv  = builtin, native
mciwave.drv             = builtin, native
mciavi.drv, mcianim.drv = native, builtin
w32skrnl                = builtin
wnaspi32, wow32         = builtin
system, display, wprocs = builtin
wineps                  = builtin

[options]
AllocSystemColors=100

[fonts]
;Read documentation/fonts before adding aliases
Resolution = 96
Default = -adobe-times-

[serialports]
Com1=/dev/ttyS0
Com2=/dev/ttyS1
Com3=/dev/modem,38400
Com4=/dev/modem

[parallelports]
Lpt1=/dev/lp0

[spooler]
LPT1:=¦lpr
```

```
LPT2:=¦gs -sDEVICE=bj200 -sOutputFile=/tmp/fred -q -
LPT3:=/dev/lp3

[ports]
;read=0x779,0x379,0x280-0x2a0
;write=0x779,0x379,0x280-0x2a0

[spy]
Exclude=WM_SIZE;WM_TIMER;

[Registry]
; Paths must be given in /dir/dir/file.reg format.
; Wine will not understand dos file names here...

;UserFileName=xxx              ; alternate registry file name (user.reg)
;LocalMachineFileName=xxx       ; (system.reg)

[Tweak.Layout]
;; WineLook=xxx   (supported styles are 'Win31'(default), 'Win95', 'Win98')
;WineLook=Win95

[programs]
Default=
Startup=

[Console]
;XtermProg=nxterm
;InitialRows=25
;InitialColumns=80
;TerminalType=nxterm
```

Most of the entries in the file are self-explanatory but, if you need more information, a Web page describing all of the entries can be found at http://www.winehq.com/wine-conf-man.html.

VMware

If you have a serious reason for window emulation, you may want to explore the MWware system at http://www2.vmware.com.

This is a commercial product, but you can download a free evaluation version for testing. It emulates Windows NT and 2000. One interesting aspect of this package is the fact that it has a family of X servers optimized for various graphics cards.

Win4Lin

Trelos is a new company that emulates a hardware configuration that will support your version of Windows. The emulator will run anything from DOS through WIN2K. You can find out more about it at http://www.trelos.com.

At this writing, the software had just reached the beta stage. While it is going to be a commercial product, the company states that it will be "extremely affordable."

Summary

There are still a lot of DOS users, and there are a lot of very useful DOS programs that have never been converted to have a GUI interface. There is even some DOS software development still underway. Except for the more exotic programs—software that deals in real-time data acquisition or does something bizarre with the hardware—all of this software is immediately available to be run under the Linux DOS emulator.

There are some Windows applications that have been run successfully under Linux, but even then it isn't quite as smooth or pretty as one would like. There needs to be a pretty compelling reason to want to execute a Windows application in a Linux environment, but it is being done more and more every day. There are something like 400 people worldwide working on WINE, so more and more of the API is conforming to the Windows version, and more applications are becoming available to WINE and Linux.

On Your Own

Set the configurations in `/etc/dosemu.conf` to address one of your floppy disk drives and, using a pre-existing DOS disk, execute a program from the floppy.

If you have a FAT formatted partition on a hard drive, configure it into `/etc/dosemu.conf` and have it appear as the `C:` drive in an X window when using the `dos`, `xdos` or `xtermdos` commands.

If you have a DOS disk drive or partition, set it up as your `C:` drive and set up a `dosemu` image as a `D:` drive (or some other letter) and verify that you can treat them both as DOS drives by copying files between them.

If you are tempted to run WINE, it's probably because there is one application you want to be able to run under Linux. Before you spend a lot of time experimenting, search the Internet for attempts by others to run the same application. There are many posted. You may find that attempts have failed, succeeded partially, or that there is no problem at all. Many people have posted configuration information that helped them succeed.

PART VI

Advanced Linux Topics

The Linux Application Development Platform

Linux is the ultimate developer's OS. The number and quality of tools available to the programmer on Linux is one of the reasons for its initial popularity. UNIX has long been known as a technical person's operating system, and Linux has long had the image as the "hacker's OS". An entire book can be written about programming under Linux, so I will narrow this chapter's information down to a few key areas:

- Tools
- Languages
- A sample program

Many of the useful programming tools available for Linux come from the Free Software Foundation. In keeping with the goals of that organization, all the tools are available free of monetary charge and come with source code that is freely modifiable within the guidelines of the GNU GPL license. Make sure you read this license carefully because it puts certain obligations on the programmer who chooses to use the FSF libraries and tools.

The core of the FSF toolset is the compiler, which is called gcc. gcc can be invoked from the command line by simply typing it. Typing gcc, along with the name of a source file, will compile that file into a program. gcc supports the standard programming concept of a makefile, which is essentially a batch script for compiling several source files and libraries into a executable program and is utilized by the GNU package make. Typing **make** at the command line in a directory with a file called Makefile will start the makefile script. Although you can use a different name, the make program defaults to using a file with this name. The output of running make is shown in Figure 22.1

There are a number of ways to get help for running gcc. Running gcc --help at the command line will display a list of command line options. Typing **man gcc** at the command line will show the gcc man page. The FSF has its own help system called info. Typing **info gcc** will take you directly to the area dealing with it. These help functions apply to all the rest of the tools described in this chapter.

In addition to make and gcc, a third component of the FSF tools is gdb, the GNU debugger. gdb is invoked in the same way as gcc, but, instead of a source file, you give

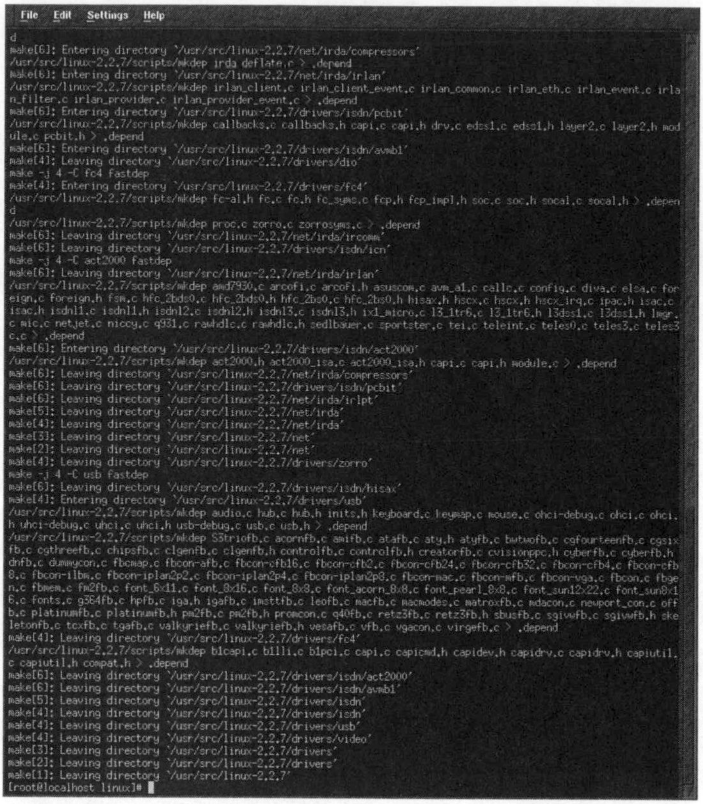

FIGURE 22.1
The output of running make.

the name of a executable program on which to operate. Additionally, gdb can operate on "core" files, which are files left over from crashed programs.

The last part of the core Linux development system is a text editor. It is crucial to pick an editor that you are intimately familiar with, because the majority of your coding time will be spent with it. Linux has few IDEs (integrated development environments), and the majority of Linux programmers eschew these programs. This is a big change for people coming from Windows or Macintosh backgrounds where programs like Visual C++ and Codewarrior are the main way to program. In general, the two main text editors for Linux and UNIX are vi and Emacs. Both are very powerful programs for editing text, but take divergent approaches to it.

Emacs is the official text editor of the GNU project and has integration with all the other GNU programming tools mentioned earlier. You can compile, debug, and edit your source files without ever leaving Emacs. This is a bit like an IDE, but Emacs does not have the elaborate system for viewing header files, class files, libraries, and other options that commercial IDEs offer.

Without going in depth on how Emacs works, other great features of this program include extensibility, self-documentation, mail and news integration, and more. It is very easy to extend Emacs' basic functionality to perform more complex custom tasks.

vi is the second major text editor for Linux, and probably the most popular in terms of use. vi lacks the integration with the GNU programming tools and other features of Emacs. vi is spare, yet powerful, and is available on just about any UNIX platform. vi may throw off novices by having two modes of operation—edit and insert. Basically, this requires you to be in one mode to insert text into a file and another to edit the text. Emacs has no such arrangement, which you may find is a more familiar approach to text editing.

Both text editors share many features in common that are useful for programmers. Options like syntax highlighting and auto indenting/formatting of source files are important. Both programs will run with GUI/X enhancements or in plain text mode. Two popular variants of these programs are vim—an enhanced vi—and XEmacs—an enhanced version of FSF Emacs.

With these tools, a Linux programmer has a powerful system for developing programs.

After you have decided on a text editor (and you are certainly not limited to the choices mentioned earlier), you can begin coding in your language of choice. Here again, Linux is head and shoulders above other OSes in terms of choice. Linux supports all the major programming languages and a plethora of lesser-know varieties. Most of the implementations come from The Free Software Foundation. Linux's core development libraries are part of the GNU project and are referred to as glibc and stdc++. These libraries support all the basic C and C++ functions, as well as the Linux-specific functionality. FSF implements Fortran, Pascal, and LISP for Linux as well. These are also many versions of Java for Linux. The standard JDK tools direct from Sun run on Linux, and there are free tools created by third parties.

Beyond the programming languages are a subset of languages called *scripting* languages. Many of these qualify as major languages as they support most, if not all, the functionality of a C or Fortran. The best known of the UNIX scripting languages is Perl. Perl is very adept at manipulating text, which makes it an excellent tool for a variety of tasks on Linux. Perl is popular with system administrators who use it to automate the tasks of maintaining the system. Perl is also popular with programmers who write Web page backend programs using CGI. Perl extends its basic functionality with a module interface. Programmers can write Perl modules in C or Perl itself. There are hundreds of modules to accomplish a dizzying array of tasks, and even novice Perl programmers can integrate these modules into their programs.

Another popular scripting language is Python. Python is similar to Perl in many ways, but is designed from the start to be an *object-oriented* language. It also avoids many of the problems that people associate with Perl in terms of readability and extensibility.

Both of these languages use the concept of an *interpreter*. When you execute a Perl or Python script, there is a program that runs it for you as opposed to it compiling the source into object code. This adds one benefit and one possible downside. The benefit is that you can take a script and run it on any platform that supports the interpreter, usually without modification. This is a lifesaver in a multiplatform environment. A downside to this approach is that the program runs slower than an actual compiled program does. To get around this, it is possible to take a Perl or Python script and compile it into an executable.

In addition to Perl and Python, there are smaller scripting environments available to the Linux programmer. sed and awk are most commonly used in small tasks like build environments and log maintenance. They harness some of the built-in programmability of the UNIX shells, like Bash and Csh. These are simple, powerful tools for automating small jobs. Linux also supports the popular Tcl/Tk combination. This is a great tool for rapidly deploying programs with a GUI for use in custom tasks. It is very easy to write a program that links several backend programs, like a database, and to have a Tk GUI front end for the end users. Perl and Python also have the ability to rapidly assemble a GUI front end for scripts.

Linux also supports specialized languages for database programming, such as SQL. There are a number of SQL databases that run on Linux, including several well-known commercial ones, such as Oracle.

Take a look at a sample program with the canonical "Hello, World" example. The first step is to open a new file in vi or Emacs at the command line, as shown in Figure 22.2 and Figure 22.3, respectively.

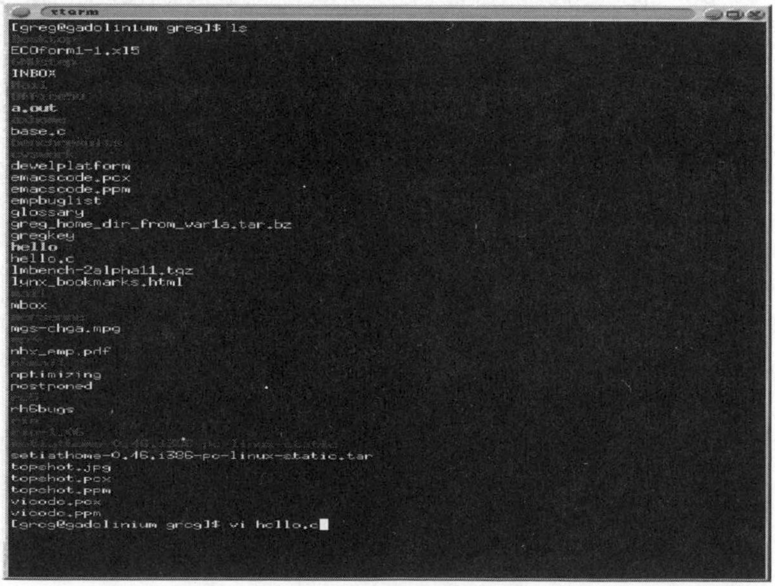

FIGURE 22.2
Opening hello.c *with* vi *from the command line.*

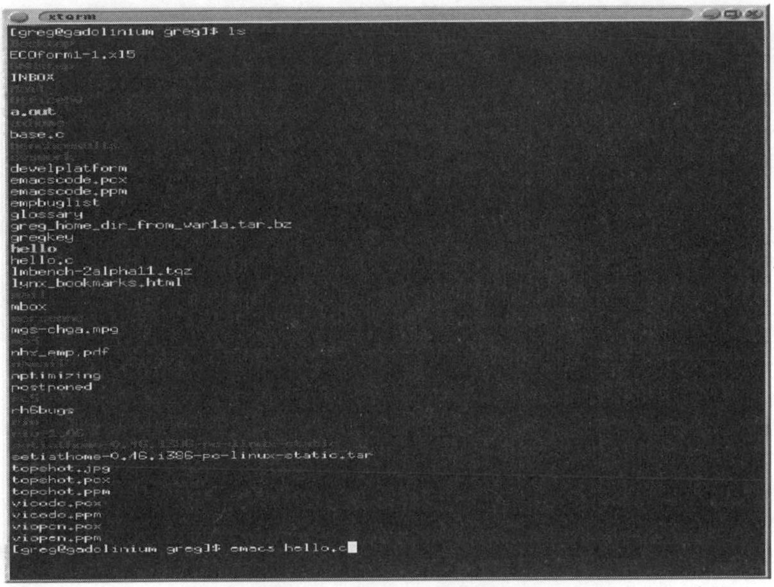

FIGURE 22.3

Opening hello.c *with* emacs *from the command line.*

After you open the file, you are now ready to edit the program. As you can see in Figures 22.4 and 22.5, vi and Emacs display this message very differently, and, at this point, you should have a good knowledge of how both work.

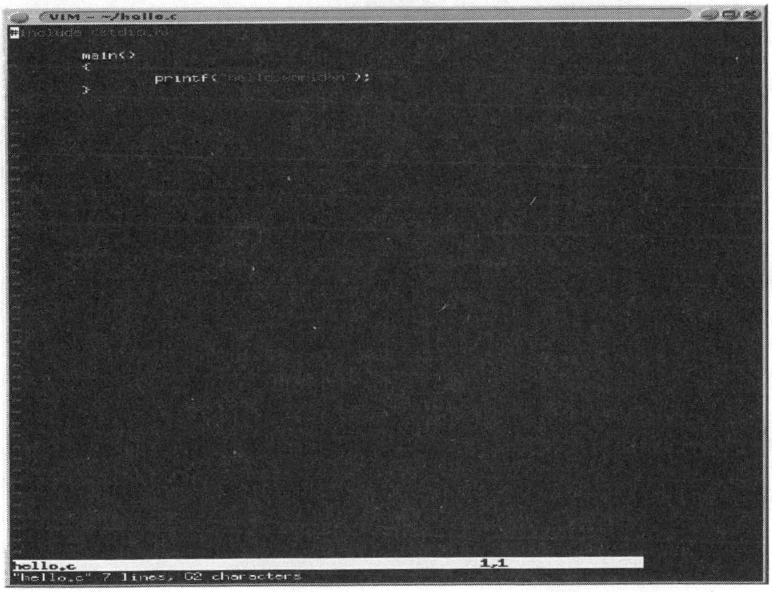

FIGURE 22.4

The hello.c *code displayed in* vi.

FIGURE 22.5
The hello.c *code displayed in* emacs.

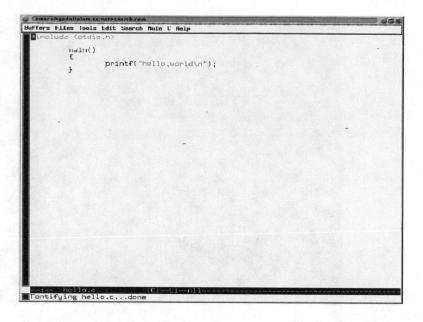

The "Hello,World" example syntax is not any different from the example first used in K&R's *The C Programming Language.*

```
#include <stdio.h>

    main()
    {
        printf("hello,world\n");
    }
```

After you enter the code, you are ready to compile using gcc. First save the program in vi or Emacs, and then quit the editor. You can actually compile right from both vi and Emacs, but, for simplicity sake, Figure 22.6 shows how to do it from the command line. Once at the command line, type **gcc -o hello hello.c**.

This will compile your program into an executable called hello, which will be put in the current directory. To run the program, just type **./hello** at the command line. If everything went well, you should get the following on the command line:

```
hello,world
```

a.out is the default filename that gcc uses when one is not specified. You can have it call the file something else by running gcc at compile time, as you did in the example in Figure 22.6.

```
gcc -o hello hello.c
```

FIGURE 22.6
Compiling and running the hello world *program.*

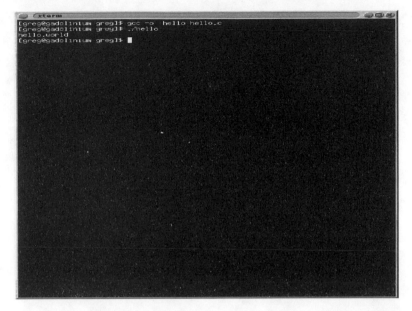

The -o option creates the executable filename that you specify as the first name with the source file you are compiling second.

Summary

This chapter mentions the power of the tools that are available to you with the Linux operating system. Although it only scratches the surface, and this is in no means a complete summary, the chapter mentions a few tools that you can use to build powerful applications. There are many more out there for you to utilize and explore.

On Your Own

Write and compile another C program using vi or Emacs.

Explore some of the other possibilities and languages available to you, such as Perl or shell scripts. Write and execute these scripts on your system.

Using Java

Java and Linux sort of grew up together. They were both kids in the early and middle 90s, so the philosophy behind them is fairly similar. It was believed by many that software innovation had been bogging down and the industry could do with alternative approaches to problems. Things only seemed to be getting worse. Java and Linux both addressed this issue, but in slightly different ways. Linux uses the open source model for rapid development and porting from one platform to another, while Java uses a standard executable file format that is the same on every computer. It seems that everyone attracted to one of these technologies is also attracted to the other. It is only natural that they would wind up working together.

There is now open source Java. Java, like much Linux software, has more than one version available. Bugs notwithstanding, all these Java implementations should do the same thing in the same way because they all follow the same specification—and the specification is rather explicit in its requirements.

How Java Works

Java was designed to be platform independent. From the beginning, the concept of Java included the ability to compile a program once and have that compiled program execute successfully on several different computers. To a large degree, it has been a success, but, like anything as complicated as a programming language with graphics, there are problems here and there. However, the problems are usually very small.

The portability is not in the language itself (although some of the language characteristics make portable code easier to generate). The portability comes from the fact that the executable object code coming out of the compiler is not hardware specific—it consists of a collection of *bytecodes* that are read and interpreted by a program designed for that purpose.

The program that interprets the bytecodes is called the Java Virtual Machine (JVM). For Java programs to execute on any particular machine, the JVM must have been ported to it. Porting the JVM to a new machine is a non-trivial manual task, but, once it has been ported, any Java program ever written can be run on it.

There is some overhead involved in loading and interpreting bytecodes. An interpreted program can never run as fast as the same program written in native object code that executes directly on the hardware. With modern computers as fast as they are, this speed difference is usually not even noticeable, but there are cases where it becomes important. To overcome the speed problem, the JVM can be given the added ability to compile bytecodes into native code whenever the bytecodes are loaded to be executed. Once the classes are loaded, the Java program can be executed at the maximum speed of the hardware. The software to do this bytecode translation is called the Just-In-Time compiler (JIT).

Java Compiles and Runs

The Java compiler takes your source code and translates it into one or more class files. The JVM is capable of loading and executing the class files. Normally, the compiler is named javac and the JVM is named java.

What follows are some examples of Java programs that show how they are compiled and executed. These examples assume the /usr/bin/javac is the java compiler and /usr/bin/java is the JVM. Depending on which version of Java you are using, the actual programs could have names that are different from the ones used here. For example, if you are using Kaffe Java, the file /usr/bin/java is a shell script that executes the JVM named /usr/bin/kaffe.

The Hello World Program

All Java source programs end with the suffix .java. Also, the name of the file is the same as the name of the class defined in the file (this makes it easy to locate classes by name). For example, a file named HelloWorld.java holds the following code:

```
class HelloWorld {
    public static void main(String arg[]) {
        System.out.println("Hello, world");
    }
}
```

This class has a main() method in it. When the JVM is started with the name of a class, it always looks for and executes the main() method. All it does is print a line of text and quit. To compile the program enter the following:

```
javac HelloWorld.java
```

This command will produce a file named HelloWorld.class that is in the form recognized by the JVM. The primary job of the JVM is to read and execute a series of 8-bit instruction codes. These instructions are known as bytecodes. To execute this example, enter the following:

```
java HelloWorld
```

Notice that, while the .java suffix is required for the compiler, the .class suffix is not specified on the command line for the JVM. If everything has gone right, the program should execute and display the following text:

```
Hello, world
```

Class File Naming

Every Java source file contains a class that has the same name as the file. For example, a file named Lance.java will contain a class named Lance, and compiling it will produce Lance.class. There are three other ways classes can be included in the same file, as demonstrated by the following example stored in a file named Multi.java:

```
class Multi {
    public static void main(String arg[]) {
        Multi multi = new Multi();
    }
    Multi() {
        Clocal cl = new Clocal();
        Cinn ci = new Cinn();
        showClass(new java.util.Date() {
            public String toString() {
                return("The anonymous class");
            }
        } );
    }
    void showClass(java.util.Date date) {
        System.out.println(date);
    }
    class Cinn {
        Cinn() {
            System.out.println("The inner class");
        }
    }
}
class Clocal {
    Clocal() {
        System.out.println("The local class");
    }
}
```

There are four classes of different types in this file. The main class displays a string from each of the other three, and the output looks like the following:

```
The local class
The inner class
The anonymous class
```

The main class is Multi; it is the one with the same name as the file. There is another class named Clocal that, if the file were renamed to Clocal.java, would be the main class. A class defined the way that Clocal is defined is normally only used by classes in the same source file—otherwise, it should have a source file of its own.

The class `Cinn` is an inner class. It is defined inside the `Multi` class and instances of it can only be created inside `Multi` unless it is made public, in which case the definition can be accessed through the dot reference `Multi.Cinn`. This kind of class can be quite handy for local data structure arrays and such.

The fourth kind of class in the example is the anonymous class created by extending a parent class named `java.util.Date`. By using the keyword `new` on the constructor, an instance of the class is created. But the instantiated class is actually an unnamed variation of the `java.util.Date` class that overrides the `toString()` method. In this example, the anonymous class is instantiated and passed to a method that displays the string.

The JVM attempts to name the class files so there are no name conflicts. There are four classes defined in the source file so, when `Multi.java` is compiled, it produces four class files:

```
Clocal.class
Multi$1$$anonymous_class0.class
Multi$Cinn.class
Multi.class
```

The `Multi` and `Clocal` classes are defined at the outermost level, so they both cause the generation of class files bearing their names. For these outer-level classes, care must be taken so that all classes have unique names. The class name `Clocal` cannot be defined in two separate files, because the last one compiled will simply overwrite the first. Using inner classes is much simpler—the Java compiler creates a new name by combining the name of the parent class, `Multi`, with the name of the inner class, `Cinn`, to produce the name `Multi$Cinn.class`. The anonymous class is named by using the name of the class in which it is declared and appending some characters that make it obvious that it is an anonymous class.

Java's Graphical User Interface

It is possible to write Java programs that run under X and have a graphical interface. There is nothing really special about the class files themselves, but they do include some classes that, at the lowest level, communicate with the X Windows System. You must have X running to run these programs.

The following is a very simple example of a Java program with a graphical interface. It displays a simple window with some labels and a single check box:

```
import java.awt.*;
import java.awt.event.*;

public class CheckMe extends Frame
        implements ItemListener {
    private Checkbox box;
    private Label north = new Label(" - - - - - -");
    private Label south = new Label(" - - - - - -");
    private Label west = new Label("<!");
```

```
        private Label east = new Label("!>");
        public static void main(String[] arg) {
            CheckMe cm = new CheckMe();
        }
        CheckMe() {
            super("CheckMe");
            initialize();
            setSize(200,100);
            box = new Checkbox("Check me!");
            box.addItemListener(this);
            add("North",north);
            add("South",south);
            add("East",east);
            add("West",west);
            add("Center",box);
            pack();
            show();
        }
        private void initialize() {
            north.setAlignment(Label.CENTER);
            south.setAlignment(Label.CENTER);
            east.setAlignment(Label.CENTER);
            west.setAlignment(Label.CENTER);
            addWindowListener(new WindowAdapter() {
                public void windowClosing(WindowEvent e)
                    { System.exit(0); } } );
        }
        public void itemStateChanged(ItemEvent event) {
            System.out.println("Checked: " + box.getState());
        }
    }
```

This class extends the Frame class so it will be a top level window. The constructor calls super() to set the title text that will display at the top of the window. After the initialize() method is called, the method setSize()—which is inherited from Frame—is called to set the height and width of the window. A Checkbox named box is created, and the CheckMe object, known inside itself as this, is added to the list of classes to be notified whenever the mouse activates the check box. The labels are added to the window using the names of the points of the compass to determine their positions. The check box is placed in the center. The call to pack() organizes the graphical elements according to the placement and size of each one, and the call to show() displays the window.

Use the following command to compile the program:

```
javac CheckMe.java
```

Although X must be running, it is still possible to start this program from the command. Open a terminal window and enter the following:

```
java CheckMe
```

The program will run and display the window shown in Figure 23.1.

FIGURE 23.1
*A Simple X
Window displayed
by Java.*

The `itemStateChanged()` method is called every time the mouse toggles the check box. In the `xterm` window that you used to start the program, the output looks like the following:

```
Checked: true
Checked: false
Checked: true
    . . .
```

The `initialize()` method sets all the labels so their text is centered, and it also establishes a way for the class to respond to the user choosing to halt the program by using the menu or the buttons at the top of the screen. This is achieved by instantiating an anonymous `WindowAdapter` class that has a `windowClosing()` method defined to shut down the process.

A Java Applet

Every modern Web browser has a JVM built into it. This includes the Netscape browser that is normally delivered with the X Windows System for Linux. For security reasons, this JVM is somewhat limited in what it is allowed to do on your local system. For example, it can have no file access on your local disk (although it can access the files on the Web site from which it was loaded).

The following is a very simple Java applet:

```
import java.awt.*;
import java.applet.*;

public class TextApplet extends Applet {
    private static final String outString = "Sized and Centered";
    private static final String fontName = "TimesRoman";
    private static final int fontSize = 42;
    private static final int fontStyle = Font.BOLD;
    private static final Color fontColor = Color.red;

    private Font font;
    private int X;
    private int Y;
```

```
    public void init() {
        font = new Font(fontName,fontStyle,fontSize);
    }
    public void paint(Graphics g) {
        Rectangle rectangle = getBounds();
        FontMetrics fm = g.getFontMetrics(font);
        X = rectangle.width;
        X -= fm.stringWidth(outString);
        X /= 2;
        Y = rectangle.height;
        Y -= fm.getAscent() + fm.getDescent();
        Y /=  2;
        Y += fm.getAscent();
        g.setColor(Color.lightGray);
        g.fillRect(0,0,rectangle.width,rectangle.height);
        g.setColor(fontColor);
        g.setFont(font);
        g.drawString(outString,X,Y);
        g.dispose();
    }
}
```

The applet `TextApplet` displays a line of text in the center of the displayed window. You can tell this is an applet because it extends the class `Applet`.

The Web browser first calls the `init()` method and then, when the time comes to display the applet, calls the `paint()` method. There are other pre-defined methods that can be included in an applet—these mostly have to do with complex initializations and animation. The `paint()` method in this example uses the size of the window (determined by the JVM, not by the applet) and the size of the character string to calculate where to write the string so it will be centered. A series of calls to methods in the `Graphics` class paints the background and draws the string characters.

It is a Web browser that displays an applet, and a Web browser gets all of its instructions through HTML. The following is an HTML file that can be used to display `TextApplet`:

```
<html>
<head>
<title> TextApplet </title>
</head>
<body>
<applet code="TextApplet.class"
    width=500
    height=200>
</applet>
</body>
</html>
```

The `<applet>` tag is used to specify the name of the class file and the width and height of the applet's display window. There can be several applets on one page. It is even possible to display the same applet several times on the same page.

There is a very simple browser called `appletviewer`. It is so simple that it ignores everything in the HTML page except the `<applet>` tag. It simply shows an applet in a window by itself. If there is more than one applet on the page, `appletviewer` opens a window for each one. To display the applet in this example, enter the following:

```
appletviewer AppletText.html
```

Note: The `appletviewer` is simply a Web browser with limited capabilities, so it needs to have the name of an HTML file, not the Java class file.

The displayed applet looks like Figure 23.2.

FIGURE 23.2
A static applet.

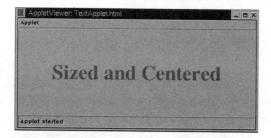

Kaffe

Kaffe is Java developed in the Linux tradition. It is an open source implementation of the JVM and the class libraries. You can find out more about it at the following Web sites:

```
http://www.kaffe.org
http://www.transvirtual.com
```

The objectives of the Kaffe project are not only to create an open source version of Java, but to do it in such a way that the software is modular and flexible. Among other things, this could lead to compilers of other languages generating bytecodes and running as portably as Java does now.

If you are going to be using Java very much, you will need to keep up with the latest version. A Java development and runtime system is very complicated, and it seems there are always things that need to be added and fixes that need to be made.

The primary concern of Kaffe is the JVM, which it calls the *OpenVM*. The name makes sense because there is nothing about the virtual machine that requires that a program be written in Java. A program can be written in any language and, as long as the compiler generates bytecodes, it can be executed by a virtual machine.

If you are interested in porting the virtual machine to another platform, you should start by reading the information on the Kaffe Web site. The Kaffe Custom Edition of OpenVM was designed to simplify the job of porting. There are several ports underway, and there are several that have been completed. Kaffe runs on almost any flavor of UNIX, and it runs on Windows 95, 98, and NT.

Installing Kaffe on Linux

The source code of Kaffe is available from a number of sources, but you should always be able to find it at www.kaffe.org.

Compiling a new version of Kaffe is very simple. Once the source files are unpacked into a directory, change to that directory and execute the script named configure. The make files will be generated. By default, Kaffe is installed in the /usr/local directory tree, but if you want to avoid conflicting with some other Java software, you can specify the location for the install by using the --prefix option. For example, to install Kaffe into /home/fred/jtest, enter the following:

```
configure --prefix /home/fred/jtest
```

> **Note:** The same source code can also be compiled for Win32. You will need to have the GNU tools gcc and gmake installed. To compile the programs, use the configure script with the --prefix option, and then use the make files to compile and install everything.

Once the make files have been created, compile and install the software with the following commands:

```
make
make install
```

Set the PATH environment variable to include the directory holding the executable programs. For example,

```
PATH=$PATH:/usr/local/bin
```

There is no real need to set the CLASSPATH variable because the JVM knows where the Java class files are located. There is an optional step you can take if you want to test your Kaffe installation. Enter the following commands:

```
make all
make check
```

The first command will compile not only Kaffe, but also a suite of test programs designed to exercise the system. The second command will run the test programs to verify that the system is correctly installed and working properly.

The Many Faces of Java

A number of projects are underway that are developing Java tools and utilities. Some of the projects have mature software, some are in early release, and others are in early development. They are all in continuing development—it seems that Java is so large that no project is ever finished.

The specification of Java requires a standard functional form for its internals, so software produced by different projects should all work together. It is possible to get a compiler from one source, a virtual machine from another, and use a JIT from yet another project. This seems to be an excellent situation to allow the best technology to succeed.

There are some circumstances that can cause one piece of Java software to be incompatible with another. For one thing, the open source model of development allows for the distribution of programs that are incomplete. An incompatibility could come about from a vague description, or an oversight, in the specification, and two separate implementers interpret the meaning differently. Also, it is unethical, but an implementer could add some special extension that renders its own version incompatible with other software. And, of course, there is the certainty of an occasional bug.

The following is a list of Java software that is currently available. This list is, of course, incomplete, because things are constantly changing. If you need to find something that isn't in the following list, you can start looking at http://www.jars.com.

There is a team of people who are constantly testing and reviewing Java software, and they post the ratings and results. This team started out as an applet rating service and spread from there to a rating service for all Java software.

Japhar

Japhar is a JVM that was built from specifications and without referring to the Sun source code. Its Web site is at http://www.japhar.org.

It is an open source project operating under the GNU license. Besides Linux, there are versions that run on FreeBSD, NetBSD, Solaris, and Win32. There are a couple of other software tools with Japhar, but it is not a software development system—it is a virtual machine. The Japhar project is active—there are major improvements and a new release every couple of months.

The design of Japhar has taken into consideration the implementation of an embedded JVM. For example, Japhar has been successfully embedded in the Mozilla (Netscape) Web browser.

GNU Classpath

This is an open source Java class library licensed under the GNU Library General Public License. Its Web site is located at http://www.gnu.org/software/classpath.

This is one of the new projects. The goal is to provide a free software replacement for the standard Java class libraries from Sun. While these classes should work with any JVM, the primary target is Japhar.

TYA

TYA is a project for a clean room version of a Just In Time (JIT) compiler. There is a Web site for it at `http://www.dragon1.net/software/tya`.

Because it is a compiler, it can only be used on an Intel-compatible CPU, and it must be a 586 or better. Special interest has been paid to the awt Java graphics package and the software built onto it.

The operation of TYA is quite straightforward. Whenever a class is loaded, its methods are quickly translated to native object code. This can be done quickly because TYA contains a table with the pre-assembled object code for each Java opcode. The calling sequences are set up so the compiled methods can be invoked, and TYA uses the hooks available in the JVM so they can be called.

There are two ways you can use TYA with your JVM. You can specify it on the command line, as shown in the following:

```
java -Djava.compiler=tya <classname>
```

Or you can set the environment variable:

```
JAVA_COMPILER=tya
export JAVA_COMPILER
```

Cygnus

Cygnus is a complete free software toolkit for Java software development. It is open source developed under the GPL license.

The Cygnus Java compiler will produce Java bytecodes, but it can also be used as a front end to the GNU C compiler gcc, enabling you to generate native code directly from Java source. For producing C code, there are also utilities that will generate C header files and an appropriate main() function.

Besides the compiler, called gcj, there is a front end library named egcs and a complete runtime library named libcj. The libcj library contains the Java class libraries and the code that communicates with the operating system. You can find out more information at the web site:

```
http://www.cygnus.com/client_services/java.html
```

To use Cygnus to compile the HelloWorld program, presented earlier in this chapter, into a native executable program, enter the following:

```
gcj --main=HelloWorld -o HelloWorld HelloWorld.java
```

The --main option specifies the entry point (that is, it names the method that is to become main()). The -o option specifies the name of the executable file.

Mauve

Mauve is a Java test suite. Its purpose is to help the "Write once, run anywhere" capability of Java. The Web site is located at http://sourceware.cygnus.com/mauve/.

This software is not really intended for an end user of Java. It is primarily for those working on compilers and virtual machines. Its purpose is to enable a high degree of compatibility among the various software projects. The suite is being built up through the cooperation of the Kaffe, GNU Classpath, and Cygnus projects. Also, Hewlett-Packard has contributed large test suites to Mauve.

FreeBuilder

FreeBuilder is a visual programming environment for Java programming. It is a Java IDE written in Java. Because it is written in Java, it will run on any computer with Java 1.1.5 or later. This is a GNU open source project. Its Web site is located at http://www.freebuilder.org.

There is only one copy of the source code because it is identical for each platform, but there are separate installation procedures for Linux, Windows, and Apple. FreeBuilder includes a compiler, debugger, and text editor.

One of the traditional impediments to programmers using an IDE is getting past the clumsiness of using a text editor. There are those who prefer the modal and cursor navigation form of vi, and there are those who have, over time, developed their own set of Emacs configuration settings. While FreeBuilder has its own text editor, it is constructed on Java Beans, so any of its built-in tools can be replaced—this includes the editor.

CACAO

CACAO is a 64-bit JIT that compiles Java into native code for the ALPHA processor. You can find information at http://www.complang.tuwien.ac.at/java/cacao.

CACAO is implemented as a complete replacement of the Java Virtual Machine. It runs under both Linux and Digital UNIX.

Harissa

Harissa translates Java bytecodes into C source code. Using this, along with the gcc compiler, you can write your program in Java and compile and run it as you would a C program. Its Web site is located at http://www.irisa.fr/compose/harissa.

The Java Virtual Machine loads classes dynamically while it runs. Harissa causes the classes to be compiled and linked into the executable; however, Harissa can also dynamically load and execute class files. Java allows class names to be specified at execution time.

Harissa is written in C, and there is a version available for both Linux and Solaris. The source code can be freely downloaded.

Jikes

Jikes is a Java compiler from IBM and can be found at
`http://alphaworks.ibm.com/formula/jikes`.

The compiler has the capability of performing incremental compilation, compiling only the necessary class much like a `make` file. Jikes also knows about `make` and is capable of producing a dependency file for it.

At the Web site, there are versions available for AIX, Windows, Linux in Intel, and Solaris on Sparc. The source code is also available.

Metrowerks

There is a version of Java 1.2 for Linux on the PowerPC found at
`http://business.tyler.wm.edu/mklinux/main.html`.

This is the full development system including a compiler, a virtual machine, and the Java 1.2 class libraries. For graphics, this version is statically linked with Motif 2.1. The PowerPC volunteer porting team has been augmented by assistance from Blackdown.

Blackdown

These are some commercial products available for Linux. The software at
`http://www.blackdown.org` was created to assist with serious Java application development.

Developers have demo versions of the commercial software available for downloading and testing, but this is not an open source project. There is a CASE tool, a RAD development environment, and more than one IDE. If you use the Emacs editor, some free software (JACOB and JDE) can be used as a Java class browser and a wrapper for command line Java.

Summary

While Java is not an integral part of Linux, it is an integral part of modern computing. Programmers have discovered that Java programs are easy to write and easy to maintain, so more and more people are moving to Java every day. And, while Java did not originate from the open source movement, it is certainly acting like a double first cousin to it. You can get a few complete (and a few not so complete) Java implementations in the open source form. These projects are making advances, and new projects are being started, so it seems that open source Java is the Java of the future.

On Your Own

A number of Java development tools are available, but none of them are from Sun. If you are serious about Java software development on Linux, it would be to your advantage to download and try as many of the tools as possible.

Write a Java program and test its speed after it has been compiled in various ways. The time command can be used to determine execution times for the program, whether it is interpreted by a JVM or executed as native code.

Kernel Hacking

This chapter describes the process of configuring and changing Linux at the most fundamental level. The kernel is the underlying program that runs everything else. It starts processes and allots memory for them. It then controls which one is running at any one time. It also provides a set of system calls used by programs that need to interface with the hardware.

Just like everything else in Linux, the kernel comes as free and open source code, and you can change it in any way you would like.

You may just need to upgrade to a later version. Each new kernel is (usually) an improvement over the previous one. There can even be circumstances where some new feature or other has been added, and some particular piece of new software won't run without it.

You may simply want to rebuild the kernel to change some option settings. There are a lot of possible options—there is an overview of them later in this chapter.

You may want to add some special feature or customize the kernel in some way. For example, if you are working with a non-standard hardware configuration that requires things to be optimized in a special way, you can modify the kernel to take advantage of it.

> **Note:** You may want to beware of the cutting-edge version. The latest release of Linux is one that has been proven to be quite stable, but there is always a pre-release version that is less than elegant. If you simply want to experiment, it doesn't really matter, but if you are trying to get some work done, you don't want to spend all your time propping up something that is incomplete.

How to Get the Source Files

If you have a Linux CD-ROM, the source is already there. However, if you want to get an update to a newer version, you will need to go to the Internet. Downloading and installing the source is a very straightforward process. There are really not that many steps, but you need to take care that you do it right.

Note: If you installed Linux from a CD-ROM, and you don't want to upgrade to a newer version, you can work from the source included on the CD-ROM. The exact form it takes will depend on the distributor of the CD-ROM, but you should expect it to be in rpm files. Look in the directory holding rpm files or something like `kernel-source*.rpm`. Use `rpm -q -l kernel*.rpm` to make sure you have the right one. And use `rpm -q -i` to find any dependency packages that must also be loaded. The only reason I can see for building this kernel would be to change some configuration settings. Most kernel builds are done for purposes of upgrading, which involves getting a new version of the source.

The source files for the Linux kernel are available everywhere. In particular, there is a large collection of mirror sites participating in the Linux Kernel Archive Mirror System. If you know your two-character country code, you find a mirror using one of these URLs:

`www.`*`xx`*`.kernel.org`

`ftp.`*`xx`*`.kernel.org`

where *xx* is your two-character country code. It could be that the site for your country code is inoperative (some have only ftp and some have only www) so you will need more information. You can find a complete list the mirror sites at `www.kernel.org/mirrors/`.

The archives of the kernel are found in the directory `/pub/linux/kernel`. There are a number of versions of the Linux kernel in the archive. The number of versions is a consequence of the "release early and release often" policy of open source software development.

Each version of the kernel has several files associated with it. For example, version 2.2.9 can have all of the following files:

```
linux-2.2.9.tar.bz2
linux-2.2.9.tar.bz2.sign
linux-2.2.9.tar.gz
linux-2.2.9.tar.gz.sign
patch-2.2.9.bz2
patch-2.2.9.bz2.sign
patch-2.2.9.gz
patch-2.2.9.gz.sign
```

To get version 2.2.9 of the kernel, you need to download either the file named `linux-2.2.9.tar.bz2` or the one named `linux-2.2.9.tar.gz`. The bz2 files are always smaller than the gz files, so, if you already have Linux running and can decompress the files using the bunzip2 utility, it may be better to get the bz2 file. The gz files can be unzipped using the GNU utility gunzip. You should store the downloaded file as either /usr/src/linux-2.2.9.tar.gz or /usr/src/linux-2.2.9.tar.bz2.

> **Note:** You can download the file directly into the /usr/src directory, or you can download it into a work directory and then copy it there. The file is quite large and may take a while to download, so it may be wise to keep a safety copy of it until you are able to verify that the source has been installed. However it is done, you need to end up with a copy of the tar file in /usr/src.

The patch files (the ones that begin with patch- instead of linux-) are updates from previous releases so you can save download time. For example, if you already have a copy of 2.2.4, you only need to download the patch file for 2.2.5 and update your existing source—a patch is a much smaller download.

The filenames that end with .sign are PGP signature files that you can use, if you want, to verify that the kernel you are downloading from the mirror site is exactly the same one found in the Linux kernel archives. If you want to get a copy of the public key required for verification, it can be found at http://www.kernel.org/signature.html.

> **Note:** From this point on you will need to proceed with care because to successfully execute many of the following steps, you will be required to have root permission. While you have these permissions, take care that commands are entered correctly, and that you have a good idea of what they will do. If you are not certain about a command, drop out of superuser mode and try the command—it may not work, but you can see what is going on without harming your system.

Once you have downloaded the bz2 or gz file and have placed it in the /usr/src directory, it is necessary to create a place to put the files. Continuing with the version number used in previous examples, change to the directory /usr/src and create a subdirectory with the following:

```
mkdir linux-2.2.9
```

If the source from another version of Linux has already been installed, you should see a directory with its version number, and there should also be a symbolic link to it named linux. If this symbolic link (also called a symlink) exists, delete it with the following command:

```
rm linux
```

Then create a symbolic link to your new directory by entering the following command:

```
ln -s linux-2.2.9 linux
```

This link gives you the ability to refer to the directory by either of two names: `linux` or `linux-2.2.9`. This convention will allow you to have more than one version of the source installed. The kernel download and build process always refers to the directory named `linux`. You can then verify that you have the correct directory setup and links by entering

```
file *
```

There may be other files and subdirectories included, but your new kernel directories should cause the output to include the following:

```
linux:        symbolic link to linux-2.2.9
linux-2.2.9: directory
```

The next step is to decompress the downloaded file. With the file in, the command will either look like

```
bunzip2 linux-2.2.9.tar.bz2
```

or like

```
gunzip linux-2.2.9.tar.gz
```

The compressed file contains source code. ASCII is one of the most compressible forms of data, so you can expect the size to be multiplied from four to seven times. The `gz` or `bz2` file should be deleted, leaving a large file named `linux-2.2.9.tar`.

There is one more step to get the source. The `tar` command is used to break out the separate source files and store them in the Linux directory. The files will be stored in a subdirectory of the current directory, so change to `/usr/src` and enter the following command:

```
tar xvf linux-2.2.9.tar
```

This command will run for a few minutes and store the output in the Linux directory, creating subdirectories as necessary. Each filename is listed as it is installed.

The installation will create the subdirectories listed in Table 25.1. These could vary over time—the table lists the main directories used at one point in time but, in later versions, there could be more or fewer directories.

Table 25.1 Subdirectories of `/usr/src/linux`

Subdirectory	Contains
Documentation	Documentation of the kernel. Every file and every subdirectory is listed in the file `00-INDEX`. There is also a `00-INDEX` file in every subdirectory. There are files of different formats, but most of them are plain ASCII text.

Subdirectory	Contains
arch	This is the hardware-specific code. This is the low-level code that does things such as field interrupts, configures I/O ports, and accesses the system clock.
extra	Software that is included to handle some special or exceptional situation.
fs	This code handles the various types of file systems. The code here is for file locking, pipes, fifo files, file status, network files, open, read, close, and so on.
include	The C header files for the source in all the other source subdirectories.
init	The code that runs immediately following boot.
ipc	Shared memory, semaphore, and ram-to-ram inner-process communications.
kernel	Starting and stopping processes, priority and schedule of running processes, timers, and signal processing.
lib	Low-level system calls such as strcmp(), memmove(), data compression, and values such as ctype and errno.
mm	Memory management such as swap file management and memory mapped files.
net	Networking such as the TCP/IP stack, IPX, decnet, appletalk, X.25, sockets, and Ethernet.
scripts	Scripts and program used to facilitate the building of a new kernel.

Tools Used to Build a New Kernel

The kernel comes to you as source code. It is necessary to configure it, compile it, link it, and put it into service. Fortunately, everything you need to get this done is supplied as a part of Linux.

Note: If you do not already have Linux running, and you intend to build the entire operating system from scratch, it would be a good idea to download an executable version to use as a bootstrap and a development platform, because Linux knows very well how to build Linux.

There is a possibility that you will be required to update some of your software—the older your version of Linux, the more likely this is to happen. In particular, there are some older versions of gcc (the C and C++ compiler) that must be upgraded before a new kernel can be built. The good news is that if you attempt to use an old compiler, the build process will notify you and refuse to continue.

There are a couple of cures for an outdated gcc. You can get a new copy of the gcc source at http://www.gnu.org/software/gcc/gcc.html.

The GNU Web site contains complete instructions for downloading and compiling a new gcc version.

However, if your compiler is old, there are probably lots of other parts of your system that are old. It is probably time to upgrade your entire system to a new version, so you should either download a new version or get a new CD-ROM. This will, of course, include a new compiler system, so you should no longer have any problems.

As you upgrade Linux from one version to the another, be sure to read the documentation that describes the changes. It is a text file named Documentation/Changes in the source file directory tree. While you read it, keep in mind the effect that changes may have on software that you have already installed. For the most part the upgrade will cause no problems, but there is an occasional oversight.

Configurables

There are a number of things that can be configured in the kernel, and, with new versions of Linux being released constantly, the list will become longer. The configurable items fall into categories.

Some of the configuration settings depend on other settings. For example, if you need to have your IDE drives simulate SCSI drives, you will need to configure the kernel with SCSI support as well as IDE support.

Processor

This is probably the fundamental configuration setting. The CPU specification can be one of several types including Alpha, ARM, Motorola 68000, Sparc, and Sparc64. The most common CPUs are Intel and AMD.

The kernel can be compiled to run on a range of Intel and AMD processors from the 386 to the Pentium family. The Linux distributors normally include a kernel that is compiled assuming the lowest common denominator, the 386. Besides the processor type, there is an option that will include math emulation for processors that don't have hardware floating points. You can also compile the kernel to support multi-processing for computers with more than one CPU.

General

There are several items that are commonly used and fall into a general category. Several of these depend on the installed hardware, such as the bus of the motherboard being PCI or Microchannel. You can also select for kernel support of the execution of ELF binaries, a.out binaries, and miscellaneous binaries. An example of a miscellaneous binary is a Java class file. Plug-and-play can be enabled or disabled.

Loadable Modules

You can configure the kernel to have or not have the capability of using loadable modules. A module is a small piece of code that can be attached to the kernel or be detached from the kernel while the kernel is running. During configuration, you will be able to select which drivers that you want to have as modules. If you do select some of them to be modules, you will also need to compile the modules as described later in this chapter.

Block Devices

A disk drive transfers blocks of data with each read and write, so it is known as a block device. A CD-ROM drive is also a block device. By setting the configuration, you can determine whether or not the floppy disk is to be supported, and what kind of hard drives and CD-ROMs are to be supported. You can control the way the kernel uses DMA (Direct Memory Address) for input and output.

The kernel can have SCSI support. You can even have the kernel make the IDE drives look as if they are SCSI drives.

Character Devices

A keyboard and a mouse transfer data in a stream with one byte behind another, so they are known as *character devices*. It is normal to configure the kernel to handle virtual terminals, and to handle terminals connected to the serial port. It is also possible to configure pseudo terminals (a client-server sort of arrangement for remote access). In addition, there is a setting in case you have a non-standard serial port. Other character devices are the timer, speech card, certain tape drives, and the joystick.

File Systems

The kernel can be configured to support several different types of file systems such as Apple Macintosh, DOS FAT, ISO 9960 (used for CD-ROMs), Minix, Microsoft NTFS, OS/2 HPFS, and more. To access one of these other files systems, they must be mounted as the correct type—the automounter can be configured into the kernel to remount the drives at boot time. You can also configure the kernel to allow you to set per-user limits on disk space.

Networking Options

The kernel is involved in TCP/IP, IPX, AppleTalk, and tunnels over IP. You can configure the kernel to be a firewall. You can also set up socket filtering to allow or disallow specific types of packets from passing through. You can optimize the kernel as a router. There are settings for multicasting, tunneling, supporting aliases, and reverse ARP (Address Resolution Protocol).

Network Device

There is support for a long list of network adapter cards, and the list is constantly growing. There is also support for different kinds of networks including Ethernet, token ring, point-to-point protocol (PPP), serial line protocol (SLIP), frame relay, FDDI, wireless LAN, ARCnet, and so on.

Miscellaneous

There are a few items that are categories of their own. There is Integrated Services Digit Networks (ISDN) support, which can be used to connect through SLIP or PPP to an Internet service provider. There is also support for amateur radio connections. The kernel can be set to deal with older CD-ROM drives—those that are not SCSI, IDE, or ATAPI. You can also configure the kernel to support sound cards.

The text mode of the local terminal can be configured to be something other than VGA. Access to the screen is necessary as part of the kernel, because the boot sequence needs someplace to display its messages.

How to Configure the New Kernel

There are an amazing number of things to be configured in the kernel. Gather up your hardware manuals—the configuration process, at some point, is sure to require something you just don't know.

There are at least four different programs that can be used to configure the Linux kernel. Configuration can be done by using a command line scroll-up list of prompts and answering questions, it can be done from a full screen text interface, or it can be done from an X application. And there is a batch utility that configures the kernel according to the contents of a file.

> **Note:** Any one of these will work, but as the software becomes more GUI, the job becomes easier. The easiest of these is the X application. If you are running the X Window System, I would suggest that you use it. If you are doing this from the command line, menuconfig will probably be the best approach.

No matter which of the options you choose, there is plenty of help available. One or more screens of text explain every option. All three of the interactive configuration programs use the same set of questions and use the same set of help files.

Linux develops quickly, especially down at this low level where the hackers all live. By the time you read this, there may be another way to configure the kernel.

Using the Command Line Configuration Utility

Working from the command line is the most straightforward way to configure your system, but it is also the most work. To use the command line, change to the /usr/src/linux directory and enter the following:

```
make config
```

Questions will appear, one after another. There are two kinds of questions—multiple choice questions (like the kind of CPU you would like to compile for) and yes-no questions (like whether or not to support networking). Fortunately, detailed help is available for each question. In fact, there is so much information available to set the configurations that the configuration process is a fairly good tutorial for a high-level understanding of the Linux kernel.

There are relatively few questions that require you to enter data, but each one is supplied with a complete list of your possible answers. For example, the CPU question looks like the following:

```
Processor family (386, 486/Cx486, 586/K5/5x86/6x86, Pentium/K6/TSC,
PPro/6x86MX) [PPro/6x86MX]
```

If you know your target processor, you can type in its name as something like **586** or **PPro**. As long as the first few characters are a unique match, it will know which one you mean. If you type anything other than one of the valid choices, you will get help—there will be one or more screens full of information to help you in making your selection. In this example, the help text describes each of the CPU types listed and then says, "If you don't know, use 386." In fact, all of the help text ends with what you should do if you don't know.

There are many more yes/no questions than there are multiple choice questions. These questions have a default value as shown by the format of the following question:

```
Symmetric multi-processing support (CONFIG_SMP) [Y/n/?]
```

This question is asking whether you want to build a kernel for a computer with a single CPU or for a computer with multiple CPUs. It also lists the name used in the code to specify the configuration. The default can be selected by simply pressing the Enter key. If the default is yes, the prompt is formatted in the following way:

```
[Y/n/?]
```

If the default is no, it looks like

```
[N/y/?]
```

The question mark is a reminder that entering anything other than y or n will cause a help screen to appear. There is another form for the prompt:

```
[Y/m/n/?]
```

I know it looks like it, but it does not mean yes, no, and maybe. This fourth option will appear for drivers (such as parallel ports, floppy disks, and UPS management) to determine how the driver is to be compiled and linked. If the answer is y, the driver will be linked to become a part of the kernel. If the answer is m, the driver will be compiled as a separate module that can be loaded and linked dynamically by a running kernel.

There are some questions that require that you enter a number. They will always have the default value as the prompt, as in the following:

```
[34]
```

> **Note:** The configuration of the kernel is in the form of a collection of #define statements in the header file include/linux/config.h. However, in any release version of Linux, this file contains nothing more than an include statement for include/linux/autoconf.h. Whenever you answer the complete set of configuration questions, a new version of autoconf.h is created.

All of the utility programs that work with the configuration settings use the same set of help files and store the current configuration in /usr/src/linux/.config. If you want to save a configuration, this is the file you want to save—the data in this file is used to generate the actual configuration files.

Using the Full Screen Configuration Utility

There are two advantages for using the full screen version instead of the scroll version. First, you can save copies of configurations and reuse them at another time. Second, you can randomly move directly to any question, allowing you make changes to only one item (instead of having to answer all the questions again just to make one or two changes).

To run the program, change to the /usr/src/linux directory and enter the following:

```
make menuconfig
```

Everything comes as source code, so if you have never run this command before, the program will first be compiled. When the program runs, the screen clears and shows you a menu of things you can configure. At the top of the screen is the information about navigating the menu and making selections. The questions and answers are the same as in the command line version but, with the random access interface, you can quickly make just a few changes.

The last two selections on the menu allow you to store your configuration definitions in a file or to load them from a previously stored file.

Using the X Configuration Utility

This is the full GUI form of the utility to set the kernel configuration options. If you are running X, you can start this program by executing the following command in the directory /usr/src/linux:

```
make xconfig
```

This command compiles the program (if necessary) and then runs it. The main window is shown in Figure 25.1. You can locate all the categories at a glance, and, once a category has been selected, all of the options for it are displayed. The list of categories will change from one version of Linux to another simply because different options will be available, and the dialog window will look different with different window managers. Figure 25.2 shows the window used to configure the mouse.

FIGURE 25.1

The X configuration utility.

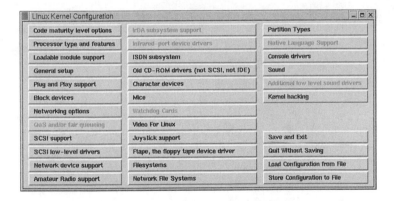

FIGURE 25.2

The X configurations mouse window.

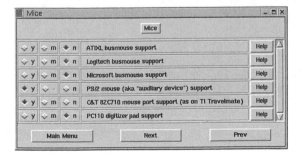

The last four menu items on the main screen are there for you to manage your configuration settings. You can save complete configurations and restore them later. This can be very handy if you want to experiment with different configuration settings, because you can save your basic configuration and just change the piece on which you are working.

Using the Batch Configuration Utility

The configuration settings are stored in the file /usr/src/linux/.config. There is a batch utility that can be used to apply the stored configuration:

```
make oldconfig
```

This command doesn't ask any questions. It just generates a complete configuration from the information stored in the file.

Setting Up the Dependencies

One of the results of defining the kernel configuration is that it also specifies which source is to be compiled and how things are to be linked. This is done automatically by changing to the /usr/src/linux directory and entering

```
make dep
```

There is nothing else you need to do. The process is entirely automatic. The actions taken are displayed in detail, so there is a lot of text scrolling up the screen as it runs. It builds its output from scratch, so you can run it more than once.

This command compiles and then runs a program called mkdep. This program searches through the source files to find out what is to be included and what is not. The process moves from one source code directory to another creating a file named .depend in each one of them. The .depend files contain a list of object file names and the header files that are included by it. It also creates the file /usr/src/linux/.hdepend that contains the header file dependencies—that is, the header files that are included by other header files.

The program has one very special capability. It recognizes the configuration definitions in config.h (normally, they are in autoconf.h) and uses them to decide which items should be included in the compilation and which should not. If, for example, CONFIG_MFP has been changed in the autoconf.h file, but no other changes were made, only programs actually using CONFIG_MFP will be recompiled.

Cleaning Up

The process of compiling and linking a new kernel creates a number of files. There is no need to do any cleanup the first time you build a kernel, but it would be a good idea if you build the kernel more than once. To make sure you are starting with a clean slate, enter

```
make clean
```

This is not so important with the newer versions of the kernel but, with any version, it does guarantee that your build will not include anything left over from a previous attempt—you will always get an absolutely new kernel.

There is another command that even does a more complete job of cleaning, but be careful how you use it:

```
make mrproper
```

The `mrproper` command does more of a "deep cleaning" than the `clean` command does. If you use `mrproper`, you will need to go all the way to defining the configuration and start over. Not only does this remove all the compiled programs, it removes the configuration settings, the dependencies, and everything else right back to the original distribution. This can be very useful if mysterious things are happening.

Building a New Kernel

There is more than one way to build and install the kernel. You can build one to be installed on your hard drive as the default boot kernel. You can also build one for a bootable floppy disk. You can also build a kernel for a system that uses LILO to manage booting multiple operating systems.

All of these things are done by using the `make` utility. For example, you could use the `make` utility to simply compile a new kernel just to verify that you get a clean compile. Once that is done, `make` can be used to create a bootable floppy disk and install the kernel on the hard drive. In fact, this is a reasonable sequence—it is probably a good idea to make sure your machine can use the kernel to boot from a floppy before you replace the one on your hard drive.

Compiling the Kernel

A kernel image file is produced with the following command:

```
make zImage
```

Depending on the size of the options you have chosen, it is possible that the kernel you are trying to produce is oversized. That is, the bootable portion of the kernel could be larger than the actual boot sector on disk. If this happens, use the following command instead:

```
make bzImage
```

The building process is quite verbose. Scrolling up on the screen is the name of every directory being entered and every file being compiled.

> **Note:** There is a lot of source code, and all this compilation takes time. Even on the fastest of machines, you should be prepared to wait for a few minutes for the entire thing to compile and link.

When Linux boots, it knows the location and the name of the kernel. To be able to boot your new kernel, you will have to replace the existing kernel with the new one.

> **Warning:** Don't be so quick to delete a kernel that works. A bad kernel could prevent the system from booting. Make a backup of the existing one before you delete it. Also, you should have a boot floppy that can be used to access the system to restore your backup. This way, you can get back into the system and fix things if need be.

A Boot Floppy

You can use the following command to build a kernel suitable for being booted from a floppy disk:

```
make zdisk
```

Although the same configuration settings can be used, there are some special options that are built into the build process—a floppy kernel is different from a normal kernel. As with the kernel for a hard drive, it is possible to produce a kernel too large for the boot sector. If this happens, use the following command to make a smaller one:

```
make bzdisk
```

The final step of this command is to copy the bootable image to the floppy disk, so, for this command to work, there must be a formatted floppy disk in the first drive. The two floppy drives are usually /dev/fd0 and /dev/fd1. Before a floppy drive can be accessed, you must configure the device node to match the hardware. For example, if your first floppy drive is a three-and-a-half inch 1.44MB floppy, the following command will configure the device node:

```
setfdprm -p /dev/fd0 1440/1440
```

If you have some other type of floppy drive, take a look a the file /etc/fdprm. This file holds configuration information for several different kinds of floppy disk drives.

A floppy disk can be formatted in the following way:

```
fdformat /dev/fd0
```

Once the disk is formatted, it can be addressed through the device name /dev/fd0.

The last thing done by either zdisk for bzdisk is to copy the kernel to the floppy disk. If you want to make other floppies using the same kernel, you can make a formatted floppy into a Linux bootable disk by simply copying the kernel to it, as shown in the following:

```
cp /usr/src/linux/arch/i386/boot/zImage /dev/fd0
```

Making an Installed Kernel

You can have the compilation process install and configure your new kernel if some basic requirements are met. Unless you have done something out of the ordinary, your system will have the correct setup. The LILO (Linux Loader) program must be /sbin/lilo, and it must have a configuration file named /etc/lilo.conf.

To create an install a new kernel, enter

```
make zlilo
```

And, as with the previous commands, if the created kernel turns out to be too large, use the following:

```
make bzlilo
```

The configuration file determines which kernel is to be used to boot the operating system. There are many options that can be included in the configuration file. The following is a typical default /etc/lilo.conf:

```
boot=/dev/hda
map=/boot/map
install=/boot/boot.b
prompt
timeout=50
image=/boot/vmlinuz-2.0.36-0.7
    label=linux
    root=/dev/hda1
    initrd=/boot/initrd-2.0.36-0.7.img
    read-only
```

Whenever you enter the lilo command, this file is used to produce a map file. The map is a file maintained by lilo that contains the name and location of the kernel or kernels to boot. In the following, the map file is /boot/map. The master boot record is on the disk partition /dev/hda. At boot time, the boot sector will be changed to /boot/boot.b.

Without the `prompt` option, the boot process continues without waiting for any user input. The `timeout` is the duration, in tenths of a second, that the boot process will wait for the user to select some image other than the first one in the list. After using `make zlilo`, you will need to edit `/etc/lilo.conf` to look something like the following:

```
boot=/dev/hda
map=/boot/map
install=/boot/boot.b
prompt
timeout=50
image=/vmlinuz
    label=linux
    root=/dev/hda1
image=/boot/vmlinuz-2.0.36-0.7
    label=2.0.36
    root=/dev/hda1
    initrd=/boot/initrd-2.0.36-0.7.img
    read-only
```

The `make zlilo` command installs the new kernel in the root directory as `vmlinuz`, so the default image (the first one in the list) is set to `/vmlinuz`. When the system starts to boot, it will prompt for the name of the image to be used for booting. You can enter the name of the image as either `linux` or `2.0.36`. If you do nothing, the default (the first image in the list) will be taken after the timeout expires. If you forget the name of the options, the tab key will cause a list of them to be displayed.

There is one more step before you can reboot. You must run `lilo`. The `lilo` command reads the contents of `/etc/lilo.conf` and uses the information to create a map file. It is the map file that is used during the boot sequence, not `lilo.conf`. To run `lilo`, enter the command with no arguments, as shown in the following:

```
lilo
```

Note: Having more than one bootable kernel configured into `lilo` is a safe way to compile and link a new kernel. Repeated use of `make zlilo` will simply replace `/vmlinux`. No `lilo` changes are necessary, and, if the something goes awry, you can always use one of the other options to get your system rebooted. As long as you can boot, you can get back in to fix any problems.

The Modules

Once you have compiled the kernel, it is time to consider the modules. If you made the choices that any parts of the kernel should be compiled as modules, you have to take a couple of extra steps. Modules are compiled and installed separately from the kernel.

This is because these modules can be recompiled and installed without changing the kernel. The following is the command to compile all the modules:

```
make modules
```

This compilation normally goes very quickly. The number of programs compiled is determined by the number of module options (the m selections) you made during configuration. After these programs are compiled, they can be installed with the following command:

```
make modules_install
```

> **Note:** If you have some piece of hardware that requires a special driver, the driver will probably be implemented as a module. Doing it this way has the advantage that a new driver can be installed dynamically without building a new kernel, but, if it is not being used, it can also be unloaded.

Summary

There are really very few steps involved with creating a new kernel from source. Once you have the source loaded, it is a matter of running one of the configuration utilities and then compiling the kernel. If you have done something about modules, you will also need to compile them. Once your compilation succeeds, the kernel can be installed. But make sure you have some other way to boot your system in case the new kernel fails.

On Your Own

If you want to get a copy of the latest, or even the experimental, version of the Linux kernel, the code can be found at www.kernel.org. There is also www.linux.org/dist/kernel.html which has quite a bit of documentation as well as links to the kernel source archives.

If you would like to become involved in a project porting the kernel to other platforms see www.linux.org/projects/ports.html.

One of the more useful and interesting capabilities of the Linux kernel is its ability to dynamically load drivers and other modules as necessary. For information on how this works and how you can use it, see http://metalab.unc.edu/LDP/HOWTO/mini/Kerneld.html.

Optimizing Linux

Optimizing Linux is something of a black art. There has been, up until recently, very little documentation in the way of optimizing Linux. Unless you were intimately familiar with the internals of the OS, the programs in question, or had learned through trial-and-error, you were in the dark.

All that has changed in the last year, thanks to the growing limelight Linux is enjoying and the need to demonstrate its superior performance against other operating systems. A wise man once said, "There are lies, damn lies, and then there are benchmarks." It is not difficult to optimize a system for a particular benchmark. However, that optimization usually is at the expense of some other area of system performance. The difficulty with optimization is getting a balanced fit for real world use.

The first step in making sure your Linux system is running at peak performance is to check that you are running the latest stable versions of software. This goes for the kernel all the way through daemons and user-level tools. Programmers are constantly at work improving their programs, so simply installing a new version can result in dramatic improvements in performance. The first area to consider is increasing performance overall for the benefit of the system users. This can mean tweaking the system in areas of file systems, kernel level tweaks, process optimization, and other areas. A good system administrator should make himself or herself familiar with some basic tools for monitoring performance under Linux. The first tool is called top. Shown in Figure 25.1, top monitors a variety of system areas such as memory, processes, and load.

FIGURE 25.1

A very useful tool to display system performance information is top.

For example, top can filter information to display the process using the most memory. It will also display CPU usage by process, and length of time the process has been running on the system. A sysadmin can kill off runaway processes or jobs that are hogging too many resources directly from top. Typing h while in top will bring up a help system. If you want to know more about where your system resources are going, get to know this program. Network-wise, a critical tool is tcpdump. This program will monitor a network interface and provide a thorough view of all network traffic going over it. In conjunction with other tools, you can determine if a performance problem is caused by faulty network configuration or an outside force wreaking havoc with your network. Syn Attacks (when someone sends thousands of invalid SYN "start connection" messages to the system) are a well-known way of bringing a system to its knees. There are other methods to attack a system in what is known as "denial of service" attacks. These problems can lead to performance degradation on a system to the point where no one can access it, and it must be restarted to be fixed.

Another great program for debugging running programs is strace. Just run strace from the command line and pass it the PID of the programs PID from top using strace -p PID. At this point, strace will display a dump of the programs calls as it is running. When it comes to performance monitoring, there are a host of programs from which to choose. If network performance is your concern, there is MRTG, The Multi Router Traffic Grapher. MRTG uses SNMP (the Simple Network Management Protocol) and Perl to monitor the traffic on your routers, as seen in Figure 25.2. The monitored data can be turned into very nice graphs for display. MRTG is written in Perl, which gives it a nice level of flexibility. Graphs can be broken out into a variety of areas such as daily, monthly, and so on. MRTG doesn't stop with router traffic. Because it is based on SNMP, any SNMP variable can be monitored and graphed. More information on MTRG can be found at `http://mrtg.hdl.com/mrtg.html`.

FIGURE 25.2
MTRG displays router traffic information for you in graph form.

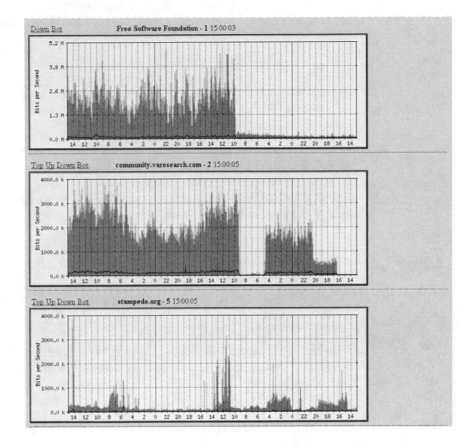

There are a variety of "realtime" programs that monitor stats in the `proc` filesystem. One of the best is `xosview`. This program displays a single window of updating graphs on things like load, swap, memory, and other areas of the system. There are many others, but `xosview` presents the most straightforward interface for keeping an eye on things. Other graphing programs are `perftool`, `perf` (a version of Sun's perf for Linux), `perfmon`, and a wealth of others. Pick one that you feel comfortable with and keep it running on your desktop. Many utilities like these and others may be included with your distribution, and others can be found by searching the Linux Software Map avalible at `http:/www.linux.org`.

The first step to a finely tuned system is to set up the hardware. Linux is very demanding of all aspects of the computer, so it is very important to start out buying the best components you can afford. For servers, focus on getting the best hardware in the areas of hard drive, RAM, motherboard, and CPU. If you are running a Linux workstation machine with you as the only user, you will want to get the best video card you can afford as well as a monitor. Note that depending on the use for your workstation (especially if you are running X), you will also want lots of RAM and a faster processor.

Start out by making sure you are running with the latest BIOS and firmware upgrades for all your hardware. Move from there to setting up your motherboard's BIOS. Some motherboards offer a ton of configuration options. To get an idea of what some of these options do, consult the manual or check out a good hardware Web site like Tom's Hardware Guide located at `http://sysdoc.pair.com`.

A utility called `hdparm` will let you set up your hard drives like a pro and give you substantial data on how Linux is set up to deal with your drive. There are a few tweaks you can perform to increase the performance of some IDE hard drives. If you have a EIDE drive, you can run `hdparm` to enable 32-bit I/O, which will increase data transfers. Simply run it from the command line, as shown in the following:

```
hdparm -c1 /dev/hda
```

This is setting up the first IDE hard drive. If you have others, run it again for their respective device names.

With UDMA IDE drives, the procedure is much the same:

```
hdparm -d1 /dev/hda
```

Some of the Linux kernels enable UDMA support by default, so running `hdparm` is not necessary. You can check on the drive's current configuration by running `hdparm` again, as shown in the following:

```
hdparm /dev/hda
```

This will show you information, such as if it is using DMA. If it doesn't look like DMA is enabled, go for it.

Another option available to you with `hdparn` is to set the get/set sector count for multiple sector I/O. This is done using the `-m` option with `hdparm`. Most drives will support the minimum settings of 2, 4, 8, or 16 sectors, and many will support 32 as well. This can result in a performance increase, but if your drive does not support it, it may lose data at some settings and result in filesystem corruption. For more information on options in `hdparam`, the man page contains useful information.

If you are trying to get maximum performance from a system, and this is especially important on server machines, you must get SCSI. IDE has the major drawback of using the CPU to do its work, but SCSI disk controllers have onboard chips to unload this work. Unfortunately, this raises the price of SCSI beyond some budgets. You will be much happier in the long run if you can get SCSI. SCSI can also handle many more drives,(15 on one controller) than IDE (4 drives total).

There are really no tweaks for SCSI similar to hdparm tricks. Controllers vary in the quality of hardware, and Linux drivers vary in completeness and support of the cards. Linux drivers focus on the controller chips themselves, so any vendor that uses a particular type of controller chip will usually be supported. Cards that use the NCR family of chips have long been favored by Linux users, as well as the Buslogic cards. Adaptec cards have been poorly supported in the past, but that is improving to the point where almost all Adaptec cards can be considered usable. Among the RAID card vendors, Mylex, DPT, and ICP/Vortex are well-supported cards. If you cannot afford a hardware RAID card, software RAID can be a reasonable option and one that can increase performance and reliability. There are several ways to set up for SoftwareRAID; check the HOWTO at http://metalab.unc.edu/LDP/HOWTO/mini/Software-RAID.html for full details. Software RAID can be used on IDE disks as well as SCSI and can really boost performance for IDE. Two cheap IDE disks running SoftwareRAID can be a very cost-effective solution for a tight budget.

Once you have decided on a disk setup, there are many considerations that can have an impact on performance and stability later. The main one is determining the type of work the system is going to be used for and then partitioning the drive accordingly. For server systems, getting a good partitioning scheme is essential. Most server applications, such as Web server, can benefit from a few good choices. A Web server puts many files into the /var partition. You can optimize the partition by moving it onto the fastest drive, if you have several, or even on a drive by itself. Mirroring the /var partition across two drives can ensure stability. There are also tweaks you can make to the filesystem during partitioning to squeeze a bit of performance out of individual partitions. If you are going to have a lot of large files, you might consider making the filesystem with the following command;

```
mke2fs -b 4096 /dev/hd*
```

where hd is your IDE drive or with /dev/sd* for some SCSI drive. This increases the block size with which the filesystem is made. When you run mke2fs without -b, it defaults to a block size of 1,024.

CPU optimization involves nothing more that making the right choice. There are many CPU models out there that run Linux, and picking the right one can give adequate performance while saving you money. If your machine's main function is going to be Web surfing, reading email, and basic application use, a cheap, low-end CPU will do the job. If you have picked an IDE, a slower CPU will feel the hit. In a low-cost machine, you will have to carefully balance the components to get the performance you want. If you settle on a lower-speed CPU, choose a UDMA IDE or other IDE drive that unloads work from the CPU, or choose a SCSI disk subsystem. If you get a nice fast CPU, you can cut costs by adding an IDE drive over SCSI. Most modern OSs hit the disk quite a bit more than the maximum power of the CPU. Linux uses the disk for virtual memory and does a lot of logging while it's running. You can add memory to decrease the amount of time that the system spends swapping to disk. Unless you are using your Linux machine to do heavy mathematical operations, such as financial or scientific applications, a high-end CPU will be more money that it's worth. Some CPUs also deliver higher performance when they have faster floating point or bigger cache sizes. A database application, for example, will benefit from a larger L2 cache; so will some scientific applications that can load bigger chunks of data into the faster cache than swapping in from disk. Faster floating point CPUs will aid in speeding up applications that utilize floating point arithmetic. Again, these are typically science and financial programs.

Another area to consider is multiple CPUs. Linux can utilize more than one CPU, the actual number depending on the platform you are running. For example, Linux can run on 8-way machines on Intel systems. Sun's can handle more than 8, and Linux can take advantage of up to 16 on any platform. Although you can modify the kernel to handle more, it is not advised that you run your Linux system with this configuration with the current versions of the kernel. While the kernel itself uses multiple CPUs by forking out a process to one or the other, applications need to be written to specifically take advantage of more than one processor. Using programming libraries, you can take advantage of multiple CPU systems. There are three main packages for doing this: LinuxThreads, PVM/MPI, and the plain old fork. LinuxThreads is a Linux implementation of Pthreads and provides shared memory for the threads and other advanced features. PVM/MPI is a package to implement parallel processing over several machines, harnessing all their CPUs for supercomputer-like performance. Almost any programmer is familiar with fork, and it can be used in the same way as any other UNIX system. Using multiple CPUs can sometimes increase performance, but more readily will increase response time.

Another area to consider, albeit very carefully, is overclocking of CPUs. Mainly, the AMD K6s and Intel celerons are capable of overclocking, and you must buy a motherboard that supports these alterations, although there are some hardware hacks that can be done to get around motherboard limits. AMD and Intel do not officially support overclocking, and Intel has taken steps to prevent it. Keep this in mind when attempting to overclock processors to squeeze that last bit of performance. While the issue of overclocking is too detailed to go into here, the Web is a good place to look for information.

- http://www.hardocp.com/   The Overclockers Comparison Page—An excellent source for overclocking just about any piece of hardware.

- http://www.aceshardware.com/   Ace's Hardware—Great hardware review site with overclocking tips and more.

- http://www.arstechnica.com/index.html   Ars Technica—Another all around fantastic site for hardware tips for the PC hobbyist.

- http://www.tomshardware.com/   Tom's Hardware Guide—The granddaddy of Web hardware review sites. Tom is the guy who finds the bugs Intel can't find themselves. Great stuff.

There are a lot more tips and tricks for tweaking hardware, too many to cover in one chapter. The previously listed Web sites are tremendous resources for getting the most out of your hardware to run Linux.

Optimizing the Kernel

Moving on from hardware-related optimization, let's get to the heart of running Linux at its best—the kernel. The first place you want to start is how you compile the kernel. The Linux kernel can be compiled to target different CPU types and use the correct optimizations for each. When running make config, the first option should ask you what "processor family" to which you want to target. The entries should look something like the following:

PPro/6x86MX

Choose which processor type fits the one you have. Another config time option to choose is MTRR. This will enable write-combining features, if available, and increase performance. Make sure you are enabling all the features of your SCSI card or IDE devices if possible, and disable any hardware drivers for stuff you don't have. If nothing else, this will decrease the size of the kernel and result in some slight memory gains. Enabling all the features of your drive controllers can significantly increase performance, as will using the right driver. There are some drivers that generically support a particular piece of hardware and some that support it specifically. For example, there are drivers for the NCR family of SCSI controllers. There is a generic driver that supports all the cards that use a particular chip. For instance, there is a generic NCR 8xx driver that supports a variety of cards from several manufacturers. There are also some specific drivers that support cards that use the NCR8xx chips and enable other vendor-specific features, as on the Symbios SCSI controllers. Check to make sure you are using the driver targeted for your hardware, and enable the kernel options available during configuration.

When you get to actually compiling a kernel, run it with make -j 5. This enables make to run several things at once and take full advantage on available system resources. Of course, this will slow things down for everything and everybody else if you are on a multiuser box.

Compiling any program with the gcc option of -06 will turn on all optimizations for that platform. This increases the size of the binaries, but also increases performance for the program. The kernel is no exception, and it will benefit from using full optimization of gcc. Most distributions are precluded from shipping a fully-optimized kernel and programs for obvious compatibility reasons. One distribution, Linux Mandrake, compiles its kernel and applications targeted for the Pentium family of CPUs. This includes Pentiums 1-3, AMD K6-K6-2, and Cyrix chips. The Linux Mandrake page claims a 5–30 percent speed increase.

Check the gcc main page for further details about the various compiler options available. For instance, running gcc with the --march=xtypeCPU will turn on everything gcc knows to optimize for that CPU.

Enabling profiling in the kernel can help you determine where the kernel is spending most of its energy. Profiling can be enabled by editing the lilo.conf file with the following line;

```
append="profile=2"
```

Verify that the System.map file matches the kernel you are using, or this will break many things. Then use the readprofile command to see what your kernel is doing.

Network Optimizations

Once you have a nice optimized kernel, tuning the network is another great way to optimize Linux. Because Linux is used primarily in server environments, an incorrectly set up network can seriously limit performance.

First, pick the right hardware for the job. Most systems today use 10/100baseT ethernet. This is usually adequate for just about any machine. It is important to note that you will get more performance out of a PCI-based Ethernet card versus an older ISA card due to the available bandwidth. If you are expecting a heavy network load, you might consider getting a gigabit ethernet card and switch. This costs more than 10/100, but the prices are coming down. Picking the best hubs, routers, and switches you can find will also help. If you are running IPv4, there are three options that can increase performance: TCP_Timestaps, TCP_windowscaling, and TCP_sack. For regular Internet connections, turning these options on can increase performance. For internal company networks, it probably do little good.

There is more through documentation on tweaking these parameters at http://www.psc.edu/networking/perf_tune.html#Linux.

The following sections will cover two of the major network applications: Apache and Sendmail. many people will tell you not to use Sendmail for the maximum performance of your mail server, because there are now more than adequate replacements for it. If you can get away with not using Sendmail, consider Qmail or Exim. You can find information about them at www.exim.org and www.qmail.org.

Sendmail can run as a daemon in the background, or as a program that gets run anytime you want to send some mail. Clearly, the most convenient and efficient method is running Sendmail as a daemon.

Sendmail uses a configuration file called sendmail.cf. This program can grow to be quite large, depending on the features you have enabled. Sendmail must parse this file when it runs, so going through the file and enabling only the features you need will result in some modest performance gains.

Apache is the second major program that can benefit from tweaking. Web serving is a high-bandwith operation and can sap the resources of your machine if not configured correctly.

A lot of Web server work involves dynamic content that is generated by CGI scripts. Apache handles the standard method of running Perl every time a CGI script invokes it. You can increase performance if you use the Apache module feature. This will load Perl as a module that gets built into Apache itself, resulting in a slower latency time for running scripts. Because the scripts are cached and the Perl interpreter is always running, you should see a performance improvement in response time. More information on mod_perl can be found at http://perl.apache.org.

Apache developer Dean Gaudet has written an excellent document on how to achieve better performance from Apache and can be read at http://www.apache.org/docs/misc/perf-tuning.html.

Linux changes all the time, and new performance tweaks are coming out with each new release of the kernel and applications. A good resource for keeping up to date with current tips and tricks is Linux.com. Its Tuning Linux section can be found at http://www.linus.com/tuneup/.

Summary

We have covered many different ways to optimize your Linux box and squeeze as much performance as possible out of the hardware you have. Using the analysis tools that are available to you, such as top and MRTG, and the tips that were discussed here can make a dramatic improvement in your system. However, you must also be careful when you start pushing the limit on your hardware. Some hardware does not support advanced modes or tweaks and these could result in hardware (or system) failure. What was discussed in this chapter is by no means all you can do to improve system performance. There are many user groups, Web sites, and mailing lists that talk about the many ways you can do this as well.

On Your Own

Use the tools such as top, tcpdump, strace, and xosview to monitor your system for potential bottlenecks and slowdowns. Determine if there is anything you can reconfigure on any found devices to increase your system's performance by using tips found here or on any Internet resource.

PART VII

Appendixes

A

The GNU License

Richard Stallman founded the GNU (GNU's Not UNIX) project in 1984 with the purpose of developing a free operating system. The operating system work became popular as the various utility programs became public. Over the years, the GNU project has produced a large number of useful utilities. To the surprise of many people, the open source development method is producing excellent software. The Emacs editor has been adopted by thousands of programmers, and the C/C++ compiler is considered to be one of the best in existence. The C/C++ compiler is now runs on more than 30 operating systems.

While the GNU utilities were becoming more respected and more widespread, there was still no operating system kernel in the early 1990s. Enter Linus Torvalds. He wrote an operating system kernel and combined it with the existing GNU tools and utilities, and Linux was born.

The GNU project prefers the term "free software," but many people are using the term "open source" to mean the same thing.

The term "free" has two meanings. In the GNU sense, it means freedom, not necessarily "without cost." You may or may not pay to get your copy of GNU software, but, once you have it, you have these freedoms:

- The freedom to run the program for any purpose
- The freedom to study how the program works and adapt it to your needs
- The freedom to redistribute copies so you can help your neighbor
- The freedom to improve the program and release your improvements to the public, so the whole community benefits

Along with the freedom to do anything you want with the software, there is also the limitation that you can do nothing to restrict anyone else's free use of it. All the freedoms and limitations are specified in the GNU General Public License. Its complete text follows.

GNU GENERAL PUBLIC LICENSE

Version 2, June 1991

Copyright (C) 1989, 1991 Free Software Foundation, Inc.

675 Mass Ave, Cambridge, MA 02139, USA

Everyone is permitted to copy and distribute verbatim copies of this license document, but changing it is not allowed.

Preamble

The licenses for most software are designed to take away your freedom to share and change it. By contrast, the GNU General Public License is intended to guarantee your freedom to share and change free software—to make sure the software is free for all its users. This General Public License applies to most of the Free Software Foundation's software and to any other program whose authors commit to using it. (Some other Free Software Foundation software is covered by the GNU Library General Public License instead.) You can apply it to your programs, too.

When we speak of free software, we are referring to freedom, not price. Our General Public Licenses are designed to make sure that you have the freedom to distribute copies of free software (and charge for this service if you wish), that you receive source code or can get it if you want it, that you can change the software or use pieces of it in new free programs; and that you know you can do these things.

To protect your rights, we need to make restrictions that forbid anyone to deny you these rights or to ask you to surrender the rights. These restrictions translate to certain responsibilities for you if you distribute copies of the software, or if you modify it.

For example, if you distribute copies of such a program, whether gratis or for a fee, you must give the recipients all the rights that you have. You must make sure that they, too, receive or can get the source code. And you must show them these terms so they know their rights.

We protect your rights with two steps: (1) copyright the software, and (2) offer you this license which gives you legal permission to copy, distribute and/or modify the software.

Also, for each author's protection and ours, we want to make certain that everyone understands that there is no warranty for this free software. If the software is modified by someone else and passed on, we want its recipients to know that what they have is not the original, so that any problems introduced by others will not reflect on the original authors' reputations.

Finally, any free program is threatened constantly by software patents. We wish to avoid the danger that redistributors of a free program will individually obtain patent licenses, in effect making the program proprietary. To prevent this, we have made it clear that any patent must be licensed for everyone's free use or not licensed at all.

The precise terms and conditions for copying, distribution and modification follow.

GNU GENERAL PUBLIC LICENSE TERMS AND CONDITIONS FOR COPYING, DISTRIBUTION AND MODIFICATION

0. This License applies to any program or other work which contains a notice placed by the copyright holder saying it may be distributed under the terms of this General Public License. The "Program", below, refers to any such program or work, and a "work based on the Program" means either the Program or any derivative work under copyright law: that is to say, a work containing the Program or a portion of it, either verbatim or with modifications and/or translated into another language. (Hereinafter, translation is included without limitation in the term "modification".) Each licensee is addressed as "you".

   Activities other than copying, distribution and modification are not covered by this License; they are outside its scope. The act of running the Program is not restricted, and the output from the Program is covered only if its contents constitute a work based on the Program (independent of having been made by running the Program). Whether that is true depends on what the Program does.

1. You may copy and distribute verbatim copies of the Program's source code as you receive it, in any medium, provided that you conspicuously and appropriately publish on each copy an appropriate copyright notice and disclaimer of warranty; keep intact all the notices that refer to this License and to the absence of any warranty; and give any other recipients of the Program a copy of this License along with the Program.

   You may charge a fee for the physical act of transferring a copy, and you may at your option offer warranty protection in exchange for a fee.

2. You may modify your copy or copies of the Program or any portion of it, thus forming a work based on the Program, and copy and distribute such modifications or work under the terms of Section 1 above, provided that you also meet all of these conditions:

   a) You must cause the modified files to carry prominent notices stating that you changed the files and the date of any change.

   b) You must cause any work that you distribute or publish, that in whole or in part contains or is derived from the Program or any part thereof, to be licensed as a whole at no charge to all third parties under the terms of this License.

   c) If the modified program normally reads commands interactively when run, you must cause it, when started running for such interactive use in the most ordinary way, to print or display an announcement including an appropriate copyright notice and a notice that there is no warranty (or else, saying that you provide a warranty) and that users may redistribute the program under these conditions, and telling the user how to view a copy of this License. (Exception: if the Program itself is interactive but does not normally print such an announcement, your work based on the Program is not required to print an announcement.)

These requirements apply to the modified work as a whole. If identifiable sections of that work are not derived from the Program, and can be reasonably considered independent and separate works in themselves, then this License, and its terms, do not apply to those sections when you distribute them as separate works. But when you distribute the same sections as part of a whole which is a work based on the Program, the distribution of the whole must be on the terms of this License, whose permissions for other licensees extend to the entire whole, and thus to each and every part regardless of who wrote it. Thus, it is not the intent of this section to claim rights or contest your rights to work written entirely by you; rather, the intent is to exercise the right to control the distribution of derivative or collective works based on the Program.

In addition, mere aggregation of another work not based on the Program with the Program (or with a work based on the Program) on a volume of a storage or distribution medium does not bring the other work under the scope of this License.

3. You may copy and distribute the Program (or a work based on it, under Section 2) in object code or executable form under the terms of Sections 1 and 2 above provided that you also do one of the following:

    a) Accompany it with the complete corresponding machine-readable source code, which must be distributed under the terms of Sections 1 and 2 above on a medium customarily used for software interchange; or,

    b) Accompany it with a written offer, valid for at least three years, to give any third party, for a charge no more than your cost of physically performing source distribution, a complete machine-readable copy of the corresponding source code, to be distributed under the terms of Sections 1 and 2 above on a medium customarily used for software interchange; or,

    c) Accompany it with the information you received as to the offer to distribute corresponding source code. (This alternative is allowed only for noncommercial distribution and only if you received the program in object code or executable form with such an offer, in accord with Subsection b above.)

    The source code for a work means the preferred form of the work for making modifications to it. For an executable work, complete source code means all the source code for all modules it contains, plus any associated interface definition files, plus the scripts used to control compilation and installation of the executable. However, as a special exception, the source code distributed need not include anything that is normally distributed (in either source or binary form) with the major components (compiler, kernel, and so on) of the operating system on which the executable runs, unless that component itself accompanies the executable.

    If distribution of executable or object code is made by offering access to copy from a designated place, then offering equivalent access to copy the source code from the same place counts as distribution of the source code, even though third parties are not compelled to copy the source along with the object code.

4. You may not copy, modify, sublicense, or distribute the Program except as expressly provided under this License. Any attempt otherwise to copy, modify, sublicense or distribute the Program is void, and will automatically terminate your rights under this License. However, parties who have received copies, or rights, from you under this License will not have their licenses terminated so long as such parties remain in full compliance.

5. You are not required to accept this License, since you have not signed it. However, nothing else grants you permission to modify or distribute the Program or its derivative works. These actions are prohibited by law if you do not accept this License. Therefore, by modifying or distributing the Program (or any work based on the Program), you indicate your acceptance of this License to do so, and all its terms and conditions for copying, distributing or modifying the Program or works based on it.

6. Each time you redistribute the Program (or any work based on the Program), the recipient automatically receives a license from the original licensor to copy, distribute or modify the Program subject to these terms and conditions. You may not impose any further restrictions on the recipients' exercise of the rights granted herein. You are not responsible for enforcing compliance by third parties to this License.

7. If, as a consequence of a court judgment or allegation of patent infringement or for any other reason (not limited to patent issues), conditions are imposed on you (whether by court order, agreement or otherwise) that contradict the conditions of this License, they do not excuse you from the conditions of this License. If you cannot distribute so as to satisfy simultaneously your obligations under this License and any other pertinent obligations, then as a consequence you may not distribute the Program at all. For example, if a patent license would not permit royalty-free redistribution of the Program by all those who receive copies directly or indirectly through you, then the only way you could satisfy both it and this License would be to refrain entirely from distribution of the Program.

If any portion of this section is held invalid or unenforceable under any particular circumstance, the balance of the section is intended to apply and the section as a whole is intended to apply in other circumstances.

It is not the purpose of this section to induce you to infringe any patents or other property right claims or to contest validity of any such claims; this section has the sole purpose of protecting the integrity of the free software distribution system, which is implemented by public license practices. Many people have made generous contributions to the wide range of software distributed through that system in reliance on consistent application of that system; it is up to the author/donor to decide if he or she is willing to distribute software through any other system and a licensee cannot impose that choice.

This section is intended to make thoroughly clear what is believed to be a consequence of the rest of this License.

8. If the distribution and/or use of the Program is restricted in certain countries either by patents or by copyrighted interfaces, the original copyright holder who places the Program under this License may add an explicit geographical distribution limitation excluding those countries, so that distribution is permitted only in or among countries not thus excluded. In such case, this License incorporates the limitation as if written in the body of this License.

9. The Free Software Foundation may publish revised and/or new versions of the General Public License from time to time. Such new versions will be similar in spirit to the present version, but may differ in detail to address new problems or concerns.

    Each version is given a distinguishing version number. If the Program specifies a version number of this License which applies to it and "any later version", you have the option of following the terms and conditions either of that version or of any later version published by the Free Software Foundation. If the Program does not specify a version number of this License, you may choose any version ever published by the Free Software Foundation.

10. If you wish to incorporate parts of the Program into other free programs whose distribution conditions are different, write to the author to ask for permission. For software which is copyrighted by the Free Software Foundation, write to the Free Software Foundation; we sometimes make exceptions for this. Our decision will be guided by the two goals of preserving the free status of all derivatives of our free software and of promoting the sharing and reuse of software generally.

NO WARRANTY

11. BECAUSE THE PROGRAM IS LICENSED FREE OF CHARGE, THERE IS NO WARRANTY FOR THE PROGRAM, TO THE EXTENT PERMITTED BY APPLICABLE LAW. EXCEPT WHEN OTHERWISE STATED IN WRITING THE COPYRIGHT HOLDERS AND/OR OTHER PARTIES PROVIDE THE PROGRAM "AS IS" WITHOUT WARRANTY OF ANY KIND, EITHER EXPRESSED OR IMPLIED, INCLUDING, BUT NOT LIMITED TO, THE IMPLIED WARRANTIES OF MERCHANTABILITY AND FITNESS FOR A PARTICULAR PURPOSE. THE ENTIRE RISK AS TO THE QUALITY AND PERFORMANCE OF THE PROGRAM IS WITH YOU. SHOULD THE PROGRAM PROVE DEFECTIVE, YOU ASSUME THE COST OF ALL NECESSARY SERVICING, REPAIR OR CORRECTION.

12. IN NO EVENT UNLESS REQUIRED BY APPLICABLE LAW OR AGREED TO IN WRITING WILL ANY COPYRIGHT HOLDER, OR ANY OTHER PARTY WHO MAY MODIFY AND/OR REDISTRIBUTE THE PROGRAM AS PERMITTED ABOVE, BE LIABLE TO YOU FOR DAMAGES, INCLUDING ANY GENERAL, SPECIAL, INCIDENTAL OR CONSEQUENTIAL DAMAGES ARISING OUT OF THE USE OR INABILITY TO USE THE PROGRAM (INCLUDING BUT NOT LIMITED TO LOSS OF DATA OR DATA BEING

RENDERED INACCURATE OR LOSSES SUSTAINED BY YOU OR THIRD PARTIES OR A FAILURE OF THE PROGRAM TO OPERATE WITH ANY OTHER PROGRAMS), EVEN IF SUCH HOLDER OR OTHER PARTY HAS BEEN ADVISED OF THE POSSIBILITY OF SUCH DAMAGES.

END OF TERMS AND CONDITIONS

Appendix: How to Apply These Terms to Your New Programs

If you develop a new program, and you want it to be of the greatest possible use to the public, the best way to achieve this is to make it free software which everyone can redistribute and change under these terms.

To do so, attach the following notices to the program. It is safest to attach them to the start of each source file to most effectively convey the exclusion of warranty; and each file should have at least the "copyright" line and a pointer to where the full notice is found.

> <one line to give the program's name and a brief idea of what it does.> Copyright (C) 19yy
>
> <name of author>
>
> This program is free software; you can redistribute it and/or modify it under the terms of the GNU General Public License as published by the Free Software Foundation; either version 2 of the License, or (at your option) any later version.
>
> This program is distributed in the hope that it will be useful, but WITHOUT ANY WARRANTY; without even the implied warranty of MERCHANTABILITY or FITNESS FOR A PARTICULAR PURPOSE. See the GNU General Public License for more details.
>
> You should have received a copy of the GNU General Public License along with this program; if not, write to the Free Software Foundation, Inc., 675 Mass Ave, Cambridge, MA 02139, USA.

Also add information on how to contact you by electronic and paper mail.

If the program is interactive, make it output a short notice like this when it starts in an interactive mode:

> Gnomovision version 69, Copyright (C) 19yy name of author Gnomovision comes with ABSOLUTELY NO WARRANTY; for details type `show w'. This is free software, and you are welcome to redistribute it under certain conditions; type `show c' for details.

The hypothetical commands `show w' and `show c' should show the appropriate parts of the General Public License. Of course, the commands you use may be called something other than `show w' and `show c'; they could even be mouse-clicks or menu items—whatever suits your program.

You should also get your employer (if you work as a programmer) or your school, if any, to sign a "copyright disclaimer" for the program, if necessary. Here is a sample; alter the names:

> Yoyodyne, Inc., hereby disclaims all copyright interest in the program `Gnomovision' (which makes passes at compilers) written by James Hacker.

> <signature of Ty Coon>, 1 April 1989
> Ty Coon, President of Vice

This General Public License does not permit incorporating your program into proprietary programs. If your program is a subroutine library, you may consider it more useful to permit linking proprietary applications with the library. If this is what you want to do, use the GNU Library General Public License instead of this License.

The Open Source Definition

The idea of open source software is not new. To some degree, programmers have been sharing code since programming began. Somewhere along the way, almost all software became proprietary—all you could get was the executable form of the program, leaving you at the mercy of the vendor. It was up to the vendor to decide whether to fix a bug, add a feature, update the software, or make it work with some other piece of software. Thousands of software customers have been trapped in the situation where the software vendor went out of business, leaving them with no support whatsoever and no possibility of ever having the bugs fixed.

In the early 1990s, the trend away from open source began to reverse itself. Primarily thanks to Linux, by the beginning of 1999, there was acceptance of open source software in hundreds of businesses around the world. The main reason: Open source software is being found to be superior to proprietary software.

Software stored and distributed as open source code will evolve over time. The bugs will be found and fixed, enhancements will be made, and its ease-of-use will increase.

It turns out that open source software is not free. You will wind up paying for it with time and effort. If you start using some open source utility program, and you find a little something that you would prefer to work differently, you'll realize that you have the source and can just change the way it works. So you make the change, start using the updated version, and share a copy of your modified source with the rest of the world. The thought and work you did to make the change is how you wind up paying your way.

Open Source Software Evolves

Open software is high quality and is developed at an astonishing rate. This happens through an evolutionary process.

How many times have you used some utility and wished you could add just one little thing (like a different display format or an option to filter out some things)? If you are working with open source, you can make the changes to your copy. You can then share your updated version with the rest of the world. Some other person may see a better approach to your idea and, after making a modification, the newly updated version is shared and you get a copy. At this point, not only do have what you wanted to have, but it is done better than you originally thought.

I saw this evolve through the GNU C and C++ compiler. The project began with the basic compiler structures (lexical scan, symbol tables, code generation, and so on). There were compiler writers all over the world who decided to contribute their best to the compiler. For example, one may have worked out a masterful way to handle symbol tables, and another may have had some real nifty code generation techniques, while another may have worked out some very smart optimization algorithms. This process continued, causing the compiler to be written by the best of the best—worldwide. There is no way that any one company can compete with that level of expertise.

The larger the problem, the more resources are applied to its solution. If the problem is that a certain option combination fails on some small utility, someone will work on that when he or she gets around to it. At the opposite extreme, a large problem has an effect on more people, so there are automatically more resources applied to it. Sure, some of the effort will be duplicated, but having more than one person work on a program stabilizes it, increasing the likelihood of it being correct.

With proprietary software, all you can do is ask the software vendor whether or not the software is Y2K compliant. He will either say, "Yes," or he will say, "No, but we have some new stuff we can sell you." The vendor fixes its own software and you pay for it.

Business

Why would a business want to use open software? There are a number of reasons. Here are the main ones.

Software needs to be reliable. It should do its job without crashing, and it should be dependable enough to do the right thing when it does run. This does not always happen with commercial software because it is developed by a room full of people doing their best to meet a deadline. Have you ever heard of a software project that came in early? "Just go ahead and ship it. We can fix it with an update later."

There will be much more security with open source than with a proprietary system. Finding a security leak is not a trial task. With open software, hundreds, or even thousands, of eyes will go over the code trying to find security loopholes.

When there is a software fix, it can be installed right away. There is no need to wait until the next release of something. If you don't need an update, skip it. There is no need to replace software that is working.

There are any number of ways to make a profit from the appropriate use of open source software. Companies are doing it now.

- There are companies that are in the business of packaging, selling, and supporting open source software. Most notable among these are Red Hat and Caldera with their Linux packages. The main product here is support; making it as easy as possible for the user. In fact, this must be done if Linux is to reach beyond the programming community.

- There are a lot of books to be published and Web sites to be designed that explain how the software is used. The information about open source software is all available, but it is not necessarily organized in a useful manner.

- The software can be treated as loss leader to attract potential customers for other business. Giving away something of value causes word of mouth to spread—the best kind of advertising in the world. This is what Netscape has done with its Web browser.

- There are computer peripherals that require the presence of a software driver to operate. Companies that manufacture hardware can profit greatly by publishing device drivers as open source. Not only will the programming community find and fix bugs, but they will also port the device driver to other operating systems, which will widen the market for the device itself.

- For the non-programming customer, there is a growing market for computers with pre-installed open source systems.

Speed and Support

Open source software is developed faster and better. There are reasons for this:

- Quite often a software developer joins a team of volunteers working on an open source project because the developer wants to have the software for his or her own use. You can see where a programmer might be interested in adding specific and useful features to a debugger or text editor, but this is also true of graphic editors and word processors.

- Another reason a software developer joins an open source project is because he has some level of expertise in one or more areas that apply to the software being developed. Because of this, it turns out that large pieces of the software are hand-crafted by experts.

- The size of the staff is in direct proportion to the size of the project. The various parts of the program are divided among as many programmers as necessary to get the job done—not too few and not too many. A software project requires a very small team at the beginning and the end, with a big bulge in the middle where the maximum number of programmers is required. With open source development, the size of the staff changes as the software development process requires. The current methods used to manage commercial and proprietary software projects simply cannot do this.

- Small companies can proceed with large software projects. No longer are staffing constraints a limiting factor.

- No software project thinks of everything. There are always necessary options and features that, during the initial design phase, no one thinks of. The more people involved in the development, the fewer pieces will drop through the cracks.

- Nobody is stuck for an answer to a question for very long. If a programmer reaches an impasse, it is a matter of asking a question on the Internet and filtering out the answers that come back. Most of these inquiry responses are from experts in the field so, here again, the software is designed and developed to be the very best.

- There is no way to develop software faster than with open source. An enormous pool of talent (the whole world) can be called on to work on each piece of the software. The development process runs continuously—all day and all night.

- Another reason open source development goes so fast is that it is so much easier to debug. There is nothing worse than calling some function in a proprietary library and discovering, usually after a time-consuming search-and-test mission, that the bug is somewhere in the binary code. It can't be changed so it must be lived with. If a workaround does not present itself, the time has come to re-invent the wheel. Again.

- It is very easy to fix bugs. If a bug is discovered and reported, it is most likely the developer of the software, or someone who knows the software and supports it, will address the bug and fix it. The expertise does not "leave the company" forcing someone to learn the software enough to apply a patch.

- The test cycle turns things around fast. People start using the software the moment you say it is ready, and your early returns are (invariably) bug reports and criticisms of the interface. You can fix these quickly, very early in the release process, and supply a corrected version immediately. Most users will never see any of the early problems.

- Upgrades happen. If there is a program out there that is showing its age and it just doesn't do everything it should, a new program will be written to replace it. Sometimes it is written as another mode or option to the existing program, sometimes it is a replacement program, and sometimes it is a new program with a different name.

- There is a certain degree of portability guaranteed by open source development. With several different developers involved, the software must be portable enough to run without problems on several different computers. In some cases, this is all the same version of the same operating system, but in other cases, it is multiple operating systems on different hardware.

- If something has already been programmed, there is really no need to do it again. The same code can be used again and again. There has always been the concept that computer hardware is more advanced than software—it is because hardware designers are able to stand on the shoulders of those who came before. It has been theorized that software can be built the same way by using well-documented binary libraries of routines. This works only in rare instances (the FORTRAN math library and the C system library seem to be the only ones). It seems that every time you need to use pre-written software, there are just one or two tweaks you need to make. You can make those tweaks if the source is open, otherwise you will spend your time producing a new wheel.

- Using the open source model to develop software is cheaper than any other way. It isn't without cost (because it is paid for with time, effort, and computer facilities), but there are enormous economies. For one thing, the number of staff on the project automatically adjusts to fit the amount of work. The quality of the software reduces the time spent on bug fixing.

Software Isn't Like That

Software is different from anything else in your experience. It has certain attributes in common with other things in your world, but there is nothing quite like it. It brings to mind a physics description of the nature of light—experts coined the word wavicle. Sometimes light acts like a wave, and sometimes it acts like a particle. Sometimes software acts like a published book or pamphlet, sometimes it acts like a service or a tool, and sometimes it acts like a physical object.

There have been any number of cases where software was looked at as a published work. This is the copyright idea. The idea is that the source code itself is the program, and anyone copying all or part of the source code is stealing the program. There are some problems with this idea. First, it is very easy to copy source code, make name changes, and put a few things in slightly different order. Only an expert, after studying the changed code for a long time, can determine whether the source has been copied. Second, it is not unusual for two programmers, working independently, to devise the same algorithm to do the same job.

Software can be thought of as a service—you buy the right to use the software, in a specifically limited manner, for a specific number of people. You don't buy the software—all you get for your money is the right to use it. Bugs and all. When software is supplied as a service, the customer is trapped into taking what the vendor is willing to supply.

The U.S. patent office treats software as if it were a physical object. All you have to do is look around for some algorithm, name it something unique, come up with a unique description for it, and you can patent it. It doesn't seem to matter how simple or basic the idea is. There are thousands and thousands of these patents. Did you know there is a patent for storing screen pixel values in memory? Whether the technology exists, or is even in common use, doesn't seem to have an affect on the process.

Some Terminology

There is a lot of variation in the amount of freedom involved in developing software. At one extreme, there is the open source model that makes software freely available to everyone. At the other extreme is commercial proprietary software that requires that the user pay for a license, and only the binaries are delivered to the user. These are some terms used to describe various kinds of software.

- *Open source software.*   This is software that comes with source code and permission to use, copy, distribute (modified or unmodified) either with no cost or for a distribution fee. This is also called free software. The word "free" refers to the user's freedom of access to the software, not the cost. This is the model used by GNU and Linux, but it is possible to have open source software that is not licensed under GNU.

- *Free software.*   This term is commonly used to mean the same thing as open source software. In fact, the term open source is probably better than free software because it implies that the source code is included with the distribution. This term is often misused to refer to a freely distributed binary-only program, but that is a different thing.

- *Public domain software.*   This is software that does not carry a copyright. Source code may or may not be included. Even if source code is included, there is nothing to prevent someone from making modifications and distributing the new version without source code. In fact, new versions could become commercial and proprietary.

- *Copyleft.*   Software that is copylefted is free software with specific restrictions on distribution: anyone making modifications and redistributing the software cannot add any restrictions. Every copy, even the ones that have been modified, must be free software. The copyleft concept comes from GNU.

- *General Public License (GPL).*   This is the name of the GNU license laying out the terms for copylefting software.

- *GNU software.*   Software released under the auspices of the GNU project is called GNU software. Most, but not all, of the software is copylefted, but it is all free software. Some is copyrighted. It is written by the staff of the Free Software Foundation and by volunteers.

- *Semi-free software.*   This is software that can be freely distributed and used, but it cannot be used for commercial purposes without a license fee being paid.

- *Non-copylefted free software.*   If software can be freely distributed and normal distribution includes the source code, but there is no restriction on redistribution, it is a special case of free software that can be used in a proprietary way. Probably the best example of this is the X Consortium, which freely distributes X11 but does not limit how it is used. Anyone can get the free version, modify it to work with a specific piece of hardware, and then treat the new version as a commercial product by charging license fees.

- *Proprietary software.* This software has been copyrighted, and the copyright is likely to be enforced. It almost never comes with source code, and it cannot be redistributed in any form. In fact, its use may be limited to one computer or even one person.

- *Freeware.* There is no clear definition of freeware except that at least some part of the software can be freely distributed. In this case the word "free" means "without cost". The distributed part may be a simple demo program, a limited version of the actual software, a complete version of the executable, or the complete source code. Most freeware allows redistribution but does not allow modification.

- *Shareware.* Shareware is software that can be freely distributed and used but, if someone continues to use the software, there will be a license fee required. This is the "try it before you buy it" software. Source code is almost never supplied.

- *Commercial software.* Commercial software is developed by a company for the purpose of making money from it. Commercial software is quite often also proprietary software, but it can be semi-free software or even free software—it can be a loss leader or a company can be in the business of providing software support.

Index

I

Get FREE books and more...when you register this book online for our Personal Bookshelf Program

http://register.samspublishing.com/

 Register online and you can sign up for our *FREE Personal Bookshelf Program...*unlimited access to the electronic version of more than 200 complete computer books—immediately! That means you'll have 100,000 pages of valuable information onscreen, at your fingertips!

 Plus, you can access product support, including complimentary downloads, technical support files, book-focused links, companion Web sites, author sites, and more!

 And you'll be automatically registered to receive a *FREE subscription to a weekly email newsletter* to help you stay current with news, announcements, sample book chapters, and special events, including sweepstakes, contests, and various product giveaways!

 We value your comments! Best of all, the entire registration process takes only a few minutes to complete, so go online and get the greatest value going—absolutely FREE!

Don't Miss Out On This Great Opportunity!

Sams is a brand of Macmillan USA.

For more information, please visit *www.mcp.com*